D1047829

Joe Cummings &
China Williams

Bangkok

standing outside a US$200-a-night hotel, or have your muscles gently kneaded for an hour and a half at Wat Pho, the oldest temple in the city, for less than the price of a cinema ticket in most Western cities. Catch a ride aboard a canal taxi from the Thonburi side of Mae Nam Chao Phraya and you can disappear down shaded waterways where modern Bangkok is soon left behind.

Viewed from above, the city resembles a quirky, skewed mandala, the quasi-circular diagram created by Buddhist artists as an object for meditation. Much like Hindu-Buddhist mythology's Mt Meru, around which the cosmos unfolds in concentric continents alternating with slender cosmic oceans, Thailand's sweltering capital straddles a vast spider's web of natural and artificial canals fanning out through sultry river delta for several hundred square miles. Crisscrossing the city in all directions, these murky green waterways conjure up a parallel universe in which 18th-century Siam collides with 21st-century Thailand.

Although today it's a city barely keeping up with the pace of its own hyper-development, Bangkok continues to lure rural Thais, Asian and Western investors, and curious visitors from around the world with its phantasmagoria of the carnal, spiritual and entrepreneurial. The capital remains easily the most exciting and dynamic city in Southeast Asia, with the region's largest foreign media correspondent base, the largest fashion industry and most active contemporary cinema. As a primary gateway for investment in neighbouring Vietnam, Cambodia, Laos and Myanmar, the city also serves as a financial hub for mainland Southeast Asia.

As the famed travel writer Pico Ayer (himself the cultural offspring of three continents) has noted about Bangkok, it is a city that is 'immutably and ineffably itself'.

JOE'S TOP BANGKOK DAY

A perfect day for me might start with a plate of fresh *kaeng mátsàman kài* (Thai Muslim chicken curry), washed down with *chaa nom ràwn* (hot milk tea) at Roti-Mataba in Banglamphu while perusing the *Bangkok Post*.

Dodging the vehicular stampede to cross the road, I'll take a leisurely stroll through Santichaiprakan Park, then cross adjacent Khlong Banglamphu and board a Chao Phraya Express boat heading downriver to Tha Wang Lang. After wandering through the classic adjacent market, I'll take in Wat Rakhang. Though it's one of the oldest and largest temples in Bangkok, you rarely see any tourists here, so it's a great spot to take in the coolness of the old ordination hall for a contemplative minute or two.

If I have company along – and what's a top day without a friend to share it? – I'll drag them to Songkran Niyomsane Forensic Medicine Museum at nearby Siriraj Hospital to see the mummified body of Si-Ouey Sae-Ung, Thailand's most notorious serial killer.

If the appetite survives, then a table overlooking the river at Khrua Rakhang Thong will do for lunch. Afterwards I'll get back to the river for a boat to Tha Tien for a long massage at the Wat Pho Thai Traditional Massage School on Th Sanam Chai.

Kicking the evening off with a quiet dinner with friends at Le Lys on Soi Lang Suan, I might divide the night's entertainment into two parts. Jamming with the house band at Ad Here the 13th comes first, and then, if I can drag myself away, I'll finish off the night with beats and bleeps at Club 87.

Essential Bangkok China Williams

- Take a **motorcycle taxi** (p210) through town – this is the closest many people will come to an extreme sport.
- Wander through **Chinatown** (p111) – impossible to navigate, this area is thoroughly entertaining to watch in its daily routine.
- Hop on the **river ferry** (p73) at sunset – through the golden haze of pollution, Bangkok is heartbreakingly beautiful.
- Ride the **Skytrain** (pp209–10)– from this vantage point, you can see into all those fortressed garden estates.
- Hang out in **MBK** (p148) – like pop music, MBK is mindless and fun.

City Life

City Life

BANGKOK TODAY

Bangkok in the 21st century remains one of Southeast Asia's most intriguing and surprising cities. Double-digit economic growth during the 1980s and '90s brought air-conditioned shopping malls, maple-and-chrome coffee shops, world-class architectural monuments and many other accoutrements of civilisation. Yet the city is as far from being 'tamed' by international ideas and technology as when it was founded more than 200 years ago.

Even the casual observer can see that Bangkok groans under the weight of an overburdened infrastructure. Road surfaces, among the world's lowest percentages relative to the overall plan for a city this size, remain insufficient for the number of Bangkok-registered cars, yet up to a thousand new vehicles climb onto the streets every day. Meanwhile the City of Angels (a translation of Krung Thep, the city's former name) is sinking at a rate of nearly one metre per year as the city's hydraulic system sucks water out from the spongy Chao Phraya flood plains upon which the city sprawls.

Yet the city continues to hold an intense allure for Thais and foreigners alike. Bangkok's legendary tolerance lends equal support to the monk and the playboy, to the beggar and the Benz dealer. You can slurp down a plate of *hǎwy thâwt* (egg-fried oysters) from a street vendor before strolling into a world-class health spa. Bid your life savings on local shares at the Stock Exchange of Thailand or take an all-day canal tour for less than the price of a cinema ticket in most world capitals. For absolutely nothing, take a meditation cell at Wat Mahathat and contemplate your life's choices for days, weeks or the rest of your life.

Even the most jaded traveller is humbled by the city's sheer cultural volume and diversity. Official estimates place Bangkok's population at eight million, though some sources claim this figure may be a million or two short. An astonishing 3600 residents compete for every square kilometre, constituting one of the highest density rates in Asia, and propelling a creative turbine that never ceases as the city's past and future co-evolve, from farms to freeways, spirit shrines to art galleries. Bangkok suburbs are now growing at a faster rate than the city centre.

As varied as it is vast, Bangkok offers residents and visitors alike the assurance they will never be bored. One can move across the city on water via 18th-century canals, in the air aboard the sleek Skytrain or below ground in the high-tech Metropolitan Rapid Transit Authority (MRTA) subway. When hunger beckons, residents are spoiled by a panoply of the finest Thai restaurants anywhere in the kingdom, along with a host of other Asian cuisines – Chinese, Japanese, Korean, Burmese, Malaysian, Sri Lankan and Indian, to name a few – and a broad range of European fare prepared by native chefs. When night falls, one can attend a classical Thai masked dance-drama performance followed by a club jaunt to hear a visiting DJ spin the latest house music.

Keeping the city vibrant at its core are the enviable freedoms that lie behind this phantasmagorical realm of choice. Metropolitan Bangkok boasts the only elected governorship in the

Hot Conversation Topics

- Closing times – the Interior Ministry wants to curb teenage drinking by closing Bangkok's bars at midnight, possibly even 10pm. The Thai public think otherwise.
- MRTA subway – will a sufficient number of Bangkokians dive 20m below street level to make it work?
- Fashion capital – PM Thaksin wants to make Bangkok a fashion centre on a par with Paris, Milan or New York, and is spending millions to buy the dream.
- Coolest new Italian restaurant – there's always a new one jockeying for position, with plenty of curbside critics ready to shoot it down.
- Mick Jagger & Angelina Jolie sightings – where will the generously lip-endowed be seen next?

A swirl of Bangkok city freeways viewed from the 87th floor of Baiyoke Tower II (p171)

nation – other provincial governors are ministry-appointed. The freedom to write just about anything one wants has made Bangkok Asia's largest base for foreign media correspondents. Thailand's openness to foreign investment has likewise developed Bangkok into the financial hub for mainland Southeast Asia, a role that has expanded quickly since Vietnam, Cambodia, Laos and Myanmar were opened up to limited travel and investment in the 1990s.

Meanwhile the city's burgeoning fine- and popular-arts scene provides a constantly changing social landscape of beauty, inspiration and challenge. More than 200 art galleries host rotating exhibitions of visual arts from both Thai and foreign artists. Public art has never been more popular, with daring neotraditional designs and colour schemes on restaurant walls, temple murals and anywhere else artists can find space.

A growing fusion of Thai ideas with global media extends from painting and architecture to Thai cinema. Recent directorial efforts have been so encouraging that Thai and foreign critics alike speak of a Thai 'new wave', almost entirely focused on Bangkok.

The city's relatively new self-consciousness as expressed in the arts has helped to boost urban pride, which in turn has led Bangkokians to put more thought into urban planning issues. Realising that late-20th-century development changed the shape of Bangkok forever, residents are now looking towards the future with an eye for doing whatever possible to make their city a more pleasant and efficient place in which to work and live.

To relieve the lack of surface streets, the city installed a system of elevated freeways that now enable commuters to leapfrog the traffic congestion below. In 1999, the city unveiled the Skytrain, an elevated rail network that has made a sizable dent in Bangkok traffic and allowed a large number of city residents to switch from the slow, often crowded city bus system. One unexpected benefit of the new system is that riding the Skytrain raises everyone 12m above street level, affording glimpses of lush greenery and old Bangkok architecture not ordinarily visible below due to high walls. During the Skytrain's first year, many Bangkokians expressed surprise that their city was actually more attractive than they'd previously believed.

The latest boon to city transport, the MRTA subway, links the 'old Bangkok' of Chinatown, Hualamphong and Banglamphu with the 'new Bangkok' further east along Th Sukhumvit, the city's longest and broadest thoroughfare. Despite the once-popular sentiment that it couldn't be done, engineers dug the MRTA tunnels 23m below street level using the same techniques as for the 'Chunnel' between France and Great Britain.

Hence Bangkokians today can traverse the city at three levels, whether above the city via the Skytrain or elevated freeways, on the traditional roadways or beneath the city via the new subway. At one spot in Bangkok, Th Phra Ram IV is surmounted by a freeway flyover and, a bit higher, the Skytrain track, while below the street runs the subway line.

Concurrent with the ongoing growth of concrete, steel and asphalt is a countering, if not equal, movement in the development of green areas and public parks. Supplementing vast Lumphini Park (144 acres) and Rama IX Park (200 acres), the latest Bangkok trend towards greenness is the creation of 'pocket parks' in unused and undeveloped areas of the city. Both of Bangkok's surviving 18th-century forts, Phra Sumen and Mahakan, have had adjacent lots planted with grass and trees to provide urbanites with relief from their mostly concrete, glass and steel existence.

All of these brave movements towards the city's future, whether in art, mass transport or urban planning, signal a new optimism for Bangkok. It's not unusual nowadays to hear a native Bangkokian comment, 'Ten years ago I was looking for another place to live in Thailand. Now I think I'll stay.'

CITY CALENDAR

Although Bangkok shares a large number of festivals and fairs with the rest of Thailand, the truth is that most Bangkokians leave town on holidays if they can. Still, something is almost always going on, especially during the November to February cool season.

Dates for festivals typically vary from year to year, either because of the lunar calendar, which isn't quite in sync with the solar calendar, or because local authorities decide to change festival days. The Tourism Authority of Thailand (TAT) publishes an up-to-date *Major Events & Festivals* calendar each year.

On dates noted as public holidays, all government offices and banks will be closed. See also Holidays, p216.

Weather-wise, the best time of year for a Bangkok visit is November to February, when temperatures drop to moderately warm and the skies are usually clear. From March through May, the heat can be quite intense, while from June to October it rains almost daily.

JANUARY

BANGKOK INTERNATIONAL FILM FESTIVAL

www.bangkokfilm.org

Despite its beginnings only two years ago, the 10-day festival screens about 140 films from around the world, with an emphasis on Asian cinema. Most screenings take place at theatres at Siam Square, Siam Discovery Center and Central World Plaza. Events end with the awarding of the festival's Golden Kinnaree in a range of categories.

LATE JANUARY–EARLY FEBRUARY

RIVER OF KINGS

www.theriverofkingsbangkok.com

Initiated by Princess Ubol Ratana, and sponsored largely by TAT, this spectacular sound-and-light show is performed for 12 consecutive nights alongside Mae Nam Chao Phraya at Tha Ratchaworadit (between Tha Tien and Tha Chang). Enhanced by the illuminated Grand Palace and Wat Phra Kaew in the background,

---

Top Five Quirky Events

- **Thai Tattoo Festival** Trance and old-fashion stylus tattooing go hand in hand at this two-day festival at Wat Bang Phra, near Nakhon Chaisi, about 20km west of Bangkok. It's usually held in March.
- **Vegetarian Festival** (Thêhtsakaan Kin Jeh) A nine-day celebration centred on Chinatown, during which devout Chinese Buddhists eat only vegetarian food. Processions to and from Chinese temples may involve acts of self-mortification. It's held from late September to early October.
- **Bangkok Gay Pride** The nearest thing Bangkok has to Mardi Gras – a week of gay parades, drag queen beauty contests, street parties, dancing, sports and cruising centred on Th Silom and Lumphini Park, and held in mid-November.
- **Fringe Festival** A celebration of nonmainstream performing arts, held at (Th Arun Amarin, Thonburi) from November to December.
- **Fat Festival** Sponsored by FAT 104.5FM radio and Heineken, Bangkok's indie-est indie bands gather for an annual mosh in early November. The venue changes from year to year.

a combination of Thai dance, music and animation makes for an intensely visual experience. The storyline, which changes every year, typically involves royal heroism.

LATE FEBRUARY–EARLY MARCH

MAGHA PUJA (MAAKHÀ BUUCHAA)

This is held on the full moon of the third lunar month to commemorate the Buddha preaching to 1250 enlightened monks who came to hear him 'without prior summons'. The festival culminates with a candle-lit walk around the main chapel at every wát.

CHINESE NEW YEAR

Bangkok's ample Thai-Chinese population celebrate their lunar new year, called Trùt Jiin in Thai, with a week of house-cleaning, lion dances and fireworks. The most impressive festivities, unsurprisingly, take place in Chinatown.

MARCH

BANGKOK INTERNATIONAL JEWELLERY FAIR

Held in several large Bangkok hotels, this is Thailand's most important annual gem and jewellery trade show. It runs concurrently with the Department of Export Promotion's Gems & Jewellery Fair.

APRIL

SONGKRAN FESTIVAL

During Thailand's lunar new year celebration, Buddha images are 'bathed', monks and elders receive the respect of younger Thais through the sprinkling of water over their hands, and a lot of water is generously tossed about for fun. Songkran generally gives everyone a chance to release their frustrations and literally cool off during the peak of the hot season. Hide out in your room or expect to be soaked – the latter is much more fun.

MAY

VISAKHA PUJA (WÍSĂAKHÀ BUUCHAA)

Falling on the 15th day of the waxing moon in the sixth lunar month, this is considered the date of the Buddha's birth, enlightenment and *parinibbana* (passing away). Activities are

centred on the local wát, with candle-lit processions, chanting and sermonising.

ROYAL PLOUGHING CEREMONY

To kick off the official rice-planting season, either the king or the crown prince participates in this ancient Brahman ritual at Sanam Luang (the large field across from Wat Phra Kaew). Thousands of Thais gather to watch, and traffic in this part of the city comes to a standstill.

JULY

ASALHA PUJA (ÀSĂANHÀ BUUCHAA)

This commemorates the day the Buddha preached his first sermon to his first five followers after attaining enlightenment. All Theravada Buddhist temples in the capital hold candle-lit processions at night.

KHAO PHANSA (KHĂO PHANSĂA)

A public holiday (p216) and the start of Buddhist *phansăa* (rains retreat), traditionally this is when young men to enter the monkhood for the rainy season and for all monks to station themselves in a monastery for the three months. It's a good time to observe a Buddhist ordination.

SEPTEMBER

WORLD GOURMET FESTIVAL

The Four Seasons (formerly the Regent) hosts this 10-day feast, bringing in international chefs from all over the world. It's Bangkok's premier food event.

OCTOBER–NOVEMBER

KATHIN (THÂWT KÀTHĬN)

A one-month period at the end of Buddhist *phansăa*, during which new monastic robes and requisites are offered to the Sangha (Buddhist community) at temples throughout Bangkok.

THAILAND INTERNATIONAL SWAN BOAT RACES

More than 20 international teams race traditional Thai-style long-boats along Mae Nam Chao Phraya and in Ayuthaya.

LOI KRATHONG (LAWY KRÀTHONG)

On the proper full-moon night (the full moon of the 12th lunar month), small lotus-shaped baskets or boats made of banana leaves containing flowers, incense, candles and a coin are floated on Thai rivers, lakes and canals. This is an intrinsically Thai festival that probably originated in Sukhothai and is best celebrated in the north. In Bangkok rather low-key celebrations take place along the banks of Mae Nam Chao Phraya.

DECEMBER

KING'S BIRTHDAY

On 5 December, King Bhumibol's birthday, the city is festooned with lights and large portraits of the king are displayed in public.

CULTURE

IDENTITY

Whether native or newcomer, virtually every Bangkokian you meet has a story. Although a majority no doubt find themselves in Bangkok owing to the simple fact that they were born in the city, a healthy percentage of the population hails from other parts of Thailand and from around the world. Some have followed the promise of work, while others have simply sought out one of the world's most vibrant social climates.

Climb into one of the capital's ubiquitous yellow-and-green taxis and the music issuing from your driver's radio or cassette player will often suggest where he's (virtually all Bangkok taxi drivers are male) from. If it's *măw lam,* with the churning sound of Thai-Lao bamboo panpipes *(khaen)* pounding out zydeco-like chord figures over a strong, simple rhythm, then chances are he moved to Bangkok from one of Thailand's distant northeastern provinces, such as Roi-Et or Sakon Nakhon. Switch to *lûuk thûng,* a unique hybrid of Thai, Indian and Latin musical influences popular with rural audiences, and the driver almost certainly comes from a province closer to Bangkok, perhaps Suphanburi or Saraburi. And if it's syrupy Thai pop or an older, crooning Bangkok style called *lûuk krung,* then you've most likely hitched a ride with a city native.

Sànùk

Although Bangkok is the most modern city in Thailand, the capital's cultural underpinnings are evident in virtually all facets of everyday life. First and foremost is the Thai sense of *sànùk,* loosely translated as 'fun'. In Thailand anything worth doing – even work – should have an element of *sànùk,* otherwise it automatically becomes drudgery. This doesn't mean Bangkokians don't work hard, just that they tend to approach tasks with a sense of playfulness. Nothing condemns an activity more than the description *mâi sànùk* (not fun). Whether in a bank or on a construction site, Bangkok Thais typically inject the activity with a little *sànùk* – flirtation between the sexes, jokes and mock insults.

Only a little more than half of the city's inhabitants are in fact true Bangkok Thais, ie those born of Thai parentage who speak Bangkok Thai as their first language. Although Thais are found in all walks of life, they are the backbone of the city's blue-collar work force, construction, automotive repair and river transport.

More than a quarter of the city's population is of Chinese or mixed Thai and Chinese descent. Many Chinese Thais in the capital can converse in at least one dialect from the old country, such as Cantonese, Hainanese, Hokkien or Chiu Chau, in addition to Thai. Although Chinese Thais live in every quarter of the sprawling city, their presence is most noticeable in a densely populated core of multistorey shophouses along Th Charoen Krung and Th Yaowarat near Mae Nam Chao Phraya, a precinct known as Yaowarat, Sampeng or 'Chinatown'. Chinese in these areas tend to be engaged in all manner of commerce, from wholesale trade in auto parts to the manufacture of high-end kitchen utensils. In other parts of the city they dominate higher education, international trade, banking and white-collar employment in general.

Also prominent are people of South Asian descent, who make up Bangkok's second-largest Asian minority. Most trace their heritage to northern India, including many Sikhs who immigrated following the 1947 Partition of India. Other South Asian nationalities found in Bangkok include Sinhalese, Bangladeshis, Nepalis and Pakistanis. Most of the city's South Asians can be found in two areas. The heaviest concentration wedge themselves in at the northern end of Th Yaowarat, between Th Chakraphet and Th Phahurat, in a neighbourhood known as Phahurat or, to English-speakers, Little India. South Asian residents are also more thinly spread along nearby Th Charoen Krung, near junctions with Th Silom and Th Surawong, an area collectively known as Bang Rak. In both areas they operate a multitude of successful retail businesses, particularly textile and tailor shops.

Malays, and Thais who are part-Malay and who adhere to Islam, make up the third-largest minority in Bangkok. Like residents of South Asian descent, many can be found living in Bang Rak, and like the majority of Thais, they tend to be found in blue-collar jobs. Other significant Asian minority groups found in Bangkok include Lao, Khmer, Vietnamese and Burmese.

Bangkok residents of European descent may number around 25,000. The vast majority, unlike their Asian counterparts, find themselves in Thailand for only a few months or years for reasons of work or study. Perhaps reflecting their significant roles in the early development of Bangkok, residents of German and British descent appear to be most prominent.

All of Bangkok's diverse cultures pay respect to the Thai king. The monarchy is considered one of the most important stabilising influences in modern Thai political and cultural life, and on Coronation Day and the King's Birthday the city is festooned with strings of lights and portraits of the King (see also the boxed text on p68).

Another cultural constant is Theravada Buddhism, the world's oldest and most traditional Buddhist sect. Around 90% of Bangkokians are Buddhists, who believe that individuals work out their own paths to *nibbana* (nirvana) through a combination of good works, meditation and study of the *dhamma* or Buddhist philosophy. The social and administrative centre for Thai Buddhism is the wát or monastery, a walled compound containing several buildings constructed in the traditional Thai style with steep, swooping rooflines and colourful interior wall murals. The most important structures will contain solemn Buddha statues cast in bronze. The sheer number of wáts scattered around the city – more than 300 – serves as a constant reminder that Buddhism retains a certain dominance even in increasingly secular Bangkok.

LIFESTYLE

Switch on the television and tune in to a Bangkok channel around eight o'clock in the evening and let Thai soap-opera plots draw a rough outline of the Bangkok story. Most series are set in the capital and although they are hardly realistic – the men are always handsome, the women beautiful, even their automobiles are spotless – the plotlines are propped up by Bangkok realities. A young Thai Isan girl from the northeastern countryside takes a cleaning job in a wealthy Bangkok household, and the resulting weekly culture clashes keep Thai viewers glued to the screen. A college student argues with his father, a *khâa râatchákaan* (civil servant), over whether he should spend a Saturday afternoon at Centrepoint, a fashionable-but-funky shopping area notorious for its tattoo parlours, punk hair salons and abundance of unaccompanied girls in revealing spaghetti-strap tops.

While there is a certain homogeneity to Bangkok Thais, individual lifestyles vary tremendously according to family background and income. If you could sneak a peek at what Bangkokians eat for breakfast, you'd have a fighting chance at guessing both. *Khâo tôm phúi,* an array of small dishes of dried fish, peanuts and pickled vegetables eaten with hot rice soup, indicates probable Chinese ancestry; add a plate of pricey sweet cured sausage and they're middle-class Chinese Thai. Spot a bowl of steaming *kaeng khíaw-wǎan* (sweet green curry) or *kaeng phèt* (red curry) over rice and it's likely your diner comes from mostly Thai genes, and prefers a basic, economic diet. The same Thai choosing ham, eggs and toast, chased with Starbucks coffee, has money and has

How Much?

- Khao San guesthouse room 200–300B
- Mid-range hotel room 800–1000B
- Skytrain ride 10–40B
- Chao Phraya Express boat ride 6B
- Cinema ticket 100B
- Large Singha beer at a restaurant 75B
- Bottle of drinking water 5–10B
- Bowl of rice noodles from street vendor 25B
- S&P food delivery, two mains plus rice 205B
- Two-hour traditional Thai massage 300B

A gathering of monks at Wat Benchamabophit (p86)

probably travelled abroad. Meanwhile a *thai pàk tâi*, or someone from southern Thailand, might be digging into *khâo yam*, a spicy salad of rice, shaved lemon grass, toasted coconut and tamarind sauce.

Walk the streets of Bangkok early in the morning and you'll catch the flash of shaved heads bobbing above bright ochre robes, as monks all over the city engage in *bindabàat*, the daily house-to-house almsfood-gathering. Thai men are expected to shave their heads and don monastic robes temporarily at least once in their lives. Some enter the monkhood twice, first as 10-vow novices in their preteen years and again as fully ordained, 227-vow monks sometime after the age of 20. Monks depend on the faithful for their daily meals, permitted only before noon and collected from lay devotees in large, black-lacquered bowls.

Green-hued onion domes looming over lower rooftops belong to mosques and mark the immediate neighbourhood as Muslim, while brightly painted and ornately carved cement spires indicate a Hindu temple. Wander down congested Th Chakraphet in the Phahurat district to find Sri Gurusingh Sabha, a Sikh temple where visitors are very welcome. A handful of steepled Christian churches, including a few historic ones, have taken root over the centuries and can be found near the banks of Mae Nam Chao Phraya. In Chinatown large, round doorways topped with heavily inscribed Chinese characters and flanked by red paper lanterns mark the location of *sǎan jâo*, Chinese temples dedicated to the worship of Buddhist, Taoist and Confucian deities.

Thai royal ceremony remains almost exclusively the domain of one of the most ancient religious traditions still functioning in the kingdom, Brahmanism. White-robed, topknotted priests of Indian descent keep alive an arcane collection of rituals that, it is generally believed, must be performed at regular intervals to sustain the three pillars of Thai nationhood, namely sovereignty, religion and the monarchy. Such rituals are performed regularly at a complex of shrines near Wat Suthat in the centre of the city. Devasathan (Abode of Gods) contains shrines to Shiva and Ganesha and thus hosts priestly ceremonies in the Shaiva tradition, while the smaller Sathan Phra Narai (Abode of Vishnu) is reserved for Vaishnava ritual.

Animism predates the arrival of all other religions in Bangkok and still plays an important role in the everyday life of most city residents. Believing that *phrá phum* or guardian spirits inhabit rivers, canals, trees and other natural features, and that these spirits must be placated whenever humans trespass upon or make use of these features, the Thais build spirit shrines to house the displaced spirits. These dollhouse-like structures perch on wood or cement pillars next to their homes and receive daily offerings of rice, fruit, flowers and water. Peek inside the smaller, more modest spirit homes and you'll typically see a collection of ceramic or plastic figurines representing the property's guardian spirits.

Larger and more elaborate spirit shrines stand alongside hotels and office buildings and may contain elaborate bronze images of Brahma or Shiva. At virtually all times of the day and night you'll see Thais kneeling before such shrines to offer stacks of flowers, incense and candles, and to pray for favours from these Indian 'spirit kings'.

One in 10 Thai citizens lives and works in Bangkok. Roughly 60% of the country's wealth is concentrated here, and per capita income runs well above the average for the rest of the country. The legal minimum daily wage in Bangkok and the adjacent provinces of Samut Prakan, Samut Sakhon, Pathum Thani, Nonthaburi and Nakhon Pathom amounted to 170B (US$4.50) in 2004, roughly 35B higher than in the rest of Thailand.

A typical civil servant in an entry-level government job earns around 7000B a month, but with promotions and extra job training may earn up to 15,000B. In the private sector an office worker starts at about the same level but will receive pay raises more quickly than those in government positions. Of course Bangkok thrives on private enterprise, from Talaat Noi junk auto-parts shops eking out a profit of less than 500B a day to huge multinational corporations whose upper-level employees drive the latest BMW sedans.

Bangkok women typically control the family finances, and are more likely than men to inherit real estate. Women constitute close to half of the city's workforce, outranking many world capitals. In fields such as economics, academia and health services, women hold a majority of the professional positions – 80% of all Thai dentists, for example, are female.

Figures on Bangkok's infamous nightlife-based economy are difficult to come by, and civic leaders prefer to keep it that way. When Longman's 1993 *Dictionary of Contemporary English* defined Bangkok as 'a place where there are a lot of prostitutes', Thais filed diplomatic protests and staged demonstrations outside the British Embassy. The publishers immediately agreed to withdraw the edition from circulation, although Longman's blunder was echoed in 2000 when Microsoft's *Encarta* extolled Bangkok as a 'commercial sex hub', resulting in a lawsuit and subsequent revision of the entry.

The infamous red-light districts that have perpetually captivated Western media attention are limited to a few areas of the city, and became further circumscribed in March 2004 when the Thai government declared that henceforth no new 'entertainment services with female hostesses' would be permitted outside of three zones: Patpong, Ratchada and Royal City Ave (RCA).

Although often linked to tourism, Bangkok's commercial sex industry actually caters far more to the local market than to foreign visitors. Modern attitudes are changing rapidly, however, and as nonpaid extramarital sex becomes increasingly common, the percentage of Thai clients in Bangkok now runs considerably lower than in other parts of the country.

With the amount of time Bangkok drivers spend stuck in traffic, it's a wonder they have time to think about sex at all. The ocean of cars, trucks, buses, motorcycles and assorted other vehicles upon which Bangkokians have set themselves adrift dominates city life during the daytime and well into the evening. Practically every activity, whether social or work-related, is planned around the ebb and flow of traffic. American road engineers in 1992 suggested that Bangkok had 'probably the worst traffic congestion of any city of similar size in the world', a claim that spurred the city to order the construction of a new set of

Dos & Don'ts

When Bangkokians greet each other, they place their palms together in the prayer-like *wâi* gesture, keeping the tips of the fingers somewhere between the chin and the nose, depending on the status of the person being greeted. If a Thai adult greets you with a *wâi*, you should *wâi* in response. Most Bangkokians are familiar with the Western-style handshake and will offer the same to a foreigner, although a *wâi* is always appreciated.

A smile and the all-purpose Thai greeting *'sawàt-dii khráp'* (if you're male) or *'sawàt-dii khâ'* (if you're female) go a long way towards smoothing any new interaction. When encounters take a turn for the worse, try to refrain from getting angry – it won't help matters, since losing one's temper means loss of face for everyone present. Talking loudly is perceived as rude behaviour by cultured Thais, whatever the situation.

The feet are the lowest part of the body (spiritually as well as physically), so don't point your feet at people or things with your feet. Don't prop your feet on chairs or tables while seated. Never touch any part of someone's body with your foot.

In the same context, the head is regarded as the highest part of the body, so don't touch Thais on the head – or ruffle their hair. If you touch someone's head accidentally, offer an immediate apology or you'll be perceived as very rude.

elevated freeways allowing vehicles to speed across at least some parts of the capital. Still, with roadways covering less than 10% of Bangkok's surface – compared to an international average of 25% – the steel-and-rubber currents remain sluggish.

Mass transit in Bangkok shows more promise than ever, however. After a slow opening year, residents are finally taking to the BTS Skytrain, and the railcars are completely packed during commute hours. At the time of writing the MRTA subway, nicknamed 'the Metro', was set to supplement the Skytrain system and make more of the capital accessible without stepping into a car, bus or taxi. Fuelling further optimism for the future, city officials recently announced plans to establish seven new light-rail lines – a circular line around Bangkok's perimeter fed by six 'spoke' lines linking the city centre with the suburbs.

FASHION

Unsurprisingly, Bangkok is Thailand's fashion hub, and in fact in all of Southeast Asia only Singapore is a serious rival. Bangkokians not only dabble in the latest American, European and Japanese designer trends, but they have an up-and-coming couture all their own. Shops run by modern Thai designers are particularly easy to find at the Emporium and Siam Center shopping centres, and in the small lanes of Siam Square. Siam Square focuses on inexpensive 'underground' Thai fashions favoured by university students and young office workers, while Emporium and Siam Center are much more upscale. Local labels to look for include Dapper, Episode, Greyhound, Jaspal and Soda. Chatuchak Weekend Market is another place to seek out Bangkok designs at bargain prices. See p144 for details on where to locate Bangkok fashions.

Take a stroll through Siam Square or Central World Plaza, especially on a weekend, and the explosion of styles and colours can't fail to impress. Even the self-tailoring applied to the black-and-white school uniforms shows a Thai sense of flair. On weekends the middle *soi* (lane) of Siam Square – an area known as Centrepoint – is filled with young Thais wearing the most outrageous clothing experiments they can create. It's not quite on a par with Tokyo's famous Harajuku district, but in a few years who knows what it may become?

Fashion shows grace the lobbies of various shopping centres around the city practically every weekend of the year. Since 1999 one of the biggest annual events has been the Elle Bangkok Fashion Week, a string of fashion shows held under a large tent in the Central Chidlom department-store parking lot each November. The Bangkok International Fashion Fair, held in January, is mostly a trade event but weekend days are usually open to the public.

Hoping to turn Bangkok into a world-class – rather than simply regional – fashion centre, the Thai government recently established the clumsily named Office of the Bangkok Fashion City to promote fashion events and construct a 'trend centre' dedicated to Thai couture. The ambitious plan aims to turn the city into a global fashion hub by 2012. However, Thailand's culture minister chastised the organisers of the 2003 Elle Bangkok Fashion Week for the skimpiness of some of the outfits displayed on the catwalks, leading many in Bangkok's fashion community to question whether the city can attain world-class status with such government interference.

SPORT

Muay Thai

The first spectator sport that comes to mind when one thinks of Bangkok is *muay thai,* also known as Thai boxing or kick boxing. Almost anything goes in this martial art, both in the ring and in the stands. If you don't mind the violence, a Thai boxing match is well worth attending for the pure spectacle – the wild musical accompaniment, the ceremonial beginning of each match and the frenzied betting throughout the stadium.

More formally known as Phahuyut (from the Pali-Sanskrit *bhahu* or 'arm' and *yodha* or 'combat'), Thailand's ancient martial art is arguably one of the kingdom's most striking national icons. Overflowing with colour and ceremony as well as exhilarating moments of clenched-teeth action, the best matches serve up a blend of such skill and tenacity that one is tempted to view the spectacle as emblematic of Thailand's centuries-old devotion to independence in a region where most other countries fell under the European colonial yoke.

Unlike some martial disciplines, such as kung fu or qi gong, *muay thai* doesn't entertain the idea that esoteric martial-arts techniques can be passed only from master to disciple in secret. Thus the *muay thai* knowledge base hasn't fossilized and in fact remains ever open to innovation, refinement and revision. Undefeated Thai champion Dieselnoi, for example, created a new approach to knee strikes that was so difficult to defend that he retired at 23 because no-one dared to fight him anymore.

One of the most famous *muay thai* champions in recent years was Parinya Kiatbusaba, a male transvestite from Chiang Mai who arrived for weigh-ins wearing lipstick and rouge. After his 1998 triumph at Lumphini, Parinya used his earnings to pay for transsexual surgery and became a consultant for 2003's *Beautiful Boxer*, a cinematic version of his life. Another notable *muay thai* event occurred in 1999 when French fighter Mourad Sari became the first non-Thai fighter to take home a weight-class championship belt from a Bangkok stadium.

Several Thai *nák muay* (fighters) have gone on to win world championships in international-style boxing. Khaosai Galaxy, the greatest Asian boxer of all time, chalked up 19 World Boxing Association bantamweight championships in a row before retiring undefeated in December 1991. At any given time Bangkok typically claims five concurrent international boxing champions, usually in the bantamweight and flyweight categories.

To find out where you can watch *muay thai* in Bangkok, see pp138–9.

Muay thai at Lumphini Stadium (p138)

Tàkrâw

Sometimes called Siamese football in old English texts, *tàkrâw* refers to a game in which a woven rattan ball about 12cm in diameter is kicked around. The rattan (or sometimes plastic) ball itself is called a *lûuk tàkrâw*. *Tàkrâw* is also popular in several neighbouring countries. It was originally introduced to the SEA Games by Thailand, and international championships tend to alternate between the Thais and Malays.

The traditional way to play *tàkrâw* in Thailand is for players to stand in a circle (the size of which depends on the number of players) and simply try to keep the ball airborne by kicking it soccer-style. Points are scored for style, difficulty and variety of kicking manoeuvres. See p139 for more details about where to see a game when visiting Thailand.

MEDIA

Thailand's 1997 constitution ensures freedom of the press, although the Royal Police Department reserves the power to suspend publishing licences for national security reasons. Editors generally exercise self-censorship in certain realms, especially with regard to the monarchy.

Thai press freedom reached its high-water mark in the mid-1990s, while Chuan Leekpai's Democrat Party was in power. Since the 1997 economic downturn and the ascension of Thaksin Shinawatra's Thai Rak Thai Party, Thailand's media have found themselves increasingly subject to interference by political and financial interests.

Before the 2001 general election, Shin Corp, a telecommunications conglomerate owned by Prime Minister Thaksin's family, bought a controlling interest in iTV, Thailand's only independent television station. Shortly thereafter, the new board sacked 23 iTV journalists who complained that the station was presenting biased coverage of the election to favour Thaksin and Thai Rak Thai. Almost overnight the station transformed from an independent, in-depth news channel to an entertainment channel with flimsy, pro-Thaksin news coverage.

Meanwhile relatives of cabinet minister and Thai Rak Thai Party secretary Suriya Jungrungreangkit purchased shares to become the third-largest shareholders of the Nation Group. Political coverage in the *Nation,* formerly known for its independent criticism of the Thai government, has since become much less aggressive.

The country's international reputation for press freedom took another serious dent in 2002 when two Western journalists were nearly expelled for reporting on a public address presented by the Thai king on his birthday, a portion of which was highly critical of PM Thaksin. In 2004 Veera Prateepchaikul, editor in chief of the *Bangkok Post*, lost his job due to direct pressure from board members with ties to Thaksin and Thai Rak Thai. Allegedly the latter were upset with *Post* criticism of the way in which the PM handled the 2003–04 bird flu crisis (see p62).

Barely a week later, Rungruang Preechakul, editor of the Thai-language *Siam Rath Weekly News,* resigned, saying he could no longer endure the intense political pressure to avoid negative news about the Thaksin administration. Four of six full-time *Siam Rath* editors followed suit, as did well-known journalist Chatcharin Chaiwat, poet laureate Praiwarin Khaongarm and 18 other writers for the magazine.

Observers agree that Thai press freedom has reached it lowest ebb since the 1970s era of Thai military dictatorship, and will probably remain there as long as Thai Rak Thai are in power.

LANGUAGE

Bangkokians conduct their daily lives using the Thai language almost exclusively. The dialect spoken in the capital is Central Thai, also known as Standard Thai, and this is the language taught in public schools throughout the country. Although as a written language Thai appears to be less than a thousand years old, the spoken language is much older. Thai has a very rich vocabulary that varies according to differences in social status, age, royal versus nonroyal and written versus spoken. See pp227–31 for a brief explanation of the pronunciation, along with a list of useful words and phrases.

Most signs around Bangkok are in Thai, although you will also see plenty of signs that mix Thai with English and, in Chinatown, with Chinese. Many Chinese or Chinese-Thai residents can speak a dialect or two of Chinese, typically Chao Zhou, Hokkien or Cantonese.

Even though English is a required subject for the first six years of school, don't expect a lot of English to be spoken. Almost everyone knows a few words in English, but apart from university English majors or Thais who are heavily involved in international tourism, you won't find many Thais who speak fluent English.

See p212 for information on studying Thai in Bangkok.

ECONOMY & COSTS

Banking, finance, wholesale and retail trade, transportation, tourism and energy dominate the immediate municipality, while the surrounding metropolitan area adds manufacturing, shipping, food processing and intensive farming to the list of top revenue producers. Per capita income in metropolitan Bangkok runs well above the average in the rest of the country (US$6900 using the purchasing power parity measure), although it's second to that found in Phuket, an island province in the south.

The bursting of Southeast Asia's economic bubble in 1997 for the most part stemmed from investor panic, with the rush to buy dollars to pay off debts creating a self-fulfilling collapse. Between 30 June and 31 October, the baht depreciated roughly 40% against the US dollar, and dollar-backed external debt rose to 52.4% of the country's GDP. Such currency problems echoed the European currency crisis of 1992–93, when sudden, unforeseen drops in the pound, lira and other currencies sounded the death knell of a long period of steady growth and economic stability.

Following the 1997 recession, the Thai economy shrank 10% in 1998, but has grown 4% to 5% per annum since 1999. This growth enabled Thailand to take an 'early exit' from the International Monetary Fund (IMF) US$17.2 billion rescue package of short-term loans in 2000. Some observers have concluded that the forced 1997–2000 'cooling off' was the best thing that could have happened to the overheated economy, giving the nation time to focus on infrastructure priorities and offering the Thai citizenry an opportunity to reassess cultural change. By the end of 2000, the economy was healthier than at any time since 1996, according to independent analysts.

The national economy is now heating up considerably, with Bangkok the primary beneficiary. Exports in 2003 increased 12%, while overall GDP increased by around 6%. Independent economic forecasts suggest this growth will continue for at least the next two years. Still, the 1997 economic crisis initiated a national discussion about Thailand's role in globalisation. Many Thais believe that the IMF somehow forced this situation upon them, and want to cut all ties with the IMF and World Bank. Some are calling for stronger tariffs on foreign goods. Others acknowledge that the reason Thailand fell into this recession in the first place was because so many middle- and upper-class Thais – not to mention banks – refused to practise any self-discipline with regard to credit. The proglobalisation camp warns that resistance to free trade and economic interdependence only widens the gap between globalisation-resistant developing countries and those who embrace free trade wholeheartedly.

As Thailand's primary commercial centre, Bangkok has always attracted Thais from poor, rural provinces. When the Thai economy collapsed in 1997, a considerable number of migrants moved back to their home provinces to live off family farms. As might be expected, when the economy bounced back in 2000, this migration reversed itself and the poorer sectors of the city's population are now facing a housing shortage.

Rural migrants have joined with urban slum-dwellers to form the Assembly of the Poor, a nongovernmental organisation that since 1999 has maintained a semipermanent encampment outside Government House, where it stages frequent demonstrations demanding that the government address its economic grievances.

King Bhumibol, in the meantime, has come out publicly in favour of a return to the relative self-sufficiency Thailand enjoyed 200 years ago or more, warning Thais that they ought to reign in their greed and practise more economic self-discipline.

GOVERNMENT & POLITICS

The Bangkok Metropolitan Administration (BMA) administers the capital, which is segmented into 50 districts covering 1569 sq km. Since 1985 metropolitan Bangkok has boasted the country's only elected governorship (provincial governors are appointed). Mid-2000 elections saw tough-talking, 10-time former MP Samak Sundaravej become Bangkok governor.

The current climate for Bangkok governance has changed considerably following the establishment, in September 1997, of a new constitution that guaranteed – at least on paper – more human and civil rights than had previously been codified in Thailand. As the first national charter to be prepared under civilian auspices, the 'people's constitution' has fostered great hope that Thailand will more quickly become a 'civic society' ruled by law rather than social hierarchies.

At the national level, politics have been dominated in recent years by the economic crisis of the late 1990s. Prime Minister Chavalit Yongchaiyudh and his New Aspiration Party took the brunt of the blame for this crisis. Chavalit's successor, Chuan Leekpai, assigned a team of economists to right the economy, but they soon came under criticism for their top-down methods that neglected the rural and urban poor. Sensing a power vacuum, billionaire telecom tycoon Thaksin Shinawatra capitalised on widespread discontent and promised 'a million baht' to every village if elected – which later turned into a 'loan'.

Chuan lost the election (the first compulsory elections held in Thailand as per the 1997 constitution) and Thaksin took power in 2001. Amid accusations of widespread vote-buying and violent protests in 16 provinces, Thailand's Election Commission launched an investigation into election conduct while the Counter-Corruption Commission (CCC) looked into allegations of graft and 'wealth concealment' in Thaksin's past. The new PM managed to escape the CCC investigation relatively unscathed.

Through a shrewd combination of financial and political manoeuvres, Thaksin has since managed to consolidate his power in a manner unprecedented for a democratically elected chief executive in Thailand. Placing political cronies and relatives in key positions in the media, government, armed forces and national police, the billionaire ruler has all but silenced public debate about his governing abilities.

Although Thaksin and his nationalist party, Thai Rak Thai (Thai Love Thai), came to power on a raft of social programmes targeted at rural villagers, their political clout took a severe hit in early 2004 when it came to light that the administration had covered up the fact that Thai poultry had been infected with the avian flu since November 2003.

While many villagers outside Bangkok remain loyal, Bangkokians appear to be rapidly losing faith in Thaksin and Thai Rak Thai. Bangkok governor Samak has gone on record criticising Thaksin's handling of the avian flu, nightclub closing times and drug suppression. When Samak runs for re-election in late 2004, he'll be facing several other candidates whose platforms also contain anti-TRT planks. It is likely that whatever the results of the next parliamentary election, Bangkok will continue to distance itself from the national government.

ENVIRONMENT

THE LAND

Occupying a space roughly midway along Thailand's 1860km north–south axis, Bangkok lies approximately 14 degrees north of the equator, putting it on a latitudinal level with Madras, Manila, Guatemala and Khartoum. The rivers and tributaries of northern and central Thailand drain into Mae Nam Chao Phraya, which in turn disgorges into the Gulf of Thailand, a vast cul-de-sac of the South China Sea. Bangkok is partly surrounded by a huge, wet, flat and extremely fertile area known as 'the rice bowl of Asia' – more rice is grown here than in any other area of comparable size in all of Asia. Thailand has, in fact, been the world's top exporter of rice for at least the last 30 years.

Metropolitan Bangkok – which covers 1569 sq km and extends into the neighbouring provinces of Nonthaburi, Samut Prakan and Samut Sakhon – sits smack in the middle of this delta area, just a few kilometres inland from the gulf. A network of natural and artificial canals crisscrosses the city, although they are fewer in number in urban Bangkok than in surrounding provinces. All feed into Thailand's hydraulic lifeline, Mae Nam Chao Phraya, which snakes through the city centre and serves as an important transport link for cargo and passenger traffic, both within the city and upcountry.

GREEN BANGKOK

The Mae Nam Chao Phraya delta's natural environment has been forever altered by the founding and ongoing development of Bangkok. All of the city's canals, as well as Mae Nam Chao Phraya itself, would be considered polluted by most definitions, although plenty of

Bangkok residents make daily use of these waterways for bathing, laundry, recreation and even drinking water (after treating it, of course). The worst water quality is found in the almost black canals on the Bangkok side of the river. The city has undertaken efforts to clean up the canals over the last couple of decades, with some limited success. Foreigners who have been visiting Thailand for 20 years or more will have noticed some incremental improvements, particularly in the river. The post-1997 budget crisis in Thailand has visibly slowed the momentum gained in this direction.

Air quality varies from precinct to precinct but is generally worse at major traffic crossings. Along with carbon monoxide, lead and other poisons produced primarily by vehicle emissions, Bangkok's air has a fairly high concentration of particulate matter, including dust and debris brought in on the wheels of cars and trucks or created by ongoing construction projects. Relative to other cities in Asia, however, Bangkok doesn't even make the United Nations Environment Programme list of the region's 10 worst cities for air pollution –

Passengers alighting from a canal boat at a Khlong Saen Saeb wharf

honours captured entirely by China and India. The worst precinct in Bangkok, Huay Khwang, has an average air quality index (AQI) of 58, which falls in the AQI scale's 'moderate quality' level.

In addition to several parks filled with trees and other vegetation, Bangkok relies on immense green areas to the west of the city as a means of detoxifying the air. One of the greatest threats to the environment is continued development, not only in the city centre, but also in outlying areas and neighbouring provinces. Realising the importance of maintaining green 'lungs' for the city, the Thai government maintains strict controls on development in these areas. They've had less success controlling development in the inner city, and almost no success controlling vehicle circulation, one of the most obvious problem areas. The 1999 introduction of the Skytrain, an elevated light-rail system that runs above some of the city's more sluggish avenues, came as a welcome relief to those who live or work in adjacent areas. It's hoped that the opening of the MRTA subway will provide yet another 'escape valve' for the traffic situation, and the city plans to construct seven commuter rail lines, in a spoke-and-wheel configuration around the city, to persuade more Bangkokians to leave their cars and motorcycles at home. See p209–10 for further Skytrain and subway information.

Ambient noise levels along main thoroughfares in Bangkok typically average 74–80dBa, slightly above the 70dBa at which researchers say hearing damage may result from long-term exposure. The BMA is currently creating legal standards for ambient noise levels that will, ideally at least, monitor construction sites, entertainment venues and other sources of ambient noise.

The public rubbish collection system in Bangkok works fairly smoothly, with the city managing to dispose of 90% of all solid waste produced, an average of 7000 tonnes per day. The piles of street rubbish commonly seen in some South and Southeast Asian capitals are noticeably fewer in Bangkok. Where the rubbish goes is another question altogether. Although some serious attempts to separate and recycle paper, glass and plastic are underway, an estimated 80% of all solid waste ends up at sanitary landfill sites outside Bangkok.

Bangkok has very strict standards for tap water and bottled drinking water. Recent tests indicate that Bangkok tap water meets minimum international health standards and is technically potable.

URBAN PLANNING & DEVELOPMENT

When Bangkok became the new royal capital in 1782, the city was originally laid out in a traditional Buddhist mandala (*monthon* in Thai) plan, inspired by earlier capitals at Ayuthaya, Sukhothai and Chiang Mai. The Lak Meuang (City Pillar), palaces and royal monasteries stood at the centre, while Khlong Rop Krung was dug around the immediate perimeters to create an island called Ko Ratanakosin. Those nobles and merchants of value to the royal court were encouraged to settle just outside Ko Ratanakosin, and other canals were dug to circumscribe this next layer out from the centre. This rough plan of inner and outer rings – land alternating with water – was a conscious attempt to pay homage to sacred Mt Meru of Hindu-Buddhist mythology.

Beginning in the early 19th century, Thai kings relinquished the mandala concept and began refashioning the city following European and American models, a process that has continued to this day. In the 1960s and '70s the capital's area doubled in size, yet scant attention was paid to managing growth. Well into the 1980s, as adjacent provinces began filling with factories, housing estates, shopping malls, amusement parks and golf courses, urban planning was virtually nonexistent.

Bangkok's first official city plan was issued in 1992, and nowadays the BMA employs engineers and urban-planning experts full-time to tackle growth and make plans for the future. So far most planning remains confined to paper – noble ideas without supporting actions. In theory city authorities have the power to regulate construction by zones, and to monitor land use, but in practice most new developments follow capital, with little thought given to such issues as parking, drainage, or social and environmental impact. For the most part city planners seem preoccupied with the immediate exigencies of maintaining basic city services.

Arts

Arts

It's no exaggeration to say that Bangkok has been Southeast Asia's contemporary art capital since the city was founded in the late 18th century. Early Chakri kings weren't satisfied to merely invite artists and artisans from previous Thai royal capitals such as Ayuthaya, Sukhothai and Chiang Mai. Whether via political coercion of neighbouring countries or seductive promises of wealth and position, Bangkok's rulers had access to the artistic cream of Cambodia, Laos and Myanmar. Mon and Khmer peoples native to the Thai kingdom also contributed much to the visual arts scene.

The great artistic traditions of India and China, the subtle renderings of Indo- and Sino-influenced art in neighbouring countries and the colonial and postcolonial cultural influx from Europe also played huge roles in early Bangkok art. In the more tightly connected modern world of aero and cyberspace, influences from just about every corner of the globe now find free play in Bangkok (see also p94).

VISUAL ARTS

Bangkok's 400-plus Buddhist temples are brimming with the figuratively imaginative but often thematically formulaic art of Thailand's foremost muralists. Always instructional in intent, such painted images range from the depiction of the *Jataka* (stories of the Buddha's past lives) and scenes from the Indian Hindu epic *Ramayana*, to elaborate scenes detailing daily life in Thailand. Artists traditionally applied natural pigments to plastered temple walls, creating a fragile medium of which very few examples remain.

The city's earliest surviving temple painting can be found at the Wat Chong Nonsi

> ### Top Five Museums & Galleries
> - **National Museum** (p75) Stodgy presentation, deluxe collection.
> - **Jim Thompson's House** (p90) The original model for expat fantasy Thai homes.
> - **Thavibu Gallery** (p94) The city's best collection of regional artists.
> - **H Gallery** (p94) Cutting-edge artists with international ambitions.
> - **Chulalongkorn Art Centre** (p94) Fast-rotating collection of Thai and international artists.

(1657–1707; p98). Nineteenth-century religious painting has fared better, and Ratanakosin-style (old Bangkok) temples are more highly esteemed for their painting than their sculpture or architecture. Typical temple murals feature rich colours and lively detail. Some of the finest are found in the National Museum's Wihan Phutthaisawan (Buddhaisawan Chapel; p75).

The study and application of mural painting remains very much alive. Modern temple projects are undertaken somewhere within the capital virtually every day of the year, often using improved techniques and paints that promise to hold fast much longer than the temple murals of old. A privileged few in Bangkok's art community receive handsome sums for painting the interior walls of well-endowed ordination halls. Chakrabhand Pasayakrit's post-modern murals at Wat Tritosathep Mahawarawihan in Banglamphu, only half completed, are being hailed as masterworks of Thai Buddhist art.

In sculpture the Thai artists have long been masters, using wood, stone, ivory, clay and metal and a variety of techniques – including carving, modelling, construction and casting – to achieve their designs. Bangkok's most famous sculptural output has been bronze Buddha images, coveted the world over for their originality and grace. Nowadays, historic bronzes have all but disappeared from the art market in Thailand. Most are zealously protected by temples, museums or private collectors.

Modern sculpture can be split into two camps, one imitating Western or Japanese trends, and the other reviving Thai themes but reinterpreting them in new ways. An example of the latter is a piece by artist Sakarin Kreu-On, who fashioned a huge, hollow Buddha head from a mixture of clay, mud, papier-mâché, glue and turmeric. Entitled *Phawang*

Si Leuang (Yellow Trance), the work was displayed lying on its side, nearly filling a small room, during a recent successful world tour.

The beginnings of Thailand's modern visual-arts movement are usually attributed to Italian artist Corrado Feroci, who was invited to Thailand by King Rama VI in 1924. In 1933 Feroci founded the country's first School of Fine Arts (SOFA), which eventually became Silpakorn University (Map p256), Thailand's premier training ground for artists and art historians. In gratitude for his contributions, the government gave Feroci the Thai name Silpa Bhirasri.

One of the most important modern movements in Thai art has been the updating of Buddhist themes, begun in the 1970s by painters Pichai Nirand, Thawan Duchanee and Prateung Emjaroen. The movement has grown stronger since their early efforts combined modern Western schemata with Thai motifs, moving from painting to sculpture and then to mixed media. Currently the most important artists working in this neo-Thai, neo-Buddhist school include Surasit Saokong, Songdej Thipthong, Monchai Kaosamang, Tawatchai Somkong and Montien Boonma. All are frequently exhibited and collected outside Thailand.

Secular sculpture and painting in Bangkok have enjoyed more limited international recognition, with Impressionism-inspired Jitr (Prakit) Buabusaya and Sriwan Janehuttakarnkit among the very few to have

Statue in Jim Thompson's House (p90)

reached this vaunted status. On Thailand's art stage, famous names include artists of the 'Fireball' school such as Vasan Sitthiket and Manit Sriwanichpoom, who specialise in politically motivated, mixed-media art installations. These artists delight in breaking Thai social codes and means of expression. Even when their purported message is Thai nationalism and self-sufficiency, they are sometimes considered 'anti-Thai'.

In Manit's infamous *Pink Man On Tour* series of art events, he dressed artist Sompong Thawee in pink from head to toe and had him parade with a shopping cart through popular tourist sites to protest the selling of Thai culture. Less well known are Manit's evocative black-and-white photographic pieces denouncing capitalism and consumerism, often identified as unwelcome Western imports. A typical Vasan work dangles cardboard silhouettes from thick steel ropes, accompanied by the title, *Committing Suicide Culture: the only way for Thai farmers to escape debt*.

Thaweesak Srithongdee, one of several newer Thai artists who manage to skirt both the neo-Buddhist and Fireball movements, paints flamboyantly iconic human figures with bulging body parts. Sculptor Manop Suwanpinta similarly moulds the human anatomy into fantastic shapes that often intersect with technological features, such as hinged faces that open to reveal inanimate content.

Modern painting and sculpture are exhibited at dozens of galleries around Bangkok, from the delicately lit darlings of Thai high society to industrially decorated spaces in empty warehouses. Other venues and sources of support for modern Thai art include the rotating displays at Bangkok's luxury hotels, particularly the Grand Hyatt Erawan (p172), the Sukhothai (pp175–6) and the Metropolitan (Map pp260–1).

ARCHITECTURE
TEMPLES, FORTS & SHOPHOUSES

When Bangkok became the capital of the kingdom of Siam in 1782, the first task set before designers of the new city was to create hallowed ground for royal palaces and Buddhist monasteries. Indian astrologers and high-ranking Buddhist monks conferred to select and consecrate the most auspicious riverside locations, marking them off with small carved stone pillars. Siam's most talented architects and artisans then weighed in, creating majestic and ornate edifices designed to astound all who ventured into the new capital.

Top Five Buildings

- **Bangkok Bank** (Map pp252–3; Cnr Soi Wanit 1 & Th Mangkhon) Classic century-old Ratanakosin, blending European and Chinese.
- **Chalermkrung Royal Theatre** (Map pp252–3; 66 Th Charoen Krung) The city's best surviving example of Thai Deco.
- **Chao Sua Son's House** (Map pp252–3; Talat Noi) With its round doorway opening on to a central U-shaped courtyard, this is one of the only examples of traditional Chinese residential architecture anywhere in Thailand.
- **Thai Wah II** (Map pp260–1; Th Sathon Tai) Although only the second-tallest, this is the most tasteful of Bangkok's superscrapers.
- **Sukhothai Hotel** (Map pp260–1; Th Sathon Tai) Fuses American architect Ed Tuttle's minimalist vision of traditional Thai temple arts with innovative hotel design.

The temples and palaces along the riverbanks of Mae Nam Chao Phraya transformed humble Bang Makok into the glitter and glory of Ko Ratanakosin (Ratanakosin Island), and their scale and intricacy continue to make a lasting impression on new arrivals. Whether approaching by river or by road, from a distance your eye is instantly caught by the sunlight refracting off the multitude of gilded spires peeking over the huge walls of Wat Phra Kaew (p78), the Temple of the Emerald Buddha. Inside the brick-and-stucco walls, you can easily lose yourself amid the million-sq-metre grounds, which bring together more than a hundred buildings and about two centuries of royal history and architectural experimentation.

Early Bangkok was both a citadel and a city of temples and palaces. Today the massive whitewashed walls of Phra Sumen Fort (p81), punctured by tiny windows, still loom over the northern end of trendy Th Phra Athit, facing Mae Nam Chao Phraya. Erected in 1783 and named for the mythical Mt Meru (Phra Sumen in Thai) of Hindu-Buddhist cosmology, the octagonal brick-and-stucco bunker was one of 14 city fortresses built along Khlong Banglamphu (Banglamphu Canal), which forms an arc carving an 'island' out of the left bank of Mae Nam Chao Phraya. Today, peaceful Santichaiprakan Park, a grassy strip lying in the the bunker's shadow, receives river breezes which cool refugees from the smoky cafés and bars of Th Phra Athit. The 7km canal curves inland towards another wall-and-bunker cluster, Pom Mahakan, thus marking the southern end of Ko Ratanakosin. Of the ramparts that once lined the entire canal, only Phra Sumen and Mahakan have been preserved to show what 18th-century Bangkok was really about – keeping foreign armies at bay.

In the 19th century, Chinese architecture began exerting a strong influence on the city. In Talat Noi (Little Market), a riverside neighbourhood just south of the older Chinese district, Yaowarat, Chinese entrepreneur Chao Sua Son founded a market where larger riverboats could offload wholesale goods to city merchants. Chao Sua Son's house still stands (Map pp252–3), a rare example of traditional Chinese architecture in Thailand. Under King Rama IV, the palace treasury found it could no longer cope with the complexities of burgeoning international trade, so the king granted a licence to Prince Mahissara Ratchaharuthai to establish the Book (as in 'bookkeeping') Club in Talat Noi. The name was later changed to Siam Commercial Bank, today one of Thailand's three leading banks. At the original office in Talat Noi, bank tellers count the money behind iron-grill windows, as customers glide in and out on old tile floors.

Open trade with the Portuguese, Dutch, English, French and Chinese made the fortifications obsolete by the mid-19th century, and most of the original city wall was demolished to make way for sealed roadways. By 1900 these roadways were lined with two-storey Sino-Gothic shophouses inspired by King Rama V's visits to Singapore and Penang.

Thais began mixing traditional Thai with European forms in the late 19th and early 20th centuries, as exemplified by Bangkok's Vimanmek Teak Mansion (p86), the Author's Wing of the Oriental Hotel (p174–5), the Chakri Mahaprasat next to Wat Phra Kaew (p78), and any number of older residences and shophouses in Bangkok. This style is usually referred to as 'old Bangkok' or 'Ratanakosin'. The Old Siam Plaza shopping centre (Map pp252–3), adjacent to Bangkok's Chalermkrung Royal Theatre (p136), is an attempt to revive the old Bangkok school.

Disembark at the Mae Nam Chao Phraya pier of Tha Tien (Map p256), weave your way through the vendor carts selling grilled squid and rice noodles, and you'll find yourself standing between two rows of shophouses of the sort once found along all the streets near the river. The deep, shaded porticoes of the ground floor, topped by upper storeys with tall, shuttered windows and delicate plaster foliage, preserve the elegance of old Bangkok's 'grand Victorian ladies'. Inside, the ground floors display multi-hued tiles of French, Italian or Dutch design, while upper floors are planked with polished teak.

South of Talat Noi, about 3km of the Mae Nam Chao Phraya riverside were formerly given over to international mercantile enterprises such as the East Asiatic Co, Chartered Bank, British Dispensary, Bombay Burmah Trading Co, Banque de l'Indochine and Messrs Howarth Erskine, as well as the Portuguese, French, Russian, British, American, German and Italian embassies. The architecture of this area – known as Bang Rak – was Bangkok's most flamboyant, a mixture of grand neoclassical fronts, shuttered Victorian windows and beaux-arts ornamentation. Many of these old buildings have survived. All have been obscured by modern structures along Th Charoen Krung, hence the best way to appreciate them as a group is by boat.

In the early 20th century, architects left the Victorian era behind, blended European Art Deco with functionalist restraint and created Thai Art Deco. Built just before WWI, an early and outstanding example of this style is Hualamphong Railway Station (p88). The station's vaulted iron roof and neoclassical portico are a testament to state-of-the-art engineering, while the patterned, two-toned skylights exemplify Dutch modernism.

Fully realised examples of Thai Deco from the 1920s and '30s can be found along China-town's main streets, particularly Th Yaowarat (Map pp252–3). Whimsical Deco-style sculptures – the Eiffel Tower, a lion, an elephant, a Moorish dome – surmount vertical towers

Phibul, Feroci & the Demo

In 1939, Thai Prime Minister Phibul Songkhram decided that Bangkok needed a national monument commemorating the 1932 revolution that overthrew Thailand's system of absolute monarchy. Phibul chose Th Ratchadamnoen – originally built for royal motorcades – as the ideal spot for this 'Democracy Monument' (p81). Whether he chose it specifically to thumb his nose at royalty, or happened to be the city's broadest avenue, is a question that's best not to ask in Thailand.

Phibul, an ardent admirer of the steely nationalism of Adolf Hitler and Benito Mussolini, chose to commission Corrado Feroci, an Italian artist who had previously designed monuments for Mussolini. Feroci, later known in Thailand by his government-conferred Thai name, Silpa Bhirasri, in turn enlisted the help of his Thai students at Bangkok's School of Fine Arts (SOFA). Together they created a monument of structural simplicity and symbolic complexity.

To start with, Feroci and the students buried 75 cannonballs in the monument's base to signify the year of the coup, BE 2475 (AD 1932). Atop the base they raised four Art Deco 'wings' to represent the role of the Thai army, navy, air force and police in the 1932 coup. Each wing stands 24m high, in homage to the date – 24 June – of the coup. The wings surround a turret containing a bronze cast of the original constitution, which has long been supplanted by others.

Four bas-relief human forms around the base of the wings represent the original coup conspirators, the Thai armed forces, the Thai people and the personification of 'Balance and Good Life'. Nowhere on the monument will you find any symbols of Buddhism or the monarchy.

Today few people know that 'the Demo', as it has been dubbed by foreign residents, was commissioned by a leader who himself had not been democratically elected. Phibul, appointed prime minister by Siam's military rulers in 1938, renamed the country 'Thailand', introduced the Western solar calendar and cooperated with the Japanese when they invaded Thailand in 1940. After the Japanese were expelled from Thailand at the end of WWII, Phibul was imprisoned and then exiled to Japan. In 1948 he returned and bullied his way into the prime minister's seat again during another military coup. Ousted by a rival military man, Field Marshal Sarith Thanarath, in 1957, Phibul returned to Japan, where he died in 1964.

The façade of the National Theatre (p136)

over doorways. Atop one commercial buildingon Th Songwat perches a rusting model of a WWII Japanese Zero warplane. Placed there by the Japanese during their brief occupation of Bangkok in 1941, it coordinates perfectly with the surrounding Thai-Deco elements. Other examples are the Chalermkrung Royal Theatre (p136), the Royal Hotel (p166), Ratchadamnoen Boxing Stadium (p138) and the Bangkok main post office (p219).

OFFICE TOWERS, HOTELS & SHOPPING CENTRES

During most of the post-WWII era, the trend in modern Thai architecture – inspired by the German Bauhaus movement – was towards a boring International-Style functionalism, and the average building looked like a giant egg carton turned on its side. The Thai aesthetic, so vibrant in prewar eras, almost disappeared in this characterless style of architecture.

The city has been moving skywards almost as quickly as it has expanded outwards. When the Dusit Thani Hotel (p174) opened in 1970 it was the capital's tallest building, and even by the end of that decade fewer than 25 buildings stood taller than six floors. By the year 2000, nearly a thousand buildings could claim that distinction, with at least 20 of them towering higher than 45 floors.

On Th Sathon Tai are the Bank of Asia headquarters (p93), known locally as the 'Robot Building'. Thai architect Sumet Jumsai combined nut-and-bolt motifs at various elevations with a pair of lightning rods on the roof (arranged to resemble sci-fi robot-like antennae) and two metallic-lidded 'eyes' staring out from the upper façade. The Robot Building represents one of the last examples of architectural modernism in Bangkok, a trend which had all but concluded by the mid-1980s.

Almost every monumental project constructed in Bangkok now falls squarely in the postmodernist camp, combining rationalism with decorative elements from the past. Proclaiming its monumental verticality like a colossal exclamation point, the 60-storey Thai Wah II building (Map pp260–1), also on Th Sathon Tai, combines rectangles and squares to create a geometric mosaic updating Egyptian Deco. At 305m, the cloud-stabbing Baiyoke Tower II (home to the Baiyoke Sky Hotel – see p171) is currently the second-tallest structure in Southeast Asia after Kuala Lumpur's Petronas Twin Towers. Stylistically it shows the inspiration of American post-Deco.

Pure verticality is now giving way to tiered skyscrapers in accordance with the city's setback regulations for allowing light into city streets. The tiered Bangkok City Tower (Map pp260–1) stacks marble, glass and granite around recessed entryways and window lines to create a stunning Mesopotamia-meets-Madison Avenue effect. Everything 'neo' is in, including neo-Thai. The Four Seasons (p171), Sukhothai (p175–6) and Grand Hyatt Erawan (p172) are all examples of hotels that make extensive use of Thai classical motifs in layout and ornamentation.

MUSIC

Throughout Bangkok you'll find a mind-bending diversity of musical genres and styles, from the serene court music that accompanies classical dance-drama to the chest-thumping house music played at dance clubs. Virtually every musical movement heard in the West has been turned upside down, and Bangkokians have piled yet more variations on top of it all.

CLASSICAL THAI

Classical central-Thai music (phleng thai doem) features a dazzling array of textures and subtleties, hair-raising tempos and pastoral melodies. The classical orchestra or pìi-phâat can include as few as five players or more than 20. Leading the band is pìi, a straight-lined woodwind instrument with a reed mouthpiece and an oboe-like tone; you'll hear it most at muay thai (Thai-boxing) matches. The four-stringed phin, plucked like a guitar, lends subtle counterpoint, while ránâat èhk, a bamboo-keyed percussion instrument resembling the xylophone, carries the main melodies. The slender saw, a bowed instrument with a coconut-shell soundbox, provides soaring embellishments, as does the khlùi or wooden Thai flute.

One of the more noticeable pìi-phâat instruments, kháwng wong yài, consists of tuned gongs arranged in a semicircle and played in simple rhythmic lines to provide the music's underlying fabric. Several types

Old & In Fashion

Classical Thai music received a huge boost in Thailand when the film Hom Rong (The Overture) was released in 2004. Based on the life story of Thai maestro Luang Pradit Phairoh (1881–1954), the film chronicles an era when Thai political leaders were trying to suppress traditional Thai music in favour of Western classical music in order to prove to would-be colonisers that Thais were 'civilised'. Despite the illicit nature of his endeavours, the hero perseveres in his study of the ránâat èhk (Thai wooden xylophone) and eventually wins over the hearts of the Thai people in restoring social status to Thai classical music. In the first few months after the film's opening, new students were practically standing in line to learn ránâat èhk at Bangkok music schools. There has been a corresponding leap in demand for the instruments.

of drums, some played with the hands, some with sticks, carry the beat, often through several tempo changes in a single song. The most important type of drum is tà-phon (or thon), a double-headed hand-drum that sets the tempo for the entire ensemble. Prior to a performance, the players offer incense and flowers to tà-phon, considered to be the conductor of the music's spiritual content.

The pìi-phâat ensemble was originally developed to accompany classical dance-drama and shadow theatre but is also commonly heard in straightforward concert performances. Classical Thai music may sound strange to Western visitors due to the use of the standard Thai scale, which divides the octave into seven full-tone intervals with no semitones. Thai scales were first transcribed by the Thai-German composer Peter Feit (whose Thai name was Phra Chen Duriyanga), who also composed Thailand's national anthem in 1932.

THAI POP

Popular Thai music has borrowed much from Western music, particularly in instrumentation, but retains a distinct flavour of its own. The bestselling of all modern musical genres in Thailand remains *lûuk thûng*. Literally 'children of the fields', *lûuk thûng* dates back to the 1940s, is analogous to country and western in the USA, and is a genre that tends to appeal most to working-class Thais. Subject matter almost always cleaves to tales of lost love, tragic early death and the dire circumstances of farmers who work day in and day out and at the end of the year still owe money to the bank.

Lûuk thûng song structures tend to be formulaic as well. There are two basic styles, the original Suphanburi style, with lyrics in standard Thai, and an Ubon style sung in Isan (northeastern) dialect. Thailand's most famous *lûuk thûng* singer, Pumpuang Duangjan (see the boxed text on p31), rated a royally sponsored cremation when she died in 1992, and a major shrine at Suphanburi's Wat Thapkradan, which receives a steady stream of worshippers.

Several popular magazines and TV programmes are dedicated to the promotion of the *lûuk thûng* industry, as well as a few Thai films. The 2002 Thai box-office hit *Mon Rak Transistor* follows the tribulations of a young *lûuk thûng* singer trying to make it in Bangkok (see also p37). Chai Muang Sing and Siriporn Amphaipong have been the most beloved *lûuk thûng* superstars for several years, with lesser lights coming and going. Other stars include former soap opera star Got Chakraband, and Monsit Khamsoi, whose trademark silky vocal style has proved enormously popular. One of the more surprising newcomers is Jonas Anderson, a blonde-haired, blue-eyed Swede who spent part of his childhood in northeastern Thailand and is now one of the hottest-selling *lûuk thûng* acts in the country.

Part of the genre's popularity is due to the spectacular *lûuk thûng* shows that tour temple fairs around Thailand, combining song, dance, comedy and large casts attired in an array of costumes – from royalty to rambutans (a popular Thai fruit). Would-be aficionados can track down modern and classical *lûuk thûng* in most Bangkok music stores.

CD warehouse in the Siam Discovery Center (p150)

Electronic Pop Queen

The popularity of *lûuk thûng* skyrocketed in the 1960s with the stardom of Suraphon Sombatjalern, a kind of Thai country Dean Martin. But the most popular *lûuk thûng* star of all was Pumpuang Duangjan, whose life mirrored the dreams and tragedies of the songs that she sang.

The illiterate daughter of a farming family, Pumpuang left her rural town of Suphanburi to seek her fortune in the city. She joined a band as a dancer at the age of 14 and soon after eloped with the saxophone player (who later ran off with her sister) before becoming the band's lead singer. She eventually became one of Thailand's most famous, if tragic, musical heroines. The extraordinary range of her voice ensured her nationwide success across all social levels; she once sang a song penned for her by Princess Sirindhorn for a royal performance. Her personal life was marked by heartbreak, and she suffered a string of much publicised failed love affairs. One of the most colourful rumours circulated was that she paid her married lover's wife so that she might keep him as her own, only to have him spend all her money, run her into debt and abandon her for his original wife.

Pumpuang peaked in the 1980s when she pioneered the pop-style electronic *lûuk thûng*. She died in 1992, at the age of 31, from an immune system–related illness.

Another genre more firmly rooted in northeastern Thailand, and nearly as popular in Bangkok, is *măw lam*. Based on the songs played on the Lao-Isan *khaen*, a wind instrument devised of a double row of bamboo-like reeds fitted into a hardwood soundbox, *măw lam* features a simple but insistent bass beat and plaintive vocal melodies. If *lûuk thûng* is Thailand's country and western, then *măw lam* is its blues. Jintara Poonlap and Chalermphol Malaikham are the reigning queen and king of *măw lam*. These and other singers also perform *lûuk thûng prá-yúk*, a blend of *lûuk thûng* and *măw lam* that is emerging as *măw lam* loses its 'country bumpkin' image. Purists eschew *lûuk thûng prá-yúk* in favour of rootsier, funkier *măw lam* artists such as Rumpan Saosanon. Meanwhile, Sommainoi Duangcharoen goes in a completely different direction, mixing a bit of jazz and even rap into his *măw lam*. Tune into Bangkok radio station Luk Thung FM (FM 95.0) for large doses of *lûuk thûng* and *măw lam*.

The 1970s ushered in a new style inspired by the politically conscious folk rock of the US and Europe, which the Thais dubbed *phleng phêua chii-wít* (literally 'music for life'). Closely identified with the Thai band Caravan – which still performs regularly – the introduction of this style was the most significant musical shift in Thailand since *lûuk thûng* arose in the 1940s. *Phleng phêua chii-wít* has political and environmental topics rather than the usual love themes. During the authoritarian dictatorships of the '70s many of Caravan's songs were banned. Following the massacre of student demonstrators in 1976, some members of the band fled to the hills to take up with armed communist groups. Another proponent of this style, Carabao, took *phleng phêua chii-wít*, fused it with *lûuk thûng*, rock and heavy metal, and spawned a whole generation of imitators as well as a chain of barn-like performance venues seating a thousand or more.

Thailand also has a thriving teen-pop industry – sometimes referred to as T-Pop – centred on artists who have been chosen for their good looks, and then matched with syrupy song arrangements. GMM Grammy, Thailand's music industry heavyweight, dominates sales and promotion. Singers who are *lûuk khrêung* – half-Thai, half-*faràng* (Western) – and sport Western names are particularly popular, for example, Tata Young, Nicole Theriault and Thongchai 'Bird' Macintyre. Teen girl pop singers Palmy and Mint play much the same musical roles in Bangkok as Britney Spears and Christina Aguilera play in the West.

Among the compact disc–buying public, karaoke CDs and VCDs comprise a huge share of the market. Many major Thai artists – even alt-rock groups – release subtitled VCDs specially formatted for karaoke-style sing-alongs.

THAI ALT/INDIE

In the 1990s an alternative pop scene – known as *klawng sĕhrii* or 'free drum' in Thailand, also *phleng tâi din*, 'underground music' – grew in Bangkok. Hip-hop/ska artist Joey Boy

Top 10 Thai CDs

Most of these CDs are available from Tower Records in the Emporium (Map pp264–5) and at Central World Plaza (Map pp262–3). You can also order online at www.nongtaprachan.com or www.ethaicd.com.

- *Bakery Music: Lust For Live* – Collection of live alt rock performances by Modern Dog, Chou Chou, Yokee Playboy, P.O.P. and Rudklao Amraticha.
- *Banyen Raggan: Khaw Du Jai Kawn* – Good introduction to *mǎw lam*.
- *Blackhead: Handmade* – Thai grunge rock.
- *Carabao: Made in Thailand* – Carabao's classic and internationally popular album.
- *Caravan: Khon Kap Khwai* – The album that kicked off the *phleng phêua chii-wít* movement.
- *Fong Nam: The Nang Hong Suite* – Brilliant Thai funeral music, but think New Orleans second-line cheer rather than dirge.
- *Joey Boy: Joey Boy's Anthology* – Thirteen ska/hip-hop tracks from Joey Boy's seven years with Bakery Music.
- *Loso: The Best of Loso* – Thai anthems of teen angst.
- *Modern Dog: Modern Dog* – The Dog's debut album is still its best.
- *Pumpuang Duangjan: Best* – Compilation of the late *lûuk thûng* diva's most famous tunes.

not only explored new musical frontiers but released lyrics that the Department of Culture banned. One song, for example, included the Thai euphemism for male masturbation, *chák wâo* (pull a kite).

Modern Dog, a Britpop-inspired band of four Chulalongkorn University graduates, is generally credited with bringing independent Thai music into the mainstream, and their success prompted an explosion of similar bands and indie recording labels. Like Joey Boy, they're on the Bakery Music label, the main alternative to GMM Grammy.

Crowd pleaser Loso (from 'low society') reinvented Carabao's Thai folk melodies and rhythms with indie guitar rock. Grammy responded with a rash of similar Thai headbangers designed to fill stadiums and outsell the indies. Major alternative acts in Thailand include Modern Dog, its Britpop-inspired rivals Pru and Day Tripper, punk metal band, Ebola, and the electronica/underground group Futon, which is made up of British, Thai and Japanese band members. Futon's remake of Iggy Pop's proto-punk classic 'I Wanna Be Your Dog' hit big in Thailand, and its album *Don't Mind the Botox* has been distributed internationally.

As in the West, some indies have been compelled to undergo mergers to survive. Bakery Music is now owned by BMG Entertainment, a division of Bertelsmann AG, the world's largest media conglomerate. Meanwhile, Grammy has developed its own subsidiary alt-rock label, Genie. Truly independent labels to look for include Rehab, Junk Food and Hualamphong Riddim. For the latest indie Thai, tune into Fat Radio, 104.5 FM.

The indie stuff is almost always reserved for concert performances or one-off club appearances. One spot with regular weekend concerts is the outdoor stage at Centrepoint, Siam Square.

JAZZ & WORLD MUSIC INFLUENCES

Yet another inspiring movement in modern Thai music has been the fusion of international jazz with Thai classical and folk styles. Fong Nam, a Thai orchestra led by US composer Bruce Gaston, performs an inspiring blend of Western and Thai classical motifs, which has become a favourite for movie soundtracks, TV commercials and tourism promotions. However, a live Fong Nam performance is not to be missed. Fong Nam play regularly at Tawan Daeng German Brewhouse (p133). Another leading exponent of this genre is the composer and instrumentalist Tewan Sapsanyakorn (also known as Tong Tewan), who plays soprano and alto sax, violin and *khlùi* with equal virtuosity. Tewan's compositions are often based on Thai melodies but the improvisations and rhythms are drawn from diverse jazz sources such as Sonny Rollins and Jean-Luc Ponty. Other notable groups fusing international jazz and indigenous Thai music include Kangsadarn and Boy Thai; the latter adds Brazilian samba and reggae to the mix.

THEATRE & DANCE

Traditional Thai theatre consists of five dramatic forms. *Khŏn* is a formal, masked dance-drama depicting scenes from the *Ramakian* (the Thai version of India's *Ramayana*), and originally performed only for the royal court. *Lákhon* is a general term that covers several types of dance-drama (usually for nonroyal occasions), including *mánohraa*, the southern Thai version based on a 2000-year-old Indian story, and Western theatre. *Lí-keh* (likay) is a partly improvised, often bawdy folk play featuring dancing, comedy, melodrama and music. *Lákhon lék* or *hùn lŭang* is puppet theatre, and *lákhon phûut* is modern spoken theatre.

KHŎN

In all *khŏn* performances, four types of characters are represented – male humans, female humans, monkeys and demons. Monkey and demon figures are always masked with the elaborate head coverings often seen in tourist promo material. Behind the masks and make-up, all actors are male. Traditional *khŏn* is very expensive to produce – Ravana's retinue alone (Ravana is the *Ramakian*'s principal villain) consists of more than a hundred demons, each with a distinctive mask.

Perhaps because it was once limited to royal venues and hence never gained a popular following, the *khŏn* or *Ramakian* dance-drama tradition nearly died out in Thailand. Bangkok's National Theatre (p136) was once the only place where *khŏn* was regularly performed for the public; the renovated Chalermkrung Royal Theatre (p136) now hosts occasional *khŏn* performances, enhanced by laser graphics and hi-tech audio.

Scenes performed in traditional *khŏn* (and *lákhon* performances – see the following section) come from the 'epic journey' tale of the *Ramayana*, with parallels in the Greek Odyssey and the myth of Jason and the Argonauts. The central story revolves around Prince Rama's search for his beloved Princess Sita, who has been abducted by the evil 10-headed demon Ravana and taken to the island of Lanka. Rama is assisted in his search and in the final battle against Ravana by a host of mythical half-animal, half-human characters including the monkey-god Hanuman (see p35 for some details on the differences between the Indian *Ramayana* and the Thai *Ramakian*).

LÁKHON

The more formal *lákhon nai* (inner *lákhon*, which means that it is performed inside the palace) was originally performed for lower nobility by all-female ensembles. Today it's a dying art, even more so than royal *khŏn*. In addition to scenes from the *Ramakian*, *lákhon nai* performances may include traditional Thai folk tales; whatever the story, text is always sung. *Lákhon nâwk* (outer *lákhon*, performed outside the palace) deals exclusively with folk tales and features a mix of sung and spoken text, sometimes with improvisation. Male and female performers are permitted. Like *khŏn* and *lákhon nai*, performances are increasingly rare.

Much more common these days is the less refined *lákhon chaatrii*, a fast-paced, costumed dance-drama usually performed at upcountry temple festivals or at shrines (commissioned by a shrine devotee whose wish was granted by the shrine deity). *Chaatrii* stories are often influenced by the older *mánohraa* theatre of southern Thailand.

Young Lákhon dancer wearing traditional costume (left).

A variation on *chaatrii* that has evolved specifically for shrine worship, *lákhon kâe bon,* involves an ensemble of about 20, including musicians. At an important shrine such as Bangkok's Lak Meuang, four *kâe bon* troupes may alternate, each for a week at a time, as each performance lasts from 9am till 3pm and there is usually a long list of worshippers waiting to hire them.

LÍ-KEH

In outlying working-class neighbourhoods of Bangkok you may be lucky enough to come across the gaudy, raucous *lí-keh.* This theatrical art form is thought to have descended from drama-rituals brought to southern Thailand by Arab and Malay traders. The first native public performance in central Thailand came about when a group of Thai Muslims staged *lí-keh* for Rama V in Bangkok during the funeral commemoration of Queen Sunantha. *Lí-keh* grew very popular under Rama VI, peaked in the early 20th century and has been fading slowly since the 1960s.

Most often performed at Buddhist festivals by troupes of travelling performers, *lí-keh* is a colourful mixture of folk and classical music, outrageous costumes, melodrama, slapstick comedy, sexual innuendo and commentary on Thai politics and society. *Faràng* – even those who speak fluent Thai – are often left behind by the highly idiomatic language and gestures. Most *lí-keh* performances begin with the *àwk khàek,* a prelude in which an actor dressed in Malay costume takes the stage to pay homage to the troupe's teacher and to narrate a brief summary of the play to the audience. For true *lí-keh* aficionados, the visit of a renowned troupe is a bigger occasion than the release of a new *Matrix* sequel at the local cinema.

LÁKHON LÉK

Lákhon lék (little theatre; also known as *hùn lǔang,* or royal puppets), like *khǒn,* was once reserved for court performances. Metre-high marionettes made of *khòi* paper and wire, wearing elaborate costumes modelled on those of the *khǒn,* were used to convey similar themes, music and dance movements.

Two to three puppet masters were required to manipulate each *hùn lǔang* – including arms, legs, hands, even fingers and eyes – by means of wires attached to long poles. Stories were drawn from Thai folk tales, particularly *Phra Aphaimani* (a classical Thai literary work), and occasionally from the *Ramakian. Hùn lǔang* is no longer performed, as the performance techniques and puppet-making skills have been lost. The *hùn lǔang* puppets themselves are highly collectable; the Bangkok National Museum has only one example in its collection. Surviving examples of a smaller, 30cm court version called *hùn lék* (little puppets) are occasionally used in live performances; only one puppeteer is required for each marionette in *hùn lék.*

Another form of Thai puppet theatre, *hùn kràbàwk* (cylinder puppets), is based on popular Hainanese puppet shows. It uses 30cm hand puppets carved from wood and viewed only from the waist up. *Hùn kràbàwk* marionettes are still crafted and used in performances today, most notably at the Joe Louis Theatre in Bangkok (see p136).

LÁKHON PHÛUT

Lákhon phûut – 'speaking theatre', or live contemporary theatre as known in the West – is enjoyed by a small elite audience in Bangkok. Virtually the entire scene, such as it is, centres on two venues, Patravadi Theatre (p137) and Bangkok Playhouse (p136).

LITERATURE
CLASSICAL

The written word has a long history in Thailand, dating back to the 11th or 12th centuries when the first Thai script was fashioned from an older Mon alphabet. Sukhothai king Phaya Lithai is thought to have composed the first work of Thai literature in 1345. This was *Traiphum Phra Ruang,* a treatise that described the three realms of existence according to Hindu–Buddhist cosmology. According to contemporary scholars, this work and its symbolism continues to have considerable influence on Thailand's art and culture.

Of all classical Thai literature, however, the *Ramakian* is the most pervasive and influential. Its Indian precursor – the *Ramayana* – came to Thailand with the Khmers 900 years ago, first appearing as stone reliefs on Prasat Hin Phimai and other Angkor temples in the northeast. Eventually, Thailand developed its own version of the epic, which was first written during the reign of Rama I. This version contains 60,000 stanzas and is a quarter again longer than the Sanskrit original.

The 30,000-line *Phra Aphaimani,* composed by poet Sunthorn Phu in the late 18th century, is Thailand's most famous classical literary work. Like many of its epic predecessors around the world, it tells the story of an exiled prince who must triumph in an odyssey of love and war before returning to his kingdom.

During the Ayuthaya period, Thailand developed a classical poetic tradition based on five types of verse – *chǎn, kàap, khlong, klawn* and *râi.* Each form uses a complex set of rules to regulate metre, rhyming patterns and number of syllables. During the political upheavals of the 1970s, several Thai newspaper editors, most notably Kukrit Pramoj, composed lightly disguised political commentary in *klawn* verse. Modern Thai poets seldom use the classical forms, preferring to compose in blank verse or with song-style rhyming.

CONTEMPORARY

The first Thai-language novel appeared only about 70 years ago, in direct imitation of Western models. Thus far, no more than 10 have been translated into English.

The first Thai novel of substance, *The Circus of Life* (Thai 1929; English 1994) by Arkartdamkeung Rapheephat, follows a young, upper-class Thai as he travels to London, Paris, the USA and China in the 1920s. The novel's existentialist tone created quite a stir in Thailand when it was released, and became an instant bestseller. The fact that the author, himself a Thai prince, took his own life at the age of 26 added to the mystique surrounding this work.

The late Kukrit Pramoj, former ambassador and Thai prime minister, novelised Bangkok court life from the late 19th century through to the 1940s in *Four Reigns* (Thai 1953; English 1981), the longest novel ever published in Thai. *The Story of Jan Darra* (Thai 1966; English 1994), by journalist and short-story writer Utsana Phleungtham, traces the sexual obsessions of a Thai aristocrat as they are passed to his son. Director/producer Nonzee Nimibutr turned the remarkable novel into a rather melodramatic film (see p37). Praphatsorn Seiwikun's rapid-paced *Time in a Bottle* (Thai 1984; English 1996) turned the dilemmas of a fictional middle-class Bangkok family into a bestseller.

Many Thai authors, including the notable Khamphoon Boonthawi *(Luk Isan)* and Chart Kobjitt *(Time),* have been honoured with the SEA Write Award, an annual prize presented to fiction writers from countries in the Association of South East Asian Nations (ASEAN). A one-stop collection of fiction thus awarded can be found in *The SEA Write Anthology of Thai Short Stories and Poems* (1996).

When it comes to novels written in English, Thai wunderkind SP Somtow has written and published more titles than any other Thai writer. Born in Bangkok, educated at Eton and Cambridge, and now a commuter between two 'cities of angels' – Los Angeles and Bangkok – Somtow's prodigious output includes a string of well-reviewed science fiction/fantasy/horror stories, including *Moon Dance, Darker Angels* and *The Vampire's Beautiful Daughter.* The Somtow novel most evocative of Thailand and Thai culture is *Jasmine Nights* (1995), which also happens to be one of his most accessible reads. Following a 12-year-old

Top Five Novels Set in Bangkok

- *A Woman of Bangkok,* Jack Reynolds (1956)
- *All Soul's Day,* Bill Morris (1997)
- *Bangkok 8,* John Burdett (2003)
- *Four Reigns,* Kukrit Pramoj (*Si Phaendin*; 1953, translated 1981)
- *Jasmine Nights,* SP Somtow (1995)

Thai boy's friendship with an African-American boy in Bangkok in the 1960s, this semi-autobiographical work blends Thai, Greek and African myths, American Civil War lore and a dollop of magic realism into a seamless whole.

All Soul's Day (1997), by Bill Morris is a sharp, well-researched historical novel set in Bangkok circa 1963. The story, which involves vintage Buicks and the pre-Second Indochina War American military build-up, would do Graham Greene proud.

Expat writer Christopher G Moore covers the Thai underworld in his 1990s novels *A Killing Smile, Spirit House, A Bewitching Smile* and a raft of others, and his anchor is firmly hooked in the go-go bar scene. His description of Bangkok's sleazy Thermae Coffee House (called 'Zeno' in *A Killing Smile*) is the closest literature comes to evoking the perpetual male adolescence to which such places cater.

Most other efforts in the 'expat-adventures-in-Bangkok' genre aren't worth looking up, though a few – particularly Jake Needham's *The Big Mango* (the first expat novel to be translated into Thai) – are entertaining. Legal thriller *Laundry Man* (2003), also by Jake Needham, is set mostly in Bangkok and would do John Grisham proud.

One recent surprise is John Burdett's *Bangkok 8* (2003), a page-turner in which a half-Thai, half-*faràng* police detective investigates the python-and-cobras murder of a US Marine in Bangkok. Along the way we're treated to vivid portraits of the gritty capital and insights into Thai Buddhism.

CINEMA

Bangkok Film launched Thailand's film industry with the first Thai-directed silent movie, *Chok Sorng Chan,* in 1927. Silent films proved to be more popular than talkies right into the 1960s, and as late as 1969, Thai studios were still producing them from 16mm stock. Perhaps partially influenced by India's famed *masala* (curry mix) movies – which enjoyed a strong following in post-WWII Bangkok – film companies blended romance, comedy, melodrama and adventure to give Thai audiences a little bit of everything.

The arrival of 35mm movies in Thailand around the same time brought a proliferation of modern cinema halls and a surge in movie-making. During this era Thai films attracted more cinema-goers than *năng faràng* (movies from Europe and America), and today many Thais consider the '60s to be a golden age of Thai cinema. More than half of the approximately 75 films produced annually during this period starred the much-admired onscreen duo Mit Chaibancha and Petchara Chaowaraj.

Despite the founding of a government committee in 1970 to promote Thai cinema, Thai film production in the '70s and early '80s was mostly limited to inexpensive action or romance stories. A notable exception, *Luk Isan* (*Child of the North-East;* 1983), based on a Thai novel of the same name, follows the ups and downs of a farming family living in drought-ridden Isan. *Luk Isan* became one of the first popular films to offer urban Thais an understanding of the hardships endured by many northeasterners, and initiated a social drama subgenre that continues to this day.

The Thai movie industry almost died during the '80s and '90s, swamped by Hollywood extravaganzas and the boom era's taste for anything imported. From a 1970s peak of about two hundred releases per year, the Thai output shrank to an average of only 10 films a year by 1997. The Southeast Asian economic crisis that year threatened to further bludgeon the ailing industry, but the lack of funding coupled with foreign competition brought about a new emphasis on quality rather than quantity. The current era boasts a new generation of seriously good Thai directors, several of whom studied film abroad during Thailand's '80s and early '90s boom period.

Recent efforts have been so encouraging that Thai and foreign critics alike speak of a current Thai 'new wave'. Avoiding the soap operatics of the past, the current crop of directors favour gritty realism, artistic innovation and a strengthened Thai identity. Pen-Ek Ratanaruang's *Fun Bar Karaoke* is a 1997 satire of Bangkok life in which the main characters are an ageing Thai playboy and his daughter; the film received critical acclaim for its true-to-life depiction of modern urban living blended with sage humour. It was the first feature-length outing by a young Thai who is fast becoming one of the kingdom's most internationally noted directors. The film played well to international audiences but achieved only limited box-office success at home. Similarly Nonzee Nimibutr's *2499 Antaphan Krong Meuang (Dang Bireley's Young Gangsters)* was hailed abroad – winning first prize at the 1997 Brussels International Film Festival – but was only modestly successful in Thailand.

A harbinger for the Thai film industry was Nonzee Nimibutr's 1998 release of *Nang Nak,* an exquisite retelling of the Mae Nak Phrakhanong legend, in which the spirit of a woman who died during childbirth haunts the home of her husband. This story has had no fewer than 20 previous cinematic renderings. *Nang Nak* not only features excellent acting and period detailing, but manages to transform Nak into a sympathetic character rather than a horrific ghost. The film became the largest-grossing film in Thai history, out-earning even *Titanic,* and earned awards for best director, best art director and best sound at the 1999 Asia-Pacific Film Festival.

Hot on the heels of *Nang Nak*'s success came the 2000 film *Satree Lex (Iron Ladies),* which humorously dramatises the real-life exploits of a Lampang volleyball team made up almost entirely of transvestites and transsexuals. At home, this Yongyoot Thongkongtoon–directed film became Thai cinema's second-largest-grossing film to date, and was the first Thai film ever to reach the art-house cinemas of Europe and the US on general release.

The next Thai film to garner international attention was 2000's *Suriyothai,* a historic epic directed by Prince Chatri Chalerm Yukol. Forty months and US$20 million in the making, the three-hour film lavishly narrates a well-known episode in Thai history in which an Ayuthaya queen sacrifices herself at the 1548 Battle of Hanthawaddy to save her king's life. Although rich in costumes and locations, it flopped overseas and was widely criticised for being ponderous and overly long. Recently, legendary American producer-director Francis Ford Coppola re-edited the film to create a shorter, more internationally palatable version, albeit of limited appeal.

The year 2000 also introduced the Oxide brothers, Danny and Pang, to Thai and foreign film festival audiences with the release of *Krung Thep Antara (Bangkok Dangerous).* Influenced in equal parts by Hong Kong director John Woo and American writer-director Quentin Tarantino, this story of a deaf-mute hit man who finds love won a Discovery award at the Toronto Film Festival and runner-up Best Director in Seattle. Although the Oxides hail from Hong Kong, Thailand has become their main cinematic inspiration.

Top Five Thai Films

- *Bangkok Dangerous*, Danny and Pang Oxide (2000)
- *Mekhong Full Moon Party*, Jira Malikul (2002)
- *Mon Rak Transistor*, Pen-Ek Ratanaruang (2002)
- *Nang Nak*, Nonzee Nimibutr (1998)
- *Satree Lex*, Yongyoot Thongkongtoon (*Iron Ladies*; 2000)

Fah Talai Jone (2000), directed by Wisit Sasanatieng, presents a campy and colourful parody of quasi-cowboy Thai melodramas of the '50s and '60s. The film received an honourable mention at Cannes (where it was quickly dubbed a 'cult hit') and took an award at the Vancouver Film Festival. When Miramax distributed the film in the USA, it was called *Tears of the Black Tiger*.

In 2001 Nonzee Nimibutr returned with *Jan Dara,* a cinematic rendition of Utsana Pleungtham's controversially erotic 1966 novel of the same name. Filmed almost entirely on sound stages save for outdoor scenes shot in Luang Prabang, Laos, the film was critically compared with Vietnam's famous *Scent of Green Papaya*.

Encouraged by critical acclaim abroad and box office receipts at home, Thai producers nearly tripled their output from a total of 12 Thai-language movies in 2001 to around 30 new productions in 2002. Quality continues to improve as well, and Thai films have assumed a newly favoured identity on the international film scene. The Vancouver International Festival, for example, increased its screening of Thai films from three in 2001 to five in 2002.

For evidence that Thailand's role in world cinema will continue to expand, you don't need to look any further than Pen-Ek's *Mon Rak Transistor*. This acclaimed film broke ground by seizing a thoroughly Thai theme – the tragic-comic odyssey of a young villager who tries to crack the big-time *lûuk thûng* music scene in Bangkok – and upgrading production values to international standards. The 2001 release was honoured with a special Directors' Fortnight showing at Cannes 2002, and went on to earn Best Asian Film at the Seattle International Film Festival '02 and the Audience Award at the Vienna International Film Festival '02. One of Thai cinema's finest moments arrived when Cannes 2002 chose *Sut Sanaeha (Blissfully Yours)* for the coveted Un Certain Regard (Of Special Consideration) screening, an event that showcases notable work by new directors. Directed by 31-year-old Apichatpong Weerasethakul, the film dramatises a budding romance between a Thai woman and an illegal Burmese immigrant.

Another favourite on the 2002 festival circuit, and a blockbuster in Thailand as well, was Jira Malikul's film *15 Kham Deuan 11 (Mekhong Full Moon Party)*. The storyline juxtaposes folk beliefs about mysterious 'dragon lights' emanating from Mekong River with the scepticism of Bangkok scientists and news media, and also with Thai Buddhism. As with *Mon Rak Transistor,* the film affectionately evokes everyday Thai culture for the whole world to enjoy. It's also the first Thai feature film where most of the script is written in the Isan dialect, necessitating Thai subtitles.

Another watershed occurred when the 2002 London Thai Film Festival screened 16 Thai films over a one-week period, the first such event outside the country. Just as significantly, the prestigious CineAsia convention and trade show, which focuses on the Asia-Pacific film market, shifted to Bangkok last year after eight years' residence in Hong Kong. One of the reasons cited for the move was the availability of more than 300 screening venues in Bangkok.

The successful inauguration of the Bangkok International Film Festival (BKKIFF) in January 2002 further demonstrates that Thailand lies at the epicentre of a growing film industry. The 2004 BKKIFF screened nearly 140 films, and American director Oliver Stone attended the gala dinner to receive a career achievement award.

Food & Drink

Food & Drink

HISTORY & CULTURE

Bangkok's cooks concoct a seemingly endless variety of dishes, whether from 300-year-old court recipes, the latest in Euro-Thai fusion or simple dishes guided by seasonal and regional necessity.

Standing at the crossroads of many ancient and culturally continuous traditions dominated by India, China and Asian Oceania, Thailand has adapted cooking techniques and ingredients from all three of these major spheres of influence, as well as the culinary kits carried by passing traders and empire-builders from the Middle East and southern Europe. Over the centuries, indigenous rudiments have fused with imported elements to produce a distinctive native cuisine that is instantly recognisable.

Appreciation of Thai food is so central to Thai cultural identity that many Thais naively assume that non-Thais are physically or mentally unable to partake of the cuisine. Foreign visitors or residents won't be asked simply whether they like to eat Thai food. Rather they will be asked *'Kin aahǎan thai pen mǎi?'* ('Do you know how to eat Thai food?') It is almost assumed that to enjoy Thai cooking you must be either born Thai or trained in the difficult art of feeling exhilarated over a plate of well-prepared *phàt thai* (rice noodles stir-fried with egg, tofu and peanuts).

Of course the one aspect of the cuisine that does require getting used to for many people, even other Asians, is Thai food's relatively high chilli content. This is why the second-most common question asked of a foreigner about to slip a spoon into a bowl of *kaeng khǐaw-wǎan* (green curry) is *'Kin phèt dâi mǎi?'* ('Can you eat spicy food?')

Unlike their Indian counterparts, Thai cooks assemble curry pastes and other relatively elaborate seasoning concoctions quickly from fresh rather than powdered, dried or preserved ingredients. Exceptions include the fermentation and pickling processes favoured for certain condiments and seasonings. In classic Thai dishes, the use of butter or lard is extremely rare, limited to East-West fusion experiments.

A vendor preparing a variety of delicious treats in Sanam Luang (p76)

You will quickly discover that eating is one of life's great pleasures in Bangkok. The average Bangkokian takes time out to eat, not three times per day, but four or five. Sitting down at a roadside *rót khěn* (vendor cart) after an evening of cinema or nightclubbing, a Thai may barely have finished one steaming bowl of noodles before ordering a second round, just to revel in the experience a little longer.

ETIQUETTE

While Thai table manners would hardly ever be described as 'formal' in the Western sense, there are plenty of subtleties to be mastered. Using the correct utensils and eating gestures will garner much respect from Thais, who generally think Western table manners are coarse.

Originally Thai food was eaten with the fingers, and it still is in certain regions of the kingdom. Some foods, such as *khâo nĭaw* (sticky rice), are eaten by hand everywhere. In the early 1900s, restaurateurs began setting their tables with fork and spoon to affect a 'royal' setting, and it wasn't long before fork-and-spoon dining became the norm in Bangkok and later spread throughout the kingdom.

The *sâwm* (fork) and *cháwn tó* (tablespoon) are placed to the left of the plate, and usually wrapped in a paper or cloth napkin. In simpler restaurants, these utensils are laid bare on the table or may not arrive until the food is served. Some restaurants place a steel or glass container on each tabletop, in which a supply of clean forks and spoons is kept.

To most Thais, pushing a fork into one's mouth is almost as uncouth as putting a knife in the mouth in Western countries. Thais use forks to steer food onto the spoon, to eat chunks of roasted meat served as *kàp klâem* (snacks eaten with drinks) and to spear sliced fruit served at the end of the meal. Even so, the fork is never placed all the way into the mouth.

Tà-kìap (chopsticks) are reserved for dining in Chinese restaurants or for eating Chinese noodle dishes. Noodle soups are eaten with a spoon in the left hand (for spooning up the broth) and chopsticks in the right.

Whether at home or in a restaurant, Thai meals are always served 'family style', that is, from common serving platters. Traditionally, the party orders one of each kind of dish, perhaps a curry, a fish, a stir-fry, a *yam* (hot and tangy salad), a vegetable dish and a soup, taking care to balance cool and hot, sour and sweet, salty and plain. One dish is generally large enough for two people. One or two extras may be ordered for a large party.

Dishes are typically served more or less all at once rather than in courses. If the host or restaurant staff can't bring them all to the table at the same time, then the diners typically wait until everything has arrived before digging in. One exception to this rule is if a *yam* or other *kàp klâem* is ordered, as these are sometimes served as an appetiser with drinks before the main meal. When these dishes come out with everything else they will be eaten first.

Thais aren't fussy about dishes being served piping hot, so no-one minds if the dishes sit untouched for a while. In fact, it's considered impolite to take a spoonful of steaming-hot food, as it implies that you're so ravenous or uncivilised that you can't wait to gorge yourself. The one exception to the cooling rule is noodle dishes, which are typically served right from the pan.

Empty plates are placed in front of every person at the beginning of the meal, and the diners take a little from each serving platter onto these plates. When serving yourself from a common platter, put no more than one spoonful onto your plate at a time. It's customary at the start of a shared meal to eat a spoonful of plain rice first – a gesture that recognises rice as the most important part of the meal.

The Right Tool for the Job

If you're not offered chopsticks, don't ask for them. Thai food is eaten with fork and spoon, not chopsticks. When *faràng* (Westerners) ask for chopsticks to eat Thai food, it only puzzles the restaurant proprietors.

Chopsticks are reserved for eating Chinese-style food from bowls, or for eating in all-Chinese restaurants. In either case you will be supplied with chopsticks without having to ask. Unlike their counterparts in many Western countries, restaurateurs in Thailand won't assume you don't know how to use them.

For the most part, *tôm yam* (chilli and lemon-grass soup) and other soups aren't served in individual bowls except in more elegant restaurants or those aimed at tourists. You serve yourself from the common bowl, spooning broth and ingredients over your rice or into your own spoon. Sometimes serving spoons are provided. If not, you simply dig in with your own spoon.

Don't pick up a serving platter to serve yourself. Proper Thai etiquette requires leaving the platter on the tabletop and reaching over to it with your spoon, even if it means stretching your arm across the table. If you can't reach the serving platter at all, it's best to hand your plate to someone near the platter, who can then place some food on your plate. Most Thais will do this automatically if they notice you're out of platter range. Whatever you do, don't incline a serving platter over your individual plate – this is considered a very rude and greedy gesture.

Never ask someone to pass food your way, but rather wait for them to offer you more. Thais are constantly looking out for each other at meal times – making sure no-one's plate is empty – and will usually give you more food than you can eat. Don't be surprised if another diner in your party spoons food directly onto your plate, just like your mother did when you were a child. This is a completely normal gesture in Thai dining custom and carries no particular import other than showing hospitality towards a foreign guest.

Thais want you to enjoy the food, and at some point in the meal your host or one of your dining companions will pause for a second, smile and ask, '*Àràwy măi?*' ('Is it delicious?') The expected answer, of course, is *àràwy* (delicious) or *àràwy mâak* (very delicious).

Always leave some food on the serving platters as well as on your plate. To clean your plate and leave nothing on the serving platters says to your hosts 'you didn't feed me enough'. This is why Thais tend to over-order at social occasions – the more food left on the table, the more generous the host appears.

Cigarettes often appear both before and after a meal, but it is considered impolite to smoke during a meal. Thais will often step away from the table to smoke, mainly because ashtrays aren't usually placed on dining tables. It's not customary in Thailand to ask permission to smoke before lighting up, though this is beginning to change in Bangkok society. To be on the safe side, always ask, '*Sùup bùrìi dâi măi?*' ('Is it OK to smoke?') Note that Thai law forbids smoking in any air-conditioned public area, including restaurants and bars.

HOW THAIS EAT

Aside from the occasional indulgence in deep-fried savouries, most Thais sustain themselves on a varied and healthy diet filled with many fruits, rice and vegetables mixed with smaller amounts of animal protein and fat. The Thais' main culinary satisfaction seems to come not from eating large amounts of food at any one meal but rather from nibbling at a variety of dishes with as many different flavours as possible throughout the day.

Thais extend a hand towards a bowl of noodles, a plate of rice or a banana-leaf-wrapped snack with amazing frequency. There are no 'typical' times for meals, though in Bangkok diners tend to cluster in local restaurants at the customary noon to 1pm lunch break. Even so, it's not at all unusual for a bank clerk or shopowner to order in a bowl of *kŭaytĭaw* (rice noodles) some time midmorning, and perhaps again around 3pm or 4pm.

Nor are certain kinds of food restricted to certain times of day. Practically anything can be eaten first thing in the morning, whether it's sweet, salty or chilli-ridden. *Khâo kaeng* (curry over rice) is a very popular morning meal, as are *khâo mŭu daeng* (red pork over rice) and *khâo man kài* (sliced steamed chicken cooked in chicken broth and garlic and served over rice).

Lighter morning choices, especially for Thais of Chinese descent, include deep-fried chunks of *paa-thâwng-kŏh* (fried wheat pastry) dipped in warm *náam tâo-hûu* (soya milk). *Kúay jáp,* a thick broth of sliced Chinese mushrooms and bits of chicken or pork, is another early-morning Bangkok favourite. Thais also eat noodles, whether fried or in soup, with great gusto in the morning, or as a substantial snack at any time of day or night.

As the staple with which almost all Thai dishes are eaten – noodles, after all, are still seen as a Chinese import – rice *(khâo)* is considered an absolutely indispensable part of the daily diet. Most Bangkok families will put on a pot of rice, or start the rice cooker, just after rising in the morning to prepare a base for the day's menu. All other dishes, aside from noodles, are considered *kàp khâo* (side dishes) that supplement this central *aahăan làk* (staple).

Plaa (fish) finds its way into almost every meal, even if it's only in the form of *náam plaa* (a thin, clear, amber sauce made from fermented anchovies), which is used to salt Thai dishes, much as soy sauce is used in eastern Asia. Chicken is the next favourite source of protein, and is prepared in a variety of fashions, from curries and stir-fries to barbecues. Pork is particularly enjoyed by Chinese Thais while shunned by most Muslim Thais. Although beef isn't as popular as fish or chicken, there are some Bangkok favourites such as *néua phàt náam-man hǎwy* (beef stir-fried in oyster sauce) and northeastern Thailand's *néua náam tòk* (literally 'waterfall beef').

Alfresco dining at Sanam Luang (p76)

Thais are prodigious consumers of fruit. You'll find vendors pushing glass-and-wood carts filled with a rainbow of fresh sliced papaya, pineapple, watermelon and coconut, and a more muted palette of salt-pickled or candied seasonal fruits. These are usually served in a small plastic bag with a thin bamboo stick to use as an eating utensil.

Because many restaurants in Thailand are able to serve dishes at an only slightly higher price than they would cost to make at home, Thais dine out far more often than their Western counterparts. Any evening of the week you'll see small groups of Thais – usually males – clustered around roadside tables or in outdoor restaurants, drinking Thai-brewed beer or rice liquor while picking from an array of common dishes, one morsel at a time. These are *kàp klâem*, dishes specifically meant to be eaten while drinking alcoholic beverages, often before an evening meal or while waiting for the larger courses to arrive. *Kàp klâem* can be as simple as a plate of *mét má-mûang thâwt* (fried cashews) or as elaborate as one of the many types of *yam*, containing a blast of lime, chilli, fresh herbs and a choice of seafood, roast vegetables, noodles or meats.

Thais tend to avoid eating alone. Dining with others is always preferred from the Thai perspective because it means everyone has a chance to sample several dishes. When forced to fly solo by circumstance – such as during lunch breaks at work – a single diner usually sticks to one-plate dishes such as fried rice or curry over rice.

STAPLES & SPECIALITIES

Just as Bangkok Thai has become 'Standard Thai' in schools and government offices throughout the country, so Bangkok Thai cooking is today considered 'classic Thai' cuisine. The region's central position, and more importantly its wealth relative to the rest of the country, means that spices, seasonings and produce hailing from any corner of the kingdom are easily available. Coconuts from the south, bamboo shoots from the north, *maeng-daa* (water beetle) from the northeast – all find their way into Bangkok markets.

RICE

Bangkok sits right in the middle of the Mae Nam Chao Phraya delta, the country's 'rice bowl'. Thailand has led the world in rice exports since the 1960s, and the quality of Thai rice, according to many discerning Asians, is considered the best in the world. Thailand's *khâo hǎwm málí* (jasmine rice) is so coveted that there is a steady underground business in smuggling bags of the fragrant grain to neighbouring countries.

Rice is so central to Thai food culture that the most common term for 'eat' is *kin khâo* (literally 'consume rice'), and one of the most common greetings is *'Kin khâo láew rĕu yang?'* ('Have you consumed rice yet?') All the dishes eaten with rice – whether curries, stir-fries, soups or other food preparations – are simply classified as *kàp khâo* (with rice). Only two dishes using rice as a principal ingredient are common in Thailand, *khâo phàt* (fried rice) and *khâo mòk kài* (chicken biryani), neither of which is native to Thailand.

NOODLES

Exactly when the noodle reached Thailand is difficult to say, but it probably arrived along trade routes from China, since the preparation styles in contemporary Thailand are similar to those of contemporary southern China.

You'll find four basic kinds of noodle in Bangkok. Hardly surprising, given the Thai fixation on rice, is the overwhelming popularity of *kŭaytĭaw*, made from pure rice flour mixed with water to form a paste, which is then steamed to form wide, flat sheets. The sheets are then folded and sliced into *sên yài* (flat 'wide line' noodles 2cm to 3cm wide), *sên lék* ('small line' noodles about 5mm wide) and *sên mìi* ('noodle line' noodles only 1mm to 2mm wide). *Sên mìi* dry out so quickly that they are sold only in their dried form.

At most restaurants or vendor stands specialising in *kŭaytĭaw*, you can choose between *sên yài* or *sên lék* noodles when ordering.

The king of Thai noodles, *kŭaytĭaw* comes as part of many dishes. The simplest, *kŭaytĭaw náam*, is *kŭaytĭaw* served in a bowl of plain chicken or beef stock with bits of meat and pickled cabbage, and coriander leaf as garnish. Season your noodle soup by choosing from a rack of small glass or metal containers on the table (see the boxed text below).

Another dish, *kŭaytĭaw phàt*, involves the quick stir-frying of the noodles in a wok with sliced meat, *phàk kha-náa* (Chinese kale), soy sauce and various seasonings. Two other ways to order Thai rice noodles are *kŭaytĭaw hâeng* (dry *kŭaytĭaw*) and *kŭaytĭaw râat nâa* (*kŭaytĭaw* with gravy). For *kŭaytĭaw hâeng*, rice noodles are momentarily doused in very hot water to heat them up and soften them, then tossed in a soup bowl with garlic oil and topped with the usual ingredients that make up *kŭaytĭaw náam*, save the broth. *Kŭaytĭaw râat nâa* involves braising the noodles in a light gravy made with cornstarch-thickened stock, adding meats and seasonings to taste and serving the finished product on an oval plate.

Chilli-heads must give *kŭaytĭaw phàt khîi mao* (drunkard's fried noodles) a try. A favourite lunch or late-night snack, this spicy stir-fry consists of wide rice noodles, fresh basil leaves, chicken or pork, seasonings and a healthy dose of fresh sliced chillies.

Perk Up Your Noodle

Much as chicken soup is viewed as something of a home cold remedy in the West, rice-noodle soups in Thailand are often eaten to ward off colds, hangovers or general malaise. When you face a bowl of noodles and the array of condiments available to season them, you must be prepared to become your own pharmacist, mixing up the ingredients to create the right flavour balance and, by implication, to set body and soul right.

If you see a steel rack containing four lidded glass bowls or jars on your table, it's proof that the restaurant you're in serves *kŭaytĭaw* (rice noodles). Typically these containers offer four choices: *náam sôm phrík* (sliced green chillies in white vinegar), *phrík náam plaa* (*phrík khîi nŭu*, or mouse-dropping chilli, in fish sauce), *phrík pon* (dried red chilli, flaked or ground to a near powder) and *náamtaan* (plain white sugar).

In typically Thai fashion, these condiments offer three ways to make the soup hotter – hot and sour, hot and salty, and just plain hot – and one to make it sweet. Some *kŭaytĭaw* vendors substitute *thùa pon* (ground peanuts) for the *phrík náam plaa*, which is provided in a separate bowl or saucer instead.

The typical noodle-eater will add a teaspoonful of each one of these condiments to the noodle soup, except for the sugar, which usually rates a full tablespoon. Until you're used to these strong seasonings, we recommend adding them a small bit at a time, tasting the soup along the way to make sure you don't go overboard. Adding sugar to soup may appear strange to some foreign palates, but it does considerably enhance the flavour of *kŭaytĭaw náam*.

In addition to the condiments rack, a conscientious *kŭaytĭaw* vendor will provide a bottle of *náam plaa* (fish sauce) for those who want to make the soup saltier without adding the spice.

Probably the most well-known *kǔaytǐaw* dish among foreigners is *kǔaytǐaw phàt thai,* usually called *phàt thai* for short, a plate of thin rice noodles stir-fried with dried or fresh shrimp, bean sprouts, fried tofu, egg and seasonings. The cook usually places little piles of ground peanuts and ground dried chilli along the edge of the plate, along with lime halves and a few stalks of spring onion, for self-seasoning.

Another kind of noodle, *khanǒm jiin,* is produced by pushing rice-flour paste through a sieve into boiling water, in much the same way as pasta is made. *Khanǒm jiin* is eaten doused with various curries. The most standard curry topping, *náam yaa* (herbal sauce), contains a strong dose of *krà-chai* (Chinese key), a root of the ginger family used as a traditional remedy for a number of gastrointestinal ailments, along with ground fish.

The third kind of noodle, *bà-mìi,* is made from wheat flour and sometimes egg (depending on the noodle-maker or the brand). It's yellowish in colour and always the same size, about 1.5mm in diameter. *Bà-mìi* is sold only in fresh bundles and, unlike both *kǔaytǐaw* and *khanǒm jiin,* it must be cooked immediately before serving. The cooking procedure is simple – plunge a bamboo-handled wire basket full of *bà-mìi* into boiling water or broth and leave it for two to three minutes. Add broth plus meat, seafood or vegetables and you have *bà-mìi náam.* Served in a bowl with a small amount of garlic oil and no liquid, it's *bà-mìi hâeng.*

Some restaurants serve both *bà-mìi* and *kǔaytǐaw,* but the best *bà-mìi* is found in shops or at vendor carts that specialise in *bà-mìi* and *kíaw. Kíaw* is a triangle of *bà-mìi* dough wrapped around ground pork or ground fish (or a vegetable substitute at Thai vegetarian restaurants). These dumplings may be boiled and added to soup, or fried to make *kíaw thâwt.* One of the most popular *bà-mìi* dishes in Bangkok is *bà-mìi kíaw puu,* a soup containing *kíaw* and *puu* (crab).

Finally there's *wún sên,* an almost clear noodle made from mung-bean starch and water. Sold only in dried bunches, *wún sên* (literally 'jelly thread') is easily prepared by soaking in hot water for 10 to 15 minutes. It's used for only three dishes in Thailand. The first and most native, *yam wún sên,* is a hot and tangy salad made with lime juice, fresh sliced *phrík khîi nǔu* (mouse-dropping chilli), mushrooms, dried or fresh shrimp, ground pork and various seasonings. A second appearance is in *wún sên òp puu,* bean-thread noodles baked in a lidded clay pot with crab and seasonings. Lastly, *wún sên* is a common ingredient in *kaeng jèut,* a bland, Chinese-influenced soup containing ground pork, soft tofu and a few vegetables.

CURRIES

In Thai, *kaeng* (rhyme it with the English 'gang') is often translated as 'curry', but it actually describes any dish with a lot of liquid and can thus refer to soups (such as *kaeng jèut*) as well as the classic chilli-based curries such as *kaeng phèt* (red curry) for which Thai cuisine is famous. The preparation of all chilli-based *kaeng* begins with a *khrêuang kaeng,* created by mashing, pounding and grinding an array of fresh ingredients with a stone mortar and pestle to form an aromatic, extremely pungent-tasting and rather thick paste. Typical ingredients in a *khrêuang kaeng* include dried chilli, galangal (also known as Thai ginger), lemon grass, kaffir lime (peel, leaves or both), shallots, garlic, shrimp paste and salt. Coriander seeds and a touch of cumin are added for green curries.

Most *kaeng* are blended in a heated pan with coconut cream, to which the chef adds the rest of the ingredients (meat, poultry, seafood and/or vegetables), along with coconut milk to further thin and flavour the *kaeng.* Some recipes will omit coconut milk entirely to produce a particularly fiery *kaeng* known as *kaeng pàa* (forest curry). Another *kaeng* that does not use coconut milk is *kaeng sôm* (sour curry), made with dried chillies, shallots, garlic and Chinese key pestled with salt, shrimp paste *(kà-pì)* and fish sauce. Cooked with tamarind juice and green papaya to create an overall tanginess, the result is a soupy, salty, sweet-and-sour ragout that most Westerners would never identify with the word 'curry'.

A few extra seasonings such as *phàk chii* (coriander leaf), *bai ma-krùt* (kaffir lime leaves), *bai hǒhráphaa* (sweet basil leaves) and *náam plaa* (fish sauce) may be added to taste just before serving. Bangkok Thais like their curries a bit sweeter than those from other regions of Thailand.

HOT & TANGY SALADS

Standing right alongside *kaeng* in terms of Thai-ness is the ubiquitous *yam,* a hot and tangy salad containing a blast of lime, chilli, fresh herbs and a choice of seafood, roast vegetables, noodles or meats. Bangkokians prize *yam* dishes so much that they are often eaten on their own, without rice, before the meal has begun.

Lime juice provides the tang, while the abundant use of fresh chilli produces the heat. Other ingredients vary considerably, but plenty of leafy vegetables and herbs are usually present, including lettuce (often lining the dish) and mint leaves. Lemon grass, shallots, kaffir lime leaves and *khêun chàai* (Chinese celery) may also come into play. Most *yam* are served at room temperature or just slightly warmed by any cooked ingredients.

On Thai menus, the *yam* section will often be the longest. Yet when these same menus are translated into English, most or all of the *yam* are omitted because Thai restaurateurs harbour the idea that the delicate *faràng* (Western) palate cannot handle the heat or pungency. The usual English menu translation is either 'Thai-style salad' or 'hot and sour salad'.

Without a doubt, *yam* are the spiciest of all Thai dishes, and *yam phrík chíi fáa* (spur chilli *yam*) is perhaps the hottest. A good *yam* to begin with if you're not so chilli-tolerant is *yam wún sên,* bean-thread noodles tossed with shrimp, ground pork, coriander leaf, lime juice and fresh sliced chilli. Another tame *yam* that tends to be a favourite among Thais and foreigners alike is *yam plaa dùk fuu,* made from fried shredded catfish, chilli and peanuts with a shredded-mango dressing on the side. Because of the city's proximity to the Gulf of Thailand, Bangkok eateries serve a wide variety of seafood *yam.* *Yam* may also be made with vegetables (*yam thùa phuu,* made with angle beans), fungi (*yam hèt hǎwm,* made with shiitake mushrooms) or fruit (*yam sôm oh,* made with pomelo).

STIR-FRIES & DEEP-FRIES

The simplest dishes in the Thai culinary repertoire are the stir-fries *(phàt),* brought to Thailand by the Chinese, who are of course world famous for being able to stir-fry a whole banquet in a single wok. Despite stir-fry's Chinese origins, *phàt* dishes are never served in Thailand with soy sauce as a condiment, except in Chinese restaurants. Instead they come with *phrík náam plaa* (mouse-dropping chilli in fish sauce) on the side.

The list of *phàt* dishes seems endless. Most are better classified as Chinese, such as *néua phàt náam-man hǎwy* (beef in oyster sauce). Some are clearly Thai-Chinese hybrids, such as *kài phàt phrík khǐng,* in which chicken is stir-fried with ginger, garlic and chilli – ingredients shared by both traditions – but seasoned with fish sauce. Also leaning towards Thai – because cashews are native to Thailand but not to China – is *kài phàt mét má-mûang hǐmáphaan* (sliced chicken stir-fried in dried chilli and cashews), a favourite with *faràng* tourists.

Perhaps the most Thai-like *phàt* dish is the faved lunch meal *phàt bai kà-phrao,* a chicken or pork stir-fry with garlic, fresh sliced chilli, soy and fish sauce, and lots of holy basil.

Another classic Thai stir-fry is *phàt phèt* (literally 'hot stir-fry'), in which the main ingredients are quickly stir-fried with red curry paste and tossed with sweet basil leaves before serving. This recipe usually includes seafood or freshwater fish, such as shrimp, squid, catfish or eel.

Stir-fry chicken, pork, beef or shrimp with black pepper and garlic and you have *phàt phrík thai krà-thiam,* a relatively mild recipe often ordered as a 'fill-in' dish during a larger meal. For lovers of fresh vegetables, *phàt phàk kha-náa* (Chinese kale stir-fried in black bean sauce) is worth looking out for, as is *phàt phàk ruam* (mixed vegetables).

Thâwt (deep-frying in oil) is mainly reserved for snacks such as *klûay thâwt* (fried bananas) or *paw pía* (egg rolls). An exception is *plaa thâwt* (fried fish), which is the most common way any fish is prepared. Many Thai recipes featuring whole fish require that it be fried first, usually in a wok filled with cooking oil (until the outside flesh is crispy to a depth of at least 1cm). Although to Western tastes this may appear to dry the fish out, in Thailand most fish fried in this way will then be topped with some sort of sauce – lime gravy or a cooked chilli-onion mixture – which will remoisten the dish. Some fish, such as mackerel, will be steamed first, then lightly pan-fried in a smaller amount of oil to seal in the moisture.

A very few dishes require ingredients to be dipped in batter and then deep-fried, such as *kài thâwt* (fried chicken) and *kûng chúp pâeng thâwt* (batter-fried shrimp).

SOUPS

Thai soups fall into two broad categories, *tôm yam* and *kaeng jèut*, that are worlds apart in terms of seasonings. *Tôm yam* is almost always made with seafood, though chicken may also be used. *Tôm yam kûng* (*tôm yam* with shrimp) can be found in nearly all Thai restaurants as well as in many serving non-Thai cuisine. It is often translated on English menus as 'hot and sour Thai soup', although this often misleads non-Thais to relate the dish to Chinese hot and sour soup, which is milder and thinner in texture, and includes vinegar.

Lemon grass, kaffir lime peel and lime juice give *tôm yam* its characteristic tang. Fuelling the fire beneath *tôm yam*'s often velvety surface are fresh *phrík khîi nǔu* and sometimes half a teaspoonful of *náam phrík phǎo* (a paste of dried chilli roasted with *kà-pì*). Improvisation comes into play with this dish as cooks try to out do one another in providing a savoury soup with at least one or two 'mystery' ingredients.

Many cooks add galangal to add fragrance to the soup. Aside from lemon grass and galangal resting on the bottom of the bowl, solids in this soup are confined to shrimp and straw mushrooms. Coriander leaf is an important garnish for both appearance and fragrance.

Tôm yam is meant to be eaten with rice, not sipped alone. The first swallow of this soup often leaves the uninitiated gasping for breath. It's not that the soup is so hot, but the chilli oils that provide the spice tend to float on top.

Of the several variations on *tôm yam* that exist, probably the most popular with Westerners is the milder *tôm khàa kài* (literally 'boiled galangal chicken', but often translated as 'chicken coconut soup'). The lime and chilli are considerably muted in this soup by the addition of coconut milk.

Kaeng jèut covers the other end of the spectrum with a soothing broth seasoned with little more than soy or fish sauce and black pepper. Although the number of variations on *kaeng jèut* are many, common ingredients include *wún sên* (mung-bean starch noodles), *tâo-hûu* (tofu), *hǔa chai tháo* (Chinese radish) and *mǔu sàp* (ground pork).

FRUIT

The omnipresent *phǒn-lá-mái* (literally 'fruit of the tree', a general term for all fruit) testifies to the Thais' great fondness for fruit, which they appear to consume at every opportunity. An evening meal is normally followed by a plate of sliced fresh fruit, not pastries or Western-style desserts – no doubt one reason Thais stay so slim, as a rule.

Other common year-rounders include *má-phráo* (coconut), *faràng* (guava; also colloquial name for Westerner), *kha-nǔn* (jackfruit), *má-khǎam* (tamarind), *sôm khǐaw-wǎan* (mandarin orange), *málákaw* (papaya), *sôm oh* (pomelo), *taeng moh* (watermelon) and *sàppàrót* (pineapple). All are most commonly eaten fresh, and sometimes dipped in a mixture of salt, sugar and ground chilli. Fruit juices of every kind are popular as beverages (see p49).

Seasonal Fruits

The watchful visitor could almost fix the calendar month in Thailand by observing the parade of fruits appearing – sweet mangoes in March, mangosteens in April, rambeh in May, custard apples in July, golden-peel oranges in November and so on.

Chom-phûu (Rose apple) Small, applelike texture, very fragrant; April to July.

Lam yai (Longan) 'Dragon's eyes'; small, brown, spherical, similar to rambutan; July to October.

Lámút (Sapodilla) Small, brown, oval, sweet but pungent smelling; July to September.

Mang-khút (Mangosteen) Round, purple fruit with juicy white flesh; April to September.

Má-fai (Rambeh) Small, reddish-brown, sweet, apricotlike; April to May.

Má-mûang (Mango) Several varieties and seasons.

Náwy nàa (Custard apple) July to October.

Ngáw (Rambutan) Red, hairy-skinned fruit with grapelike flesh; July to September.

No discussion of Thai fruit is complete without a mention of durian *(thúrian)*, dubbed the king of fruits by most Southeast Asians yet despised by many foreigners. A member of the aptly named *Bombacaceae* family, this heavy, spiked orb resembles an ancient piece of medieval weaponry. Inside the thick shell lie five sections of plump, buttery and pungent flesh. Legions of connoisseurs as well as detractors have laboured to describe the durian's complex flavour. Probably the best description is that from 19th-century British natural historian and obvious durian devotee Alfred Russell Wallace:

…CUSTARD FLAVOURED WITH ALMONDS, INTERMINGLED WITH WAFTS OF FLAVOUR THAT CALL TO MIND CREAM CHEESE, ONION SAUCE, BROWN SHERRY AND OTHER INCONGRUITIES…NEITHER ACID, NOR SWEET, NOR JUICY, YET ONE FEELS THE WANT OF NONE OF THESE QUALITIES FOR IT IS PERFECT AS IT IS.

The durian's ammonia-like aroma is so strong that many hotels in Thailand, as well as Thai Airways International, ban the fruit from their premises.

Durian seasons come and go throughout the year depending on the variety. One of the largest and most expensive durians, native to Thailand and widely exported, is the *mǎwn thawng* or 'golden pillow'.

SWEETS

English-language Thai menus often have a section called 'Desserts', even though the concept doesn't exist in Thai cuisine, nor is there a translation for the word. The closest equivalent, *khǎwng wǎan*, simply means 'sweet stuff' and refers to all foods whose primary flavour characteristic is sweetness. Sweets mostly work their way into the daily Thai diet in the form of between-meal snacks, so you won't find *khǎwng wǎan* in a traditional Thai restaurant at all. Instead, they're prepared and sold by market vendors or, more rarely, by shops specialising in *khǎwng wǎan*.

Khǎwng wǎan recipes and preparation techniques tend to require more skill than other dishes. The cook spends the morning making up *khǎwng wǎan*, which are bundled into banana leaves, poured into pandanus-leaf cups or cut into colourful squares. These are then arranged on large trays and taken to local markets or wheeled on carts through the streets to be sold by the *chín* (piece).

Prime ingredients for many Thai sweets include grated coconut, coconut milk, rice flour (from white rice or sticky rice), cooked sticky rice (whole grains), tapioca, mung-bean starch, boiled taro and various fruits. For added texture and crunch, some sweets may also contain fresh corn kernels, sugar-palm kernels, lotus seeds, cooked black beans and chopped water chestnuts. Egg yolks are a popular ingredient for *khǎwng wǎan* – including the ubiquitous *fǎwy thawng* (literally 'golden threads') – probably influenced by Portuguese desserts and pastries introduced during the early Ayuthaya era.

Thai sweets similar to the European concept of 'sweet pastry' are called *khanǒm*. Here again the kitchen-astute Portuguese were influential. Probably the most popular type of *khanǒm* in Thailand are the bite-sized items wrapped in banana or pandanus leaves, especially *khâo tôm kà-thí* and *khâo tôm mát*. Both consist of sticky rice grains steamed with

Top Five Thai Taste Sensations

- **Kaeng phèt kài nàw mái** Chicken and bamboo-shoot curry, a working-class mainstay at *rǎan khâo kaeng* (rice and curry shops).
- **Miang kham** Tiny chunks of lime, ginger and shallot, toasted grated coconut, roasted peanuts, fresh sliced chilli and dried shrimp, all wrapped up in a wild tea leaf with sweet-sour tamarind sauce. Bite into a wad and it shouts 'Thailand'.
- **Plaa dàet diaw** 'Once-sunned fish', a whole fish split down the middle, sun-dried for half a day, then deep-fried and served with a mango-peanut sauce.
- **Sǎngkhayǎa fák thawng** Creamy egg-and-palm-sugar custard baked inside a Thai pumpkin.
- **Tôm yam pó tàek** When you tire of *tôm yam kûng*, try *pó tàek* – 'broken fish trap' – which uses a similar broth with the addition of basil and assorted seafood.

kà-thí (coconut milk) inside a banana-leaf wrapper to form a solid, almost taffy-like, mass. *Khâo tôm kà-thí* also contains fresh grated coconut, while *khâo tôm mát* usually contains a few black beans or banana. *Tà-kôh,* a very simple but popular steamed sweet made from tapioca flour and coconut milk over a layer of sweetened seaweed gelatine, comes in small cups made from pandanus leaves. A similar blend, minus the gelatine and steamed in tiny porcelain cups, is called *khanŏm thûay* (cup pastry).

Coconut milk also features prominently in several soupier sweets with colourful names. In the enormously popular *klûay bùat chii* (bananas ordaining as nuns), banana chunks float in a white syrup of sweetened and slightly salted coconut milk. *Bua láwy* (floating lotus) consists of boiled sticky rice dumplings in a similar coconut sauce. Substitute red-dyed chunks of fresh water chestnut and you have *tháp thim kràwp* (crisp rubies). As at a modern ice-cream parlour, you can often order extra ingredients, such as black beans, sugar-palm kernels or corn kernels, to be added to the mix. Crushed ice is often added to cool the mixture.

Cooking kha-nŏm khrŏk on Th Chakrawat

DRINKS

FRUIT DRINKS

With the abundance of fruit growing in Thailand, the variety of juices and shakes available in markets, street stalls and restaurants is extensive. The all-purpose term for fruit juice is *náam phŏn-lá-mái.* When a blender or extractor is used, you've got *náam khán* (squeezed juice), hence *náam sàppàrót khán* is freshly squeezed pineapple juice. *Náam âwy* (sugar-cane juice) is a Thai favourite and a very refreshing accompaniment to *kaeng* dishes. A similar juice from the sugar palm, *náam taan sòt,* is also very good, and both are full of vitamins and minerals. Mixed fruit blended with ice is *náam pon* (literally 'mixed juice'), as in *náam málákaw pon,* a papaya shake.

BEER

Advertised with such slogans as *'pràthêht rao, bia rao'* ('our land, our beer'), the Singha label is considered the quintessential Thai beer by *faràng* and locals alike. Pronounced *sĭng,* it claims about half the domestic market. Singha's original recipe was formulated in 1934 by Thai nobleman Phya Bhirom Bhakdi, the first Thai to earn a brewmaster's diploma in Germany. Many beer-drinkers believe the strong, hoppy brew to be one of the best produced in Asia. The barley for Singha is grown in Thailand, the hops are imported from Germany and the alcohol content is a heady 6%. It is sold in brown glass bottles (both 33cl and 66cl) with a shiny gold lion on the label as well as cans. It is available on tap as *ia sòt* (draught beer) – much tastier than either bottled or canned brew – in many Bangkok pubs and restaurants.

Kloster, similarly inspired by German brewing recipes, is a notch smoother and lighter than Singha, has an alcohol content of 4.7% and generally costs about 5B to 10B more per bottle. Look for a straight-sided green bottle with a label that looks like it was designed in 18th- or 19th-century Germany.

Singha's biggest rival, Beer Chang, matches the hoppy taste of Singha but pumps the alcohol content up to 7%. Beer Chang has managed to gain an impressive following mainly because it retails at a significantly lower price than Singha and thus offers more bang per baht.

Boon Rawd (the makers of Singha) responded with its own cheaper brand, Leo. Sporting a black-and-red leopard label, Leo costs only slightly more than Beer Chang but is similarly high in alcohol. More variation in Thai beer brands is likely in the coming years as manufacturers scramble to command market share by offering a variety of flavours and prices.

Dutch-licensed but Thailand-brewed Heineken comes third after Singha and Chang in sales rankings.

RICE WHISKY

Rice whisky is a favourite of the working class in Bangkok, since it's more affordable than beer. It has a sharp, sweet taste not unlike rum, with an alcohol content of 35%. The most famous brand, Mekong (pronounced *mâe khŏhng*), costs around 120B for a large bottle *(klom)* or 60B for a flask-sized bottle *(baen)*. Also popular is the slightly more expensive Sang Som.

More expensive Thai whiskies produced from barley and appealing to the can't-afford-Johnnie-Walker-yet set include Blue Eagle, 100 Pipers and Spey Royal, each with a 40% alcohol content. These come dressed up in shiny boxes, much like the expensive imported whiskies they're imitating.

CELEBRATING WITH FOOD

During Trùt Jiin (Chinese New Year), Bangkok's Chinese population celebrates with a week of house-cleaning, lion dances, fireworks and restaurant feasting. Naturally the most impressive festivities take place in Chinatown. Favourite foods eaten during Trùt Jiin include 'mooncakes' – thick, circular pastries filled with sweetened bean paste or salted pork – and lots of noodles.

During the famous Vegetarian Festival, Thêhtsakaan Kin Jeh, also centred on Chinatown, virtually every Chinese eatery in the city puts on a lengthy Chinese vegetarian menu, advertised by yellow-and-red pennants in front of the restaurants.

1 Traders jostle for space at the famously popular Damnoen Saduak Floating Market (p200) 2 A ferry on Mae Nam Chao Phraya (p65) passes the distinctly Thai-shaped Wat Arun (Temple of Dawn, p77) 3 Buddhist monks stand in front of Wat Saket near Golden Mount (p83) 4 Posters of royal portraits for sale – the King's Birthday is a popular celebration (p12)

1 The chedi (stupa) of Wat Saket (p83) gleams in the afternoon sun, from the vantage point of the Khlong Saen Saeb 2 Túk-túks zip around Th Khao San (p80) in monsoon rain 3 Dressed to soak – part of the watery celebrations during the Songkran Festival, Thai New Year (p11) 4 Th Silom stalls (p151) sell a quirky mix, including dishwashing detergent and ready-made flower offerings for the many temples in town

1 Traffic streams past the commercial development on Th Sathon Neua and Th Sathon Tai (p92) 2 Sparks fly at a metalworks in Chinatown (p87) 3 A pool game steams up in a bar on Th Sukhumvit (p128) 4 Elvis, alive and well, belts out a tune at Radio City (p133)

1 Some like it hot – Thai food's key ingredient, chilli (p40)
2 Steamed fish on display at one of Bangkok's many food markets
3 Rhambutans galore can be found at a market in Banglamphu (p108)
4 The aroma of barbecued fish tantalises passers-by at a street market

1 & 2 Mouth-watering delights on display at night markets across town *3* Southern-style kaeng sôm (sour curry) is a meal in a soup (p107) *4* Creamy Thai taste sensation sǎngkhayǎa fák thawng, *which is egg-and-palm sugar custard baked inside a Thai pumpkin (p48)*

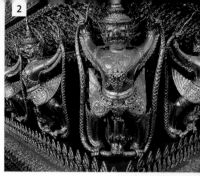

1 At Wat Benchamabophit (p86), Dusit, a resplendent Buddha, with right palm down, subdues the demons of the earth **2** Garuda statues guard the Grand Palace and adjoining Wat Phra Kaew (Temple of the Emerald Buddha, p78), Ko Ratanakosin **3** Intricate murals depicting scenes from the Ramakian at the Grand Palace compound (p78) **4** Wat Ratchanatda (p82) makes for a spectacular sight when it is illuminated at night

1 Buddhist monks at morning prayers in the sermon hall at Wat Pho (Temple of the Reclining Buddha, p79), the oldest and largest wát 2 Stunningly lit chedi (stupas) of Wat Pho shine in the evening (p79) 3 Pounding out a tune on the traditional Thai ránâat èhk, a xylophone-style instrument (p29) 4 The Thai wâi – a woman demonstrates the traditional prayer-like greeting (p15)

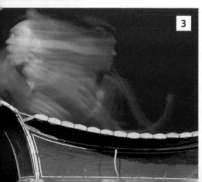

1 Traditional dancers perform at the Sala Rim Nam restaurant at the Oriental Hotel (p137)
2 Hand-painted movie posters on Bangkok's streets help to promote Thailand's 'new wave' of movie-making (p36) **3** Alms bowls on a wood fire at the Monk's Bowl Village (p81), where they are still made in the traditional way
4 Traditional beliefs go hand in hand with a modern landscape – this shrine is outside Central World Plaza

History

History

THE RECENT PAST

Bangkok finished the last millennium riding a tide of events that have set new ways of governing and living in the capital. Most significantly, after a seemingly endless succession of military coups dating back to the early 20th century, a democratically elected civilian coalition took control of the national government in 1992. Thailand had been governed democratically before, but few regimes had lasted more than three years. Twelve years on, the Thai military appears to have resigned itself to serving rather than ruling the nation.

A second watershed occurred in July 1997 when, after several months of warning signs that were ignored by almost everyone in Thailand and the international community (see p19), the Thai currency went into a deflationary tailspin and the national economy screeched to a virtual halt. Bangkok, which rode at the forefront of the 1980s double-digit economic boom, was more adversely affected than elsewhere in the country in job losses and income erosion.

Two months after the crash, the Thai parliament voted in a new constitution that guaranteed – at least on paper – more human and civil rights than had hitherto been codified in Thailand. The 'people's constitution' fostered great hope in a population emotionally battered by the 1997 economic crisis.

When Prime Minister Chavalit Yongchaiyudh failed to deal effectively with the economy, he was forced to resign. An election brought former prime minister Chuan Leekpai back into office, and he handled the crisis reasonably well. By early 2000, following a financial

Bangkok's Bull Governor

When Samak Sundaravej, a political warhorse who over the course of 32 years had served as an elected member of Thai parliament 10 times, stood for Bangkok governor in 2000 he was expected to win simply because he was better known than his Thai Rak Thai (Thai Love Thai) party rival. The outspoken conservative, alleged to have supported military coups in the '70s and '80s, further alienated progressives when he and his Thai Citizens Party abstained from voting for watershed constitutional reforms that same year.

With Bangkok leaning towards the liberal side of Thailand's political spectrum, it was assumed that victory wouldn't come easily to the right-wing dinosaur. His main rival, media-dubbed 'wonder woman' Sudarat Keyuraphan, had the backing of the new technocrat-styled Thai Rak Thai party, fast gaining support in provincial election campaigns.

When the July election was held, Samak annihilated his opponents, garnering nearly twice the combined total votes of the other 22 candidates. The 58% voter turnout was the highest since the capital's first local-government elections in 1985.

His rivals may have underestimated Samak's tremendous *baawrámii* (charisma) with the voting public, and he has without doubt been the most colourful character yet to assume the governorship. When his political tactics to stamp out Bangkok police corruption didn't yield results, for example, he arranged for a spirit curse to be placed on all crooked cops. He regularly appears on TV talk shows to air his views on metropolitan and national policy.

An avid amateur chef, Samak hosted his own cooking programme on national television each weekend until the Thaksin administration ordered him to stop, claiming it took time from his official duties. Samak retaliated during the 2004 avian flu crisis by upstaging Prime Minister Thaksin's 'Eat Chicken' promotional campaign. With the Thaksin event scheduled to begin in the early evening, Samak rallied his supporters and threw a larger bash starting at 7am the same day. The governor himself manned one of the booths, wok-frying enough chicken to feed thousands. By the time Thaksin's evening event rolled around, the crowd had eaten its fill and the evening attendance was embarrassingly low.

1548	1767
Thonburi Si Mahasamut founded on the right bank of Mae Nam Chao Phraya as a trade centre for Siam	Ayuthaya, Siam's royal capital, is sacked by the Burmese

The Skytrain leaving Nana station

restructuring coached by the International Monetary Fund (IMF), Bangkok's economy began to show signs of recovery.

Bangkok local-government elections in mid-2000 found Thai Citizen Party candidate Samak Sundaravej elected to office in a surprise landslide. Among Samak's first official acts was a crackdown on police who were extorting money from street vendors. Although the campaign had little demonstrable effect on corruption, it won the hearts of many residents. Samak also made the support and expansion of the Bangkok Mass Transit System (BTS) Skytrain and Metropolitan Rapid Transport Authority (MRTA) subway a major priority and promised to build affordable flats for low-income residents.

In January 2001, billionaire Thaksin Shinawatra became prime minister after winning a landslide victory in compulsory nationwide elections – the first in Thailand to be held under the strict guidelines established in the 1997 constitution. Thaksin's party Thai Rak Thai (TRT; Thai Love Thai) espouses a populist platform at odds with the man's enormous wealth and influence. The sixth-richest ruler in the world as of late 2003, Thaksin owns the country's only private radio station and his family owns the largest Thai telecommunications company, which has lucrative coverage not only in Thailand but in India and Myanmar as well. He has publicly stated his ambition to stay in office for five consecutive terms, a total of 20 years.

Many Thai citizens have become fed up with the government's slowness to right perceived wrongs in the countryside and continue to plague the administration with regular large-scale demonstrations. A coalition of northeastern Thai farmers calling themselves the Assembly of the Poor established a permanent tent-and-shanty encampment outside Bangkok's Government House in 1999 to make their grievances known around the clock via colourful protest banners. The common demand is for the government to dismantle World Bank or Asian Development projects – such as Kheuan Pak Mun (Pak Mun Dam) – which were established without the consent of the coalition. In early 2003 Governor Samak ordered 10,000 Bangkok Metropolitan Administration (BMA) workers to dismantle

1781	1782
Phaya Taksin takes the Siamese throne and moves the capital to Thonburi	Phaya Chakri crowned; founds new capital at Bang Makok

Soapland Saga

A major political scandal rocked Bangkok in 2003 when 43-year-old Chuwit Kamolvisit, owner of half a dozen high-end massage parlours in the notorious Ratchada district, went on record confirming that such establishments do indeed sell sex – something everyone knew already but which was seldom publicly acknowledged.

That announcement might have gone relatively unnoticed if Chuwit hadn't also mentioned he paid an average 12 million baht a month in bribes to police and local politicians to stay in business, and that many of these same officials visited Chuwit's parlours regularly for free sex, booze and food. The clever Thammasat University graduate had kept a diary with names and dates, and when police escalated their demands for bribes, he decided to go public.

The act was a direct provocation to Prime Minister Thaksin, a former police colonel who campaigned on his ability to wipe out police corruption. Police commissioner Sant Sarutanond was publicly humiliated when it was revealed that he himself had a four-million-baht investment in a Ratchada hotel and ties to two massage parlours on the 5km neon-lit strip known as 'Soapland'. While investigating Chuwit's claims, the Thaksin administration suspended nearly 90 police officers of high and low rank.

Shortly after this news broke, Chuwit disappeared for two days, only to turn up walking alongside a suburban Bangkok highway in a daze. Claiming he'd been kidnapped, drugged and beaten by police, Chuwit launched a media blitz designed to raise his profile even further.

In late 2003 Chuwit formed his own Ton Trakun Thai (Thai Ancestry) party and announced his bid to campaign for the next Bangkok governorship. Within a week his party had registered 50,000 members who marched in the streets to his campaign slogans 'Dare to Think, Dare to Talk, Dare to Do', and 'Stop the Government Corrupting Our Country Now!'

To help finance his campaign, Chuwit published two bestselling books, an exposé of the massage parlour industry entitled *The Golden Bath*, and a detailed look at police corruption, *My Confession: One Day I Will Commit Suicide*. Further funds, he says, will come from the sale of his massage businesses.

---

the encampment and bus many of the 1200 inhabitants to Ubon Ratchatani Province in northeastern Thailand.

The Tourism Authority of Thailand (TAT) wants to clear 'unwanted buildings and communities' from Ko Ratanakosin (Ratanakosin Island) and the Mae Nam Chao Phraya riverside to create an area of landscaped parks and sweeping river views. Among the buildings targeted for demolition or relocation are the Office of the Council of State, the National Theatre, the Thai Dancing School, Thammasat University, the Navy Club, Talat Pak Khlong, and illegal businesses and residences at Tha Phra Chan and Tha Chang. When plans materialise, these ideas will no doubt meet with fierce protest from local communities.

In early 2004 three crises in public confidence shook Bangkok and the nation. Firstly, avian influenza turned up in Thailand's bird population and, when it became known that the administration had been aware of the infections since November 2003, the EU and Japan banned all imports of Thai chicken. Large neighbourhoods in Bangkok were quarantined, particularly near Chatuchak Weekend Market in northern Bangkok, where live birds and fighting cocks are sold. Fearing that droppings could contaminate the capital, city workers captured and killed tens of thousands of pigeons in central Bangkok as well. Although there was no evidence to suggest that eating cooked chicken put people at risk, Bangkok restaurants suffered a huge loss of custom, and most were forced to quit serving chicken altogether. By mid-2004 the epidemic had cost the Thai economy 19 billion baht.

Just as the bird flu seemed under control, the Interior Ministry announced that, as of 1 March 2004, all entertainment establishments in Thailand would be required to close at midnight. In Bangkok the government exempted three districts – Patpong, Ratchada and Royal City Avenue (RCA) – in an all-too-apparent attempt to appease the city's most

1893–1910	1932
Siam accedes border territories to the French and British empires	People's Party launches bloodless revolution; Siam becomes a constitutional monarchy

powerful mafia dons. Public reaction against this decision was so strong (mafia figures who control other areas of the city reportedly announced a billion-baht price on the prime minister's head) that the government back-pedalled, allowing nightspots to stay open till 1am, regardless of zoning.

Immediately on the heels of the uproar over new closing hours came the government's announcement that the Electricity Generating Authority of Thailand (EGAT) and other state enterprises were being put on an accelerated schedule for privatisation. Tens of thousands of government employees demonstrated in Bangkok streets and, once again, the government backtracked, putting privatisation plans on hold for the time being.

When the next general election comes in February 2005, the Thaksin administration will be called to account for its bungling of the bird flu, bar closing and privatisation crises. Then again, the opposition Democrats have yet to put forth a positive platform that will prevent Thaksin and TRT from fulfilling their ambition to remain in power another 16 years.

FROM THE BEGINNING
AYUTHAYA & THONBURI

Before it became the capital of Thailand in 1782, the tiny settlement known as Bang Makok was merely a backwater village opposite Thonburi Si Mahasamut on the banks of Mae Nam Chao Phraya, not far from the Gulf of Siam.

Thonburi Si Mahasamut itself had been founded on the right bank by a group of wealthy Thais during the reign of King Chakkaphat (1548–68) as an important relay point for sea- and riverborne trade between the Gulf of Siam and Ayuthaya, 86km upriver. Ayuthaya served as the royal capital of Siam – as Thailand was then known – from 1350 to 1767. Encircled by rivers with access to the Gulf, Ayuthaya flourished as a river port courted by Dutch, Portuguese, French, English, Chinese and Japanese merchants. By the end of the 17th century the city's population had reached a million and Ayuthaya was one of the wealthiest and most powerful cities in Asia.

Throughout four centuries of Ayuthaya reign, European powers tried without success to colonise the kingdom of Siam. An Asian power finally subdued the capital when the Burmese sacked Ayuthaya in 1767, destroying most of its Buddhist temples and royal edifices. Many Siamese were marched off to Pegu (Bago, Myanmar today), where they were forced to serve the Burmese court.

Four years after this devastating defeat, the Siamese regrouped under Phaya Taksin, a half-Chinese, half-Thai general who decided to move the capital to Thonburi. Taksin, whose behaviour had become in-creasingly violent and bizarre, eventually came to regard himself as the next Buddha. Disapproving of his religious fantasies, his ministers deposed him and then executed him in the custom reserved for royalty – by beating him to death in a velvet sack so that no royal blood touched the ground – in 1782.

River Reality

One of the main physical transformations the city underwent during the 16th-century founding of Thonburi was the digging of a canal to short cut a large bend in Mae Nam Chao Phraya, thus hastening water transport to Siam's capital to the north, Ayuthaya.

Much of the volume of Mae Nam Chao Phraya's original rivercourse gradually diverted to the canal short-cut. Today most visitors and residents are unaware that the section of river running along the western edge of Ko Ratanakosin is a canal. The original river loop, now assumed to be a *khlong* (canal), has taken on the name Khlong Bangkok Noi.

1938	1941
Phibul Songkhram becomes Siam's first prime minister, changes country's name to Thailand and builds Bangkok's Democracy Monument	Japanese invade, first bombing and then occupying Bangkok; Phibul collaborates

THE CHAKRI DYNASTY & THE PORT OF BANGKOK

One of Taksin's key generals, Phaya Chakri, came to power and was crowned in 1782 as Phra Yot Fa. Fearing Thonburi to be vulnerable to Burmese attack from the west, Chakri moved the Siamese capital across the river to a smaller settlement known as Bang Makok (Olive Plum River bank), named for the trees which grew there in abundance. As the first monarch of the new Chakri royal dynasty – which continues to this day – Phaya Chakri was later dubbed King Rama I.

The first task set before the planners of the new city was to create hallowed ground for royal palaces and Buddhist monasteries. Astrologers divined that construction on the new royal palace should begin on 6 May 1782, and ceremonies consecrated Rama I's transfer to a temporary new residence a month later. Construction of permanent throne halls, residence halls and palace temples followed. The plan of the original buildings, their position relative to the river and the royal chapel, and the royal parade and cremation grounds to the north of the palace (today's Sanam Luang) exactly copied the royal compound at Ayuthaya.

Upon completion of the royal district in 1785, at a three-day consecration ceremony attended by tens of thousands of Siamese, the city was given a new name: 'Krungthep mahanakhon amonratanakosin mahintara ayuthaya mahadilok popnopparat ratchathani burirom udomratchaniwet mahasathan amonpiman avatansathit sakkathattiya witsanu-kamprasit'. This lexical gymnastic feat translates roughly as: 'Great City of Angels, the Repository of Divine Gems, the Great Land Unconquerable, the Grand and Prominent Realm, the Royal and Delightful Capital City full of Nine Noble Gems, the Highest Royal Dwelling and Grand Palace, the Divine Shelter and Living Place of Reincarnated Spirits.'

Foreign traders continued to call the capital Bang Makok, which eventually truncated itself to 'Bangkok', the name most commonly known to the outside world.

The break with Ayuthaya was ideological as well as temporal. As Chakri shared no blood-line with earlier royalty, he garnered loyalty by modelling himself as a Dhammaraja (*dhamma* king) supporting Buddhist law rather than a Devaraja (god king) linked to the divine.

Ayuthaya's control of tribute states in Laos and western Cambodia (including Angkor, ruled by the Siamese from 1432 to 1859) was transferred to Bangkok, and thousands of prisoners of war were brought to the capital to work as coolie labour. Bangkok also had ample access to free Thai labour via the *phrai lŭang* (commoner/noble) system, under which all commoners were required to provide labour to the state in lieu of taxes.

Using this immense pool of labour, Rama I augmented Bangkok's natural canal-and-river system with hundreds of artificial waterways feeding into Thailand's hydraulic lifeline, the broad Mae Nam Chao Phraya. Chakri also ordered the construction of 10km of city walls and *khlong rop krung* (canals round the city), to create a royal 'island' – Ko Ratanakosin – between Mae Nam Chao Phraya and the canal loop. Sections of the 4.5m-thick walls still stand in Wat Saket and the Golden Mount, and water still flows, albeit sluggishly, in the canals of the original royal district.

Canal boats on Khlong Saen Saeb

1957	1964–73
Field Marshal Sarit Thanarat seizes power in coup d'état	Military dictators allow the USA to establish several army bases; period of Communist insurgency begins

Temple construction remained the highlight of early development in Bangkok until the reign of Rama III (1824–51), when attention turned to upgrading the port for international sea trade. The city soon became a regional centre for Chinese trading ships, slowly surpassing even the British port at Singapore.

By the mid-19th century Western naval shipping technology had eclipsed the Chinese junk fleets. Bangkok's rulers began to feel threatened as the British and French made colonial inroads into Cambodia, Laos and Burma. This prompted the suspension of a great iron chain across Mae Nam Chao Phraya to guard against the entry of unauthorised ships.

WATERWAYS & ROADWAYS

During the reign of the first five Chakri kings, canal building comprised the lion's share of public works projects, changing the natural geography of the city, and city planners added two lengthy canals to one of the river's largest natural curves. The canals Khlong Rop Krung (today's Khlong Banglamphu) and Khlong Ong Ang were built to create Ko Ratanakosin. The island quickly accumulated an impressive architectural portfolio centred on the Grand Palace, political hub of the new Siamese capital, and the adjacent royal monastery, Wat Phra Kaew.

Throughout the early history of the Chakri Dynasty, royal administrations added to the system. Khlong Mahawawat was excavated during the reign of King Rama IV to link Mae Nam Chao Phraya with Mae Nam Tha Chin, thus expanding the canal-and-river system by hundreds of kilometres. Lined with fruit orchards and stilted houses draped with fishing nets, Khlong Mahawawat remains one of the most traditional and least visited of the Bangkok canals.

Khlong Saen Saeb was built to shorten travel between Mae Nam Chao Phraya and Mae Nam Bang Pakong, and today is heavily used by boat-taxi commuters moving across the city. Likewise Khlong Sunak Hon and Khlong Damoen Saduak link up the Tha Chin and Mae Klong. Khlong Prem Prachakon was dug purely to facilitate travel for Rama V between Bangkok and Ayutthaya, while Khlong Prawet Burirom shortened the distance between Samut Prakan and Chachoengsao provinces.

In 1861 Bangkok's European diplomats and merchants delivered a petition to Rama IV requesting roadways so that they could enjoy horseback riding for physical fitness and pleasure. The royal government acquiesced, and established a handful of roads suitable for horse-drawn carriages and rickshaws. The first – and the most ambitious road project for nearly a century to come – was Th Charoen Krung (also known by its English name, New Rd), which extended 10km south from Wat Pho along the east bank of Mae Nam Chao Phraya. This swath of hand-laid cobblestone, which took nearly four years to finish, eventually accommodated a tramway as well as early automobiles.

Waterworld

Portuguese priest Fernão Mendez Pinto was the first to use the epithet 'Venice of the East', referring not to Bangkok but to Ayuthaya, in a letter to the Society of Jesus in Lisbon in 1554. Two hundred years later it came to be used to describe Bangkok as well. In 1855, British envoy Sir John Bowring noted in his reports: 'The highways of Bangkok are not streets or roads but the river and the canals. Boats are the universal means of conveyance and communication.'

On the eve of the coronation of Rama VI in 1911, a young and adventurous Italian nobleman named Salvatore Besso wrote:

The Venice of the Far East – the capital still wrapped in mystery, in spite of the thousand efforts of modernism amid its maze of canals, and in spite of the popularity of the reigning monarch...From the crowded dock-roads of the River...which reminds one of the Giudecca, across the intricate mass of... the Chinese quarter...which, whilst resembling Canton, is still more Venetian. Were it not for the queues, almond eyes and odours, decidedly Oriental, the illusion would very often be complete...

1973	1976
Kukrit Pramoj's civilian government takes charge	Paramilitary groups kill hundreds of demonstrators at Thammasat University; military regains government control

Top Five Nonfiction Books about Bangkok

- *Bangkok: Place, Practice and Representation,* Marc Askew (2002) – A detailed look at how geography, culture and politics shaped the capital from its founding to the present day.
- *Bangkok: The Story of a City,* Alec Waugh (1971) – Fascinating account of the city and its residents in the 1960s. Paul Bowles originally came to Bangkok to write this book but, when his wife's illness forced him to return to Tangiers, he suggested that novelist and travel writer Alec Waugh (the less famous brother of Evelyn Waugh) finish the job.
- *Bangkok, Vol. 1,* William Warren (2002) – Warren, an American resident of Bangkok for nearly half a century, has written several titles with Bangkok as a theme. His latest blends personal impressions with accounts of some of the city's most celebrated personalities, from Anna Leonowens (of *The King & I* fame) to silk magnate Jim Thompson.
- *Old Bangkok,* Michael Smithies (1986) – Smithies, an independent academic and long-time resident of Thailand, delves deep into the stories behind the capital's historical districts.
- *The Intimate Economies of Bangkok: Tomboys, Tycoons, and Avon Ladies in the Global City,* Ara Wilson (2004) – A historically based ethnography that combines feminist theory with mainstream anthropology.

Shortly thereafter Rama IV ordered the construction of the much shorter Bamrung Meuang and Feuang Nakhon roads to provide access to royal temples from Charoen Krung. His successor Rama V (King Chulalongkorn; 1868–1910) added the much wider Th Ratchadamnoen Klang to provide a suitably royal promenade between the Grand Palace and the expanding commercial centre to the east of Ko Ratanakosin.

RESISTANCE TO COLONIALISM & THE 1932 REVOLUTION

Towards the end of the 19th century, Bangkok's city limits encompassed no more than a dozen square kilometres, with a population of about half a million. Despite its modest size, the capital successfully administered the much larger kingdom of Siam – which then extended into what today are Laos, western Cambodia and northern Malaysia. Even more impressively, Siamese rulers were able to stave off intense pressure from the Portuguese, the Dutch, the French and the English, all of whom at one time or another harboured desires to add Siam to their colonial portfolios. By the end of the century, France and England had established a strong presence in every one of Siam's neighbouring countries – the French in Laos and Cambodia, and the British in Burma and Malaya.

Facing increasing pressure from British colonies in neighbouring Burma and Malaya, Rama IV signed the 1855 Bowring Treaty with Britain to reduce import-export duties and to allow access to former trade monopolies. Wishing to head off any potential invasion plans, Rama V acceded Laos and Cambodia to the French and northern Malaya to the British between 1893 and 1910. The two European powers, for their part, were happy to use Thailand as a buffer state between their respective colonial domains.

Siam's future seemingly secured, Rama V gave Bangkok 120 new roads during his reign, inspired by street plans from Batavia (the Dutch colonial centre now known as Jakarta), Calcutta, Penang and Singapore. Germans were hired to design and build railways emanating from the capital, while the Dutch contributed the design of Bangkok's Hualamphong Railway Station, today considered a minor masterpiece of civic Art Deco.

In 1893 Bangkok opened its first railway line, extending 22km from Bangkok to Pak Nam, where Mae Nam Chao Phraya enters the Gulf of Thailand; at that time it cost just 1B to travel in first class. A 20km electric tramway opened the following year, paralleling the left bank of Mae Nam Chao Phraya. By 1904 three more rail lines out of Bangkok had been added: northeast to Khorat (306km), with a branch line to Lopburi (42km); south-southwest to Phetchaburi (151km); and south to Tha Chin (34km).

Italian sculptor Corrado Feroci contributed several national monuments to the city and helped found the country's first fine-arts university. Americans established Siam's first

1982	1992
General amnesty ends Communist insurgency, but civilian and military interests continue to vie for control	General Suchinda Kraprayoon ousted; civilians regain government

printing press along with the kingdom's first newspaper in 1864. The first Thai-language newspaper, *Darunovadha*, came along in 1874, and by 1900 Bangkok boasted three daily English-language newspapers, the *Bangkok Times, Siam Observer* and *Siam Free Press.*

As Bangkok prospered, many wealthy merchant families sent their children to study in Europe. Students of humbler socioeconomic status who excelled at school had access to government scholarships for overseas study as well. In 1924 a handful of Thai students in Paris formed the Promoters of Political Change, a group that met to discuss ideas for a future Siamese government modelled on Western democracy.

After finishing their studies and returning to Bangkok, three of the 'Promoters', lawyer Pridi Banomyong and military officers Phibul Songkhram and Prayoon Phamonmontri, organised an underground 'People's Party' dedicated to the overthrow of the Siamese system of government. The People's Party found a willing accomplice in Rama VII, and a bloodless revolution in 1932 transformed Thailand from an absolute monarchy into a constitutional one. Bangkok thus found itself the nerve centre of a vast new civil service, which, coupled with its growing success as a world port, transformed the city into a mecca for Thais seeking economic opportunities.

WWII & THE STRUGGLE FOR DEMOCRACY

Phibul Songkhram, appointed prime minister by the People's Party in December 1938, changed the country's name from Siam to Thailand and introduced the Western solar calendar. When the Japanese invaded Southeast Asia in 1941, outflanking Allied troops in Malaya and Burma, Phibul allowed Japanese regiments access to the Gulf of Thailand. Japanese troops bombed and briefly occupied parts of Bangkok on their way to the Thai-Burmese border to fight the British in Burma and, as a result of public insecurity, the Thai economy stagnated.

Phibul resigned in 1944 under pressure from the Thai underground resistance, and after V-J Day in 1945 was exiled to Japan. Bangkok resumed its pace towards modernisation, even after Phibul returned to Thailand in 1948 and took over the leadership again via a military coup. Over the next 15 years, bridges were built over Mae Nam Chao Phraya, canals were filled in to provide space for new roads and multistorey buildings began crowding out traditional teak structures.

Another coup installed Field Marshal Sarit Thanarat in 1957, and Phibul Songkhram once again found himself exiled to Japan, where he died in 1964. From 1964 to 1973 – the peak years of the 1962–75 Indochina War – Thai army officers Thanom Kittikachorn and Praphat Charusathien ruled Thailand and allowed the US to establish several army bases within Thai borders to support the US campaign in Indochina. During this time Bangkok gained notoriety as a 'rest and recreation' (R&R) spot for foreign troops stationed in Southeast Asia.

In October 1973 the Thai military brutally suppressed a large prodemocracy student demonstration at Thammasat University in Bangkok, but King Bhumibol and General Krit Sivara, who sympathised with the students, refused to support further bloodshed, forcing Thanom and Praphat to leave Thailand. Oxford-educated Kukrit Pramoj took charge of a 14-party coalition government and steered a leftist agenda past the conservative parliament. Among Kukrit's lasting achievements were a national minimum wage, the repeal of anticommunist laws and the ejection of US military forces from Thailand.

The military regained control in 1976 after right-wing, paramilitary civilian groups assaulted a group of 2000 students holding a sit-in at Thammasat, killing hundreds. Many students fled Bangkok and joined the People's Liberation Army of Thailand (PLAT), an armed communist insurgency based in the hills, which had been active in Thailand since the 1930s.

Bangkok continued to seesaw between civilian and military rule for the next 15 years. Although a general amnesty in 1982 brought an end to the PLAT, and students, workers and farmers returned to their homes, a new era of political tolerance exposed the military once again to civilian fire.

1997	1999
Baht crashes; new democratic constitution unveiled	BTS Skytrain opens; Assembly of the Poor establish tent-and-shanty camp outside Government House

The King

If you see a yellow Rolls Royce flashing by along city avenues, accompanied by a police, you've just caught a glimpse of Thailand's longest-reigning monarch – and the longest-reigning living monarch in the world – King Bhumibol Adulyadej. Also known as Rama IX (the ninth king of the Chakri dynasty), Bhumibol was born in the US in 1927, while his father Prince Mahidol was studying medicine at Harvard University.

Fluent in English, French, German and Thai, His Majesty ascended the throne in 1946 following the death of his brother Rama VIII (King Ananda Mahidol), who reigned for only one year before dying in a handgun accident.

An ardent jazz composer and saxophonist when he was younger, King Bhumibol has hosted jam sessions with the likes of jazz greats Woody Herman and Benny Goodman. His compositions are often played on Thai radio.

His Majesty administers royal duties from Chitralada Palace in the city's Dusit precinct, north of Ko Ratanakosin. As protector of both nation and religion, King Bhumibol presides over several important Buddhist and Brahmanist ceremonies during the year. Among the more colourful are the seasonal robe-changing of the jade Buddha in Wat Phra Kaew and the annual Royal Ploughing Ceremony, in which ceremonial rice is sowed to insure a robust economy for the coming year, at Sanam Luang.

The king and Queen Sirikit have four children: Princess Ubol Ratana (born 1951), Crown Prince Maha Vajiralongkorn (1952), Princess Mahachakri Sirindhorn (1955) and Princess Chulabhorn (1957).

Along with nation and religion, the monarchy is very highly regarded in Thai society – negative comment about the king or any member of the royal family is a social as well as legal taboo.

In May 1992 several huge demonstrations demanding the resignation of the latest dictator, General Suchinda Kraprayoon, rocked Bangkok and the large provincial capitals. Charismatic Bangkok governor Chamlong Srimuang, winner of the 1992 Magsaysay Award (a humanitarian service award issued in the Philippines) for his role in galvanising the public to reject Suchinda, led the protests. After confrontations between the protesters and the military near the Democracy Monument resulted in nearly 50 deaths and hundreds of injuries, King Bhumibol summoned both Suchinda and Chamlong for a rare public scolding. Suchinda resigned, having been in power for less than six weeks, and Chamlong's career was all but finished.

During the 20th century Bangkok grew from a mere 13 sq km in 1900 to an astounding metropolitan area of more than 330 sq km by the turn of the century. Today the city encompasses not only Bangkok proper, but also the former capital of Thonburi, across Mae Nam Chao Phraya to the west, along with the densely populated 'suburb' provinces, Samut Prakan to the east and Nonthaburi to the north. More than half of Thailand's urban population lives in Bangkok.

2001	2004
Tycoon Thaksin Shinawatra elected PM, attempts to run Thailand 'CEO'-style	MRTA subway opens

Neighbourhoods

Neighbourhoods

A simple sketch of Bangkok's layout does a real injustice to the chaos that the city has effortlessly acquired, first along its original streets, the *khlong* (canals), and then along their modern replacements, asphalt roads. Major street names are unpronounceable to newcomers and compounded by the inconsistency of Romanised Thai spellings. In between the major arteries, *soi* (small lanes) run in serpentine patterns like unfettered rivers, and rarely deliver you where a map so boldly hypothesised. Almost every new outing is a wild goose chase, rarely resulting in a deliberate course. So many errands result in a dead end that thankfully a food vendor is nearby to provide edible solace. In this frustrated, sweaty state, embracing the Buddhist precept of being in the present rather than looking forwards or backwards is Bangkok's greatest gift to recent arrivals. Urban adrenalin-junkies will also see it as a never-ending adventure. As the doyen of expat authors in Thailand, William Warren, has said, 'The gift Bangkok offers me is the assurance I will never be bored'.

To the west and south, Mae Nam Chao Phraya defines the city's only tangible boundary. To the north and east, the city just pours forward like an endless concrete spill. Within the densest or central portion, Bangkok can be divided into east and west by the main railway line, which feeds in and out of Hualamphong Railway Station. Sandwiched between the western side of the tracks and the river is the older part of the city, Ko Ratanakosin, crowded with historical temples, bustling Chinatown and the popular travellers' centre of Banglamphu. The regal enclave of Dusit sits like a crown on the northern apex of Banglamphu, with residential Thewet to its west. The western part of town is less urban, relatively speaking, with low-slung residential homes and shops built along the *khlong*. This is old Bangkok, a medieval city of ancient guilds and traditional customs.

East of the railway line is the new city, devoted to commerce and its attendant temples of skyscrapers and shopping centres. Th Phra Ram I feeds into Siam Square and Pratunam, a popular shopping district, and eventually turns into Th Sukhumvit, a busy commercial centre. Between Siam Square and Th Sukhumvit, Th Withayu shelters many of the city's foreign embassies. South of these districts, Th Silom and Th Surawong house another concentration of high-rise hotels and multinational business offices.

River traffic moving past Wat Arun (p77) on Mae Nam Chao Phraya

ITINERARIES
One Day
Early in the morning, before the day gets steamy, go to **Wat Phra Kaew** (p78) and the **Grand Palace** (p78). These buildings form the pinnacle of Thai religious architecture and make a visual assault on short-term visitors. Afterwards, stroll down to **Wat Pho** (p79), which has enough quirky corners to accommodate huge crowds of gawkers, or to the **Amulet Market** (p78), which is so cramped with commerce that pavements become makeshift stores. When you're ready to see something else, charter a long-tail boat for a tour of Thonburi's **river canals** (p71), bordered by elegant and dilapidated houses balancing effortlessly over watery yards. Most boat drivers will make a stop at **Wat Arun** (p77), which would nicely complete a morning's temple consumption. Have the driver drop you off at Tha Phra Athit for a stroll through the charming neighbourhood of **Banglamphu** (p80). Graze your way through lunch by sampling all the streetside snacks: pineapple, iced Thai coffee, satay, deep-fried bananas, more fruit. If you aren't already planted on Th Khao San, do a fly-through for a glimpse of the round-the-clock freak show or to pick up some cheap souvenirs.

For dinner, head to one of the riverside restaurants for a side order of scenery or to one of the traditional Thai restaurants in the Silom-Surawong neighbourhood. If you opt for the latter, you're perfectly positioned for a night on the town in the notorious **Patpong district** (p92). From go-go bars to a market selling pirated goods, Patpong will make you feel naughty without damaging your soul. If you're killing time before an early flight, stop in at one of the discos on Soi Patpong 2 and Silom Soi 4, or have a beer at one of the nearby bars. Before you call it quits, do as the Thais do and grab one final meal from a vendor stall as an insurance policy against a hangover.

Three Days
With the cultural obligations out of the way, you can devote more time to the unofficial national sport – shopping. **Siam Square** (p89) has the largest concentration of shopping malls, ranging from mall-rat traps to label-whore temples. You can temporarily interrupt your shopping pilgrimage with a trip to **Jim Thompson's House** (p90), a serene example of old-style Bangkok living. It will make you dream of becoming a Bangkok transplant. Be sure to ride the Skytrain, a sleek, elevated tram that gives a bird's-eye view into the city's fortressed compounds and high-rise balconies. If working those bargaining muscles has worn you out, treat yourself to a cheap and rejuvenating Thai massage.

For dinner head to Th Sukhumvit, where you'll find **Vientiane Kitchen** (p125) and **Hua Lamphong Food Station** (p122), two of Bangkok's best restaurants for nontouristy traditional music. After dinner, explore the cosmopolitan side of Bangkok at **Q Bar** (p134) or go for gaudy disco fare at **Narcissus** (p134).

One Week
Now that you're accustomed to the noise, pollution and traffic, **Chinatown** (p87) should be added to your itinerary. A whole day can be spent here wandering the narrow streets, where commerce is elevated to an ancient art. Work your way over to **Phahurat** (p87), the Indian district, for lunch – one can't live on Thai food alone.

On the weekend, take the Skytrain to **Chatuchak Weekend Market** (p154) for intensive souvenir hunting. Past the kitchen supplies is an area where fighting cocks and fighting fish are as proudly displayed as antique Buddhas and used blue jeans.

For a little R&R, take a river ferry to **Ko Kret** (p98), a carless island north of central Bangkok that defines relaxation. In open-air studios, Ko Kret artisans continue the age-old tradition of hand-thrown terracotta pottery. Their meditative process is the most intensive activity on the island.

With one week, you will also have time to peruse the goings-on about town, such as a traditional arts performance or a visiting DJ at a local club. You can also find a favourite street vendor, the best souvenir of all.

ORGANISED TOURS

In 1855 British envoy Sir John Bowring wrote: 'The highways of Bangkok are not streets or roads but the river and the canals. Boats are the universal means of conveyance and communication.' The wheeled motor vehicle has long since become Bangkok's conveyance of choice, but fortunately it hasn't yet become universal. A vast network of canals and river tributaries surrounding Bangkok still carry a motley fleet of watercraft, from paddled canoes to rice barges. In these areas many homes, trading houses and temples remain oriented towards water life and provide a fascinating glimpse into the past, when Thais still considered themselves *jâo náam* (water lords).

You can observe urban river life from the water for several hours by boarding a Chao Phraya Express boat at any *tha* (pier) and taking it in either direction to its final stop. The trip is the cheapest introduction to one of Bangkok's most photogenic aspects. Boats pass children swimming in the muddy waters, huge cargo ships groaning under the weight of sand being shipped to construction sites, and wake-skipping long-tailed boats. At sunset the famed missile-shaped *prang* (tall Hindu-Khmer-style stupa) of Wat Arun (p77) and the riverside towers of the luxury hotels are bathed in ethereal red-and-orange hues.

Bosom Brothers

If it weren't for an English trader taking a quiet stroll along the river one afternoon in 1824, probably Siamese twins would be known by an entirely different name. Robert Hunter spied an eight-limbed and two-headed creature in the water and was astonished to discover it was two conjoined 13-year-old boys, called Chang and Eng. The brothers became celebrities in the best freak-show tradition of the times, touring Europe and the USA, and featuring in PT Barnum's museum. They eventually settled in North Carolina, where they married sisters, produced 22 children and died within hours of each other.

The terminus for most northbound boats is Tha Nonthaburi; for most southbound boats it's Tha Sathon (also called Central Pier), close to the Saphan Taksin Skytrain station, or Wat Ratchasingkhon, which is further south. See p209 for information on fares and timetables.

Another good boat trip is through Khlong Bangkok Noi, just across the river in the area known as Thonburi. The further up the *khlong* you go, the better the scenery, with teak houses on stilts, old temples and plenty of greenery. After just a five-minute ride, you are far removed from the concrete entanglements of central Bangkok.

Long-tail public boats (60B) leave from Tha Chang and travel to Bang Yai, a district in Nonthaburi, dropping off residents along the way. They operate from 8am to 3pm Monday to Friday. Sightseers are discouraged from using this boat, but if you forget that you aren't a local, take it all the way to the final stop (Bang Yai) and wait approximately an hour for a return boat.

Trips along Khlong Bangkok Yai pass Wat Intharam, where a *chedi* (stupa) contains the ashes of Thonburi's King Taksin, who was assassinated in 1782. Fine gold-and-black lacquerwork adorning the main *bòt* (chapel) doors depicts the mythical *naariiphŏn* tree, which bears fruit shaped like beautiful maidens. Durian plantations line picturesque Khlong Om, which loops back to the river from Khlong Bangkok Noi. Khlong Mon, between Bangkok Noi and Bangkok Yai, offers more typical canal scenery, including orchid farms.

Those interested in seeing Bangkok's deep-water port can hire long-tail boats to Khlong Toey or as far downriver as Pak Nam, which means 'river mouth' in Thai. It's about two hours each way by boat, or a bit quicker if you take a bus or taxi one way.

You can charter a boat (400B to 500B per hour) from any pier to travel into any of these canals. Many boats will also stop at Wat Arun (p77), the Royal Barges National Museum (p76) or a weekend floating market. Rates and routes are highly negotiable, so shop around and make sure all parties are agreed before climbing aboard. And don't forget to buy your boat driver a drink from one of the floating vendors. Tha Chang has the largest selection of boat-tour operators, but most piers offer boat hire. You might be able to shave a few baht off the deal if you negotiate directly with a boat driver, but you'll need to speak some Thai and be able to dodge the pesky operators whose sole job is to intercept you.

River Tours

CHAO PHRAYA EXPRESS BOAT

☎ 0 2623 6001, 0 2623 6143; www.chaophrayaboat
.com; round trip adult/child 350/250B, one way
250/150B; ⏰ 8am-6pm Sun; from Tha Maharat

The company that manages the river express
boats also provides a Sunday tour of the Royal
Folk Arts & Handicrafts Centre in Bang Sai,
Bang Pa-In Palace near Ayuthaya and the bird
sanctuary at Wat Phailom in Pathum Thani
Province. The tour price does not include
lunch or admission fees. You can also use this
service one way for an independent trip to
Ayuthaya (pp184–88).

MANOHRA 2

☎ 0 2677 6240; fax 0 2677 6246; Bangkok Marriott
Resort & Spa, 257/1-3 Th Charoen Nakorn; admission
US$480

The Manohra 2 and Mekhala (see below) are
restored teak rice barges that have been transformed into luxury cabin cruisers that travel to
and from Ayuthaya. Decorated with antiques
and Persian carpets, these craft represent the
ultimate in Mae Nam Chao Phraya luxury, the
nautical equivalent of the *Eastern & Oriental
Express* train.

A three-day trip to Bang Pa-In and Ayuthaya aboard *Manohra 2* stops en route at
Ko Kret and overnights in front of a temple
along the river. In the morning guests 'make
merit' and continue on to visit Bang Pa-In
and Ayuthaya. On the third day the tour visits
Bang Sai.

MEKHALA

☎ 0 2688 1000; fax 0 2291 9400; Menam Riverside
Hotel, 2074 Th Charoen Krung; adult US$250-280, child
US$117-199

A two-day trip to Ayuthaya and Bang Pa-In
aboard *Mekhala* includes an overnight stay on
the boat with a candle-lit dinner at the foot
of a picturesque temple. A minibus returns
guests to Bangkok. The trip can also be done in
reverse with a minivan to Ayuthaya and return
by boat cruise.

ORIENTAL QUEEN

☎ 0 2236 0400; Oriental Hotel, Soi Oriental, Th Charoen
Krung; admission 1600B; ⏰ 7.30am-4.30pm

The Oriental Hotel organises tours to Bang
Pa-In as well as Ayuthaya. These tours depart
from the hotel by bus and return by way of
the river on the luxurious, air-conditioned
Oriental Queen. Lunch and a guide are also
provided.

RIVER SUN CRUISE

☎ 0 2266 9316; River City Complex, 721/5 Th Si
Phraya; adult/child 1600/1100B; ⏰ 8am-4.30pm

Departing from the River City Complex (Map
pp252–3), tours travel by bus to Ayuthaya and
Bang Pa-In, where they return to Bangkok by
boat.

Bicycle Tours

ABC AMAZING BANGKOK CYCLIST TOUR

☎ 0 2712 9301; fax 0 2712 9310; www.realasia.net;
1000B incl equipment & insurance

Several Dutch cyclists organise daily bike
tours through a riverside neighbourhood in
Thonburi. You travel by long-tail boat to the
location, which is crisscrossed by *khlong* and
narrow concrete platforms. The company
promises that instead of Bangkok's traffic
jams you will see fruit plantations and village
life.

KO RATANAKOSIN

Shopping p145

Bordering the eastern bank of Mae Nam Chao Phraya, this area is a veritable Vatican City of Thai Buddhism filled with some of the country's most honoured and holy sites: Wat Phra Kaew, the Grand Palace and Wat Pho. These are also the most spectacular tourist attractions the city has to offer and a must for even the most unmotivated students of culture and history.

This collection of religious and architectural treasures wasn't accidental. Rama I intended to recreate the glory of the sacked Siamese capital of Ayuthaya by constructing a new island city – one that would be fortified against future attacks by the Burmese and elevate the newly established dynasty. Both intentions succeeded. The Burmese never staged an assault on the new capital and the Chakri dynasty survives to the present day.

Transport Ko Ratanakosin

Bus Air-con 506 & 507, ordinary 1, 3, 15, 30 & 33
Ferry Chao Phraya Express to Tha Maharat, Tha Chang & Tha Tien

The ancient city has matured in modern times to a lively district of contradictions that only Thailand can elegantly juggle. The temples, with their heavenly status, are tethered to earth by nearby food markets that spring up like small mushroom villages after rain. Rip-off artists prowl the tourist strip, using the country's legendary hospitality to earn a dishonest day's wages (see p76). In the shadows of the whitewashed temple walls are Buddhism's ancient companions – the animistic spirits who govern fortune and fate, neatly packaged into amulets that are traded with as much esoteric knowledge as ancient coins.

Come here to survey the street life as much as the famed attractions. In the cool season, medicinal bowls of ginger-infused broth are sold from steaming caldrons to stave off winter colds. Stray dogs are covered with old T-shirts by merit-making residents hoping to provide the animals with added warmth. The narrow alleys between the Amulet Market and Thammasat University are endless mazes of urban landscape.

Orientation

Forming almost a tear-drop shape, Ko Ratanakosin's boundaries are defined by Mae Nam Chao Phraya on the western side, Th Phra Pin Klao on the northern side and Th Atsadang, which follows Khlong Lawt, on the eastern side. The district's attractions are concentrated in the area south of Sanam Luang, making for a walkable outing. Two main river piers – Tha Chang and Tha Maharat – service this district, making transport a scenic and relaxed experience. This is also a popular area from which to hire boats for tours into Thonburi's canals.

The area is best visited early in the morning, before the sun reaches its maximum strength. The wide pavements that circumnavigate the major sights and the inside courtyards of the temples are unfortunately devoid of shade, a necessary refuge from the tropical sun. Some of the more elegant visitors carry a sun umbrella to preserve their pampered skin.

South of Th Na Phra Lan is primarily a tourist zone with a few warehouses abutting the river as reminders that daily life still exists. For unstructured strolls through more local-friendly areas, head north of Th Na Phra Lan along Th Maharat, where students, office workers and monks stroll the pedestrian paths. In the small *soi* that entangle themselves near Thammasat University are the best cheap lunch eats the neighbourhood has to offer, and some of these ramshackle shops have river views.

East of Thammasat University is Sanam Luang, an oval park where joggers shuffle along in the early morning hours. Alongside Sanam Luang the National Museum and the National Theatre stand with stoic resolve.

On the far eastern side of Wat Phra Kaew are government ministry buildings reflecting a pronounced Western architectural influence – an interesting contrast to the flamboyant traditional Thai architecture demonstrated by the temples.

LAK MEUANG Map p256

ศาลหลักเมือง

Cnr Th Ratchadamnoen Nai & Th Lak Meuang; admission free; 8.30am-5.30pm; ferry Tha Chang, air-con bus 506 & 507

The City Pillar is across the street from the eastern wall of Wat Phra Kaew, at the southern end of Sanam Luang. This shrine encloses a wooden pillar erected by Rama I in 1782 to represent the founding of the new Bangkok capital. Later, during the reign of Rama V (King Chulalongkorn), five other idols were added to the shrine. The spirit of the pillar, Phra Sayam Thewathirat (Venerable Siam Deity of the State), is considered the city's guardian deity and receives the daily supplications of countless Thai worshippers, some of whom commission classical Thai dancers to perform *lákhon kâe bon* (shrine dancing) at the shrine. Some of the offerings include severed pigs' heads with sticks of incense sprouting from their foreheads.

NATIONAL GALLERY Map p256

หอศิลปแห่งชาติ

0 2282 8525, 0 2281 2224; Th Chao Fa; admission 30B; 9am-4pm Wed-Sun; ferry Tha Phra Athit, air-con bus 506, ordinary bus 30

Housed in an early Ratanakosin-era building near the National Theatre, the National Gallery displays traditional and contemporary art, mostly by artists receiving government support. The general view is that it's not Thailand's best, but the gallery is worth a visit for die-hard art fans or those who find themselves nearby.

NATIONAL MUSEUM Map p256

พิพิธภัณฑสถานแห่งชาติ

0 2224 1370; Th Na Phra That; admission 40B; 9am-4pm Wed-Sun; air-con bus 507

Thailand's National Museum is the largest museum in Southeast Asia and an excellent place to learn about Thai art. All periods and styles are represented, from Dvaravati to Ratanakosin, and there's also a well-maintained collection of traditional musical instruments from Thailand, Laos, Cambodia and Indonesia. Other permanent exhibits include ceramics, clothing and textiles, woodcarving, royal regalia, Chinese art and weaponry.

In addition to the exhibition halls, the museum grounds contain the restored **Phutthaisawan (Buddhaisawan) Chapel**. Inside the chapel (built in 1795) are some well-preserved original murals and one of the country's most revered Buddha images, Phra Phuttha Sihing. Legend

The National Museum (left)

claims the image came from Ceylon, but art historians attribute it to the 13th-century Sukhothai period.

The museum buildings were originally built in 1782 as the palace of Rama I's viceroy, Prince Wang Na. Rama V turned it into a museum in 1884.

Keep in mind that the museum is not air-conditioned and that signage in English is sporadic. Taking a foreign-language tour will contribute greatly to your appreciation of the museum and of Thailand's rich artistic history. Free tours are given in English on Wednesday (focusing on Buddhism) and Thursday (Thai art, religion and culture). Tours in German (Thursday), French (Wednesday) and Japanese (Wednesday) are also available. All tours start from the ticket pavilion at 9.30am.

Ko Ratanakosin Top Five

- **Wat Mahathat** (p77) Monks and academics flock to this Buddhist centre and browse the amulet market.
- **Lak Meuang** (p75) Best when a shrine dance has been commissioned.
- **Wat Arun** (p70) Everyone's favourite phallus.
- **Wat Phra Kaew & Grand Palace** (p78) The Hollywood blockbusters of Thai architecture.
- **Wat Pho** (p79) A rambling complex of hidden sights and corners.

ROYAL BARGES NATIONAL MUSEUM

Map p256

เรือพระที่นั่ง

☎ 0 2424 0004; Thonburi; admission 30B, photography fee 100B; ⏰ 9am-5pm; tourist shuttle boat from Tha Phra Athit to museum

The royal barges are long, fantastically ornamented boats used in ceremonial processions on the river. The largest is 50m long and requires a rowing crew of 50 men, plus seven umbrella bearers, two helmsmen and two navigators, as well as a flagbearer, rhythm-keeper and chanter.

The barges are kept in sheds on the Thonburi side of the river, next to Khlong Bangkok Noi. *Suphannahong*, the king's personal barge, is the most important of the boats; made from a single piece of timber, it's the largest dugout in the world. The name means 'golden swan', and a huge swan's head has been carved into the bow. Lesser barges feature bows carved into other Hindu-Buddhist mythological shapes such as the *naga* (sea dragon) and the *garuda* (Vishnu's bird mount).

One of the best times to see the fleet in action on the river is during the royal *kàthîn* ceremony at the end of *phansǎa* (the Buddhist rains retreat, ending with an October or November new moon), when new robes are offered to the monastic contingent.

SANAM LUANG Map p256

สนามหลวง

ferry Tha Chang, air-con bus 503, 506, 507, 511 & 512, ordinary bus 33 & 59

On a hot day, Sanam Luang (Royal Field), just north of Wat Phra Kaew, is far from charming – a great expanse of dying grass, ringed by scraggly shade trees, great flocks of pigeons and a universe of heavy characters. Despite its modern role as an urban wasteland, Sanam Luang also enjoys a royal appointment as the traditional site for royal cremations and for the annual Royal Ploughing Ceremony, in which the king officially initiates the rice-growing season (p11). The most recent ceremonial cremation took place here in March 1996, when the king presided over funeral rites for his mother. Before that the most recent Sanam Luang cremations were held in 1976 for Thai students killed in demonstrations.

A **statue of Mae Thorani**, the earth goddess (borrowed from Hindu mythology's Dharani), stands in a white pavilion at the northern end

of the field. Erected in the late 19th century by Rama V, the statue was originally attached to a well that provided drinking water to the public.

Until 1982, Bangkok's famous Weekend Market was regularly held at Sanam Luang (it's now at Chatuchak Park; see p154). Nowadays, the large field is most popularly used as a picnic and recreational area. A large kite-flying competition is held here during the kite-flying season (mid-February to April). Matches are held between many teams, who fly either a 'male' or 'female' kite and are assigned a particular territory, winning points if they can force a competitor into their zone.

SONGKRAN NIYOMSANE FORENSIC MEDICINE MUSEUM Map p256

พิพิธภัณฑ์นิติเวชศาสตร์สงกรานต์ นิยมเสน

☎ 0 2419 7000; Forensic Medicine Building, Siriraj Hospital, Th Phrannok, Thonburi; admission free; ⏰ 9am-4pm Mon-Fri; ferry Tha Rot Fai

Near the Thonburi (Bangkok Noi) train station, this museum is the most famous of 10 medical museums on the hospital premises. Among the grisly displays are the preserved bodies of famous Thai murderers. The best way to get here is to take a river ferry to Tha Rot Fai (Railway Station Pier) in Thonburi and follow the road to the second entrance into the Siriraj Hospital campus. The museum building will be on your left.

Warning

Many tourist are caught by scams in Thailand. Near popular temples, you could be approached by a well-dressed Thai person who speaks your native tongue masterfully. The person seems nice and trustworthy and advises you that a temple is closed today. This could be the beginning of a slow and costly con game. Your new friend might tell you about some other temples to visit, or about a one-day-only gem fair, or about a really great tailor – all things you've wanted to check out but weren't sure where to start. Sadly, if you agree to accompany them you might get hustled into buying fake gems, overpriced suits or a variety of other expensive mistakes. While the Thai people are very friendly and hospitable, most honest individuals are not likely to be hanging around the heavily touristed sites. Keep on your guard. See p220 for more details.

WAT ARUN Map pp248–9

วัดอรุณฯ

☎ 0 2466 3167; Th Arun Amarin, Thonburi; admission 20B; ⏱ 8.30am-5.30pm; cross-river ferry from Tha Tien to Tha Thai Wang

The missile-shaped temple that flanks Mae Nam Chao Phraya is referred to as the Temple of Dawn, named after the Indian god of dawn, Aruna. It was here that King Taksin stumbled upon a small shrine used by the local people and interpreted the discovery as an auspicious sign for building a new Thai capital in Thonburi after Ayuthaya was sacked by the Burmese. King Taksin used the site for a palace, royal temple and home of the Emerald Buddha before relocating (along with the capital) to Bangkok.

The 82m *prang* was constructed during the first half of the 19th century by Rama II and Rama III. The unique design elongates the typical Khmer *prang* into a distinctly Thai shape. Its brick core has a plaster covering embedded with a mosaic of broken, multihued Chinese porcelain, a common temple ornamentation in the early Ratanakosin period, when Chinese ships calling at Bangkok used tonnes of old porcelain as ballast. Steep stairs reach a lookout point about halfway up the *prang*, from where there are fine views of Thonburi and the river. During certain festivals, hundreds of lights illuminate the outline of the *prang* at night.

Also worth a look is the interior of the *bòt*. The main Buddha image is said to have been designed by Rama II himself. The murals date to the reign of Rama V; particularly impressive is one that depicts Prince Siddhartha (the Buddha) encountering examples of birth, old age, sickness and death outside his palace walls, an experience that led him to abandon the worldly life. The ashes of Rama II are interred in the base of the *bòt*'s presiding Buddha image.

On the periphery of the temple grounds are simple wooden cutouts of Thai dancers luring visitors to take photographs of their mugs imposed onto the figures. A fairly innocuous scam is at work here: after the camera has clicked a hawker emerges to collect a fee of 40B, although no charge is posted in front of the figures.

WAT MAHATHAT Map p256

วัดมหาธาตุ

☎ 0 2222 6011; Th Mahathat; admission free; ⏱ 9am-5pm; ferry Tha Maharat, air-con bus 8 & 12

Founded in the 1700s, Wat Mahathat is a national centre for the Mahanikai monastic sect and houses one of Bangkok's two Buddhist universities, Mahathat Rajavidyalaya. The university is the most important place of Buddhist learning in mainland Southeast Asia – the Lao, Vietnamese and Cambodian governments send selected monks to further their studies here.

What's a Wát?

Planning to conquer Bangkok's temples? With this handy guide, you'll be able to collect your wits about you and know your wát from your elbow.

- **bòt** – a consecrated chapel where monastic ordinations are held
- **jeh-dii** (commonly spelled *chedi; stupa*) – a large bell-shaped tower usually containing five structural elements symbolising (from bottom to top) earth, water, fire, wind and void; relics of the Buddha or a Thai king are housed inside
- **prang** – a towering phallic spire of Khmer origin serving the same religious purpose as a *chedi*
- **wát** – temple monastery
- **wíhǎan** – the main sanctuary for the temple's Buddha sculpture and where laypeople come to make their offerings; classic architecture typically has a three-tiered roof representing the triple gems, Buddha (the teacher), Dharma (the teaching) and Brotherhood (the followers)

Buddha Images

Elongated earlobes, no evidence of bone or muscle, arms that reach to the knees, a third eye: these are some of the 32 rules, originating from 3rd-century India, that govern the depiction of Buddha in sculpture. With such rules in place, why are some Buddhas sitting, others walking? Known as 'postures', the poses depict periods in the life of Buddha.

- **sitting** – Buddha teaching or meditating. If the right hand is pointed towards the earth, Buddha is shown subduing the demons of desire. If the hands are folded in the lap, Buddha is meditating
- **reclining** – the exact moment of Buddha's passing into *parinibanna* (postdeath nirvana)
- **standing** – Buddha bestowing blessings or taming evil forces
- **walking** – Buddha after his return to earth from heaven

Temple Etiquette

Wáts are sacred places and should be treated with respect and formality. Wat Phra Kaew, especially, is very strict in its dress code. You may not enter the temple grounds if wearing shorts or a sleeveless shirt. The temple does have sarongs and baggy pants that are sometimes available on loan at the entrance. For walking in the courtyard areas you must wear shoes with closed heels and toes – sandals and flip-flops aren't permitted for foreigners. As in any temple compound, shoes should be removed before entering any building.

Mahathat and the surrounding area have developed into an informal Thai cultural centre of sorts, though this may not be obvious at first glance. A daily **open-air market** features traditional Thai herbal medicine, and out on the street you'll find a string of shops selling herbal cures and offering Thai massage. On weekends a large produce market held on the temple grounds brings people from all over Bangkok and beyond. Opposite the main entrance, on the other side of Th Maharat, is a large religious amulet market (talàat phrá khrêuang).

The monastery offers meditation instruction in English (see p212).

WAT PHRA KAEW & GRAND PALACE

Map p256

วัดพระแก้ว/พระมหาราชวัง

☎ 0 2623 5500; admission to both 200B, 2hr guided tours 100B; ☻ 8.30am-3.30pm; ferry Tha Chang, air-con bus 508 & 512

Wat Phra Kaew (Temple of the Emerald Buddha) is an architectural wonder of gleaming, gilded chedi seemingly buoyed above the ground, polished orange-and-green roof tiles piercing the humid sky, mosaic-encrusted pillars and rich marble pediments. The highly stylised shrine houses the much revered Emerald Buddha and is bestowed with a fitting official name – Wat Phra Si Ratana Satsadaram (which has the same meaning of Temple of the Emerald Buddha).

The fantastical ornamentation of the temple does an excellent job of distracting first-time visitors from paying their respects to the Emerald Buddha. It is quite easy to tour the grounds in a sort of daze, enamoured and confused by Thai Buddhism, and not realise until much later that you didn't see the eponymous figure. Here's why: the Emerald Buddha is only 66cm high and sits so high above worshippers in the main temple building that the gilded shrine is more striking than the small figure it cradles.

The Emerald Buddha's lofty perch signifies its high status as the 'talisman' of the Thai kingdom and legitimiser of Thai sovereignty. Neither the origin nor the sculptor of the Buddha is certain, but it first appeared on record in 15th-century Chiang Rai in northern Thailand. Legend says it was sculpted in India and brought to Siam by way of Ceylon, but stylistically it seems to belong to Thai artistic periods of the 13th to 14th centuries.

Sometime in the 15th century, this Buddha is said to have been covered with plaster and gold leaf and placed in Chiang Rai's own Wat Phra Kaew. While being transported to a new location after a storm had damaged the chedi containing the Buddha, it supposedly lost its plaster covering in a fall, revealing a brilliant green figure (the Emerald Buddha is actually carved from nephrite, a type of jade). This is a great portent in the life of Buddha figures. Lao invaders took the figure from Chiang Mai in the mid-16th century and brought it to their homeland.

When Thailand waged war against Laos 200 years later, the Emerald Buddha was seized and taken back to the then Thai capital of Thonburi. Here is where the image achieves its modern significance: the Thai general who retrieved the image later succeeded the throne and established the present Chakri dynasty as Rama I.

Rama I had the Emerald Buddha moved to the new Thai capital in Bangkok and had two royal robes made for it, one to be worn in the hot season and one for the rainy season. Rama III added another seasonal robe, to be worn in the cool season. The three robes are still solemnly changed at the beginning of each season by the king himself.

Extensive murals depicting scenes from the Ramakian (the Thai version of the Indian Ramayana epic) line the cloisters along the inside walls of the compound. Divided into 178 sections, the murals illustrate the epic in its entirety, beginning at the north gate and moving clockwise around the compound.

Adjoining Wat Phra Kaew is the Grand Palace (Phra Borom Maharatchawong), a former royal residence which today is used by the king only for certain ceremonial occasions. The current monarch lives in Chitralada Palace, in the Dusit area and closed to the public. The exteriors of the four Grand Palace buildings are worth a swift perusal, however, for their royal bombast.

At the eastern end, **Borombhiman Hall**, a French-inspired structure that served as a residence for Rama VI, is occasionally used to house visiting foreign dignitaries. In April 1981 General San Chitpatima used it as headquarters for an attempted coup. **Amarindra Hall**, to the west, was originally a hall of justice but is used today for coronation ceremonies.

The largest of the palace buildings is the triple-winged **Chakri Mahaprasat** (Grand Palace Hall). Designed in 1882 by British architects, the exterior shows a peculiar blend of Italian Renaissance and traditional Thai architecture, a style often referred to as *faràng sài chá-daa* (Westerner wearing a Thai classical dancer's headdress), because each wing is topped by a *mondòp* (a layered, heavily ornamented spire). The tallest of the *mondòp*, in the centre, contains the ashes of Chakri kings; the flanking *mondòp* enshrine the ashes of Chakri princes who failed to inherit the throne.

Thai kings traditionally housed their huge harems in the inner palace area, which was guarded by combat-trained female sentries. The intrigue and rituals that occurred within the walls of this once-cloistered community are relatively silent to the modern visitor. A fictionalised version is told in the trilogy *Four Reigns*, by Kukrit Pramoj, which follows a young girl named Ploi growing up within the Royal City.

The last building to the west is the Ratanakosin-style **Dusit Hall**, which initially served as a venue for royal audiences and later as a royal funerary hall.

You enter the Wat Phra Kaew and Grand Palace complex through the third gate from the river pier. Tickets are purchased inside the complex. If anyone outside the complex tells you that it is closed, proceed to the official ticket window to confirm. The admission fee also includes entry to the Vimanmek Teak Mansion (p86) and Abhisek Dusit Throne Hall (p85).

WAT PHO Map p256

วัดโพธิ์(วัดพระเชตุพน)

☎ 0 2221 9911; Th Sanam Chai; admission 20B, 40min guided tours 150-200B; 🕑 8am-6pm; ferry Tha Tien, air-con bus 508 & 512, ordinary bus 44

This temple has a long list of credits: the oldest and largest wát in Bangkok, the longest reclining Buddha and the largest collection of Buddha images in Thailand, and the earliest centre for public education.

As a temple site, Wat Pho (Temple of the Reclining Buddha) dates to the 16th century, but its current history really begins in 1781 with the complete rebuilding of the original monastery. Narrow Th Chetuphon divides the grounds in two, with each section surrounded by huge, whitewashed walls. The most interesting part is the northern compound, which includes a gallery of Buddha images, four large *chedi* commemorating the first three Chakri kings (Rama III has two *chedi*), 91 smaller *chedi*, an old *tripitaka* (Buddhist scriptures) library, and a large structure that houses the reclining Buddha.

The tremendous **reclining Buddha**, 46m long and 15m high, illustrates the passing of the Buddha into nirvana. The figure is modelled out of plaster around a brick core and finished in gold leaf. Mother-of-pearl inlay adorns the eyes and feet of this colossal figure, with the feet displaying 108 different auspicious *laksana* (characteristics of a Buddha).

The images on display in the four *wíhăan* (sanctuaries) surrounding the main *bòt* in the eastern part of the compound are interesting. Particularly beautiful are the Phra Jinnarat and Phra Jinachi Buddhas, in the western and southern chapels, both from Sukhothai. The galleries extending between the four chapels feature no fewer than 394 gilded Buddha images. Rama I's remains are interred in the base of the presiding Buddha figure in the *bòt*.

During Rama III's reign, Wat Pho was an open university, and it maintains that tradition today as the national headquarters for the teaching and preservation of traditional Thai medicine, including Thai massage. The massage school, which is across the street from the temple, offers daily massages as well as courses in traditional techniques (see p212).

The ceramic animal figures scattered about the temple grounds arrived in Thailand as ballast on Chinese junks. The temple rubbings for sale at Wat Pho and elsewhere in Thailand come from the 152 *Ramakian* reliefs, carved in marble and obtained from the ruins of Ayuthaya, which line the base of the large *bòt*. The rubbings are no longer taken directly from the panels but are rubbed from cement casts made years ago.

You, You, Where You Go?

A direct translation of a standard Thai inquiry *('Pai năi?')*, the English phrase 'Where you go?' will be hurled at you by money-struck *túk-túk* and taxi drivers as if it were a military interrogation technique. The best answer is to master the public transportation system, which is cheap and reliable, and won't steer you to its cousin's tailor shop. See the transport boxed texts in each neighbourhood section, or individual entries, for public transport options.

BANGLAMPHU

Eating p108; Shopping p145; Sleeping p165

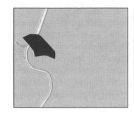

One of the oldest districts in Bangkok, Banglamphu was originally settled by Thai farmers and produce merchants from Ayuthaya who followed the transfer of the royal court to Bangkok in the late 18th century. The name means 'Place of Lamphu', a reference to the *lamphuu* tree *(Duabanga grandiflora)* once prevalent in the area. By the time of King Rama IV (1851–68), Banglamphu had developed into a thriving commercial district by day and an entertainment spot by night.

The district is most famous for **Th Khao San**, the backpacker enclave of cheap guesthouses and travellers' amenities. Demonstrating the herd mentality of even the most independent types, Th Khao San's guesthouse scene has expanded beyond its namesake street, even swallowing up a primary school located nearby. The municipal government announced the school closure as a way to shield the children from the backpackers' public drunkenness, but critics point to the monetary incentive of transforming a public school into a lucrative guesthouse or bar.

The neighbourhood continues to evolve, based on its popularity with foreign visitors and the changing tastes of its residents. In the small wooden shops, some traditional crafts still endure, while the majority of stores have responded to modern demands. A cluster of boutiques sell Western-style wedding dresses, providing a momentary pang of homeland *déjà vu* to a recent arrival. Internet shops are usually crammed with foreigners checking their email or neighbourhood kids playing shoot-'em-up computer games. Despite the school closing, there are still several stores specialising in the government-issued school uniforms, consisting of black pants and skirts, white button-down shirts, Mary Jane shoes and faux-leather book satchels.

This neighbourhood is one of the most charming districts of the city, thanks to these surviving family businesses. Every store is decorated with terracotta water gardens or potted plants and low-hanging shades that block the mean sun. The commercial collection is most entertaining around Chinese New Year, when the merchants conduct 'spring cleaning'. Swarms of workers scour the pavements, mop the floors and polish the neon signs. Once all the soap is rinsed away, the scene looks inexplicably like it did before.

Transport Banglamphu

Bus Air-con 506, 511 & 512, ordinary 3, 15, 30, 32 & 53
Ferry Tha Phra Athit (aka Tha Banglamphu)
Boat Khlong Saen Saeb taxi from pier near Wat Saket to Tha Ratchathewi near Siam Square (6B)

Orientation

Banglamphu spreads from the river north of Th Phra Pin Klao and eventually melts into Dusit and Thewet around Th Krung Kasem. The neighbourhood's eastern boundary is ill-defined, but many point to the intersection of Khlong Banglamphu with Khlong Saen Saeb or Th Maha Chai as a good marker. Bookended by the major roads of Th Phra Athit and Th Ratchadamnoen Klang, the backpacker universe starts on Th Khao San and spreads down Soi Rambutri, Th Rambutri and even over the *khlong* to the residential *soi* off Th Samsen.

Banglamphu is one of the best neighbourhoods for vendor hopping, as the streets are shady and the traffic is minimal (comparatively so), making a pavement luncheon a pleasant affair. It is easy to lose direction in this neighbourhood where streets more closely mimic a maze than a thoroughfare. Luckily there is always a vendor at the end of each wrong turn as a reward for getting lost.

Although life-sentence expats deride the backpacker clones in Banglamphu, the services and affordability here are unrivalled in the city. All along the guesthouse strip you can check your email, eat a banana pancake (a popular home-replacement meal) and have a friendly chat with a fellow traveller on how to get to the Cambodian border. A staging ground for trips elsewhere, Banglamphu creates an instant camaraderie that emerges to pacify the anxiety of plunging into the unknown.

Neighbourhoods – Banglamphu

Beyond the safety zone of the backpacker camp, the major roads that meet at the Democracy Monument form a street-level highway that detracts from the district's otherwise amiability to pedestrians. For strolls beyond Th Khao San, stick to the small roads and *soi* to see more street life.

On Th Bamrung Meuang between Sao Ching-Cha and Monk's Bowl Village are several shops selling monks' robes, Buddha figures and other religious paraphernalia not found in other parts of the city. Teak shops line Th Burapha and make for a nice diversion if visiting Monk's Bowl Village.

An interesting transport option is the canal taxi that runs from the pier near Wat Ratchanatda along Khlong Banglamphu to Khlong Saen Saeb, and on to Siam Square and Th Sukhumvit.

Banglamphu Top Five

- **Santichaiprakan Park** (p81) A perfect spot for evening sunsets and cool river breezes.
- **Street stalls** (p80) Graze the informal buffet of Banglamphu's street food.
- **Th Khao San** (p80) Backpacker mecca and daily freak show.
- **Wat Ratchanatda** (p82) A grand temple complex with a popular amulet market.
- **Wat Saket & Golden Mount** (p83) Gain a little altitude in this flat city.

DEMOCRACY MONUMENT Map pp254–5
อนุสาวรีย์ประชาธิปไตย
Traffic circle of Th Ratchadamnoen Klang, Th Din So & Th Prachatipatai; air-con bus 511 & 512, ordinary bus 2, 39 & 44

Four dismembered angel wings planted in a circle form Thailand's most stunning monument to the modern age. Erected in 1932 to commemorate Thailand's momentous transformation from absolute to constitutional monarchy, the monument was designed by Italian artist Corrado Feroci, who buried 75 cannonballs in its base to signify the year BE (Buddhist Era) 2475 (AD 1932). Before immigrating to Thailand to become the nation's 'father of modern art', Feroci designed monuments for Italian dictator Benito Mussolini.

In recent years the 'Demo' has become a favourite spot for public demonstrations, most notably during the antimilitary, prodemocratic protests of 1992.

MONK'S BOWL VILLAGE Map pp254–5
บ้านบาตร
Soi Ban Baht, Th Borphat; air-con bus 508

This is the only remaining village of three established in Bangkok by Rama I for the purpose of handcrafting *bàat* (monk's bowls). The black *bàat*, used by Thai monks to receive almsfood from faithful Buddhists every morning, are still made here in the traditional manner. Due to the expense of purchasing a handmade bowl, the 'village' has been reduced to a single alley in a district known as Ban Baht (*bâan bàat* or Monk's Bowl Village). About half a dozen families still hammer the bowls together from eight separate pieces of steel said to represent Buddhism's Eightfold

Path. The joints are fused in a wood fire with bits of copper, and the bowl is polished and coated with several layers of black lacquer. A typical *bàat*-smith's output is one bowl per day.

To find the village, walk south on Th Boriphat, south of Th Bamrung Meuang, then turn left onto Soi Ban Baht. The artisans who fashion the bowls are not always at work, so it's largely a matter of luck whether or not you'll see them in action. At any of the houses that make them, you can purchase a fine-quality alms bowl for around 600B to 800B.

PHRA SUMEN FORT & SANTICHAIPRAKAN PARK Map pp254–5
ป้อมพระสุเมรุ
cnr Th Phra Sumen & Th Phra Athit; ⏰ 5am-10pm; ferry Tha Phra Athit, ordinary bus 30 & 53

Next to Mae Nam Chao Phraya in Banglamphu stands one of Bangkok's original 18th-century forts. Built in 1783 to defend against potential naval invasions, and named for the mythical Mt Sumeru (Meru) of Hindu-Buddhist cosmology, the octagonal, brick-and-stucco bunker was one of 14 city fortresses constructed alongside Khlong Rop Krung (now Khlong Banglamphu).

Alongside the fort, and fronting the river, are a small, grassy park and open-air Thai pavilion that make a good stop for river views, cool breezes or a picnic. Daily aerobics classes are held here in the evenings and attract as many spectators as participants. An intoxicating spirit of community haphazardly forms when the adept aerobics performers move in time with the thumping bass music, surrounded by an amused audience.

Phra Sumen Fort (p81)

A walkway zigzags along the river – and in some cases is suspended right over it – from the fort all the way to Saphan Phra Pin Klao. Follow this walk and along the way you can catch glimpses of old Ratanakosin-style buildings not visible from the street, such as those housing parts of the Buddhist Society of Thailand and the Food & Agriculture Organization. See p104 for details.

SAO CHING-CHA Map pp254–5
เสาชิงช้า
☎ 0 2281 2831; Th Botphram, btwn Th Tri Thong & Th Burapha; air-con bus 508

A spectacular Brahman festival in honour of the Hindu god Shiva used to take place at Sao Ching-Cha (Giant Swing) each year until it was stopped during the reign of Rama VII. Participants would swing in ever-heightening arcs in an effort to reach a bag of gold suspended from a 15m bamboo pole – many died trying. Sao Ching-Cha is two blocks south of the Democracy Monument. The framework of the giant swing still remains, and it's worth visiting to take a few pictures of this unusual site.

WAT BOWONNIWET Map pp254–5
วัดบวรนิเวศ
☎ 0 2281 2831; Th Phra Sumen; admission free; 8am-5pm; air-con bus 511, ordinary bus 53

Wat Bowonniwet (also spelled Wat Bovornives or shortened to Wat Bowon) is the national headquarters for the Thammayut monastic sect, the minority sect in Thai Buddhism. King Mongkut, founder of the Thammayuts, began a royal tradition by residing here as a monk – in fact he was the abbot of Wat Bowon for several years. King Bhumibol and Crown Prince Vajiralongkorn, as well as several other males in the royal family, have been temporarily ordained as monks here. The temple was founded in 1826, when it was known as Wat Mai.

Bangkok's second Buddhist university, Mahamakut University, is housed at Wat Bowon. Selected monks are sent from India, Nepal and Sri Lanka to study here.

Because of its royal status, visitors should be particularly careful to dress properly for admittance to this wát – no shorts or sleeveless clothing are allowed.

WAT INTHARAWIHAN Map pp254–5
วัดอินทรวิหาร
☎ 0 2281 1406; Th Wisut Kasat; admission by donation; 8am-5pm; ordinary bus 30, 53 & 49

Marked by its enormous, modern-style, 32m standing Buddha, Wat Intharawihan is at the northern edge of Banglamphu. It's worth seeing the hollow air-conditioned stupa with a lifelike image of the standing Buddha called Luang Phaw Toh.

WAT RATCHANATDA Map pp254–5
วัดราชนัดดา

☎ 0 2224 8807; Th Mahachai; admission free; ⏰ 8am–5pm; air-con bus 511 & 512, ordinary bus 39 & 44

Across Th Mahachai from Wat Saket, this temple dates from the mid-19th century, and was built under Rama III in honour of his granddaughter. Also spelled Wat Rajanadda, this wát was possibly influenced by Burmese models.

The wát has a well-known market selling Buddhist *phrá khrêuang* (amulets) in all sizes, shapes and styles. The amulets feature not only images of the Buddha, but also famous Thai monks and Indian deities. Full Buddha images are also for sale. This is an expensive place to purchase a charm, but a good place to look.

WAT SAKET & GOLDEN MOUNT

Map pp254–5

วัดสระเกศ

☎ 0 2223 4561; Th Worachak; admission to summit of Golden Mount 10B; ⏰ 8am–5pm; air-con bus 511 & 512, ordinary bus 39 & 44

Like all worthy summits, Golden Mount (Phu Khao Thong), which is visible from Th Ratchadamnoen Klang and situated on the western side of Wat Saket's grounds, plays a good game of optical illusion, appearing closer than it really is. Serpentine steps wind through an artificial hill shaded by gnarled trees, some of which are signed in English, and past small tombstones accompanied by photos of the deceased.

This artificial hill was created when a large *chedi* under construction by Rama III collapsed because the soft soil would not support it. The resulting mud-and-brick hill was left to sprout weeds until Rama IV built a small *chedi* on its crest. Rama V later added to the structure and housed a Buddha relic from India (given to him by the British government) in the *chedi*. The concrete walls were added during WWII to prevent the hill from eroding.

Frank Vincent, an American writer, describes his 1871 ascent in *The Land of the White Elephant*:

From the summit...may be obtained a fine view of the city of Bangkok and its surroundings; though this is hardly a correct statement, for you see very few of the dwelling-houses of the city; here and there a wat, the river with its shipping, the palace of the King, and a waving sea of cocoa-nut and betel-nut palms, is about all that distinctly appears. The general appearance of Bangkok is that of a large, primitive village, situated in and mostly concealed by a virgin forest of almost impenetrable density.

Every November there is a big festival in the grounds of Wat Saket, which includes an enchanting candle-lit procession up the Golden Mount.

Top Five for Children

- **Bangkok Doll Factory & Museum** (p90) This is a fairy-tale place for little girls (or boys) who love dolls.
- **Children's Discovery Museum** (p97) Learn how things work at this hands-on educational museum.
- **Dusit Zoo** (p85) Meet and greet zoo animals, picnic beside a lake or run around in a traffic-free zone.
- **Safari World** (p98) Go on safari in Thailand at this huge complex of African and Asian animals.
- **World Ice Skating** (p91) The best way to beat the heat is to go ice-skating.

WAT SUTHAT Map pp254–5

วัดสุทัศน์

☎ 0 2224 9845; Th Botphram; admission free; ⏰ 8.30am–5.30pm; air-con bus 508

Across from Sao Ching-Cha (p82), this temple boasts a *wíhǎan* with gilded bronze Buddha images (including Phra Si Sakayamuni, Thailand's largest surviving Sukhothai-period bronze) and colourful *Jataka* murals depicting scenes from the Buddha's life. One of the oldest Ratanakosin-era religious structures in Bangkok, the *wíhǎan* bears wooden doors carved by several artisans, including Rama II himself.

Wat Suthat maintains a special place in the national religion because of its association with Brahman priests, who perform important ceremonies such as the Royal Ploughing Ceremony in May (p11). These priests perform religious rites at two Hindu shrines near the wát – the Thewa Sathaan (Deva Shrine) across the street to the northwest and the smaller Saan Jao Phitsanu (Vishnu Shrine) located to the east. The former shrine contains images of Shiva and Ganesha while the latter is dedicated to Vishnu.

Wat Suthat holds the rank of Rachavoramahavihan, the highest royal temple grade. The ashes of Rama VIII (Ananda Mahidol, the current king's deceased older brother) are contained in the base of the main Buddha image in the *wíhǎan*.

THEWET & DUSIT

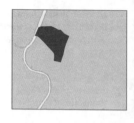

Shopping p146; Sleeping p168

Once a fruit orchard, Dusit was transformed into a mini European city by Rama V. Like London and Paris, Dusit is bisected by wide, deliberate avenues and lined with shady walkways. The effect is familiar and elegant but hollow. You can walk for blocks and blocks and not spot all the things that make Bangkok wonderful: street vendors, motorcycle taxis, random stores with blaring music. Somerset Maugham said it better in 1923 when driving through Dusit's main streets: 'They seem to await ceremonies and procession. They are like the deserted avenues in the park of a fallen monarch.'

Devotion to the venerated monarch is the primary purpose of an average Bangkokian's visit to Dusit. Many people come to make merit at the bronze statue of Rama V, which stands in military garb at the Royal Plaza, opposite Vimanmek Teak Mansion and Abhisek Dusit Throne Hall, from where the king once ruled the kingdom. Although originally intended as mere historical commemoration, the statue has quite literally become a religious shrine, where every Tuesday evening thousands of Bangkok residents come to offer candles, flowers (predominantly pink roses), incense and bottles of whisky. Even in the hot noon sun, an imported luxury car might park along the avenue to pray in front of the proud statue.

Rama V is also honoured with an annual festival acknowledging his accomplishments of modernising the country, abolishing slavery and maintaining the country's independence as other Southeast Asian countries were being colonised. During this festival huge numbers of visitors converge on the plaza, accompanied by cacophonous loudspeakers and attendant food vendors, momentarily breaking Dusit's aloofness with Bangkok's engaging chaos.

For a temporary visitor used to more subdued spaces, Dusit and its well-maintained green spaces will provide a necessary break from the coughing *túk-túk* and suffocating pavements.

The riverside section of the district is referred to as Thewet and shelters a quiet backpacker scene as well as a popular flower market. Although guesthouses claim almost an entire *soi*, the neighbourhood seems oblivious to the money-making opportunities that come from catering to foreigners. Instead vendors prefer to follow the traditional course of business with Thais, allowing the foreigners to adjust to local customs. Largely a residential neighbourhood, Thewet is packed at rush hour with uniform-clad residents climbing aboard rickety buses for a sweaty commute to the office districts of Silom or Th Sukhumvit. At rush hour, Th Samsen is a near continuous stream of rattletrap buses and screaming *túk-túk*.

Transport Thewet & Dusit

Bus Air-con 505, 506 & 510, ordinary 3, 16, 30, 32, 33, 53, 70 & 72
Ferry Tha Thewet

Orientation

Cradled between Th Samsen and the river, Thewet consists of a series of small *soi* and its name comes from the nearby temple, Wat Ratchathewet. Thewet's pavements are packed with vendors, making for an interesting stroll but an aggravating delay if you're in a rush.

Dusit begins east of Th Samsen and follows Th Phitsanulok and Th Si Ayuthaya to the district's most famous sites of Vimanmek Teak Mansion, Abhisek Dusit Throne Hall, Dusit Zoo and Wat Benchamabophit. Further east is the present monarch's residence of Chitralada Palace, which is not open to the public. Although the sites are clustered together on the map, the distances between them are long dull stretches that make walking seem like crossing a desert. Taxis and buses zoom down the main avenues at regular frequencies to speed you to your next destination.

Street stalls and food markets are most prolific near Thewet, but eating opportunities dry up quickly as you plunge into the hallowed promenades of Dusit. Be sure to be well watered and fed before embarking into Dusit on foot.

ABHISEK DUSIT THRONE HALL

Map pp250–1

พระที่นั่งอภิเศกดุสิต

☎ 0 2628 6300; Th U-Thong Nai; adult/child 100/75B, admission free with Wat Phra Kaew & Grand Palace ticket; ☽ 9.30am-3pm; air-con bus 503 & 510

Located in the Dusit palace grounds, this East-meets-West royal building is a classic example of Rama V taking much inspiration from his European tutors. Visions of Moorish palaces and Victorian mansions must have still been spinning around in his head when he commissioned the throne hall (completed in 1904), as it is a stunning, intricate building that, despite all its porticoes and other Western influences, has a distinctly Thai exterior. Built as the throne hall for the palace (they are separated by a canal), it opens onto a big stretch of lawn and flowerbeds, just like any important European building.

Inside, the heavy ornamentation of the white main room is quite extraordinary, especially if you've been visiting a lot of overwhelmingly gold temples or traditional wooden buildings. Look up to just below the ceiling to see the line of brightly coloured, stained-glass panels in Moorish patterns.

The hall displays regional handiwork crafted by members of the Promotion of Supplementary Occupations & Related Techniques (SUPPORT) charity foundation sponsored by Queen Sirikit. Among the exhibits are mát-mìi cotton and silk, málaeng tháp collages (made from metallic, multicoloured beetle wings), damascene and nielloware, and yaan lípao basketry.

Tickets also cover admission to the Vimanmek Teak Mansion (p86) and the Royal Elephant Museum (below).

CHURCH OF THE IMMACULATE CONCEPTION Map pp250–1

วัดบ้านญวน

Soi 11, Th Samsen; admission by donation; ☽ sunrise to sunset; ferry Tha Thewet, air-con bus 506, ordinary bus 53 & 30

South of Saphan Krungthon, this church was founded by the Portuguese and later taken over by Cambodians fleeing civil war. The present building is an 1837 reconstruction on the site of the original 1674 church. One of the original buildings survives and is now used as a museum housing holy relics.

DUSIT ZOO Map pp250–1

สวนสัตว์ดุสิต(เขาดิน)

☎ 0 2281 2000; Th Ratwithi; adult/child 30/5B; ☽ 8.30am-6pm; air-con bus 510, ordinary bus 18 & 28

The collection of animals at Bangkok's 19-hectare zoo comprises more than 300 mammals, 200 reptiles and 800 birds, including relatively rare indigenous species. Originally a private botanical garden for Rama V, Dusit Zoo (Suan Sat Dusit or khào din) was opened in 1938 and is now one of the premier zoological facilities in Southeast Asia. The shady grounds feature trees labelled in English, Thai and Latin, plus a lake in the centre with paddle boats for rent. There's also a small children's playground.

If nothing else, the zoo is a nice place to get away from the noise of the city and observe how the Thais amuse themselves – mainly by eating. A couple of lakeside restaurants serve good, inexpensive Thai food. Sunday can be a bit crowded – if you want the zoo mostly to yourself, go on a weekday.

NATIONAL LIBRARY Map pp250–1

หอสมุดแห่งชาติ

☎ 0 2281 5212; Th Samsen; admission free; ☽ 10am-3pm; ferry Tha Thewet, air-con bus 506, ordinary bus 53 & 30

Housed in a grand edifice, the National Library has a huge collection of Thai material dating back several centuries as well as smaller numbers of foreign-language books and magazines.

ROYAL ELEPHANT MUSEUM Map pp250–1

พิพิธภัณฑ์ช้างต้น

☎ 0 2628 6300; Th U-Thong Nai; adult/child 100/75B, admission free with Wat Phra Kaew & Grand Palace ticket; ☽ 9.30am-3pm; air-con bus 503 & 510

On the same grounds as the Vimanmek Teak Mansion and Abhisek Dusit Throne Hall, two large stables that once housed three 'white' elephants – animals whose auspicious albinism automatically made them crown property – are now a museum. One of the structures contains photos and artefacts outlining the importance of elephants in Thai history, and explains their various rankings according to physical characteristics. The second stable holds a sculptural representation of a living royal white elephant kept at Chitralada Palace, home to the current Thai king. Draped in royal vestments, the statue is more or less treated as a shrine by the visiting Thai public.

Tickets also cover admission to the Abhisek Dusit Throne Hall (p85) and the Vimanmek Teak Mansion (below).

VIMANMEK TEAK MANSION Map pp250–1
พระที่นั่งวิมานเมฆ

☎ 0 2628 6300; Th U-Thong Nai; adult/child 100/75B, admission free with Wat Phra Kaew & Grand Palace ticket; ☼ 9.30am-3pm, tours every half-hour; air-con bus 503 & 510

Said to be the world's largest golden teak building, this beautiful three-storey mansion has huge staircases, octagonal rooms and lattice walls that are nothing short of magnificent, but surprisingly serene and intimate.

Originally constructed on Ko Si Chang in 1868 and moved to the present site in 1910, Vimanmek was the first permanent building on the Dusit palace grounds. It served as Rama V's residence in the early 1900s. The interior of the mansion contains various personal effects of the king, and a treasure-trove of early Ratanakosin art objects and antiques. Smaller adjacent buildings display historic photography documenting the Chakri dynasty.

Traditional Thai classical and folk dances are performed at 10.30am and 2pm in a pavilion on the canal side of the mansion.

As this is royal property, visitors wearing shorts or sleeveless shirts will be refused entry. Tickets also cover admission to the Abhisek Dusit Throne Hall (p85) and the Royal Elephant Museum (p85).

WAT BENCHAMABOPHIT Map pp250–1
วัดเบญจมบพิตร (วัดเบญฯ)

☎ 0 2282 7413; cnr Th Si Ayuthaya & Th Phra Ram V; admission 20B; ☼ 8am-5.30pm; air-con bus 503, ordinary bus 72

The closest Thailand will come to an ice palace, this temple of white Carrara marble (hence its alternate name, 'Marble Temple') was built at the turn of the century under Rama V. The large cruciform *bòt* is a prime example of modern Thai *wát* architecture. The base of the central Buddha image, a copy of Phra Phuttha Chinnarat in Phitsanulok, holds the ashes of Rama V. The courtyard behind the *bòt* has 53 Buddha images (33 originals and 20 copies) representing famous figures and styles from across Thailand and other Buddhist countries – it's a great way to compare Buddhist iconography. If religious details aren't for you, this temple offers a pleasant stroll beside landscaped *khlong* filled with blooming lotus and Chinese-style footbridges.

The majestic Vimanmek Teak Mansion located in Dusit Gardens (above)

CHINATOWN

Eating p111; Shopping p147; Sleeping p169

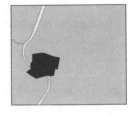

Bangkok's oldest residential and business district was originally inhabited by Chinese residents who were moved out of Ko Ratanakosin to make way for royal temples and palaces in the late 18th century. Today the umbilical cord to the cultural motherland is so strong that Chinese is the district's primary language, sometimes mixed with Thai to form a motley language-soup spoken in the depths of the winding neighbourhood *soi*. Not learning Thai as an infant adds a distinct accent to Chinatown-born Bangkokians, who are not considered wholly Thai by their non-Chinese compatriots.

Despite the cultural divide, the commercial success of this district, from the major power players to the solo import-exporters, helps fuel the country's overall economy. Observable at street level are middle-class enterprises such as the family-owned jewellery shops along Th Yaowarat and Th Charoen Krung, painted blood red and with neatly polished display cases selling yellow gold. Occupying the empty corners of the pavements are the do-it-yourself vendors selling red-and-gold talismans and accoutrements for Chinese festivals. The neighbourhood is self-segregated by profession with whole streets or blocks dedicated to sign-making, gold and jewellery stores, and machine and tyre shops.

During the Chinese New Year the neighbourhood swings into a joyous mood, with an increased presence of vendors and shoppers haggling over auspicious gifts and tokens. Chinese calligraphers also join the pavement commerce.

In the crowded alleys between these main roads, particularly along Sampeng Lane, the daily business revolves around wholesale food, plastic toys, stuffed animals, pens and pencils – the variety is astounding. And the routine of stocking these cramped stores is an even bigger accomplishment: scrappy delivery kids wheel overloaded carts through throngs of people with surgical precision.

At the western edge of Chinatown, around the intersection of Th Phahurat and Th Chakraphet, is a small but thriving Indian district, generally called Phahurat or Little India.

Orientation

Chinatown fans out along Mae Nam Chao Phraya between Saphan Buddha Yotha to the west and Hualamphong Railway Station to the east. Th Yaowarat and Th Charoen Krung are Chinatown's main arteries and provide the greatest diversity of services, from shopping to eating to promenading in the styles popular on the Chinese mainland, such as oversized designer sunglasses and chest-high pants. At night the district feels like a carnival, with the merriment of banquet dining and the dazzling spectacle of neon lights.

Getting into and out of the area by bus or cab is nearly impossible due to an impenetrable stream of traffic. The best transport is the river ferry, which will deliver you within a short walk of the heart of Chinatown. Walking is the most efficient and entertaining way to get around the neighbourhood. Follow the little *soi* into the claustrophobic pathways past warehouses and trinket shops, or walk west to see the subtle transition from Chinatown to Phahurat. The dim alleys and affinity for commerce tie these two heritages together, although the particular expressions provide a fascinating diversity.

Until the subway is fully operational, Hualamphong Railway Station will remain inconveniently consumed by Chinatown's signature traffic. Many layover hotels stand sentry around the train station as an alternative to making a cross-town approach.

Chinatown Top Five

- **Holy Rosary Church** (p88) A good excuse to wander the neighbourhood of cramped lanes and machine shops.
- **Phahurat** (p88) Bollywood-style markets of flashy colours and sequins galore.
- **Sampeng Lane** (p147) Regimented chaos and commerce staged deep in the bowels of an exotic other-world.
- **Walking Tour** (p102) Dive into the sights and smells of real live commerce.
- **Wat Traimit** (p88) Meet the handsome golden Buddha.

Transport Chinatown

Bus Air-con 507, ordinary 53
Ferry Tha Ratchawong

HOLY ROSARY CHURCH Map pp252–3
โบสถ์กาลาหว่าน

☎ 0 2266 4849; admission by donation; cnr Th Yotha & Th Charoen Phanit; ☺ 9am-5pm; ferry Tha River City

Near the River City Complex, this Catholic church (also called Wat Kalawan, from the Portuguese 'Calvario') was originally built in 1787 by the Portuguese. It was later rebuilt by Vietnamese and Cambodian Catholics around the turn of the 20th century, hence the French inscriptions beneath the stations of the cross. This old church has a splendid set of Romanesque stained-glass windows, gilded ceilings and a very old statue of Christ that is carried through the streets during Easter celebrations. The alley leading to the church is lined with Ratanakosin shophouse architecture.

HUALAMPHONG RAILWAY STATION
Map pp252–3
พิพิธภัณฑ์รถไฟ

Th Phra Ram IV; air-con bus 501 & 507, ordinary bus 25, 40 & 109

At the southeastern edge of Chinatown, Bangkok's main train station was built by Dutch architects and engineers just before WWI. One of the city's earliest and most outstanding examples of the movement towards Thai Art Deco, the vaulted iron roof and neoclassical portico demonstrate an engineering feat that was state-of-the-art in its time, while the patterned, two-toned skylights exemplify pure de Stijl Dutch modernism.

Beneath the Surface

Deep inside the maze of Chinatown, a secretive world of action-movie fodder still conducts its ancient rituals. An 1880 census found 245 opium dens, 154 pawnshops, 69 gambling establishments and 26 brothels. Pawnshops, along with myriad gold shops, remain a popular Chinatown business, while the other three vices have gone underground: brothels continue to exist under the guise of rohng chaa (tea halls), back-street heroin vendors have replaced the opium dens, and illicit card games convene in the private upstairs rooms of certain restaurants.

PHAHURAT Map pp252–3
พาหุรัด

West of Th Chakraphet; ferry Tha Saphan Phut, ordinary bus 40 & 53

Dozens of Indian-owned shops sell all kinds of fabric and clothes here. Behind the more obvious storefronts along these streets, in the 'bowels' of the blocks, is a seemingly endless Indian bazaar.

Just off Th Chakraphet is a **Sikh temple** (Sri Gurusingh Sabha) where visitors are welcome. Basically it's a large hall, somewhat reminiscent of a mosque interior, devoted to the worship of the *Guru Granth Sahib*, the 16th-century Sikh holy book which is itself considered the last of the religion's 10 great gurus or teachers. *Prasada* (literally 'blessed food offered to Hindu or Sikh temple attendees') is distributed among devotees every morning around 9am, and if you arrive on a Sikh festival day you can partake in the langar (communal Sikh meal) served in the temple.

TALAAT NOI
ตลาดน้อย

Bounded by the river, Th Songwat, Th Charoen Krung and Th Yotha

This microcosm of *soi* life is named after a little market between Soi 22 and Soi 20, off Th Charoen Krung. The lanes weave through people's living rooms, noodle shops and junk collections. Opposite the Riverview Guesthouse, **San Jao Sien Khong** (unnamed *soi*; admission by donation; ☺ 6am-6pm) is one of the city's oldest Chinese shrines.

WAT TRAIMIT Map pp252–3
วัดไตรมิตร

☎ 0 2623 1226; cnr Th Yaowarat & Th Charoen Krung; admission 20B; ☺ 9am-5pm; ferry Tha Ratchawong, ordinary bus 25, 40 & 53

The attraction at Wat Traimit (Temple of the Golden Buddha) is the gleaming, 3m-tall, 5.5-tonne, solid-gold Buddha image. Sculpted in the graceful Sukhothai style (notice the hair curls and elongated earlobes), the image was 'rediscovered' some 40 years ago beneath a plaster exterior when it fell from a crane while being moved to a new building within the temple compound. It has been theorised that the covering was added to protect it from marauding hordes, either during the late Sukhothai period or later in the Ayuthaya period when the city was under siege by the Burmese. The temple itself is said to date from the early 13th century.

SIAM SQUARE & PRATUNAM

Eating p113; Shopping p147; Sleeping p170

The centre of teenage culture, Siam Square seems centuries removed from the older sections of town. Boxy shopping centres – such as MBK, Siam Discovery Center and Central World Plaza – dominate the landscape, bisected by elevated footpaths to deliver Skytrain riders immediately into air-conditioned comfort. Fashionable youngsters float effortlessly across the concrete pathways, breaking every social more their ancestors ever created. Female students wear barely-there miniskirts and strappy heels, cutesy couples stroll hand-in-hand, quiet arty types assume gangsta styles from ghettos they've only read about. The pop tunes of Japan and the West serve as their urban soundtracks.

Behind the modern façade is a simple village of modest means centred on one of Bangkok's most famous canals, the soot-coloured Khlong Saen Saeb. Lined with rickety wooden shacks, drying laundry and the exposed interior of daily life, the *khlong* is the primary plumbing for many of its residents. Kids bathe in the water as morning commuter boats buzz by, housewives rinse out the family's dishes, and unwanted items are discarded into the murky depths. Baan Krua, originally founded by immigrants from Cambodia and one of the city's most famous slums, has successfully fought off highway-construction plans to remain an intact village. The silk-weaving skills of early occupants caught the attention of Jim Thompson, a long-time Bangkok resident who developed the village's woven work into an international commodity.

Orientation

Siam Square radiates out from the intersection of multilane Th Phayathai and Th Phra Ram I. The area derives its name from the low-slung shopping arcade wedged between MBK shopping centre and Chulalongkorn University. Across busy Th Phra Ram I are the Siam Center and Siam Discovery Center. Elevated footpaths cross the district's busy roads and provide great photo opportunities of an almost unending line of idling cars.

Transport Siam Square & Pratunam

Bus Air-con 508, 515 & 529, ordinary 15, 16, 25 & 40
Skytrain Siam, National Stadium, Chitlom & Ploenchit stations
Khlong taxi Tha Ratchathewi

Also included in this section is the area extending east along Th Phloenchit and Th Withayu (Wireless Rd), where many embassies and expatriates reside. Nearby is the upscale dining zone of Soi Lang Suan. North of Khlong Saen Saeb, the area known as Pratunam begins and crawls northwards. Pratunam is home to many high-rise hotels, including Thailand's tallest skyscraper, the Baiyoke Tower. The huge shopping centres dissipate here into smaller markets and cottage industries, and wandering the *soi* offers an exploration of a human-sized environment.

The Skytrain is the best transport through Siam Square and Pratunam, with stations conveniently located near major shopping centres. Although the area is well served by buses, it is easy to ignore this outmoded method because of the ease of the Skytrain.

Shopping is the main draw here, with multistorey centres specialising in designer imports, all-purpose items and youth fashion. Every shopping centre has an interior food court that replicates the Thai tradition of a market without the drawbacks of noise, heat and pollution.

The ever-present noise and suffocating exhaust fumes that clog this district fuel Bangkok's image as a third-world cesspool. To spare their tender lungs, many residents wear surgical-style face masks with as much ease as Easter bonnets. Oblivious to the pollution, pavement food vendors and shoe repairers return to their open-air shops every day, taking little or no health precautions.

Siam Square & Pratunam Top Five

- **Bangkok Doll Factory & Museum** (below) This museum of Thai and foreign dolls is a real treasure.
- **Erawan Shrine** (p91) A modern expression of religion in the landscape.
- **Jim Thompson's House** (below) Teak mansion with a junglelike garden and informative tours.
- **Khlong Saen Saeb Canal Taxi** (p89) Cigarette-thin boats ply the polluted waters of this ageing canal, past humble yet proud homesteads.
- **MBK & Siam Discovery Center** (p148) Everything gross and seductive about the modern world, from plastic junk to junk food.

BANGKOK DOLL FACTORY & MUSEUM Map pp248–9

พิพิธภัณฑ์ตุ๊กตาบางกอกดอล

☎ 0 2245 3008; 85 Soi Ratchataphan (Soi Mo Leng), Th Ratchaprarop; admission free; 🕒 8am-5pm Mon-Sat; ordinary bus 63

Khungying Tongkorn Chandevimol became interested in dolls while living in Japan. Upon her return to Thailand, she began researching and making dolls, drawing from Thai mythology and historical periods. Today her personal collection of dolls from all over the world and important dolls from her own workshop are on display. You can also view the small factory where 20 family members continue to craft the figures that are now replicated and sold throughout Thailand's tourist markets. A large selection of her dolls are also for sale.

It is almost impossible to locate this well-hidden spot, but perseverance will reward any doll lover, especially the pint-sized connoisseurs. The museum is in Pratunam and is best approached via Th Si Ayuthaya heading east. Cross under the expressway past the intersection with Th Ratchaparrop and take the *soi* to the right of the post office. Follow this windy street until you start seeing signs.

JIM THOMPSON'S HOUSE Map pp262–3

บ้านจิมทอมป์สัน

☎ 0 2216 7368, 0 2215 0122; www.jimthompsonhouse.org; 6 Soi Kasem San 2, Th Phra Ram I; adult/child 100/50B; 🕒 9am-5pm; khlong taxi Tha Ratchathewi, Skytrain National Stadium

Though it may sound corny when described, this is a great spot to visit for authentic Thai residential architecture and Southeast Asian art. Located at the end of an undistinguished *soi* next to Khlong Saen Saeb, the premises once belonged to the American silk entrepreneur Jim Thompson, who deserves most of the credit for the worldwide popularity of Thai silk.

Born in Delaware in 1906, Thompson was a New York architect who briefly served in the Office of Strategic Services (forerunner of the CIA) in Thailand during WWII. After the war he found New York too tame and moved to Bangkok. Thai silk caught his eye and he sent samples to fashion houses in Milan, London and Paris, gradually building a worldwide clientele for a craft that had been in danger of dying out.

A tireless promoter of traditional Thai arts and culture, Thompson collected parts of various derelict Thai homes in central Thailand and had them reassembled in the current location in 1959. Although for the most part they're assembled in typical Thai style, one striking departure from tradition is the way each wall has its exterior side facing the house's interior, thus exposing the wall's bracing system.

On display in the main house are Thompson's small but splendid Asian art collection and his personal belongings. The Jim Thompson Foundation has a table at the front where you can buy prints of old Siam maps and Siamese horoscopes in postcard and poster form, and you can shop for silks at an adjacent outlet of Jim Thompson Silk Co. A plush bar overlooking the canal offers cold drinks and occasional live jazz.

While out for an afternoon walk in the Cameron Highlands of western Malaysia in 1967, Thompson disappeared under mysterious circumstances and has never been heard from since. That same year his sister was murdered in the USA, fuelling various conspiracy theories to explain the disappearance. Was it communist spies? Business rivals? A man-eating tiger? The most recent theory (for which there is apparently some hard evidence) is that the silk magnate was accidentally run over by a Malaysian truck driver who hid his remains.

The Legendary American: The Remarkable Career & Strange Disappearance of Jim Thompson, by William Warren, is an excellent book on Thomspon, career, house and intriguing disappearance. In Thailand it has been republished as *Jim Thompson: The Legendary American of Thailand* (Jim Thompson Thai Silk Co, Bangkok).

The *khlong* at the end of the *soi* is one of Bangkok's liveliest. Beware of well-dressed touts in the *soi* who will tell you Thompson's house is closed – it's just a ruse to take you on a buying spree. Admission proceeds go to Bangkok's School for the Blind.

Hotel & Shopping Centre Shrines

Seamlessly weaving traditional beliefs into a modern landscape, Bangkok's hotels and shopping centres devoted space to religious shrines to mediate mishaps during construction and ensure the projects' success. These shrines were often adopted by the local residents as focal points for religious devotion.

One of the most famous shrines, **Erawan Shrine** (Saan Phra Phrom; Map pp262–3; cnr Th Ratchadamri & Th Ploenchit; Skytrain Chitlom), next to the Grand Hyatt Erawan, was originally built to ward off bad luck during the construction of the first Erawan Hotel (torn down to make way for the Grand Hyatt Erawan some years ago). The four-headed deity at the centre of the shrine is Brahma (Phra Phrom), the Hindu god of creation. Apparently the developers of the original Erawan (named after Indra's three-headed elephant mount) first erected a typical Thai spirit house but decided to replace it with the impressive Brahman shrine after several serious mishaps delayed the hotel's construction. The construction workers and contractors who first erected the shrine are long gone, and it's now the supplicating spot for ordinary Bangkokians, who make a human traffic jam circling the shrine and laying down marigold garlands or raising a cluster of joss sticks to their foreheads in prayer. They come to ask for good luck, health, wealth and love. When wishes are granted, the worshippers show their gratitude by commissioning shrine musicians and dancers for an impromptu performance. The tinkling tempo, throaty bass and colourful dancers elevate the crowd beyond the ordinary street corner surrounded by idling cars and self-absorbed shoppers.

The **Lingam Shrine** (Saan Jao Mae Thap Thim; Map pp262-3; Nai Lert Park Hotel, Th Withayu; Skytrain Ploenchit) is another hotel shrine worth seeing. Clusters of carved stone and wooden phalluses surround a spirit house and shrine built by millionaire businessman Nai Loet to honour Jao Mae Thap Thim, a female deity thought to reside in the old banyan tree on the site. Someone who made an offering shortly after the shrine was built had a baby, and the shrine has received a steady stream of worshippers – mostly young women seeking fertility – ever since. Facing the entrance of the hotel, follow the small concrete pathway to the right, which winds down into the guts of the building beside the car park. The shrine is at the end of the building next to the *khlong*.

WANG SUAN PHAKKAT Map pp248–9
วังสวนผักกาด

☎ 0 2245 4934; Th Si Ayuthaya, btwn Th Phayathai & Th Ratchaprarop; admission 100B; 🕙 9am-4pm; Skytrain Phayathai

The Lettuce Farm Palace, at one time the residence of Princess Chumbon of Nakhon Sawan, is a collection of five traditional wooden Thai houses containing varied displays of art, antiques and furnishings. The landscaped grounds are a peaceful oasis complete with ducks, swans and a semienclosed, Japanese-style garden.

The diminutive **Lacquer Pavilion** at the back of the complex dates from the Ayuthaya period (the building originally sat in a monastery compound on the banks of Mae Nam Chao Phraya, just south of Ayuthaya) and features gold-leaf *Jataka* and *Ramayana* murals as well as scenes from daily Ayuthaya life. Larger residential structures at the front of the complex contain displays of Khmer Hindu and Buddhist art, Ban Chiang ceramics and a decent collection of historic Buddhas, including a beautiful late–U Thong–style image. In the noise and confusion of Bangkok, the gardens offer a tranquil retreat.

Gong at Lettuce Farm Palace (above)

WORLD ICE SKATING Map pp262–3
เซ็นทรัลเวิลด์ไอซสเก็ตติ้ง

☎ 0 2255 9500; 7th fl, Central World Plaza; Th Phra Ram 1; rental 150B; 🕙 10am-9pm Mon-Fri; Skytrain Chitlom

To spit in the face of humidity, come to this public ice-skating rink on top of the Central World Plaza shopping centre. You'll be surprised how adept on the ice these unwintered Thais can be.

SILOM & SURAWONG

Eating p115; Shopping p151; Sleeping p173

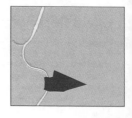

Often referred to as Bang Rak (Village of Love), the area running along the river was the European merchant quarter and, in 1861, the site of Bangkok's first road (Th Charoen Krung). Today the Oriental Hotel, French Embassy and Catholic churches are the surviving remnants of the city's early relationship with the West. An Indian and Muslim community now claims the storefronts along Th Charoen Krung, selling silks and jewellery to wealthy tourists staying at the riverside luxury hotels. Surrounding the commerce of Th Charoen Krung is the residential section of the Muslim community, where curry shops are more likely to serve roti than rice and culturally mandated silken headdresses frame the Muslim women's angelic faces.

Reflecting the shift away from shipping, the business district has moved inland along the thoroughfare of Th Silom. During the day, foreigners sweat in their imported cotton suits, maintaining the corporate appearance of New York and London in styles that are ill-suited for the tropics. Thai workers prefer polyester suits that are sold off the rack at small markets, alongside bulk toiletries and thick-heeled sandals. Workers returning to the office after lunch are usually loaded down with plastic bags of food for mid-afternoon snacks: in Thailand the snack table is the equivalent of the Western water cooler.

In the heart of the business zone is Bangkok's most infamous attraction, the strip clubs of Patpong. Mainly the stuff of pulp fiction, Patpong donates loads of war stories to the foreigners who partake in its naughty nightlife. It is no accident that this skin party occurs so close to the buttoned-down world of international business. Accommodating Bangkok knows what displaced foreigners will desire for after-work entertainment.

More family-friendly outings include the Patpong Night Market (p151), which sets up in the neighbouring *soi*, and the new government venture of Suan Lum Night Bazaar (p152), which is slowly gaining a following despite Bangkok's resistance to regimented activities.

Orientation

The main roads of this district are the namesake Th Silom and Th Surawong, which form right angles with Th Charoen Krung. These parallel streets connect the river to a congested business district terminating at Th Phra Ram IV.

Th Silom is hopelessly backed up with traffic and is best avoided at almost every hour but daybreak. The Skytrain is a better alternative for reaching destinations on this street. Traffic moves more regularly on Th Sathon, which runs parallel to Th Silom, if you need to take a cab in or out of the area quickly. Th Sathon is a divided road with traffic segregated into northbound (Th Sathon Neua) and southbound (Th Sathon Tai) lanes. On a small street off Th Sathon is the Immigration Office, a frequent pilgrimage site for every foreigner living in Bangkok. Other embassies fan out along Th Sathon and into the area known as Soi Ngam Duphli, the backpacker predecessor of Th Khao San's guesthouse scene.

The area between Th Convent and Th Sala Daeng, off Th Silom, has become a culinary alley with creative fusion and royal Thai restaurants dolled up in stylish décor. During the lunch-time crush whole alleys become makeshift canteens for small armies of office workers. On the other side of Th Silom, Patpong and Silom Soi 4 form the nightlife nexus of the district. Shopping is prolific in this neighbourhood, from the Patpong Night Market to Soi Lalai Sap (p152).

On the eastern side of the district is the city's prettiest green space, Lumphini Park, bounded by Th Sarasin, Th Phra Ram IV, Th Withayu and Th Ratchadamri. East of the park is the new night bazaar and the boxing stadium.

> ### Transport Silom & Surawong
>
> **Bus** Air-con 502, 504 & 505, ordinary 15
> **Skytrain** Sala Daeng, Chong Nonsi & Surasak stations

Silom & Surawong Top Five

- **H Gallery** (p94) Emerging Thai artists receive the attention of an international art dealer in a charming restored teak house.
- **Lumphini Park** (below) A peaceful park for exercisers and exercise-observers.
- **Patpong** (p92) Take in one of Bangkok's legendary sex shows.
- **Queen Saovabha Memorial Institute** (Snake Farm; below) Confront your fear of these legless creatures at this humanitarian facility.
- **Sri Mariamman Temple** (p95) Thai temples will look subdued after you've visited this riotously coloured Hindu temple.

BANK OF ASIA Map pp257–9
ธนาคารเอเชีย

cnr Th Sathon Tai & Soi Pikun; air-con bus 15 & 67, Skytrain Chong Nonsi

During the crazy 1980s, when no building project was too outlandish or expensive, architect Sumet Jumsai created his now-famous 'Robot Building' for the Bank of Asia. Few were keen on it at the time, but now it seems quaint and retro. The building's whimsical façade is best viewed on the Skytrain between Surasak and Chong Nonsi stations.

CHRIST CHURCH Map pp260–1
ไครส์ตเชิช

☎ 0 2234 3634; 11 Th Convent, cnr Th Sathon Neua; admission by donation; ⏱ 9am-6pm; Skytrain Sala Daeng

Next to the Bangkok Nursing Home, Christ Church was established as English Chapel in 1864. The current Gothic-style structure, opened in 1904, features thick walls and a tiled roof braced with teak beams. The carved teak ceiling fans date to 1919.

LUMPHINI PARK Map pp260–1
สวนลุมพินี

Skytrain Sala Daeng & Ratchadamri

Named after Buddha's birthplace in Nepal, this is Bangkok's largest and most popular park. A big artificial lake in the centre is surrounded by broad, well-tended lawns, wooded areas and walking paths – it's the best outdoor escape from Bangkok without leaving town.

One of the best times to visit the park is in the early morning before 7am, when the air is fresh (well, relatively so for Bangkok)

and legions of Chinese are practising t'ai chi. Meanwhile, vendors set up tables to dispense fresh snake's blood and bile, considered health tonics by many Thais and Chinese. A weight-lifting area in one section becomes a miniature 'muscle beach' on weekends. Facilities include a snack bar, an asphalt jogging track, a picnic area, restrooms and a couple of tables where women serve Chinese tea.

During the kite-flying season (mid-February to April), Lumphini becomes a favoured flight zone, with kites (*wâo*) for sale in the park.

M R KUKRIT PRAMOJ HOUSE
Map pp257–9

บ้านหม่อมราชวงศ์คึกฤทธิ์ปราโมช

☎ 0 2286 8185; Soi 7 (Phra Phinij), Th Narathiwat Ratchanakhon; admission 50B; ⏱ 10am-5pm Sat & Sun; Skytrain Chong Nonsi

Author and statesman Mom Ratchawong Kukrit Pramoj once resided in this charming complex now open to the public for tours. Surrounded by a manicured garden, five teak buildings introduce visitors to traditional Thai architecture and to the former resident, who authored more than 150 books (including *Four Reigns*) and served as prime minister of Thailand.

QUEEN SAOVABHA MEMORIAL INSTITUTE (SNAKE FARM) Map pp257–9
สถานเสาวภา

☎ 0 2252 0161; 1871 Th Phra Ram IV; admission 70B; ⏱ 8.30am-4.30pm Mon-Fri, 8.30am-noon Sat & Sun; air-con bus 507, ordinary bus 50, Skytrain Sala Daeng

Venomous snakes – such as the formidable cobra and pit viper – live a peaceful and altruistic existence at this farm affiliated with the Thai Red Cross. The snakes are milked daily to make snake-bite antivenins, which are distributed throughout the country. When the institute was founded in 1923, it was only the second of its kind in the world (the first was in Brazil).

Tourists are welcome to view the milkings (11am and 2.30pm Monday to Friday, 11am Saturday and Sunday) and feedings (2.30pm Monday to Friday) or to stroll the small garden complex where the snakes are kept in escape-proof cages. The snakes tend to be camera-shy during nonperformance times, although it is exhilarating to spot a camouflaged king cobra poised to strike.

The booklet titled *Guide to Healthy Living in Thailand*, published by the Thai Red Cross in conjunction with the US embassy, is available here for 450B. At the neighbouring clinic, you can get common vaccinations against cholera, typhoid, rabies, tetanus, polio, encephalitis, meningitis, smallpox, and hepatitis A and B.

This institution received its historical name in honour of Queen Saovabha, wife of Rama V, who championed a wide variety of medical causes and education, including a school for midwives and other modern birthing practices.

Art Appreciation

For a new arrival, Bangkok's modern-art scene offers more than pretty pictures. In the exhibition spaces, art restaurants or commercial galleries throughout the city, artists use a variety of media to debate a quickly morphing Thailand. Emerging Thai artists, drawing from a repository of religious art, have turned to modern symbols to express the psychological and spiritual effects of rapid industrialisation and globalisation. Like the Romantics of the Western Industrial Revolution, many modern Thai artists are drawn to the mythic ideals of village life: an interconnected devotion to the land, ancient customs and religious spirituality. Gumsak Atipiboonson, for example, uses colourful geometric shapes to juxtapose the urban and rural landscapes, making the viewer ache for the innocent green of the rice field. Other artists, such as Thaweesak Srithongdee, use pop sensibilities to mock and embrace modernity. Thaweesak's human forms morph into surreal superheroes posing in front of floral patterns borrowed from market sarongs.

In typical Bangkok fashion, the art scene lacks a centre, with artists and galleries peppered throughout the city. Socially, many artists and their work gather at the cafés along Th Phra Athit, while the galleries prefer the business districts of Silom and Th Sukhumvit. **Eat Me Restaurant** (p117) extends dinner invitations to rotating exhibits organised by H Gallery, and photography gets its just desserts at **Gallery F-Stop**, which shares space with **Tamarind Café** (p125). Pick up a copy of the free *Art Connection* brochure for a map and listings of exhibits.

While most venues keep standard business hours for viewing, an exhibit's opening provides the added dimension of mingling with bohemian artists, well-scrubbed cosmopolitans and free-booze moochers. Despite the air of sophistication, openings pour liberal doses of Thailand's famed hospitality. Refer to Bangkok's *Metro* magazine for a calendar of exhibition openings.

The following is a list of noteworthy galleries:

About Studio/About Café (Map pp252–3; ☎ 0 2623 3927; 418 Th Maitrichit; ☾ hours vary) Cutting-edge Thai artists, working in alternative and experimental media.

Alliance Française Bangkok (Map pp260–1; ☎ 0 2670 4200; www.alliance-francaise.or.th; 29 Th Sathon Tai; ☾ 8am-6.30pm Mon-Fri, 8.30am-5pm Sat, 8.30am-noon Sun) Artists-in-residence programmes, and Thai and French film retrospectives.

Chulalongkorn Art Centre (Map pp262–3; ☎ 0 2218 2964; 7th flr, Library Building, Chulalongkorn University, Th Phayathai; ☾ 8am-7pm Mon-Fri, 8am-4pm Sat) Major names in the modern art scene, as well as international artists.

Goethe Institut (Map pp260–1; ☎ 0 2287 0942; 18/1 Soi Goethe, off Soi 1/Atthakarn Prasit, Th Sathon Tai; ☾ 8am-4.30pm Mon-Fri) Thai art gallery; patron and organiser of December Art & Fun Fair.

H Gallery (Map pp257–9; ☎ 0 1310 4428; 201 Soi 12, Th Sathon; ☾ noon-6pm Wed-Sat) Leading commercial gallery for emerging Thai abstract painters.

Japan Foundation (Map pp264–5; ☎ 0 2260 8560; Soi 21, Th Sukhumvit; ☾ 9am-7pm Mon-Fri, 9am-5pm Sat) Japanese artists, film festivals and an annual comic-book show.

Neilson Hays Library Rotunda Gallery (Map pp257–9; ☎ 0 2233 1731; 195 Th Surawong; ☾ hours vary) Handicrafts, Thai antiques and works by British artists.

Silpakorn University (Map p256; ☎ 0 2225 4350; Silpakorn Th Na Phra Lan; ☾ 8am-7pm Mon-Fri, 8am-4pm Sat & Sun) Bangkok's premier fine-arts university and gallery of student works.

Tadu Contemporary Art (Map pp246–7; ☎ 0 2203 0927; Pavilion Y, Royal City Ave; ☾ 10am-7pm Tue-Sat) Artists from Southeast and South Asia.

Tang Gallery (Map pp257–9; ☎ 0 2630 1114; basement, Silom Galleria, 91 9/1 Th Silom; ☾ 11am-7pm Tue-Sat, noon-6pm Sun) Chinese modern artists.

Thavibu Gallery (Map pp257–9; ☎ 0 2266 5454; 3rd fl, Silom Galleria, 91 9/1 Th Silom; ☾ 11am-7pm Tue-Sat, noon-6pm Sun) Artists from Cambodia, Thailand and Myanmar.

SRI MARIAMMAN TEMPLE Map pp257–9

วัดพระศรีมหาอุมาเทวี(วัดแขก)

☎ 0 2238 4007; cnr Th Silom & Th Pan; ⏱ 6am-8pm;
ferry Tha Oriental, Skytrain Chong Nonsi

Called Wat Phra Si Maha Umathewi in Thai, this small Hindu temple anchors the surrounding Indian neighbourhood. The principal temple structure, built in the 1860s by Tamil immigrants, features a 6m façade of intertwined, full-colour Hindu deities, topped by a gold-plated copper dome. The temple's main shrine contains three main deities: Jao Mae Maha Umathewi (Uma Devi; also known as Shakti, Shiva's consort) at the centre; her son Phra Khanthakuman (Khanthakumara or Subramaniam) on the right; and her elephant-headed son Phra Phikkhanesawora (Ganesha) on the left. Along the left interior wall sit rows of Shivas, Vishnus and other Hindu deities, as well as a few Buddhas, so that just about any non-Muslim, non-Judaeo-Christian Asian can worship here – Thai and Chinese devotees come to pray along with Indians. Bright-yellow marigold garlands are sold at the entrance for use as offerings to the deity images inside.

Thais also call this temple by its colloquial name Wat Khaek– khàek is a colloquial expression for people of Indian descent. The literal translation is 'guest', an obvious euphemism for a group of people you don't particularly want as permanent residents; hence most Indian Thais don't appreciate the term.

TH SUKHUMVIT

Eating p121; Shopping p153; Sleeping p177

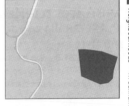

One of the first suburbs for Bangkok's emerging car culture in the mid-20th century, Th Sukhumvit is the primary address for the city's most recent expatriates, from Japanese engineers to Lebanese importers. Whole neighbourhoods are populated by company families temporarily transplanted to the tropics. Homesickness is a tangible sentiment in the grocery-store aisles filled with American breakfast cereal and English marmalade. Middle-class lives in the West are transformed into upper-class status in Thailand, and foreign families are expected to contribute to the local economy by hiring maids, gardeners and other household staff. These new-found privileges and cultural demands are handled with varying degrees of success by the newcomers. Some slide into step, while others fumble with the differences. These minidramas are observable in the Emporium, an upscale shopping mall, and in the neighbourhood's many international restaurants.

Th Sukhumvit also has a fair number of mansions (inhabited by the city's elite) that are hidden from the public eye by large concrete walls and junglelike gardens. The bird's-eye view from the Skytrain gives an unprecedented glimpse into these grand estates. The younger money lives in high-rise condos, but everyone still descends from their cocoons to eat at the local street vendor parked under a shady tree.

Like the city as a whole, Th Sukhumvit lacks a centre and instead spreads out along a stretch of asphalt, with neighbourhood streets branching off at right angles to form what must look like a felled tree from an aerial view.

A guiding principle in Bangkok's social landscape is the close proximity of business districts to strip clubs. Multinational office towers line Th Sukhumvit, blocking the sun and adding to a crowded skyscape of concrete towers. And in the shadows are two renowned girlie-bar centres, Nana Entertainment Plaza and Soi Cowboy, which have been so successful in their chosen professions that sex tourists rarely venture far from these dedicated areas.

Orientation

Th Sukhumvit starts on the eastern side of Chalerm Mahanakhon Expressway and travels east past the city limits to the Bay of Thailand. The *soi* that branch off Th Sukhumvit are conveniently numbered, with the even-numbered *soi* occupying the southern side of the street, and the odd-numbered *soi* occupying the northern side. The drawback to such an uncharacteristically simple design is that the even- and odd-numbered *soi* don't line up numerically (Soi 11 lies directly opposite Soi 8). Also, some *soi* are better known by an alternative name, such as Soi Asoke or Soi Nana – these instances have been indicated on the map.

Transport Th Sukhumvit

Bus Air-con 501, 508, 511 & 513, ordinary 2, 25, 38 & 40

Skytrain from Nana to On Nut stations

When venturing down the *soi*, try to determine how far your destination is located from the main road, as landmarks and building numbers are difficult to ascertain. Motorcycle taxis usually camp out at the beginning of the *soi* to shuttle residents the last kilometres home. They typically charge 10B and are usually young single guys who like motorcycles as much as watching the world go by.

The tourist scene of Th Sukhumvit is concentrated on the lower-numbered *soi* near Nana Entertainment Plaza and Soi Cowboy. East of Soi Asoke, the area is claimed by expats and families.

The best way to get around Th Sukhumvit is the Skytrain, which follows the start of the district all the way to Soi On Nut. The Skytrain also links to the Eastern Bus Terminal, for trips to Ko Samet and Pattaya. As with other parts of the city, Th Sukhumvit is almost always congested with traffic, especially at rush hour and at bar-closing time. A short cut through the back *soi*, known as the 'Green Route', is used by savvy cabs and locals to circumvent the creeping pace of Th Sukhumvit.

MUSEUM OF SCIENCE & PLANETARIUM Map pp264–5
ท้องฟ้าจำลอง

☎ 0 2392 5951; Building 2, 928 Th Sukhumvit, btwn Soi 40 & Soi 42; adult/child under 12 40/10B; ◷ 9am-4.30pm Tue-Sun; Skytrain Ekamai

In the National Science Centre for Education complex, this hands-on museum has general science exhibitions, an aquatic-life arena and a planetarium. When you enter the campus, the museum is the first building on your left.

SIAM SOCIETY & BAN KAMTHIENG
Map pp264–5
สยามสมาคม/บ้านคำเที่ยง

☎ 02661 6470; 131 Soi Asoke (Soi 21), Th Sukhumvit; Ban Kamthieng admission 100B; ◷ 9am-5pm daily (Ban Kamthieng), 9am-5pm Tue-Sat (Siam Society); Skytrain Asoke

Past the elevated Skytrain tracks and the roar of traffic, the Siam Society transports visitors to a northern Thai village with its excellent Ban Kamthieng house museum. Recently renovated, Ban Kamthieng is a traditional 19th-century home that was located on the banks of Mae Ping in Chiang Mai. Now relocated to Bangkok, the house presents the daily customs and spiritual beliefs of the Lanna tradition. Communicating all the hard facts of a sterile museum (with detailed English signage and engaging video installations), Ban Kamthieng instils in the visitor a sense of place, from the attached rice granary and handmade tools to the wooden loom and woven silks.

Next door to Ban Kamthieng are the headquarters of the prestigious Siam Society, pub-

Th Sukhumvit Top Five

- **Ban Kamthieng** (below) Cultural studies amid a pretty teak house makes learning not so taxing.
- **Clubbing** (p134) Q Bar, Narcissus and other night spots attract a happening crowd of expats and Bangkok locals.
- **Emporium Shopping Centre** (p153) High-powered shopaholics get their fix at this glamorous high-rise.
- **International Cuisine** (p121) Craving nachos, kidney pie or pasta *primavera*? All can be rustled up at Th Sukhumvit's many international restaurants.
- **Skytrain Rides** (above) This elevated tram gives a peek into the neighbourhood's many fortressed mansions.

lisher of the renowned *Journal of the Siam Society* and a valiant preserver of traditional Thai culture. This is a good place to visit for those with a serious interest in Thailand. A reference library is open to visitors and Siam Society monographs are for sale. Almost anything you'd want to know about Thailand (outside the political sphere, since the society is sponsored by the royal family) can be researched here.

WAT THAMMAMONGKHON Map pp246–7
วัดธรรมมงคล

Soi 101, Th Sukhumvit; admission by donation; ◷ 6am-6pm; Skytrain On Nut then air-con bus 507 or 502

East of Bangkok, this 95m-high *chedi* grew from a monk's vision. While meditating in 1991, Phra Viriyang Sirintharo saw a giant jade boulder; simultaneously a 32-tonne block of solid jade was found in a Canadian riverbed. Viriyang raised more than US$500,000 to buy the block and commissioned a 14-tonne Buddha sculpture (carried out by Carrara sculptors) to go in a pavilion at Thammamongkhon. An image of this size deserved a massive *chedi*. The *chedi*, which contains a hair of the Buddha presented to Thailand by Bangladesh's Sangharaja (head of a Theravada monastic order), has a lift so you can ride to the top. The opening ceremony for the *chedi* was held in 1993.

A leftover 10-tonne chunk of jade was carved into Kuan Yin (the Chinese Buddhist goddess of compassion). Smaller leftovers – totalling nearly eight tonnes – were used for amulets and sold to worshippers for US$20 each, to raise money for 5000 daycare centres throughout Thailand.

GREATER BANGKOK

Surrounding the previously defined neighbourhoods are residential suburbs with a few scattered attractions. Once rice fields, voracious Bangkok has expanded in every possible direction with little alluring charm. Chatuchak, in the northern section of the city, is one noteworthy area with a popular weekend market and several child-friendly museums. Other attractions listed here are located in otherwise uneventful areas.

Orientation

Many of these sites lie beyond the inner-city expressway. Chatuchak is in the northern section of town en route to the airport and the Royal Thai Air Force Museum. Once impossible to reach because of traffic, Chatuchak is now a hassle-free journey aboard the Skytrain. The other attractions listed here will require several forms of public transportation (and lots of time and patience) or personal transportation. The prisons are located west of Chatuchak and the river and north of central Bangkok. In the far eastern part of town is Bangkok's newest park, Rama IX.

BANG KWANG & KHLONG PREM PRISONS Map pp246–7

เรือนจำบางขวางและคลองเปรม

Bang Kwang: ☎ 0 2967 3311; fax 0 2967 3313; Nonthaburi Road, Nonthaburi; 🕙 visiting hours vary; ferry Nonthaburi Khlong Prem: ☎ 0 2580 0975; 33/3 Ngam Wang Wan Rd, Chatuchak; 🕙 visiting hours vary; ferry Nonthaburi, Skytrain Mo Chit

Thailand's permissive image is juxtaposed by strict antidrug laws that often land foreign nationals in Bangkok's prison system with feudal-style conditions. A sobering expedition is to visit an inmate, bringing them news of the outside, basic supplies and reading materials. The regulations for visitations are quite involved and require pre-arrival research (see p217). You must dress respectfully (long sleeves and long pants), bring your passport for registration purposes and have the name and building number of the inmate you plan to visit. Inmate information can be obtained from most embassies. Visiting hours and days vary depending on the building the inmate is housed in.

Male inmates who have received sentences of 40 years to life (often for drug offences) are detained in Bang Kwang Prison, north of central Bangkok. To reach the prison, take the Mae Nam Chao Phraya ferry north to Nonthaburi (the last stop); the prison is 500m from the pier.

Greater Bangkok Top Five

- **Chatuchak Weekend Market** (p154) So much stuff to buy and so little time.
- **Children's Discovery Museum** (below) A place where kids can touch everything – what a relief.
- **Ko Kret** (p98) Relax on this laid-back island light years behind bustling Bangkok.
- **Safari World** (p98) When the jungles of Bangkok become too ordinary, take the kids to the African savanna on the outskirts of town.
- **Victory Point** (p126) This night market around Victory Monument is exemplifies the provinces.

Women are detained in the Bang Khen section of Khlong Prem Prison. From Nonthaburi, take a minibus (10B to15B) to the prison, or take the Skytrain to Mo Chit and then a taxi to the prison gates.

CHILDREN'S DISCOVERY MUSEUM
Map pp246-7

พิพิธภัณฑ์เด็กกรุงเทพมหานคร

☎ 0 2615 7333; Queen Sirikit Park, Th Kamphaeng Phet 4; adult/child 70/50B; 🕙 9am-5pm Tue-Fri, 10am-6pm Sat & Sun; Skytrain Mo Chit

Through hands-on activities, learning is well disguised as fun at this museum opposite

Chatuchak Weekend Market. Kids can stand inside a bubble, see how an engine works, or role-play as a fire-fighter, supermarket cashier or café waiter. Most activities are geared to primary school–aged children. There is also a toddlers' playground at the back of the main building.

HALL OF RAILWAY HERITAGE
Map pp246–7

พิพิธภัณฑ์รถไฟ

☎ 0 2243 2037; Th Kamphaeng Phet 3, Chatuchak Park; admission free; ☽ 5am-3pm Sat & Sun; Skytrain Mo Chit
This museum has steam locomotives, model trains and other artefacts related to Thai railroad history.

KO KRET Map pp246–7

เกาะเกร็ด

Public boat from Tha Nonthaburi, one way 10B, then cross-river ferry, one way 1B, to Tha Pa Fai on island
This carless island in the middle of Mae Nam Chao Phraya at Bangkok's northern edge is the paragon of calm. A small path circles the island, leading past a village of expert nappers and lazy water buffalo submerged in mud. Even the life of a stray dog on Ko Kret seems enviable.

The most activity arises from the island's ancient art of throwing pots. Home to one of Thailand's oldest Mon settlements, who between the 6th and 10th centuries AD were the dominant culture in Central Thailand, Ko Kret remains one of the oldest and largest sources of earthenware in the region. You will have seen and maybe ignored this terracotta pottery in every tourist market in Bangkok, but seeing its birthplace adds a dimension of beauty to the pieces. There are two pottery centres on the island where you can buy the earthenware and watch the potters work. To find them, head in either direction from Wat Paramai Yikawat, also known simply as Wat Mon. Poke your head into the wát to see a Mon-style marble Buddha.

The easiest way to reach Ko Kret is to take a northbound Chao Phraya Express boat to Nonthaburi and then hire a long-tail boat (300B per person for two hours) from there. Another option is the equivalent of sneaking in the back door. From Tha Nonthaburi, dodge the pesky tour operators and hop on a public Laem Thong boat (10B) continuing north. Disembark at Tha Pak Kret and wait for a cross-river ferry to Ko Kret (1B), which is just across the way. Voilà, you're on the island and you did it all by yourself. Ko Kret has several piers, so remember to return to Tha Pa Fai for your indirect trip home.

RAMA IX ROYAL PARK Map pp246–7

สวนหลวง ร.๙

Soi 103 (Soi Udom Sak), Th Sukhumvit; admission 10B; ☽ 5am-6pm; ordinary bus 2, 23 & 25, transfer to green minibus at Soi 103
Opened in 1987 to commemorate King Bhumibol's 60th birthday, Bangkok's newest green area covers 81 hectares and has a water park and botanical garden. Since its opening, the garden has become a significant horticultural research centre. A museum with an exhibition on the king's life sits at the park's centre. There are resident lizards, tortoises and birds. A flower and plant sale is held here in December.

ROYAL THAI AIR FORCE MUSEUM
Map pp246–7

พิพิธภัณฑ์กองทัพอากาศ

☎ 0 2534 1764; Th Phahonyothin, near Wing 6 of Bangkok International Airport; admission free; ☽ 8.30am-4.30pm; air-con bus 504 & 510, ordinary bus 29 & 59, train to Don Muang
Military aircraft aficionados shouldn't miss this museum. Among the world-class collection of historic aircraft is the only existing Japanese Tachikawa trainer, along with a Spitfire and several Nieuports and Breguets.

SAFARI WORLD Map pp246–7

ซาฟารีเวิลด์

☎ 0 2518 1000; www.safariworld.com; 99 Th Ramindra 1, Miniburi; adult/child 780/570B; ☽ 9am-5pm
Claiming to be world's largest 'open zoo', Safari World is divided into two parts, the drive-through Safari Park and the Marine Park. In the Safari Park, visitors drive through eight habitats with giraffes, lions, zebras, elephants, orangutans, and other African and Asian animals. A panda house displays rare white pandas. The Marine Park focuses on stunts by dolphins and other trained animals. Safari World is 45km northeast of Bangkok, and best reached by car.

WAT CHONG NONSI Map pp246–7

วัดช่องนนทรีย์

Th Ratchadaphisek; admission by donation; ☽ 6am-6pm; ordinary bus 102 & 205
Near the Bangkok side of the river, this temple has *Jataka* murals painted between 1657 and 1707. It is the only surviving Ayuthaya-era temple with the murals and architecture from the same period with no renovations. As a single, 'pure' architectural and painting unit, it has importance for the study of late Ayuthaya art.

Walking Tours

Walking Tours

Walk through the world's worst traffic jam? Sounds absurd, but Bangkok really is charming by foot. Without a doubt, every block will be filled with something you've never seen before – blind troubadours with portable karaoke machines, stray dogs wearing T-shirts, vendors selling everything plus the kitchen sink. The added challenge is that Bangkok's pavements are as traffic-clogged as its roads, turning a leisurely stroll into an adventure sport of dodging broken asphalt and inexplicable puddles, ducking under huge umbrellas or canvas awnings anchored right at your forehead, or squeezing through a bottleneck at a stall selling desserts that look like tacos.

KO RATANAKOSIN STROLL

This walk covers Ko Ratanakosin (Ratanakosin Island), which rests in a bend of the river in the middle of Bangkok and contains some of the city's most historic architecture. Despite its name, Ko Ratanakosin is not actually an island, though in the days when Bangkok was known as the 'Venice of the East', Khlong Banglamphu and Khlong Ong Ang – two lengthy adjoining canals to the east – were probably large enough for the area to seem like an island. The canals were enlarged in the early period of the city in an effort to re-create the island-city of Ayuthaya (Thailand's former capital, which was sacked by the Burmese).

Walk Facts

Start Tha Chang ferry stop
End Sanam Luang bus stop or Tha Phra Chan ferry stop
Distance 2.5km
Duration 1 to 3 hours
Fuel Stop Trok Nakhon food vendors

This circular walk starts at Tha Chang, accessible by Chao Phraya river ferries. From the pier, file east past the market toward Th Na Phra Lan. On your left-hand side is **Silpakorn University** 1 (p94), Thailand's premier fine-arts university. Founded as the School of Fine Arts by Italian artist Corrado Feroci, the university campus includes part of an old Rama I palace and an art gallery showing works by students and professors. A small **bookshop** 2 next door to the campus stocks English-language books on Thai art.

Just past the intersection with Th Na Phra That is the third gate and the official tourist entrance to Thailand's holiest temple, **Wat Phra Kaew** 3 (p78), and the formal royal residence, the **Grand Palace** 4 (p78). All visitors to the palace and temple grounds must be appropriately attired – no shorts, tank tops or other dress considered unacceptable for temple visits. Temple staff can provide wraparound sarongs for bare legs.

Exiting via the same gate, take a right and cross Th Ratchadamnoen Nai to reach **Lak Meuang** 5 (City Pillar; p75), a shrine to Bangkok's city spirit. Traditionally, every city in Thailand must have a foundation stone that embodies the city's guardian deity and from which intercity distances are measured. This shrine is Bangkok's most important site of animistic worship; believers throng the area day and night, bringing offerings of flowers, incense, whisky, fruit and even cooked food.

From Lak Meuang, follow Th Sanamchai south with the Grand Palace and Wat Phra Kaew to your right until you come to Th Chetuphon (the second street after the palace walls end, approximately 600m from the pillar). Turn right on to Th Chetuphon and enter **Wat Pho** 6 (p79) through the second portico. Meander through the grounds, working your way to the massive reclining Buddha just barely fitting in its shelter. Exit via the same door and turn right on to Th Chetuphon, heading towards the river. The small *soi* (lane) directly in front of you is the newest address of the **Wat Pho Thai traditional massage school** 7 (p142), whose doors are always open to weary foot soldiers.

If you've still got stamina, turn right at Th Maharat and stroll north, passing the market area to your left. At the end of this block, Th Maharat crosses Th Thai Wang. On the southwestern corner is an older branch of the Bangkok Bank, where you can turn left on Th Thai Wang to glimpse a row of rare, early Ratanakosin-era shophouses. If you continue along Th Thai Wang to the river you'll arrive at Tha Tien pier stop for the Chao Phraya Express. From an adjacent pier you can catch one of the regular cross-river ferries to **Wat Arun** 8 (p77), which features one of Bangkok's most striking *praang*, a tall Hindu/Khmer-style stupa.

Back on the east side of the river, retrace your steps along Th Thai Wang to Th Maharat and turn left to continue the walking tour. About 500m from the Th Thai Wang intersection, Th Maharat crosses Th Na Phra Lan. From here turn left to reach Tha Chang and return home, or keep pushing northward.

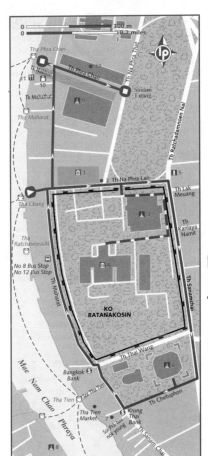

North of Th Na Phra Lan, Th Maharat becomes an informal healing centre of herbal apothecaries and pavement amulet sellers, for the health of one's body and spirit. On your right is **Wat Mahathat** 9 (p77), Thailand's most respected Buddhist university. Take a left into the narrow alley immediately after Trok Mahathat to find a warren of vendors selling *phrá khrêuang* (religious amulets) representing various Hindu and Buddhist deities. Follow the alley towards the river to appreciate how extensive the **amulet market** 10 (p145) is.

If you're hungry, snake your way back to Th Mahathat and continue to the next alley, Trok Nakhon, which leads past more amulet stalls and stores selling graduation gowns, to a dim alternative world of **food vendors** 11, some of whom sport a river view. The food here is very good and inexpensive – to order, all you'll need is a pointing index finger.

Renewed and refuelled, follow the last stretch of Th Maharat to the gates of **Thammasat University** 12, which is known for its law and political science faculties. It was also the site of the bloody prodemocracy demonstrations of October 1976, when hundreds of Thai students were killed or wounded by military troops. Hang a right on to Th Phra Chan towards Sanam Luang to return home by bus (air-con bus 506, 507, 509, 511 or 512, or ordinary bus 39, 44 or 47). Alternatively you could turn left on to Th Phra Chan and take a cross-river ferry from Tha Phra Chan to Tha Bangkok Noi, where you can pick up the Chao Phraya Express in either direction.

CHINATOWN SHOPPING SPREE

Chinatown is packed – every inch of it is used to make a living. From the fresh food market festooned with carcasses to the plastic beeping toy stores, commerce never rests. This walking tour plunges you into crowded claustrophobic alleys lined with vendors selling a greater variety of goods than the modern shopping centres. At points you'll be shocked, disgusted and thoroughly amazed – just come prepared for crowds and smells.

Start at Tha Ratchawong, along the banks of Mae Nam Chao Phraya and reached via river taxi. Walk along Th Ratchawong, the main street leading away from the pier. Here are established vendors selling wholesale products you've seen in smaller quantities at other markets – bulk plastic bags, handbags, calculators and hairpins. Turn right at Sampeng Lane (Soi Wanit 1; p147); you won't see a street sign here because the corner is packed with vendors' stalls, but you'll know it by the queue of people slowly shuffling into the alley. You have now entered the shopping fun house, where the sky is completely obscured and bargains lie in ambush – that is if you really want 500 Hello Kitty pens, a tonne of stuffed animals and books of stickers.

After about 100m, Sampeng Lane crosses Th Mangkon. On either side of the intersection are two of Bangkok's oldest commercial buildings, a **Bangkok Bank** 1 and the venerable **Tang To Kang** 2 gold shop, which are both more than 100 years old. The exteriors of the buildings are classic early Ratanakosin, showing lots of European influence; the interiors are heavy with hardwood panelling. Good luck spotting these as you squeeze against your neighbour to allow a delivery of overstuffed boxes to pass.

Walk Facts

Start Tha Ratchawong ferry stop
End Th Charoen Krung
Distance 1.5km
Duration 1 hour
Fuel Stop Hong Kong Noodles

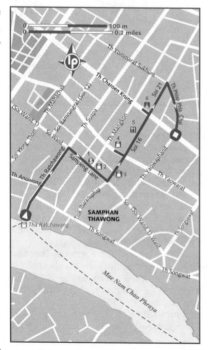

Continue walking another 60m or so to Trok Itsaranuphap, where you'll take a left on to a wider lane past rows of vendors selling huge bags of fried pork skins, dried fish and other delicacies. Down the lane on your right is **Talaat Kao** 3 (Old Market) – the entrance is ornamented in Chinese style. This market has been operating continuously for more than 200 years. All manner and size of freshwater and saltwater fish and shellfish are displayed here, alive or filleted – or, as is sometimes the case, half alive and half filleted.

From Trok Itsaranuphap, continue to **Th Yaowarat** 4, (p87), a main Chinatown thoroughfare This section of Th Yaowarat is lined with large and small gold shops; for price and selection, this is probably the best place in Thailand to purchase a gold chain (sold by the *bàat*, a unit of weight equal to 15g). To cross the road, shadow a few savvy Thai shoppers possessing that innate Bangkok ability to dodge traffic.

Trok Itsaranuphap continues now in the guise of Soi 16, according to the street sign. This section is lined with vendors purveying cleaned chickens, freshly plucked ducks, descaled fish, unnaturally coloured vats of pickled food, prepackaged snacks – hungry yet? **Hong Kong Noodles 5** (p111), on the left side of the alley, does a rollicking business catering to appetites aroused by the sight of such raw ingredients. A popular souvenir item here is fresh cashews, sold by the kilo.

Cross the next major intersection, Th Charoen Krung, and turn left. Continue for 20m to **Wat Mangkon Kamalawat 6** (Neng Noi Yee), one of Chinatown's largest and liveliest temples; the name means Dragon Lotus Temple. Along this stretch of Th Charoen Krung, neighbouring shops sell fruit, cakes, incense and ritual burning paper for offering at the temple. Inscriptions at the entrance to Wat Mangkon Kamalawat are in Chinese and Tibetan, while the labyrinthine interior features a succession of Buddhist, Taoist and Confucian altars. At virtually any time of day or night this temple is packed with worshippers lighting incense, filling the ever-burning altar lamps with oil and praying to their ancestors.

Work your way back to Trok Itsaranuphap, which has now changed its name to Soi 21, and continue past funerary stalls selling the paper versions of 21st-century necessities and niceties to be ritualistically burned so the dearly departed are accompanied in the next life. Slide your way past the jerky vendor who is fending off devoted fans to the termination of the *soi* at Th Yommarat Sukhum. Turn right on to Th Phlap Phla Chai and follow the bend in the road into the blazing hot sun, past more religious shops, back to Th Charoen Krung. About midblock, this tour poetically ends beside a coffin shop.

If the commingling of death and commerce has you energised, take your wallet on an outing to other outdoor markets (p147) in Chinatown.

OLD BANGLAMPHU WALK

Beyond Banglamphu's manic scene of Th Khao San, the neighbourhood makes for a charming wander. Start on Th Din So directly across from the **Democracy Monument 1** (p81). From 'the Demo', walk north along the left-hand side of Th Din So. Many of the shophouses that line the road here date to the reigns of Rama V (1868–1910) and Rama VII (1925–34). Since the entire block to the northwest of the Democracy Monument belongs to Wat Bowonniwet, the shop owners pay rent directly to the temple.

Turn left on to Th Phra Sumen and immediately on your left you'll notice a short row of shops selling Thai flags and Thai regalia, including orange Buddhist flags, photos of the royal family and window stickers reading *song phrá jaroen* (long live the king). The long wall on your left encloses **Wat Bowonniwet 2** (p82), one of the most highly venerated Buddhist monasteries in Bangkok and headquarters for the strict Thammayut monastic sect. Opposite the monastery on the north side of the street, wedged between shophouses and Khlong

> ## Walk Facts
>
> **Start** Democracy Monument air-con bus 511, 512, ordinary bus 2, 39, 44
> **End** Bangkok Tourist Bureau
> **Distance** 1.5km
> **Duration** 1 to 1½ hours
> **Fuel Stop** Ton Pho

Banglamphu, stands an **old city gate 3**, one of Bangkok's original 16. Once built of timber, it was replaced by this larger brick-and-stucco version during the reign of Rama V and restored in 1981.

Further along Th Phra Sumen, after crossing Th Bowonniwet and Th Chakaphong, you'll pass a ruined brick **palace gate 4** on your left. Although the 18th-century palace, once the residence of Rama I's youngest brother, is long gone, local residents maintain a small spirit house in front of the gate out of respect for the Chakri dynasty.

As Th Phra Sumen approaches Mae Nam Chao Phraya, it bends southward and its name changes to Th Phra Athit. Looming over the riverine corner formed by Mae Nam Chao Phraya and Khlong Banglamphu, 18th-century **Phra Sumen Fort 5** (p81) is the centrepiece of the recently developed Santichaiprakan Park. The small, grassy park makes a good stop for river views and cooling breezes. Standing in the park are Banglamphu's last two remaining *lamphuu* trees, from which the area derives its name. A riverfront promenade follows Mae Nam Chao Phraya southwest from the park to Tha Phra Athit and **Ton Pho 6** (p111), an outdoor restaurant with water views.

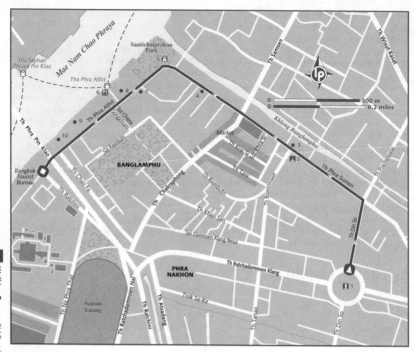

If, from Santchaiprakan Park, you continue walking southwest along Th Phra Athit, you'll pass a mixture of modern shophouses and old mansions on either side of the road, the latter built to house Thai nobility during the late 19th and early 20th centuries. **Ban Phra Athit 7**, at No 201/1, once belonged to Chao Phraya Vorapongpipat, finance minister during the reigns of Ramas V, VI and VII. One of the most splendidly restored Ratanakosin-era buildings in the neighbourhood, it now belongs to a private company, but is easily viewed from the street or from the coffee shop next door.

On the opposite side of the street is the **Buddhist Society of Thailand 8** (p82), which is housed in an attractive Ratanakosin-era building. The society has a library and other services geared primarily to Thais; foreigners interested in Buddhism should visit the World Fellowship of Buddhists, near Soi 24, Th Sukhumvit (p212).

Further southwest on the river side of Th Phra Athit stands **Ban Maliwan 9**, a striking mansion designed and built from 1910 to 1925 by Italian architect Ercole Manfredi. Today Ban Maliwan contains the Asia–Pacific offices of the UN Food & Agriculture Organization. Since the entrance to Ban Maliwan faces the river, the architecture is best appreciated from the riverfront promenade.

Another international organisation, **UNICEF 10**, occupies the former palace of HRH Prince Nareswororit, a son of King Rama IV and his Queen consort. Originally built during the Fourth regnum (1851–68), the palace served as a command post for the Seri Thai (Free Thai) movement towards the end of WWII.

Just a bit further south down Th Phra Athit, you'll pass under Saphan Phra Pin Klao and come to the well-staffed Bangkok Tourist Bureau. From here you can link to the Ko Ratanakosin walking tour (p100), or you could walk back to Th Ratchadamnoen Klang or Th Khao San.

Eating

Eating

Wherever you go in Bangkok, there is food. *Rót khěn* (vendor carts) deploy across the city outfitted with portable woks, charcoal stoves or deep-fryers ready to whip up a quick snack or a sit-down meal. There is so much variety on the streets themselves that you can go weeks without stepping inside a restaurant.

When you make the leap inside, your choices are just as astounding. Even the shopping malls are known for their food centres, which bring the traditional Thai market inside. Then there are the simple canteen shops, where you select a dish from a display case of premade options, or the open-air restaurants that are known city-wide for a particular speciality.

As a cosmopolitan centre, Bangkok also has many stylish spots that set a mood with a riverside view, traditional antiques or modern minimalism. These restaurants lead diners on a tour through Thai dishes once reserved only for the royal family or to regional cuisines outside the capital.

Although Thai food might be sufficiently exotic, Bangkok offers an international menu prepared by its many immigrant communities. Chinatown is naturally a good area for Chinese food. In a corner of Chinatown known as Phahurat and around Th Silom Indian residents keep themselves and the culinary traveller well fed in closet-sized restaurants. In the crowded bazaar-like area of Little Arabia, just off Th Sukhumvit, there is Muslim cuisine from every far-flung corner of the region. There's also a variety of Western food, from Italian to American and from *haute cuisine* for power players to pub grub to cure homesickness.

Opening Hours

Restaurants serving Thai food are generally open from 10am to 8 or 9pm, although some places are open later. Foreign-cuisine restaurants tend to keep only dinner hours, although this varies. Thais are consummate eaters and are always within reach of a snack or a light meal, so meal times are quite flexible.

Busy cooking up a storm in a Bangkok restaurant

The Soup That is Like Eating a Meal

Thailand's best-known food exports are its curries *(kaeng)*, which come in a variety of neon colours with a sublime interplay of spicy, sweet, salty and sour. Reflecting Thai cuisine's emphasis on fresh vibrant flavours, Thai curries derive their complexity from native seasonings such as lemon grass, kaffir lime leaves and galangal, as well as a base of shrimp paste and chilli peppers. Some recipes, such as *kaeng khǐaw wǎan* (green curry), add coconut milk for a rich and creamy dimension, while other curries, such as *kaeng sôm* (sour curry), omit the coconut milk for more of a soup-like quality.

The term *kaeng* is broadly used to refer to any dish with a lot of liquid, and certain dishes are translated into English as 'soups', introducing the misconception that they should be eaten directly from the bowl, like Western-style soups. Regardless of its consistency, *kaeng* is always eaten like a meal. When eating in a restaurant, *kaeng* is served in a rounded bowl, and diners serve themselves individual bowls which are then ladled over rice and eaten like any communal Thai dish. At rice-and-curry shops *(ráan khâo kaeng)*, you pick a curry from a selection of premade options – typically *kaeng kài* (chicken), *kaeng plaa* (fish) and *kaeng sôm* – that are served directly over the rice. Eating rice with curry helps dilute the spiciness and, according to Thais, aids in digestion.

Muslim-run restaurants sometimes close in observance of religious or cultural holidays, but most Thai and Chinese restaurants view holidays as a chance to feed more customers.

How Much?

A bowl of noodles or a stir-fry dish bought from a street vendor should cost 20B to 25B, depending on the portion size and ingredients. Climbing up the scale are the canteen shops that have a selection of premade dishes, sturdier chairs and a roof. For these luxuries, you'll probably pay 30B.

Thai restaurants with an army of servers and laminated menus usually offer main dishes for around 80B to 150B. Add ambience, air-con and fancy uniforms, and a main jumps to about 120B to 200B. Anything above 300B will deliver you into the arms of some of the city's fanciest restaurants. An exception is the restaurants in top-end hotels, which feature prices close to what you'd expect to pay at any flash hotel in the world.

In most parts of the city, Western food occupies the high end of the scale, costing from 200B to 350B. One obvious exception is Banglamphu, where *faràng* (Western) food comes in under 200B a plate.

Booking Tables

If you have a lot of friends in tow or will be attending a formal restaurant (including hotel restaurants), reservations are recommended. Bookings are also recommended for Sunday brunch and dinner cruises.

Otherwise, you shouldn't have a problem scoring a table at most restaurants in the city, especially if you arrive during off-peak hours. Following the European tradition (or because of the wretched evening commute), peak dinner time starts around 8pm. The lunch-time crush typically starts around noon and lasts close to an hour.

Tipping

You shouldn't be surprised to learn that tipping in Thailand isn't as exact a science as it is in Europe (tip no-one) or the USA (tip everyone every chance you get). Thailand falls somewhere in between, and some areas are left open to interpretation. Everyone agrees that you don't tip streetside vendors (although some vendors add a little surcharge when tallying up a bill for a foreigner. To avoid getting annoyed about this double-pricing scheme, consider it an implicit tip).

When eating at a restaurant, tipping becomes more a game of finesse. Some people leave behind roughly 10% at any sit-down restaurant where someone fills their glass every time they take a sip. Others don't. Most upscale restaurants will apply a 10% service charge to the bill. Some patrons leave extra on top of the service charge; others don't. The choice is up to you.

BANGLAMPHU

With more village-like qualities than other parts of Bangkok, this area's strengths lie in its abundant street food. Every alley wide enough to hold a wok is claimed as a makeshift dining room. Because of the backpacker presence, Western and vegetarian food is plentiful and cheap.

ARAWY Map pp254–5   *Vegetarian Thai*
152 Th Din So; dishes 35B; ◷ 7am-7pm; ordinary bus 10, 19 & 42

Just opposite the City Hall and a few doors from a 7-Eleven store, this mama of veggie spots is marked by a Roman-script sign that reads 'Alloy' ('delicious'). It is one of the best Thai vegetarian restaurants, with real veggie flavour rather than the tasteless oil spill that often accompanies vegetarian dishes. This was one of Bangkok's first Thai nonmeat restaurants, inspired by the strict vegetarianism of the ex-governor of Bangkok, Chamlong Srimuang.

BAAN PHANFAH RESTAURANT
Map pp254–5   *Thai*
☎ 0 2281 6237; 591 Th Phra Sumen; dishes 150-300B; ◷ 6pm-2am; air-con bus 511, ordinary bus 2

Overlooking Khlong Banglamphu, this chic restaurant occupies a classic Sino-Portuguese house of white walls and gracious louvred windows. The backyard dining area has dramatic lighting with sleek furniture and hip tunes that make even the plastic-bottle-filled canal seem magical. If you have something to celebrate, clean yourself up and strike a pose.

CHABAD HOUSE Map pp254–5   *Israeli*
☎ 0 2282 6388; Th Rambutri; dishes 100-200B; ◷ noon-9pm Sun-Thu, noon-4.30pm Fri; ferry Tha Phra Athit, air-con bus 506, ordinary bus 56

This well-scrubbed shopfront is a Jewish place of worship (upstairs), but the downstairs café serves Israeli-style kosher food in a sedate environment as part of its nonprofit community outreach.

ISAN RESTAURANTS Map pp254–5   *Thai*
Th Ratchadamnoen Nok; mains 50-100B; ◷ 11am-10pm; air-con bus 503 & 509, ordinary bus 70 & 201

A fight night tradition, these neighbours to the Ratchadamnoen Boxing Stadium serve the hallmarks of Isan (northeastern Thai) cuisine: *kài yâang* (grilled chicken), *lâap* (spicy meat salad) and *sôm-tam* (papaya salad). The crowds squeezing into the restaurants and the frenzied betting activity around the stadium help buoy the food above mediocre.

JEY HOY Map pp254–5   *Thai-Chinese*
Soi 2, Th Samsen; dishes 50-100B; ◷ 6pm-midnight; ferry Tha Phra Athit, air-con bus 506, ordinary bus 53

Just over the *khlong* bridge, this popular open-air restaurant commandeers the corner with a big tray of fresh seafood displayed on a bed of ice. The iron chef beats mercilessly at the prominently displayed wok, creating lickety-split Hokkien specials, such as *puu phàt phõng kàrìi* (crab stir-fried with curry powder and egg). You might want to hit it early in the evening when Thai families dominate the place. Later on, backpackers swarm in and accomplish amazing faux pas, such as drinking directly from the big bottles of Singha rather than from a glass – an obvious example of a DUI (drinking under the influence) of Khao San.

KHRUA NOPPARAT Map pp254–5   *Thai*
Th Phra Athit; dishes 60-100B; ◷ 10.30am-9.30pm Mon-Sat; ferry Tha Phra Athit, ordinary bus 53

On a bohemian strip of arty restaurants and bars, Khrua Nopparat (Nopparat's Kitchen) is a decidedly unhip, but utterly delicious, spot. This plain Jane is filled with fluorescent lighting and cheap furniture, which leaves more resources for the food. The plates are small, so don't shy away from the Thai tradition of overordering. Winners include the *kûng chúp pâeng thâwt* (deep-fried shrimp) or *phat phàk khánáa* (stir-fried Chinese kale), or more traditional Thai dishes such as *yam plaa sãmlii* (spicy cottonfish salad); *hàw mòk plaa châwn* (thick fish curry steamed in banana leaves) and *kaeng khïaw-wãan kài* (green chicken curry).

Top Five Banglamphu Eats

- **Arawy** (above) Vegetarian food that, as the restaurant's name suggests, really is delicious.
- **Jey Hoy** (above) A streetside salute to seafood and wok wonders.
- **Khrua Nopparat** (above) All the Thai classics by a true master.
- **Roti-Mataba** (p110) Thai-Muslim flavours without the long bus ride south.
- **Ton Pho** (p111) No-frills riverside eating with powerful flavours.

Top Five Street Snacks

The original fast-food, these street snacks can be found all over the city and demonstrate Thais' great talent for snacking between meals. The following snacks are the simple reasons why many foreigners can never leave Thailand.

Kaafae yen (iced Thai coffee) – Skip the instant stuff that is served to foreigners in guesthouses and hit the streets for this jolt of joe – filtered coffee mixed with sweetened condensed milk and sugar poured into a portable bag filled with ice. You'll be buzzing like a hummingbird from this dynamic caffeine-sugar duo, and your waistline will never forgive you. This is also available as *kaafae ráwn* (hot coffee), served tableside in a glass.

Khànòm khrók – Keep an eye out for a griddle with semicircular dimples into which a batter of coconut milk and rice flour is poured. These bite-sized pudding bits are sweet and slightly salty. More savoury varieties are garnished with corn and green onions. Be sure to buy them fresh off the griddle for a creamier texture.

Klûay thâwt (deep-fried bananas) – Doing a deep-fried world tour? Add these finger-sized snacks to the constellation of deep-fried delicacies. These vendors won't be hard to spot – look for a bubbling vat of oil. Sometimes taro and sweet potatoes are sold alongside the bananas.

Sàp-pàrót (pineapple) – If Thailand wanted to invade the world, its secret weapon could be pineapple. Juicy, sweet and tangy, this exotic fruit could persuade the pineapple-deprived people of the world to lay down arms in submission. Served freshly carved from glass-cased carts, pineapple shares space with other tropical fruits *(phŏn-lá-mái)* such as guava, papaya and watermelon.

Satay – Dainty yet masculine, satay exerts a strong magnetic force on foraging foreigners. Originally a Malay-Indonesian recipe, short skewers of meat (beef, pork or chicken) are grilled over a mesquite barbecue and served with a sweet and spicy sauce.

KHRUA RAKHANG THONG

Map pp254–5   *Thai*

Soi Tambon Wang Lang 1; dishes under 150B; noon-10pm; ferry Tha Wang Lang from Tha Chang

This is the trailer-park neighbour to the well-maintained Supatra River House. With similar (and cheaper) river views, Khrua Rakhang Thong has excellent Thai food, including a wide choice of vegetarian dishes. Especially tasty is the *sôm-tam yâwt máphráo àwn* (spicy coconut shoots salad). A small outdoor area upstairs has a few tables, plus one or two with the famous dual-temple view. The restaurant is a great walk from Tha Wang Lang (reached from the Bangkok side by a cross-river ferry at Tha Chang); from the pier turn left at the first through-street past the market full of veggie sellers and vendors glued to TV soap operas. The restaurant is marked by a Roman-script sign that reads 'River View'.

KUAY TIAW MAE Map pp254–5   *Thai*

Th Phra Athit; mains 30-50B; 10.30am-7.30pm; ferry Tha Phra Athit, ordinary bus 53

Two doors down from Roti-Mataba, this shady storefront might be the most stylish *kŭaytĭaw* (rice noodles) shop in the universe, with wooden benches lining the walls and deliberate, artistic wall hangings. The *kŭaytĭaw tôm yam* (rice noodles in a spicy lemon-grass broth) with pork or tofu substitution keeps noodle fans reverently bowed over steaming bowls.

MAY KAIDEE'S

Map pp254–5   *Vegetarian Thai-Chinese*

sub-soi off Soi Damnoen Klang Neua; mains 20-50B; 11am-9.30pm; ferry Tha Phra Athit, air-con bus 506, ordinary bus 56

For an all-veggie menu at low prices, seek out the string of vegetarian restaurants near Srinthip Guest House. May Kaidee's is the best of the bunch. To find it, turn right on to Th Tanao at the eastern end of Th Khao San, cross the street then take the first left.

METHAVALAI SORN DAENG

Map pp254–5   *Thai*

☎ 0 2224 3088; Democracy Monument; dishes 80-200B; 11am-11pm; air-con bus 511 & 512, ordinary bus 2, 39, 10 & 12

Similar in sensibilities to Vijit (see p111), Sorn Daeng is decorated with lacy curtains and has a staid atmosphere. If you like *thâwt man plaa* (fried spicy fishcakes), Sorn Daeng makes some of the best in the city. At lunchtime, the restaurant gets crowded with local government office workers.

PHON SAWAN

Map pp254–5   *Vegetarian Thai-Chinese*

80 Th Samsen; dishes 35B; 10am-8pm; Tha Phra Athit, air-con bus 506, ordinary bus 53

Directly across from the Bangkok Bank, this simple place feeds Banglamphu expats tofu-based

Day & Night Food on the Go

Th Khao San used to be a desert for good Thai food, but thanks to the increasing presence of partying Thais, the standards have been improving. Amid the nightly parade you can forage for great late-night snacking: fresh fruit, spring rolls and *shwarma* sandwiches. The best places to get *phàt thai* (fried rice noodles with vegetables, egg and tofu) in the neighbourhood are from the simple pushcarts (without seating) that are loaded with piles of noodles and vegetables. Near the 7-Eleven on Th Rambutri, post-imbibing Thais fend off a hangover with a bowl of *jóhk* (rice porridge). Soi Rambutri has more streetside eating, with grilled fish, chicken and cold beer.

Night-time stalls on **Th Samsen**, between Soi 2 and Soi 8, serve *sômtam* (papaya salad), *kŭaytĭaw* and *râat nâa* (noodles with gravy). Just look for the stall with the most devoted eaters. The *sômtam* stalls are frequented by former Isan (northeast) residents who meticulously direct the vendor as to the precise portions of seasonings. Until you're able to squat with your heels to the floor, just specify the variety of *sômtam* (Thai or Lao).

Lots of daytime vendors are hidden down the neighbourhood's myriad *soi* and alleys. A few Muslim vendors occupy **Trok Surat**, which is between the shoe shops on the western side of Th Chakraphong between Th Tani and Th Rambutri. The noodle vendor down this *soi* does semivegetarian noodles with fluffy cubes of tofu and seafood.

Thai-Chinese dishes, served on a bed of hearty *khâo klâwng* (brown rice). Once you pass Soi 4 on Th Samsen, keep an eye out for a handwritten 'Vegetarian Food' sign inside the simple storefront. There are a couple of copy-cat restaurants nearby that are worth a venture as well.

PRAKORP'S HOUSE

Map pp254–5   *Western & Thai*
☎ 0 2281 1345; 52 Th Khao San; dishes 50-100B;
🕑 8am-10pm; ferry Tha Phra Athit, air-con bus 506, ordinary bus 56

Exceptionally good guesthouse fare is served at this age-old denizen. A huge menu covers all the Southeast Asian interpretations of Western breakfasts, but the real winner is the chewy cup of hot coffee.

RANEE'S GUESTHOUSE

Map pp254–5   *Vegetarian Thai*
77 Trok Mayom; dishes 70-120B; 🕑 7am-midnight;
ferry Tha Phra Athit, air-con bus 506, ordinary bus 56

Quantity-loving vegetarians will appreciate this guesthouse kitchen, which serves large portions of vegetable dishes. Vegetable stir-fries are cooked to perfection and can be enjoyed in a quiet garden courtyard where the owner's children play. Specify if you want brown rice.

ROTI-MATABA Map pp254–5   *Muslim Thai*
Cnr Th Phra Athit & Th Phra Sumen; dishes 50-80B;
🕑 7am-8pm Tue-Sun; ferry Tha Phra Athit, ordinary bus 53

Opposite Phra Sumen Fort, this claustrophobic spot does delicious roti, *kaeng mátsàmàn* (Muslim-style curry), chicken korma and chicken or vegetable *mátàbà* (a sort of stuffed Indian pancake). It has a bilingual menu and a gruff army of aproned young servers. An upstairs air-con dining area and outdoor tables barely provide enough seating for its loyal fans. The procedure for eating and paying requires telepathic Thai abilities: you seat yourself and flag down one of the waitresses (who will pretend that you don't exist), but you pay downstairs where miraculously they have a bill waiting. Wonders never cease.

Roti Mataba Restaurant (left)

SAFFRON BAKERY Map p256 *Bakery*
Th Phra Athit;dishes 50-80B; 🕑 **9am-5pm; ferry Tha Phra Athit, ordinary bus 53**

This bright and cheery little place, opposite the Food & Agriculture Organization, has good pastries and fresh coffee, but only a few tables.

SILVER SPOON Map pp250–1 *Thai & Western*
☎ **0 2281 2900; Th Krung Kasem; dishes 70-200B;** 🕑 **5-11pm; ferry Tha Thewet, air-con bus 506, ordinary bus 53**

Next door to Tha Thewet, Silver Spoon (Chon-Ngern) has a magnificent view of the elegant Saphan Phra Ram XIII (King Rama XIII Bridge). Dining is casual and relaxed, and satisfying dishes won't hurt your wallet. Nothing says Thailand like picking tender meat off a whole fish, and this restaurant is known for its *plaa kàphong nêun mánao* (steamed sea bass with lemon).

TON PHO Map pp254–5 *Thai*
☎ **0 2280 0452; Th Phra Athit; dishes 60-100B;** 🕑 **10am-10pm; ferry Tha Phra Athit**

This dockside restaurant, overlooking the muddy Mae Nam Chao Phraya, is an excellent stop for authentic Thai. The restaurant's décor has as much charm as a school cafeteria, adding anecdotal evidence to the irrational conviction that good food in Thailand has an inverse relationship to the restaurant's interior decorations. The restaurant has no Roman-script sign.

VIJIT Map pp254–5 *Thai*
☎ **0 2255 9529; Democracy Monument; dishes 70-200B;** 🕑 **11am-11pm; air-con bus 511 & 512, ordinary bus 2, 39, 10 & 12**

This old-school restaurant, anchored by a prominent stage for nightly crooners, reportedly has the best *yam plaa dùk fuu* (deep-fried catfish salad) in town.

CHINATOWN
Bored with Thai food already? Without leaving the city, you can take a culinary trip to China and India with a visit to Chinatown and Phahurat.

CHIANG KII Map pp252–3 *Chinese*
54 Soi Bamrungrat; mains 100B; 🕑 **9am-7pm; ferry Tha Ratchawong**

It is easy to walk by and assume this makeshift soup-house is a private residence. But if the doors are open, stop by for a bowl of the best *khâo tôm plaa* (rice soup with fish) in town.

HONG KONG NOODLES
Map pp252–3 *Chinese*
136 Trok Itsaranuphap, Th Charoen Krung; 🕑 **10am-8pm; ferry Tha Ratchawong**

Deep in the heart of a vendor-lined *soi*, Hong Kong Noodles does a busy trade in steaming bowls of roast duck noodles. If you can find a seat, there's a nice vista of the surrounding commerce.

LAEM THONG Map pp252–3 *Chinese*
☎ **0 2224 3591; 38 Soi Bamrungrat, Th Charoen Krung; mains 20-25B;** 🕑 **9am-7pm; ferry Tha Ratchawong**

A small, glass-enclosed, canteen-style shop, Laem Thong specialises in southern Chinese cuisine with a wide assortment of seafood, rice noodles and dumplings. You just point and order.

Eating – Chinatown

Kin Khâo – Eating Rice

In Thailand, eating is a social occasion to be shared with as many people as possible. Usually the head of the table orders a soup, a vegetable dish and a few stir-fries or curries. All the dishes are set in the middle of the table, and everyone takes a spoonful of whatever dish looks interesting on to their personal plate of rice. Since the dishes are communal, the kitchen rarely delivers items all at once.

When adhering to their own customs of ordering individually, Westerners find the staggered arrival of dishes to be especially frustrating. The solution is simple: share and share alike.

Thais eat with a spoon and a fork, using the fork to push food on to the spoon. To them, putting a fork into the mouth is the height of bad manners. It's okay to use your hands when eating sticky rice – roll the rice into a ball and eat it with your right hand. You'll be offered chopsticks only with Chinese meals or *kǔaytiaw* (noodle soups).

Although eating is communal, bill paying is not. Traditionally the eldest at the table picks up the check. But 'American share' (splitting the bill) is becoming more common among younger diners who don't have as much cash to kick around.

OLD SIAM PLAZA

Map pp254–5 *Thai & Chinese*

cnr Th Phahurat & Th Triphet; mains 30-40B; 🕙 10am-5pm; ferry Tha Saphan Phut

Wedged between the western edge of Chinatown and the northern edge of Phahurat, this three-storey shopping plaza has a 3rd-floor food centre serving Thai and Chinese food. The 1st floor provides a quick lesson in Thai desserts, with vendors selling all the streetside sweets within a quieter space.

PET TUN JAO THA Map pp252–3 *Thai*

n945 Soi Wanit 2; mains 30B; 🕙 closed Sun; ferry Tha Si Phraya

Across from the Harbour Department, this modest storefront (signed in English) has a geographically name that literally translates as 'Harbour Department Stewed Duck'. The speciality is *kŭaytĭaw* served with duck or goose, either roasted or stewed. Other Thai and Chinese dishes are available – just name it and the cooks can probably make it.

ROYAL INDIA Map pp252–3 *Indian*

☎ 0 2221 6565; 392/1 Th Chakraphet; mains 150-300B; 🕙 10am-10pm; ferry Tha Saphan Phut

One of the best northern Indian restaurants in Bangkok, Royal India huddles in the shadows of a small *soi*. It can be very crowded at lunchtime, almost exclusively with Indian diners, but everyone is open to sharing tables and swapping tales. The lunch thali (vegetarian/nonvegetarian 150/200B) is an excellent introduction to the menu. The accompanying dessert of the day is hard to ignore. Other hits include curries (both vegetarian and nonvegetarian), dhal, Indian breads, raita and lassi. Royal India also has a **branch** in Banglamphu (on Th Khao San) but it's not as good.

Top Five Chinatown Eats

- **Hong Kong Noodles** (p111) Take a break from market-mania with their steamy energisers.
- **Old Siam Plaza** (left) The first stop for educating your sweet tooth to Thai desserts.
- **Pet Tun Jao Tha** (left) To feed a noodle addiction provides a great excuse to come to this well-hidden neighbourhood.
- **Royal India** (left) Homesick Indians adopt this den as a stand-in kitchen.
- **White Orchid Restaurant** (below) Everything a Chinese banquet house should be.

SHANGARILA RESTAURANT

Map pp252–3 *Chinese*

☎ 0 2235 7493; 206 Th Yaowarat; dishes 220-500B; 🕙 11am-10pm; ferry Tha Ratchawong

This massive, banquet-style restaurant prepares a variety of Cantonese cuisine for ravenous families. The dim sum lunches are worth muscling your way past the outdoor steam tables.

WHITE ORCHID RESTAURANT

Map pp252–3 *Chinese*

☎ 0 2226 0026; 2nd fl, White Orchid Hotel, 409-21 Th Yaowarat; mains 180-250B; 🕙 10.30am-11pm; ferry Tha Ratchawong

Welcome to a rough approximation of Hong Kong circa 1988. White Orchid's cluelessly retro interior is further enhanced by its lunch-time dim sum process: ordering from 20 baskets filled with plastic imitation food of dubious artistic quality. But persevere, because you'll soon be congratulating yourself on your accidental choice of prawn dumplings and minced crab rolls.

Chinatown's Medley of Flavours

All-night **food hawkers** set up along the intersection of Th Yaowarat and Th Ratchawong. This is the least expensive place to dine out in Chinatown – and on weekends parts of these two streets are turned into a pedestrian-only mall.

On either side of Th Chakraphet near the ATM Building are several small **teahouses** with inexpensive Indian and Nepali food, including lots of fresh chapatis and strong milk tea. In the afternoons, vegetarian samosas are sold from a pushcart at the end of Soi ATM (which is marked by a 'Thai-Sikh Internal Security' sign); these deep-fried friends are often cited as the best in Bangkok.

During the annual Vegetarian Festival (in September/October; see boxed text p10), Bangkok's Chinatown becomes a virtual orgy of vegetarian Thai and Chinese cuisine. The festivities centre on Wat Mangkon Kamalawat, on Th Charoen Krung between Th Mangkon and Soi 16, but food shops all over the neighbourhood offer hundreds of different meat-free dishes; just keep an eye out for the yellow and red banners.

SIAM SQUARE & PRATUNAM

When you just can't stomach another meal of rice, take yourself immediately to Siam Square for wickedly irresistible American fast food. These spiffy air-con joints overflow with Thai students more adept at handling a hamburger than most *faràng* are with chopsticks. Fear not for mediocrity: Siam Square also boasts a veritable restaurant row around Soi Lang Suan, off Th Ploenchit.

AUBERGE DAB Map pp262–3 *French*
☎ 0 2658 6222; Mercury Tower, 540 Th Ploenchit; dishes 400-175B, set menu 950B; ◷ 11am-10pm; Skytrain Chitlom

Sharing the ground floor with Fabb Fashion Café, this very plush French place has crystal chandeliers, fine wine and an impressive menu of steak and Atlantic seafood. Try the steak stuffed with foie gras and truffles. Another speciality is the fresh oysters from Brittany.

BAAN KHANITHA & GALLERY
Map pp262–3 *Thai*
☎ 0 2253 4638; 49 Soi Ruam Rudi, Th Ploenchit; dishes 150-360B; ◷ 11am-2pm & 6-11pm; Skytrain Ploenchit

East and West come together like bosom buddies at this expat favourite. The setting is a pleasant Thai-style house of soaring eaves and honest dining rooms decorated with stone carvings, wide plank floors and soothing earth tones. The staff orchestrate a crush of diners with flawless English, and deliver Thailand's greatest dishes accommodated to tender *faràng* palates without jeopardising the subtle complexity of flavours. The wing bean salad and deep-fried squid curry will engender near marital fidelity to this restaurant. There's another **branch** on Soi 23, Th Sukhumvit (☎ 0 2258 4181).

BAN KHUN MAE Map pp262–3 *Thai*
☎ 0 2658 4112; Soi 8, Siam Square; dishes 50-90B; ◷ 11am-10pm daily; Skytrain Siam

Welcome to Mama's House. Directly across the street from the Novotel Hotel, this rambling restaurant does straightforward Thai dishes for the country's recent arrivals. Once you master this menu, you are ready to strike out on your own into the vendor stalls where the same quality is delivered for half the price.

CENTRAL WORLD PLAZA
Map pp262–3 *Thai & Fast Food*
cnr Th Ploenchit & Th Ratchadamri; ◷ 10am-9pm; Skytrain Chitlom

Formerly the World Trade Center, this shopping complex has a more suburban feeling than the urban, zit-popping energy of MBK (see p114). The restaurants reflect the same sensibilities, targeting multigenerational families with special events to celebrate. **Kroissant House** (ground floor, snacks 60-100B) serves coffee, pastries and *gelato*, and its companion **La Fontana** is an Italian bistro (dishes 100-200B). The 6th floor features **Lai-Lai**, a sumptuous Chinese banquet restaurant with a set dim sum lunch (75-115B). There are also two **food centres** on the 6th floor serving standard Thai and Chinese dishes. In the cool season, Central's outdoor **beer garden** is the best in the city, with a front-row view of the leather-clad crooners on stage and the ant-farm parade of late-night shoppers.

FABB FASHION CAFÉ Map pp262–3 *Italian*
☎ 0 2658 6200; Mercury Tower, 540 Th Ploenchit; dishes 390-520B; ◷ 11am-midnight; Skytrain Chitlom

Despite the tacky name, this is actually a rather classy Italian restaurant. Serenaded by a smooth jazz band, well-heeled bilinguals enjoy the height of Thai service.

HARD ROCK CAFÉ Map pp262–3 *Western*
☎ 0 2254 0830; Soi 11, Siam Square; dishes from 200B; ◷ until 2am; Skytrain Siam

The Bangkok branch of this international homage to rock-and-roll does a decent batch of American and Thai food. Eaters who have the girth to prove it swear by Hard Rock's nachos.

> ## Top Five Siam Square & Pratunam Eats
>
> - **Baan Khanitha & Gallery** (left) High-powered Thai food in a classic setting.
> - **Le Lys** (p114) A culinary elixir to frenetic Bangkok.
> - **Ngwan Lee Lang Suan** (p114) Pig out at this unadorned seafood mess hall.
> - **Siam Center & Discovery Center** (p115) Because a *faràng* can't live on rice alone, there is fast food and Western chains.
> - **Whole Earth Restaurant** (p115) The Goldilocks of Thai vegetarian food – not too spicy, not too greasy.

High Tea

Although Thailand was never a British colony (or anyone's colony for that matter), influences from nearby Kuala Lumpur and Singapore have made afternoon tea a custom at the more ritzy hotels. Tea is typically served between 2pm and 4pm and costs 300B to 500B.

Authors Lounge (Map pp257-9; ☎ 0 2659 9000; Oriental Hotel, Soi Oriental, Th Charoen Krung) Serves a range of sweet and savoury delights and has one of the best tea assortments in Bangkok, all taken in the quasi-colonial atmosphere enjoyed by Maugham, Coward and Greene.

Four Seasons Hotel (Map pp262-3; ☎ 0 2250 1000; 155 Th Ratchadamri) Has one of the best spreads, where you'll find a selection of herbal, fruit, Japanese, Chinese and Indian teas, plus a variety of hot scones, Devonshire cream, jam, cakes, biscuits and sandwiches. A string quartet provides atmosphere.

Shangri-La Hotel (Map pp257-9; ☎ 0 2236 7777; 89 Soi Wat Suan Phlu, Th Charoen Krung) Recommended for its lavish 40-item high-tea buffet on Sunday accompanied by the Bangkok Symphony Light Orchestra and ballroom dancing.

The Lobby Salon (Map pp260-1; ☎ 0 2287 0222; Sukhothai Hotel, 13/3 Th Sathon Tai) Serves a chocolate buffet amid its Asian minimalism.

(Beware of ordering nachos elsewhere as the term is liberally translated as meaning four soggy chips with a dollop of salsa.) Look for the túk-túk captioned 'God is my co-pilot' coming out of the building's façade.

KHAO MAN KAI SIAM Map pp262-3   *Thai*
Siam Chicken (on front door); 280 Th Phra Ram I; dishes 35-50B; ⊙ **10am-9pm; Skytrain Siam**

On the Siam Square side of Th Phra Ram I and in the shadow of the Siam Skytrain station, this slick and sterile spot still maintains the calling card of a traditional *khâo man kài* shop: dangling chicken carcasses in front of the kitchen. The fresh lemongrass broth and spicy dipping sauce keep the traditions of this time-honoured comfort food, and you can eat here free from car exhaust fumes.

LE LYS Map pp262-3   *French-Thai*
☎ **0 2652 2401; 75 Sub-Soi 3, Soi Lang Suan; dishes 80-200B;** ⊙ **11am-10.30pm; Skytrain Chitlom**

A soothing respite from Bangkok's traffic and the pressures of formality, Le Lys is tucked into a breezy colonial house guarded by a dense garden. Superb Thai dishes, such as *kaeng phèt mǔu yâang bai chà-om* (roast pork curry with acacia leaves), are easily chosen from a menu accompanied by appetising photos. Some diners snack and drink between sets of *pétanque* (French bowling) in the restaurant's backyard.

MAHBOONKRONG (MBK) SHOPPING CENTER Map pp262-3   *Thai & Fast Food*
Cnr Th Phayathai & Th Phra Ram I; food centre dishes

30B, chain dishes 150-200B; ⊙ 10am-10pm; Skytrain Siam

It sounds ridiculous to recommend eating at a shopping mall in such a culinary capital, but before you hurl this book into the nearest *khlong*, investigate Bangkok's unique version of mall eating. Besides the international chains, every mall sports a food centre with outdoor-market variety and prices but cradled in soothing air conditioning. See, the modern world isn't so bad. The food court is on the 4th floor, and the more popular vendors run out of food as early as 8.30pm or 9pm. On the 3rd floor are several popular Japanese restaurant chains.

NGWAN LEE LANG SUAN
Map pp260-1   *Thai*
☎ **0 2250 0936; cnr Soi Lang Suan and Soi Sarasin; dishes 150-200B; Skytrain Chitlom**

You've got to catch this place at night when the fluorescent lights make the open-air dining room look like a carnival and the undistracted diners look like sweating, bloated pigs. Join the mess hall for a huge variety of Chinese-style seafood and *kài lǎo daeng* (chicken steamed in Chinese herbs). Referring to the English menu will be more helpful than the illuminated pictures of dishes that have become indistinguishable with age.

NOODDI Map pp262-3   *Thai*
Mid-block Soi 4, Siam Square; dishes 80-120B; ⊙ **10am-9pm; Skytrain Siam**

This is a modern noodle bar serving all kinds of fresh Thai noodles and Italian pastas.

SARA-JANE'S Map pp262–3 *Italian & Thai*

☎ 0 2650 9992; Sindhorn Building, 130-132 Th Withayu; dishes 35-175B; ☻ 11am-10.30pm; Skytrain Ploenchit

Despite its *faràng* name, Sara-Jane's serves very good Isan and Italian cuisine in a casual, air-con dining room. The restaurant is inside the Sindhorn Building towards the back. There's a **second location** (Map pp007-00) on Th Narathiwat Ratchanakharin, near Th Sathon Tai.

SIAM CENTER & DISCOVERY CENTER
Map pp262–3 *Fast Food & International*

cnr Th Phayathai & Th Phra Ram I; food centre dishes 30-40B; restaurant dishes 100-300B; ☻ 10am-10pm; Skytrain Siam

Sober Siam Center and its attached tower, Discovery Center, have several stylish chain restaurants, including the coffee-dictator **Starbucks** (ground fl, Siam Center; ☻ 7am-midnight); **S&P Restaurant & Bakery** (ground fl, Siam Center), a regional chain with affordable Thai and Japanese dishes; and **Vietnam Cuisine** (4th fl, Siam Center), which has tasty Vietnamese dishes. The food centre is on the 3rd floor of Siam Center. Good luck figuring out where Siam Center ends and Discovery Center begins; even Bangkok's seemingly organised shopping malls retain the city's signature ability to defy navigational ease.

WHOLE EARTH RESTAURANT
Map pp262–3 *Vegetarian Thai*

☎ 0 2252 5574; 93/3 Soi Lang Suan; dishes 120-200B; ☻ 11.30am-2pm & 5.30-11pm; Skytrain Chitlom

This is a good Thai vegetarian restaurant (non-veg dishes are also served) with service to match. The upstairs room features low tables with floor cushions. A **second branch** (Map pp264-5;

Whole Earth Restaurant (below)

☎ 0 2258 4900; 71 Soi 26, Th Sukhumvit) serves both Thai and Indian vegetarian dishes.

SILOM & SURAWONG

In the heart of the financial district, Silom has a lot more variety than a hungry business suit would assume. At lunchtime Silom goes into a feeding frenzy, with whole shanty villages of lunchtime vendors or set-menus and buffets at the nearby English-Irish pubs. Dinner offerings take on a more gourmet attire, with a handful of elegant restaurants preparing fusion and royal Thai cuisine.

Towards the western end of Th Silom and Th Surawong, in an area known as Bang Rak, Indian eateries begin making an appearance. Unlike in Indian restaurants elsewhere in Bangkok, the menus in Bang Rak don't necessarily exhibit the usual, boring predilection towards North Indian Moghul-style cuisine.

BAAN RIM NAM Map pp257–9 *Thai*

☎ 0 2860 4500; 723 Th Charoen Nakhon, Thonburi; dishes 150-250B; ☻ 5-10pm; river ferry to Thonburi

Across the river from Central Bangkok, this riverside restaurant has an open-air dining pavilion overlooking the bright lights of the Shangri-La and Oriental Hotels. Take a cross-river ferry (2B) from the end of the *soi* in front of the Shangri-La Hotel to the wooden pier on the Thonburi shore. Wind through the narrow lanes until you come to a main road (Th Charoen Nakhon), then turn left. Near a large shopping centre, follow the signs to the restaurant.

Bangkok's Culinary Superstars

You haven't really experienced Thai food until you graze from the street vendors, who are considered the stalwarts of the cuisine. Outfitted with a portable cart, vendors are well versed in typical staples but usually define themselves with a particular speciality. A vast word-of-mouth network connects the demanding Thai eater with the best vendor for every imaginable dish. This eating subculture allows for a prosperous cottage industry or side job (many civil servants moonlight as street vendors) that brings capable cooks out of private homes for everyone to enjoy.

A few hits of the streetside parade include the following:

- *khâo phàt* – fried rice
- *khâo phàt bai kàphrao* – a fiery stir-fry of chopped chicken, chilli, garlic and fresh holy basil
- *phàt phàk kha-náa* – stir-fried Chinese greens, simple but delicious
- *phàt phàk ruam* – stir-fried mixed vegetables
- *phàt phrík thai kràthiam* – stir-fried chicken or pork with black pepper and garlic
- *phàt thai* –fried rice noodles, bean sprouts, peanuts, eggs, chilli and often prawns

BAN CHIANG Map pp257–9   *Thai*
☎ 0 2236 7045, 14 Soi Th Wiang, Th Surasak; dishes 90-150B; ⏰ 11.30am-9.30pm; Skytrain Surasak
Named after the archaeological site in north-eastern Thailand, Ban Chiang is a great place for traditional Thai and Isan cuisine. Occupying a restored wooden house with eclectic décor, this restaurant calms urban-frayed nerves with *yam plaa duk foo*, *phàt phàk khánáa* and *kài phàt khĭng hèt hăwm* (chicken stir-fried with mushroom and ginger). Once you pass the Holiday Inn Hotel, hang a left on Soi Si Wiang and look for the jungle-like garden barely tamed by an overwhelmed wooden fence.

BLUE ELEPHANT Map pp262–3   *Thai*
☎ 0 2673 9353; 233 Th Sathon Tai; dishes 200-500B; ⏰ 11am-2pm & 5-11pm; Skytrain Surasak
The Blue Elephant got its start in Brussels more than two decades ago as an exotic outpost of royal Thai cuisine. After spreading to other foreign cities, the Blue Elephant boldly chose Bangkok, the cuisine's birth mother, as its 9th location. Set in a refurbished Sino-Thai colonial building with service fit for royalty, this newcomer promises fine dining within striking distance of the city's luxury hotels. Many visiting businesspeople are wined and dined here.

Skip the set meals and choose wisely from the extensive menu of modernised traditional dishes – which range from simple to elaborate. *Lâap salmon* (salad with mint leaves) and mesquite-flavoured *phàk bûng fai daeng* (stir-fried greens) are divine, while the *kaeng mátsàmàn* (Muslim lamb curry) is too sweet. The Blue Elephant is near St Louis Hospital.

BUSSARACUM Map pp257–9   *Thai*
☎ 0 2266 6312, Sethiwan Bldg; 139 Th Pan off Th Silom; dishes 250-500B; ⏰ 11am-2pm & 5-11pm; Skytrain Surasak
Pronounced 'boot-sa-ra-kam', this restaurant's speciality is royal Thai cuisine. It uses recipes that were created for the royal court in days past and kept secret from commoners until late last century. Every dish (like the carved squash gourd stuffed with seafood) is supposedly prepared only when ordered, from fresh ingredients and freshly ground spices. Live classical Thai music adds to the elegance of the restaurant.

CHAII KARR Map pp257–9   *Thai*
☎ 0 2233 2549; Th Silom; ⏰ 10.30am-9.30pm; Skytrain Surasak
Across from the Holiday Inn and a few shops east of Central department store, this restaurant is a solid choice for Thai food. The Thai mango salad and spicy seafood soup get rave reviews, as do the 19 varieties of brewed coffee. Thai folk music plays in the background, and the dining room is decorated in a wooden Thai-country style.

CHENNAI CHETTINADUMESS
Map pp257–9   *Indian*
☎ 0 2635 6609; 68 Soi 22, Th Silom; dishes 70-100B; ⏰ 11am-8pm; ferry Tha Oriental
Down a small *soi* opposite the Sri Mariamman Temple, this modest South Indian establishment

---

Top Five Silom & Surawong Eats

- **Ban Chiang** (left) A dressed-up version of northeastern Thai cuisine.
- **Chennai Chettinadumess** (above) For a taste of India, stop into this simple storefront.
- **Eat Me Restaurant** (p117) Creative fusion with urban sensibilities.
- **Harmonique** (p117) A refreshing refuelling station.
- **Muslim Restaurant** (p118) Point, sit and eat – easier than an automatic camera.

has delicious vegetarian thali. Although it's not a Sri Lankan restaurant *per se*, authentic string hoppers and a few other Sinhalese specialities are also on the menu.

EAT ME RESTAURANT

Map pp257–9   *International*

☎ 0 2238 0931; Soi Phiphat 2, off Th Convent; dishes 200-400B; ⏰ 6pm-1am; Skytrain Sala Daeng

The facilitator of Bangkok's emergence as a cosmopolitan diva, Eat Me Restaurant creatively merges the denizens' cuisines into a riveting fusion meal. Try the luscious tuna tartare, glass-noodle spring rolls and five-lettuce salad. Chic, minimalist décor is accessorised by a quick-draw cell-phone crowd and a bimonthly rotation of contemporary Thai art. A weekend jazz band fills the spaces in between.

FOLIES CAFÉ-PATISSERIE

Map pp260–1   *French Bakery*

☎ 0 2678 4100; ground fl, Alliance Française, 29 Th Sathon Tai; dishes 50-100B; ⏰ 11am-2pm; ordinary bus 17

Delicate pastries and other French treats are served in this air-conditioned bakery graced with voluptuous display cases and small café tables. An out-of-the-way spot to visit on its own, Folies is a fabulous midday repose for guests at the nearby Sukhothai and Banyan Tree Hotels.

HARMONIQUE Map pp257–9   *Thai*

☎ 0 2237 8175; Soi 34, Th Charoen Krung; dishes 60-150B; ⏰ 11am-10pm Mon-Sat; ferry Tha Oriental or Tha Meaung Khae

The entrance of this *soi* is marked by a psychedelic candy cane arch which belongs to the nearby temple. Down the *soi* on the right is this tiny but refreshing oasis, set in a former Chinese residence. European-managed and unobtrusive, Harmonique serves Thai food, French and Chinese bread plus a variety of tea, fruit shakes and coffee to be enjoyed at Hokkien-style marble-topped tables – a comfortable spot to read while quenching your thirst.

HIMALI CHA-CHA Map pp257–9   *Indian*

☎ 0 2235 1569; 1229/11 Th Charoen Krung; dishes 135-215B; ⏰ 11am-3.30pm & 6-10.30pm; ferry Tha Oriental

Featuring North Indian cuisine (veggie and meat options), Himali Cha-Cha is reminiscent

Street Food in Silom

The **Soi Pradit (Soi 20) Market** assembles in front of the Masjid Mirasuddeen mosque every day. Daytime vendors sell fresh fruit, takeaway meals and quick noodle dishes. The street really comes alive at night when more sit-down stalls appear. **Talat ITF (Soi 10)** has a string of foodstalls running the length of the *soi*, purveying pots of curry and miles of noodles. Lunch time eats can also be found on Soi Sala Daeng 2 and on Soi 7. A midday vendor ekes out a small business selling *khâo mòk kài* (chicken biryani) in front the Irish X-Change. **Talat Sam Yan (Map pp257-9; cnr Th Phayathai & Th Rama IV; ⏰ noon-midnight)** has glorious food stalls on the ground floor.

of college-town Indian joints where the décor mimics the hippy students' dorm rooms and the food is exciting to diners who have just escaped mama's kitchen. The founder, Cha-Cha, worked as a chef for India's last Viceroy; his son has taken over the kitchen here. The staff are conscientious about timing the arrival of dishes to coincide with Western customs of ordering separately. There are also **branches** on Th Convent (☎ 0 2238 1478) and Soi 35, Th Sukhumvit (☎ 0 2258 8843).

INDIA HUT Map pp257–9   *Indian*

☎ 0 2635 7876; Th Surawong; dishes 90-250B; ⏰ 11am-10pm; ferry Tha Oriental

Bearing a self-styled logo that blatantly rips off Pizza Hut, this Indian restaurant, across the freeway from the Manorha Hotel, specialises in Nawabi (Lucknow) cuisine. Try the vegetarian samosas, fresh prawns cooked with ginger or the homemade *paneer* in tomato and onion curry. The modern Indian décor (translation: stiff white tablecloths, upholstered chairs and shopping-mall sterility) is stifling when the restaurant isn't crowded, but once the tables fill up, the place feels like a palace.

IRISH X-CHANGE Map pp257–9   *Western*

☎ 0 2266 7160; 1-4 Sivadon Building, Th Convent; dishes 200-380B; ⏰ lunch & dinner; Skytrain Sala Daeng

Western businesspeople beat a path to this Irish pub, formerly named Shenanigans, for the set lunch buffet (270B; Monday to Friday). Other Western dishes are the perfect companion for a tall glass of suds.

Eating – Silom & Surawong

KHUN CHURN

Map pp257–9   *Vegetarian Thai*

☎ 0 2236 9410; Soi 10, Th Sathon Neua; dishes 30–65B; ☽ 11am-8pm; Skytrain Chong Nonsi

The eponymous movie star, who played the Little Mermaid in the Thai adaptation, owns this low-key vegetarian restaurant in the grounds of the Saengaroom Ashram. Mushrooms play a starring role in many of the dishes, and meat has been totally blacklisted.

MANGO TREE Map pp257–9   *Thai*

☎ 0 2236 2820; 37 Soi Than Tawan, Th Surawong; dishes from 150B; ☽ 11am-10pm; Skytrain Sala Daeng

In an elegant wooden Thai house, Mango Tree is cultured and serene, with evening sessions of traditional Thai music. Recommended dishes include *plaa sãmlii dàet diaw* (half-dried, half-fried cottonfish with spicy mango salad) and *kài bai toei* (chicken baked in pandanus leaves). Mango Tree can also be approached by Soi 6, Th Silom.

MATOI CHAYA Map pp257–9   *Japanese*

☎ 0 2632 7853; 9/16-17 Soi Thaniya; mains 80-250B; Skytrain Sala Daeng

For authentic and inexpensive sushi, head to this old-style sushi bar at the Th Surawong end of Soi Thaniya. Just look for the giant fibreglass model of Godzilla outside.

MIZU'S KITCHEN Map pp257–9   *Japanese*

☎ 0 2233 6447; Soi Patpong 1, Th Silom; dishes 150-200B ; ☽ 11am-3pm; Skytrain Sala Daeng

With a loyal Japanese and Thai following, Mizu's pleases with inexpensive but good Japanese-style steak. The place accidentally evokes an Italian trattoria with chequered tablecloths and a crooning Sinatra as background music. Just as Mizu's locks its heavy wooden door, its neighbouring go-go bars are waking up for another night of ping-pong shows.

MUSLIM RESTAURANT

Map pp257–9   *Muslim*

1356 Th Charoen Krung; dishes under 40B; ☽ 10am-8pm; ferry Tha Oriental

Near the intersection of Th Charoen Krung and Th Silom, this aptly named restaurant has been feeding various Lonely Planet authors for more than 20 years. The faded walls and stainless-steel tables are the opposite of smart décor, but an assortment of curries and roti are displayed in a clean glass case for easy pointing and eye-catching allure.

NAAZ Map pp257–9   *Muslim-Thai*

Soi 43/Soi Saphan Yao, Th Charoen Krung; dishes 50-70B; ☽ 7.30am-10.30pm Mon-Sat; ferry Tha Oriental

Around the corner from the central post office is the popular but basic Naaz (pronounced

---

Hotel Restaurants

Before Bangkok really grew into its urban skin, the luxury hotels provided the city with the most elaborate and sophisticated dining. The restaurants were lavishly decorated and subsidised by the hotel, and provided quality on par with their Western counterparts. But now, as independent restaurants push Bangkok into culinary frontiers, the hotel restaurants have assumed a more traditional role of catering to out-of-town guests, as venues for business meetings and as status symbols. One area where the hotel restaurants still excel is the buffet (lunch, dinner and Sunday brunch). The huge spread offers a one-stop introduction to Thai food, a homesick splurge for Western fare or a user-friendly dim sum exploration. Reservations are recommended.

Angelini (Map pp257-9; ☎ 0 2236 7777; Shangri-La Hotel, 89 Soi Wat Suan Phlu; mains 500B) Manages to be simultaneously grand and relaxed, with excellent décor and Italian cuisine, and an intimate setting overlooking the river. Too bad there is no buffet to ease the bill blow.

Colonnade Restaurant (Map pp260-3; ☎ 0 2287 0222; 1st fl, Sukhothai Hotel, 13/3 Th Sathon; set menu 1200-1500B; Sun brunch 11am-3pm) Offers a cultishly popular Sunday brunch with free-flowing champagne and exquisite selections: made-to-order lobster bisque, caviar, imported cheeses and foie gras. A jazz trio supplies background music.

Emperor Chinese Restaurant (Map pp257-9; ☎ 0 2962 2824; Montien Hotel, Th Rama III; daily lunch buffet 700-900B) Does a relaxed but impressive dim sum buffet.

JW (Map pp264-5; ☎ 0 2656 7700; JW Marriott, 4 Soi 2, Th Sukhumvit; buffet 900B) Has American-style abundance with fresh oysters, seafood, pasta and Japanese food at its daily buffet.

Lord Jim's (Map pp257-9; ☎ 0 2236 0400; Oriental Hotel, Soi Oriental, Th Charoen Krung; lunch buffet 900B) A river-view restaurant designed to imitate the interior of a 19th-century Asian steamer; the menu focuses on seafood.

Dinner Cruises

The river is lovely in the evenings, with the skyscrapers' lights twinkling in the distance and a cool breeze lulling Bangkok to sleep. A dozen or more companies run regular dinner cruises along Mae Nam Chao Phraya. Some are mammoth boats so brightly lit inside that you'd never know you were on the water; others are more sedate and intimate, allowing patrons to see the surroundings. Several of the dinner boats cruise under the well-lit Saphan Phra Ram IX, the longest single-span cable-suspension bridge in the world.

Loy Nava (Map pp246-7; ☎ 0 2437 4932, 0 2437 7329; set menu 1120B, alcohol extra; dinner 6-8pm & 8-10pm) Travels from Tha Si Phraya and offers a more swanky dinner cruise.

Manohra (Map pp246-7; ☎ 0 2677 6240; fax 0 2677 6246; Bangkok Marriott Resort & Spa, 257/1-3 Th Charoen Nakorn; 1650B, plus tax & service; dinner 7.30-10pm) A restored rice barge, Manohra is the grandest of them all.

Yok Yor Restaurant (Map pp257-9; ☎ 0 2437 1121; dishes 100-200B; dinner 8-10pm) A floating restaurant on the Thonburi side of the river (Tha Wisut Kasat) also runs a dinner cruise to Saphan Phra Ram IX. You order from a regular menu – try the *hàw mòk* (fish curry) – and pay a nominal charge for the boat service.

'Naat' in Thai), with the richest *khâo mòk kài* (Thai Muslim-style chicken biryani) in the city. The milk tea is also very good, and daily specials include chicken *masala* and mutton korma. For dessert, the house speciality is *firni*, a Middle Eastern pudding spiced with coconut, almonds, cardamom and saffron.

NEW MADRAS CAFÉ Map pp257–9 *Indian*
☎ 0 2635 0956; 31/10-11 Soi 13 (Trok Vaithi), Th Silom; dishes 30-70B; ⏲ 9.30am-10pm; Skytrain Chong Nonsi
At the end of the *soi*, this Indian restaurant recently received the inexplicable prefix of

'New'. It still operates out of the converted living room of an Indian guesthouse where homestyle South Indian food (such as *dosa*, *idli*, and *vada*) is served. Part of the charm here is the outgoing Indian lodgers who are happy to wave in a new face.

O'REILLY'S IRISH PUB
Map pp257–9 *Western*
☎ 0 2632 7515; 62/1-2 Th Silom at Soi Thaniya; ⏲ 11am-2am; Skytrain Sala Daeng
At the entrance to Thaniya Plaza, this 'Thairish' pub, a Thai-Irish hybrid, features a popular lunch

Food stalls line the Nonthaburi riverside promenade

Culinary Reader

If you can tear yourself away from the B-grade movies on Star channel, a cerebral pastime is to learn to read Thai. A serious study session with the curly script might not engender an understanding of the newspaper or sacred texts, but you will gain the tools to read something more useful: a Thai menu. Scrawled on poster boards in simple food shops, illuminated in signs affixed to *rot khěn* (vendor carts) and printed in well-thumbed menus, a treasure-trove of food possibilities will deliver you from the monotony of ordering *khâo phàt* (fried rice) or *phàt thai* (fried noodles with vegetables, egg and tofu) every time you sidle up to a plastic table. You'll also be able to track down the names of some of those incredible dishes shared with Thais that too much Singha made you forget as soon as you asked.

A useful study aid is a menu with pictures and names of dishes written in Thai and a Roman transliteration (or English translation). Once you start sounding out the Thai, you'll realise that *'kaeng jèut'* sounds so much more appetising than 'bland soup'.

buffet (195B) and has an evening happy hour. Bring something long-sleeved as the air-con turns the well-polished room into an arctic zone.

RAMENTEI Map pp257–9 *Japanese*
☎ 0 2234 8082; Soi 6 (Than Tawan), Th Silom; mains 100-140B; ⏰ 6-11pm; Skytrain Sala Daeng
For no-nonsense Japanese fast food, go to this busy canteen on Soi 6. Tables are arranged around a large open kitchen, and the ramen noodles come fast and furious. There are **branches** on Soi Thaniya (Map pp007-00) and Soi Lang Suan (Map pp009-00).

SALLIM RESTAURANT
Map pp257–9 *Muslim*
☎ 0 2237 1060; Soi 32, Th Charoen Krung; dishes 50-80B; ⏰ 11am-9pm; ferry Tha Si Phraya
This could easily win the dubious and challenging award for the dirtiest restaurant in Thailand, but the food is fabulous. Don't even bother looking at the English menu, which in no way corresponds to the daily offerings. Instead leap into one of the meat curries (*kaeng kài, néua* or *plaa*) served with your choice of rice or roti.

SILOM VILLAGE TRADE CENTRE
Map pp257–9 *Thai*
☎ 0 2234 4448; dishes 150-400B; ⏰ 6-10pm; ferry Tha Oriental

The centrepiece of a mini resort, Silom Village's open-air restaurant is an unabashed tourist spot that maintains fairly high standards. Serenaded by traditional Thai musicians, diners partake in fresh seafood and Chinese, Thai and Japanese dishes.

SOMBOON SEAFOOD Map pp257–9 *Thai*
☎ 0 2233 3104; cnr Th Surawong & Th Narathiwat Ratchanakharin; dishes 150-250B; ⏰ 4pm-midnight; Skytrain Sala Daeng
Towards the eastern end of Th Surawong, about a 10-minute walk west of Montien Hotel, Somboon's is known for having the best crab curry in town. Soy-steamed seabass (*plaa kà-phong nêung sii-íu*) is also a speciality. The dining room is a human-sized version of the fish tanks where the daily specials bide their time, making diners wonder if they are on display as tasty evening morsels.

SOI NGAM DUPHLI
This traveller enclave doesn't deserve a trip just to sample the food, but if you find yourself nearby there are several neighbourhood standards that are worth chewing on.

JUST ONE Map pp260–1 *Thai*
☎ 0 2679 7932; 58 Soi 1, Th Sathon Tai; dishes 50-100B; ⏰ 8am-7pm; air-con bus 507, ordinary bus 13, 14, 74, 109, 115 & 116
A popular lunch spot, Just One woks up the Thai standards in the parking lot across from the Tungmahamek Privacy Hotel and beside the Malaysia Hotel.

MALI Map pp260–1 *Thai & Western*
☎ 0 2679 8693; Soi 1 Th Sathon; dishes 50-150B; ⏰ 11am-10pm; air-con bus 507, ordinary bus 13, 14, 74, 109, 115 & 116
The regular neighbourhood characters stop into this homely restaurant serving Thai and Western food. Inside the restaurant, each surface is covered with knick-knacks, posters and Thai handicrafts celebrating a 1950s revival.

RATSSTUBE Map pp260–1 *German*
☎ 0 2287 2822; Soi Goethe; dishes 200-350B; ⏰ 11am-2.30pm & 5.30-10pm Mon-Fri, 11am-10pm Sat & Sun; air-con bus 507, ordinary bus 13, 14, 74, 109, 115 & 116
Next door to the Goethe Institut, off Soi Atakanprasit, this German restaurant makes homemade sausages and offers hearty set lunches (120B) to a large and sturdy clientele. The softly lit Euro-Asian décor borders on rococo.

TH SUKHUMVIT

Th Sukhumvit, stretching east all the way to the city limits, is the most international in Bangkok in its culinary landscape, thanks to the various expat enclaves of Westerners, Japanese and Middle Easterners. Oddly, Sukhumvit has few Thai restaurants other than the ubiquitous food stalls. Except for the restaurants in Little Arabia and a few notables, you'll be happier with your food hunting if you travel to the higher-numbered *soi* beyond Soi Asoke. Lower Sukhumvit gets such a deluge of sex tourists that restaurants just adopt a German-sounding name and reap the profits.

AYUBOWAN Map pp264–5 *Sri Lankan*

☎ 0 2253 2757; 43 Soi 8, Th Sukhumvit; mains 100–180B; ☷ 6-11pm; Skytrain Nana

Hidden away in a mammoth private house off Soi 8, this restaurant provides fine-quality Sri Lankan cuisine. The red-hot fish curries are accompanied with Sri Lankan hoppers, which are pancakes made of rice flour and coconut milk.

BEI OTTO Map pp264–5 *German*

☎ 0 2262 0892; 1 Soi 20 (Soi Nam Phung), Th Sukhumvit; mains 300-500B; ☷ 6-11pm Mon-Sat, 11.30am-2.30pm Sun; Skytrain Phrom Phong

Amid speeding motorcycle taxis and hulking pushcarts, this cute Bavarian-style cottage is as out of place as Dorothy's hurricane-blown house in The Wizard of Oz. Claiming a Bangkok residence for nearly 20 years, Bei Otto's major culinary bragging point is its pork knuckles, reputedly the best in town. There is also a comfortable bar with the requisite German beers and an attached bakery, deli and butcher shop.

BIER-KUTSCHE Map pp264–5 *German*

☎ 0 2252 5776; 4 Soi 15, Th Sukhumvit; dishes 120-200B; ☷ breakfast, lunch & dinner; Skytrain Asoke

Formerly Haus Munchen, this comfortable restaurant serves big plates of German and Austrian food and home-brewed beer.

BOURBON ST BAR & RESTAURANT

Map pp264–5 *American*

☎ 0 2259 0328; 29/4-6 Soi 22, behind Washington Theatre; mains 150-300B; ☷ breakfast, lunch & dinner; Skytrain Asoke & Phrom Phong

Guide to Kŭaytĭaw

The *kŭaytĭaw* (rice noodle) addiction takes a while to cultivate, but once it clicks you'll spend all of your time searching for the perfect bowl of noodles. Now you've joined an unofficial sport in Thailand, the noodle hunt, or more precisely, the broth hunt. Meaty, salty and complex, a good broth is the foundation upon which the other ingredients display their personality.

What is truly amazing about such a simple dish (noodles, broth and sundries) is the nearly infinite variation. The starter set is *kŭaytĭaw náam*, noodles with chicken or beef broth and *phák chii* (coriander leaf). The steaming bowl is then seasoned to taste with a little fish sauce, sugar, chilli and vinegar.

The biggest choice at this level is the size of the rice noodle: *sên yài* (flat and wide), *sên lék* (thin) and *sên mǐi* (extra thin, usually dried). Most vendors offer *kŭaytĭaw lûuk chín plaa* (noodles with fishballs), but they come with a warning: fishballs can be an acquired taste. This basic noodle dish can be found on any street corner or market, day or night.

Another kind of noodles are wheat and egg noodles *(bàmìi)*, which are usually corkscrew-shaped and yellowish in colour. *Bàmìi* come in two varieties (flat and round) and usually star alongside duck *(bàmìi pèt)*. One well-known duck noodle vendor is tucked into a little *soi* off Th Chakraphong, near Th Khao San (Map pp254–5). Look for a Converse shoe sign that marks the entry to the *soi*. **Pet Tun Jao Tha** (see p112) specialises in duck and goose with *kŭaytĭaw*.

Once you've taken this step in your noodle evolution, it is time to explore other meat options. Hanging in the glass display cases like a leathery shoe sole dipped in red paint, *mùu daeng* (barbecued pork) is your next assignment. If you're in the neighbourhood, a noodle vendor on Soi 71, Th Sukhumvit, does a tasty *bàmìi mùu daeng* (Map pp264–5), but there are plenty of other vendors all over town. A noodle shop on Th Phra Athit, near Soi Chana Songkhram, does a famous bowl of *kŭaytĭaw néua* (beef noodles); the meat is so silky and tender and the broth so flavourful that you barely need to spice it with the provided condiments. Other noteworthy noodle vendors set up on Soi 38, Th Sukhumvit, at night (see p264–5).

Ascending one more rung to noodle nirvana is the highly acquired taste of *yen taa foh* (pickled squid and a kind of tofu). You'll be able to spot this by the pinkish hue imparted to the bowl of noodles by the food colouring added to the tofu. This dish isn't for everyone, however, so tread lightly. A **Yan Tah Noodle Shop** (Map pp254-5), on Th Samsen between Soi 8 and Soi 10 is so swamped with *yen-taa-foh* lovers that the servers plead for the customers to be patient *(jai yen)* as bowls are given to earlier arrivals.

- **Crepes & Co** (below) Sunday brunch and light Mediterranean fare served in a relaxed garden villa.
- **Govinda** (right) Rescuing vegetarians from culinary doldroms, this is Italian without the meat.
- **La Piola** (p123) The best Italian food this side of the boot.
- **Le Dalat** (p123) A flashback to colonial Vietnam through sight and taste.
- **Vientiane Kitchen** (p125) Like a trip to the provinces, with nightly music too.

Nostalgic visitors from the USA, especially those from the south, will appreciate this well-run Creole outpost. Barbecue ribs, blackened shrimp and catfish are so finger-lickin' good that even Thais feel proud to be American here. A few Mexican items have emigrated on to the menu, and the salsa is the best in town. The breakfast staff get kudos for mastering the ability to deliver warm toast.

CABBAGES & CONDOMS

Map pp264–5 *Thai*
☎ 0 2229 4611; Soi 12, Th Sukhumvit; dishes 150-200B; ☺ 11am-10pm; Skytrain Asoke

'Be fed and be sheathed' is the motto of the restaurant outreach program of the Population & Community Development Association (PDA), a sex education-AIDs prevention organisation. The restaurant cooks with familiar vegetables, such as celery and tomatoes, to create sufficiently complex flavours for those 'wading' into Thai food. Dishes like *yam wún sên* (mung-bean noodle salad) provide a source of raw vegetables. Instead of after-meal mints, diners get packaged condoms; all proceeds go towards PDA educational programmes in Thailand.

CHINA JOURNAL Map pp264–5 *Chinese*
☎ 0 2712 8589; 41 Soi 55 (Thong Lor), Th Sukhumvit; dishes 150-250B; ☺ 10am-9pm; Skytrain Thong Lor

This Shanghai-inspired tea room brews a meditative pot that claims ancestry from China, Japan and Thailand.

CREPES & CO Map pp264–5 *French*
☎ 0 2653 3990; 18/1 Soi 12, Th Sukhumvit; dishes 140-280B; ☺ 9am-midnight; Skytrain Asoke

This cute cottage creperie, another 50m down the same *soi* as Cabbages & Condoms, invokes involuntary drooling from Bangkok foodies. Crepes of all kinds, brunch classics and a nice selection of Mediterranean dishes are delivered to garden-view tables. A Moroccan menu occasionally makes an appearance.

EMPORIUM SHOPPING CENTER

Map pp264–5 *International*
Soi 24, Th Sukhumvit; ☺ 10am-10pm; Skytrain Phrom Phong

You haven't really earned your stripes as an expat until you know your way around this shopping centre, which does a remarkable job of channelling Los Angeles (minus the blonde bimbos). Conspicuous consumption is on every menu, especially the trendy **Greyhound Café** (2nd fl; dishes 120-200B) with highly prized seating along the main pedestrian hallway – the better view to be seen. Greyhound's hybrid menu emphasises updated Thai standards supplemented by Italian and Mediterranean cuisine; the salads get rave reviews. **Fuji Japanese Restaurant** (4th fl) is always packed with Japanese families. There is also an upmarket food centre on the 5th floor.

GOVINDA Map pp264–5 *Italian Vegetarian*
☎ 0 2663 4970; Soi 22, Th Sukhumvit; mains 150-300B; ☺ 6-11pm; Skytrain Phrom Phong

Recently voted Bangkok's best veggie restaurant, this place cooks up splendid Italian food based on soya and unusual vegetables. The food is so delicious that you'll barely notice there's no meat. The restaurant is near the mouth of the *soi* in the shopping complex, before Larry's Dive Shop.

HUA LAMPHONG FOOD STATION

Map pp264–5 *Thai*
☎ 0 2661 3538; 92/1 Soi 34, Th Sukhumvit; dishes 150-330B; ☺ 6-11pm; Skytrain Thong Lor

Nowhere near Bangkok's main railway station despite the name, Hua Lamphong is so well hidden that your arrival is like a journey to the provinces. Decorated with country Thai furnishings, Hua Lamphong serves delicious Isan and northern Thai food, and has traditional music nightly from 8pm to 10pm. From Th Sukhumvit, take a motorcycle taxi to the restaurant, which is difficult to find on foot.

JOOL'S BAR & RESTAURANT

Map pp264–5 *British*
☎ 0 2252 6413; Soi 4 (Soi Nana Tai); mains 250-300B; ☺ 11am-midnight; Skytrain Ploenchit & Nana

This British-style pub offers huge plates of chilly-weather specialities that square-shouldered expats and their demure Thai girlfriends scoff down without a lick of trouble. Being so close to Nana Entertainment Plaza, this place is often visited for a meal before seeing a strip show.

KUPPA Map pp264–5 *International*
☎ 0 2663 0450-4; 39 Soi 16, Th Sukhumvit; mains 150-490B; closed Mon; Skytrain Asoke

Voted Bangkok's best café, this sublime brick-and-wood place is tucked away on Soi 16, but it's worth going out of your way for the fine Pacific rim cuisine. The steaks here are excellent. The restaurant is anchored deep down into the soi, so don't get discouraged too quickly.

LA PIOLA Map pp264–5 *Italian*
☎ 0 2253 8295; 32 Soi 13, Th Sukhumvit; set menu 1170B; 6-10pm Tue-Sat; Skytrain Nana

It might be sacrilegious to say so, but this Italian eatery is one of Bangkok's best restaurants. Take a seat in the little basement-level dining area among diners speaking every imaginable language and begin the feasting. There is no menu; the only choice you make is what to drink. Three courses, including antipasto, three pasta mains and dessert, will effortlessly

Kuppa received Bangkok's vote (above)

appear while the crowd is serenaded with Italian karaoke. You'll leave unimaginably full and drunk with flavours.

LAICRAM Map pp264–5 *Thai*
☎ 0 2204 1069; Soi 23, Th Sukhumvit; mains 200-300B; 10am-9pm; Skytrain Asoke

A well-hidden gem, opposite Tia Maria, Laicram offers authentic gourmet Thai at sensible prices. The house specialities include hàw mòk hǎwy, a thick fish curry steamed with mussels, and sôm-tam served with khâo man (rice cooked with coconut milk and pandanus leaf).

LE BANYAN Map pp264–5 *French*
☎ 0 2253 5556; 59 Soi 8 (Soi Prida), Th Sukhumvit; dishes 390-450B; 6.30-9.30pm Mon-Sat; Skytrain Nana

One of Bangkok's top French restaurants in the city, Le Banyan is poised in a charming early-Ratanakosin-style house. The kitchen is French-managed, and the menu covers the territory from *ragout d'escargot* (snails in pastry) to *canard maigret avec foie gras* (wild duck with goose liver), complemented by a superb wine list. The restaurant is further down the *soi* than you would expect; keep an eye out for the artistically trimmed bamboo hedge.

LE DALAT Map pp264–5 *Vietnamese*
☎ 0 2258 4192, 0 2260 1849; 14 Soi 23, Th Sukhumvit; dishes 200-600B; 11.30am-2.30pm & 6-10pm; Skytrain Asoke

The city's most celebrated Vietnamese cuisine is served here in a gracious wooden house in a garden compound. Don't overlook *nǎem neuang*, grilled meatballs that you place on steamed rice-flour wrappers, adding chunks of garlic, chilli, ginger, starfruit and mango along with a tamarind sauce, before wrapping the whole thing into a lettuce bundle and popping it in your mouth. There's another **branch** further up the road at 47/1 Soi 23, Th Sukhumvit, that looks so similar you'll feel Vietnamese-inspired *déjà vu*.

LITTLE ARABIA Map pp264–5 *Arabic*
Btwn Soi 3 (Soi Nana Neua) & Soi 3/1, Th Sukhumvit; Skytrain Nana

Little Arabia is a dense bazaar of restaurants run by nationals from Egypt, Nigeria, Pakistan and Lebanon, to name a few. **Al Hussain** (75/7 Soi 3/1; dishes 100-200B), a covered outdoor café, prepares a range of vegetarian, chicken,

Eating – Th Sukhumvit

Le Dalat is renowned for its Vietnamese cuisine (opposite)

mutton and fish curries, along with dhal, *aloo gobi* (spicy potatoes and cauliflower), naan and rice. Across the street are several hookah restaurants where Middle Eastern gentlemen while away the afternoon. The Indian subcontinent claims a few restaurants on the western side of Soi 3 (Soi Nana Neua). When the area is in full swing, it is pretty tough to differentiate one restaurant from another – go with a spirit of adventure.

MOUSSES & MERINGUES

Map pp264–5 *Western*
☎ 0 2662 1290; fax 0 2662 1290; 245 Soi 31 (Sawasdee), Th Sukhumvit; cakes 25B per piece, 700B whole; 10am-7pm; Skytrain Phrom Phong
Not that you need help finding desserts in Thailand, but if your cravings crawl towards cakes and pastries, this neighbourhood bakery can fill the void. With gleaming display cases full of decadent treats, Mousses is a popular stop for the borrowed tradition of birthday cakes. If you're treating a Thai, try the strawberry cake, which is in high demand. But be warned: these delicacies will swoon like a Southern belle in the tropical heat.

MRS BALBIR'S Map pp264–5 *Indian*
☎ 0 2651 0498; 155/18 Soi 11/1, Th Sukhumvit; dishes 120-270B; noon-10.30pm Tue-Sun; Skytrain Nana

Beside the Swiss Park Hotel, Mrs Balbir's offers vegetarian and nonvegetarian Indian food (mostly North Indian) to a predominantly tourist crowd. But don't write off the food. The Mrs still knows her stuff; she has been teaching Indian and Thai cooking for many years and has her own TV show. Cooking classes are offered on weekends if you become a devoted fan.

POMODORO Map pp264–5 *Italian*
☎ 0 2655 1248; 2 Sukhumvit, btwn Soi 7 & Soi 7/1; dishes 110-200B; 10am-10pm; Skytrain Nana
Part of a city-wide chain, Pomodoro specialises in Sardinian cuisine and has more than 25 pasta dishes. The wine list encompasses vintages from nine regions in Italy, along with others from France, Australia and the USA; the house red isn't bad. There is another **branch** on the ground floor of the Nai Lert Building on Th Sukhumvit (between Soi 3 and Soi 5).

RANG MAHAL Map pp264–5 *Indian*
☎ 0 2261 7100; Soi 18, Th Sukhumvit, Rembrandt Hotel; dishes 150-230B; 11am-11pm; Skytrain Asoke
With sky-high dining and an all-you-can-eat buffet, Bangkok really is the 'City of Angels'. Atop the Rembrandt Hotel, Rang Mahal specialises in northern and southern Indian 'royal cuisine', and the buffet is offered every Sunday

(adult/child 575/295B; 🕐 11am-2pm). During the week, set lunches of nonvegetarian (350B) and vegetarian (325B) dishes are available in addition to an à la carte menu. An open-air observation platform on the same floor is reason enough for a visit.

SEÑOR PICO'S OF LOS ANGELES

Map pp264–5 *Mexican*
☎ 0 2261 7100; 2nd fl, Rembrandt Hotel, Soi 18, Th Sukhumvit; dishes 250-500B; 🕐 6-11pm; Skytrain Asoke

If you're looking for Mexican food, the city's best can be found at Señor Pico's. This brightly decorated, festive restaurant offers reasonably authentic Tex-Mex cuisine, including fajitas, *carnitas* and nachos. Live Latin music is the norm most evenings; the dress code prohibits sleeveless shirts or sandals.

SOI 38 NIGHT MARKET

Map pp264–5 *Thai-Chinese*
Soi 38, Th Sukhumvit; 🕐 8am-midnight; Skytrain Thong Lor

Night noshing happens with panache at this gourmet night market. Taste a crowded bowl of *kŭaytĭaw* Hong Kong or Chinese-style spring rolls.

SONIE'S Map pp264–5 *Japanese*
☎ 0 2258 8336; 9/2 Soi 39 (Soi Phrompong), Th Sukhumvit; mains 150-220B; 🕐 11.30am-2pm & 5.30-10pm Tue-Sun; Skytrain Phrom Phong

Japanese-Thai fusion gets invited to a family dinner at this informal café. The din of eating and conversation will meet you like an exuberant puppy.

TAMARIND CAFÉ

Map pp264–5 *International Vegetarian*
☎ 0 2663 7421; 27 Soi 20, Th Sukhumvit; mains 200-250B; 🕐 11am-9pm; Skytrain Asoke

Pacific Rim cuisine goes vegetarian at this sleek eatery. Imaginative fresh juice concoctions will stave off a cold or transport you to a long-forgotten beach vacation. Main dishes fuse Asia's heavyweight cuisines with a Californian sensibility for freshness and flavour. The less health-conscious drool over the highly praised cheesecakes. Tamarind also shares space with Gallery F-Stop, which presents rotating photography exhibits. Unlike other restaurant galleries in town, Tamarind allows visitors to approach the artwork without peering over a fellow diner's shoulder.

Wine Pairings

Experts in matters of wine and food have noted that Thai food is tricky to match. But they do offer a few basic guiding principals: choose an acidic Chardonnay for fried dishes and a medium-bodied Merlot for duck.

Another word of advice is to stick to younger vintages that are less fragile than older ones. Thailand's tropical climate and inconsistent attention to storage can quickly ruin an easily bruised (older) wine.

THONGLEE Map pp264–5 *Thai*
☎ 0 2258 1983; Soi 20, Th Sukhumvit; mains 40-70B; 🕐 9am-8pm; closed 3rd Sun of the month; Skytrain Asoke

In any other neighbourhood, Thonglee would be nearly indistinguishable from all the other shopfront wok shops. Instead of being transformed into a massage parlour or visa-wedding service, Thonglee offers a more nutritious service: rice and curries.

VEGA CAFÉ Map pp264–5 *Thai*
☎ 0 2258 8273, 0 2662 6471; 32/1 Soi 39, Th Sukhumvit; dishes 80-150B; 🕐 6pm-midnight; Skytrain Phrom Phong

This casual restaurant is lesbian-owned and a low-key gathering place for Thai lesbians. A keyboardist and singer serenade the crowd during dinner, and an upstairs lounge has karaoke.

VIENTIANE KITCHEN

Map pp264–5 *Northeastern Thai*
☎ 0 2258 6171; 8 Soi 36, Th Sukhumvit; dishes 120-200B; 🕐 11am-midnight; Skytrain Thong Lor

Near the beginning of the *soi*, Vientiane Kitchen is easier to find than Hua Lamphong Food Station (see p122). You'll find all the Isan and Lao 'soul-food' standards, such as *lâap* with duck lips, fried frog and deep-fried chicken innards. Smothered in chilli peppers, you'll swear you're eating chicken breast. For the less daring, there are plenty of middle-of-the-road options too. A *măw lam* band, seating on the floor and rotating fans create an amazing approximation of Isan and a relaxed cultural display, but the hallucinatory spiciness of the food and sweaty bottles of Chang beer might be more to blame. Be sure to tip the band on your way out; no matter the amount, they'll announce to the crowd that it was 1000B.

GREATER BANGKOK

The area around Victory Monument has some interesting food options and is easily accessible on the Skytrain. You'll be sharing stools with local university students and hardly a foreigner in sight.

PICKLE FACTORY

Map pp248–9   *International*

☎ 0 2246 3036; 55 Soi 21, Th Ratwithi; dishes 150-200B; ⊙ 5.30-11.30pm; Skytrain Victory Monument

---

Dining with a View

- **Crepes & Co** (p122) An idyllic view of a cottage tropical garden surrounds this breezy restaurant.
- **Little Arabia restaurants** (p123) People of all shapes, ethnicities and sizes file through this narrow marketplace.
- **Rang Mahal** (p124) A sea of concrete towers meets the horizon from this rooftop perch.
- **Ton Pho** (p111) Watch the muddy Mekhong, hulking barge boats and zippy long-tail boats.
- **Victory Point** (right) From here the view of a provincial-style night bazaar is an eyeful.

A bit of a trek outside your normal sphere, the Pickle Factory occupies a 1970s-vintage Thai house that has been converted into a cosy restaurant, replete with indoor sofa-seating areas, outdoor tables, fully stocked bar and a swimming pool – in short, the perfect place to kick back for an evening with friends. The menu includes Western dishes such as Chiang Mai sausage pizzas, smoked chicken wings and stuffed mussels, as well as Thai mango salads. Take a taxi or the long, dreary walk and the threat of *soi* dogs might drive you away empty-handed.

VICTORY POINT Map pp248–9   *Thai*
Th Phayathai & Th Ratwithi; mains 25-30B;
⊙ 6am-10pm; Skytrain Victory Monument

Lining the busy roundabout is a squat village of concrete stalls lit in neon under the collective title 'Victory Point'. A mix of food and market-goods vendors open their stalls after dark, feeding the hungry residents of Victory Monument. Overhead, the real drama unfolds as university students cruise the elevated walkways in an age-old mating ritual. Bad boys show off their break-dancing moves or their disaffected Sid Vicious sneers, and the girls just melt over a wild one.

Entertainment

Entertainment

Bangkok's entertainment scene goes well beyond its naughty-nightlife image, a hangover from the days when the City of Angels was an R&R stop for GIs serving in Vietnam. Today, Bangkok offers a vast assortment of entertainment venues, from no-nonsense boozing to unabashed flash. Thai students and fashionable yuppies are the greatest consumers of nightlife, allowing Bangkok to develop a home-grown clutch of nightspots.

Parts of Banglamphu near the tourist strip of Th Khao San make up one big outdoor party, where small stalls set up tables and chairs for a night of Beer Chang drinking. A more local scene can be found on weekends at the restaurant-bars along Th Phra Athit (see boxed text, p131).

Lower Th Sukhumvit is a men's playground obsessed with the hostess and go-go bars at Soi Cowboy and Nana Entertainment Plaza (p135). Women might want to venture to upper Sukhumvit where a more diverse expat and yuppie crowd sips wine and fancy cocktails.

> ### Trend Spotter & Event Listings
>
> To get an idea of current happenings around town, check the daily entertainment listings in the *Bangkok Post* and the *Nation* or the monthly *Metro* (www .bkkmetro.com). These publications not only list cultural events, they also report on the latest trends to invade the city. The best source for the line-up at the city's live music clubs is the website www.bangkok gigguide.com.

Th Silom has a number of contrasting night-crawling options, including the go-go-bar-cum-tourist bazaar of Patpong, low-key English-style pubs and unpretentious dance clubs.

Under the Thaksin administration, Bangkok's all-night extravaganza has been put on a tight leash. All bars and clubs are supposed to close at 1am. Despite the city's accommodating nature, the curfew is strictly enforced by stoney-faced policemen who usher out dazed customers. A more conservative measure, which was heroically defeated, proposed a 10.30pm curfew so that patrons would be bright-eyed for morning visits to the temples.

Bartender mixing drinks at Q Bar (p134)

DRINKING

Covering the spectrum from English-style pubs to trendy display cases, Bangkok's watering holes usually provide a laundry list of beers, imported liquor and house cocktails, which despite their various names all taste like Tom Collins mix. Because food is so integral to any Thai outing, most bars have tasty dishes that are absent-mindedly nibbled between toasts. Bars don't have cover charges, but dance clubs generally do and these prices are included in the reviews.

ANA'S GARDEN Map pp264-5
☎ 0 2391 1786; 67 Soi 55 (Thong Lor), Th Sukhumvit;
🕑 5pm-midnight; Skytrain Thong Lor

Ana's lush garden of broad-leafed palms and purring fountains attractively masks the fact that you might have turned into a lush while living in the tropics. Funky house music, an occasional breeze and a table filled with dishes to peck will melt into a sensory tapestry.

BANGKOK BAR Map pp254-5

☎ 0 2629 4443; 149 Soi Rambutri, Banglamphu;
🕐 6pm-midnight; ferry Tha Phra Athit

Next door to Sawasdee House, a little slice of
urban chic has slid into this ratty backpacker
zone. Before the night gets started, smooth
samba beats waft like incense over the bar's
cosy corners where mixed *faràng* (Western)
and Thai couples sip cocktails. As the witch-
ing hour commences, the music picks up
momentum with hip-hop and techno, and
there's a steady stream of cool Thai kids. Most
entertaining are the impassioned pleas from
under-agers to the door enforcer.

BANGKOK BAR Map pp264-5

☎ 0 2391 8346; Soi 2, off of Soi 63 (Ekamai), Th
Sukhumvit; 🕐 6pm-midnight; Skytrain Ekamai

Part of the fashionable Ekamai Soi 2 strip, this
restaurant-bar has outdoor seating, a reserved
atmosphere and a Spanish-Thai menu. DJs
make weekend appearances, creating a more
electric mood. Don't confuse this spot with
the similarly named bar in Banglamphu (see
above).

BARBICAN BAR Map pp257-9

☎ 0 2234 3590; 9 Soi Thaniya, Th Silom;
🕐 6pm-1am; Skytrain Sala Daeng

If you ever feel down about life in sweaty
Bangkok, go directly to the Barbican. How
many cities in the world have an upmarket
yuppie bar in the same block as massage
parlours for Japanese businessmen? Where
else could you suck down a few cocktails with
friends from Thailand, Singapore and Norway,
and then stumble out to find a line of Thai
women dressed like cheap prom dates recit-
ing 'Hello, massage' in faulty Japanese?

BAR-BU-REE Map pp264-5

☎ 0 2392 4976; 59 Soi 63 (Ekamai), Th Sukhumvit;
🕐 6pm-midnight; Skytrain Ekamai

An updated version of a slick Thai nightclub,
Bar-Bu-Ree continues the black-and-chrome
tradition with rollicking house bands, but the
crowd is treated to some unusual pop covers,
such as Blondie's 'The Tide is High'. An outdoor
garden area provides a more romantic setting
and an escape route if the band turns to ballads. Despite the pretentious neighbourhood,
Bar-Bu-Ree isn't painted up with barely clad
pixies; the bartenders and the patrons lean
more towards beast than beauty.

BULL'S HEAD & ANGUS STEAKHOUSE
Map pp264-5

☎ 0 2259 4444; Soi 33/1, Th Sukhumvit; 🕐 6pm-
midnight; Skytrain Phrom Phong

This is a beautiful galleried bar that's well suited
to imagining foggy London nights. Happy
hours, quiz nights and comedy shows provide
much-needed stimulus if your vocabulary is
morphing into Tinglish (Thai-English – dropped
tenses, swapped 'l's and 'r's).

CHEAP CHARLIE'S Map pp264-5

Soi 11, Th Sukhumvit; 🕐 closed Sun; Skytrain Nana

What are all those foreigners doing standing
around that wooden shack? If it looks like fun
(and it is), grab yourself a stool at this neighbourhood beer stall on a sub-*soi* off Soi 11.
Charlie's started out selling cigarettes, gradu-
ated to beer and now has a faithful following
of local characters who stop in after work. Look
for the 'Sabai Sabai Massage' sign to find the
sub-*soi*.

DONG DEA MOON Map pp254-5

☎ 02333 4280; 54/1 Soi Rambutri; 🕐 11am-mid-
night; ferry Tha Phra Athit

From your privileged 2nd-floor perch, you can
heckle the penny-pinching commoners below
or enjoy good tunes and free games of pool.
To reach the open-air balcony, pass through

Top 10 Drinking & Clubbing Spots

- **Ad Here the 13th** (p131) A laid-back tippling spot with a rockin' house band
- **Bamboo Bar** (p132) Great date bar
- **Barbican Bar** (left) Yuppie hang-out amidst a massage parlour strip
- **Cheap Charlie's** (above) Neighbourhood slum-ming and the cheapest beer in Th Sukhumvit
- **Lucifer** (p134) The prince of darkness would be pleased by this rockin' disco
- **Nang Nual Riverside Pub** (p130) Go Thai-style with food, booze and river views
- **Q Bar** (p134) Urban chic delivers Bangkok from third-world exile
- **Saxophone Pub & Restaurant** (p133) Great live music every night
- **Th Khao San** (boxed text on p131) Unrepentant freak show
- **Vertigo** (p131) Drink in the scenery from this sky-high bar

the sweaty Korean restaurant on the ground floor and go up the back stairs.

GULLIVER'S TRAVELER'S TAVERN

Map pp254-5

cnr Th Khao San & Th Chakraphong, Banglamphu; 🕙 11am-midnight; ferry Tha Phra Athit

A lot like your home-town sports bar, Gulliver's woos the crowd with blasting air con and all the must-see football matches. When you tire of contemplating the shape of your beer bottle, turn your skills to the pool tables.

HARD ROCK CAFE Map pp262-3

☎ 0 2254 0830; Soi 11, Siam Square; 🕙 11am-midnight; Skytrain Siam

It gets lonesome in Siam Square after dark, but this global giant, part of the Hard Rock empire, gives night owls something to toast. The guitar-shaped bar features the full range of cocktails and a small assortment of local and imported beers. The crowd is a changing parade of Thais, expats and tourists, and there's live music from 10pm.

IRISH X-CHANGE Map pp257-9

☎ 0 2266 7160; 1-4 Sivadon Building, Th Convent; 🕙 11-1am; Skytrain Sala Daeng

Around the corner from Th Silom, this Irish-style pub serves meaty Guinness draughts. The wooden panels, mirrors and bench seating were all custom-made in Ireland. Bands of varying quality play from Tuesday to Saturday, and the place is often full from 6pm until closing.

Colliding Glasses

Although beer, imported liquor and wine have a strong following among Bangkokians, Thailand's personality emerges in the consumption of rice whisky. Ritualised and communal, whisky is usually sold in a set *(chút)*, which includes a bottle of rice liquor (known by brand names such as Sang Som and Mekong), soda water, cola and ice. Usually the youngest in the group (or a server) is responsible for the preparation and topping off. A glass is filled to the rim with ice, about two fingers of whisky, and soda water with a splash of cola. The combination is refreshing for a hot climate and smoothly intoxicating as the mixers and the whisky quickly disappear. The first sip is usually celebrated with a toast. Thais say *'chon kâew'* (literally 'colliding glasses') for 'cheers'. When clinking glasses together during a toast, keep your glass slightly lower than those of your elders – you'll get kudos for polite tippling.

LARRY'S DIVE CENTER, BAR & GRILL

Map pp264-5

☎ 0 2663 4563; 8/3 Soi 22, Th Sukhumvit; 🕙 11am-midnight; Skytrain Phrom Phong

A bright-yellow building, Larry's Dive Center serves Key West ambience with Canadian humour. Before you dismiss this as an oxymoron, stop in for the weekly specials such as drink-and-dive night (the price of beer drops as the night progresses) or to peruse the fake newspaper menu ('largest circulation of any newspaper on Soi 22'). The signature Canadian drink is the little-known Bloody Caesar (vodka and clam-and-tomato juice) – a post-op version of the Bloody Mary. There's an attached dive shop, should you get the urge to go snorkelling in a nearby canal.

LONDONER BREW PUB Map pp264-5

☎ 0 2261 0238; Soi 33, Th Sukhumvit; 🕙 11am-midnight; Skytrain Phrom Phong

In the basement of the UBC II Building, the Londoner brews its own beers and ales and runs a bevy of promotions to entertain the swillers. Quiz nights, daily happy hours and promotions for expat English-language teachers bring in the crowds. Football matches and rock bands complete the bar's weekly engagements.

NANG NUAL RIVERSIDE PUB

Map pp252-3

☎ 0 2223 7686; Trok Krai, Th Mahachak; 🕙 4pm-midnight; ferry Tha Saphan Phut or Tha Ratchawong

Is it a bar or a restaurant? This outdoor riverside deck is a quintessential example of Thai *sanùk* (fun). This is a drinking and snacking spot where groups of friends gather around the whisky set and plates of *kàp klâem* (drinking food), such as spicy salads *kài sǎam yàang* (grilled chicken with ginger, chilli and lime). If you hit this spot at the right time, the bar's blaring pop music will be competing for valuable air space with the Muslim call to prayer from the temple across the river. Equally impressive is the golden sunset bathing Bangkok's concrete mountain range of skyscrapers.

O'REILLY'S IRISH PUB Map pp257-9

☎ 0 2632 7515; 62/1-2 Th Silom cnr Soi Thaniya; 🕙 11-1am; Skytrain Sala Daeng

Across the *soi* from Thaniya Plaza, O'Reilly's draws a slow pint of Guinness or Kilkenny in a comparatively low-key setting. A Beatles tribute band plays here on weekends.

Top Party Streets

From oversized Euros headbutting each other to sashaying *kàthoey* (transvestites and transsexuals), the nightly carnival on Th Khao San in Banglamphu is as intoxicating as the cheap beer. The sheer number of bodies, variety of languages and untiring dedication to drunkenness on display every night is dazzling – endurance unmatched at other spots in the city. At no point in your time in Bangkok should you develop disdain for this alternative universe (but feel free to jeer at the faux dreadlocks). If you begin to feel jaded, park yourself at one of the pavement tables at Center Khao Sarn, or a similar place, for a front-row homage to the backpacker in us all.

For a different kind of ambience, head east to Th Phra Athit, where a charming stretch of wooden shophouses has been converted into stylish bars and cafés, popular among Thai university students and arty types. Exuding a bohemian confidence, these bars usually host a solo singer and his weeping guitar while patrons share plates of food or plough through bottles of whisky. Most bars are open until midnight.

SHIP INN Map pp264-5
9/1 Soi 23, Th Sukhumvit; 🕙 **11am-midnight; Skytrain Asoke**

Just around the corner from Soi Cowboy, Ship Inn provides a mature embrace for a quiet drinking crowd. The bar is as well stocked as a ship captain's quarters, and the music is at an easy-listening volume.

SUAN AHAHN PA LOET ROT Map pp264-5
☎ **0 2258 5070; Soi 33/1, Th Sukhumvit;** 🕙 **11am-midnight; Skytrain Phrom Phong**

Two doors from Bull's Head, this outdoor restaurant-bar offers escapism for displaced rural Thais. Shaded by the hairlike tendrils of an ancient banyan tree, tipplers are temporarily transported to the drinking dens of the Thai countryside. (Even the squat toilets provide a touch of the country.) Order a whisky set and sweat the night away.

SUSIE PUB & AUSTIN PUB Map pp254-5
☎ **0 2282 4459; Off Th Khao San, Banglamphu;** 🕙 **6am-midnight; ferry Tha Phra Athit**

With teeny-bopper exuberance, these sister pubs are popular with Thai university students celebrating birthdays or just getting hammered. Both are beautiful bars, but the music tends towards too-sweet Western pop music. Susie is on a small *soi* between Th Khao San and Th Rambutri, past Nat Guesthouse. Austin Pub is on a *soi* on the opposite side of Th Khao San, past Siam Oriental Guesthouse.

VERTIGO Map pp260-1
☎ **0 2679 1200; Banyan Tree Hotel, Th Sathon Tai;** 🕙 **weather permitting**

Of all the overhyped hotel bars, Vertigo has the upper hand. This sky-high, open-air bar-restaurant will literally take your breath away. From ground level, the elevator delivers you to the 59th floor, where you weave your way through dimly lit hallways, *wai*-ing attendants and narrow sets of stairs, emerging to the roar of Bangkok traffic far below. Come at sunset and grab a coveted seat to the right of the bar for more impressive views. Don't come thirsty, however, because service is atrocious.

MUSIC

Bangkok's live-music scene has expanded rapidly over the past decade. Most bands, with varying degrees of success, are tributes to Western music; but even if the accent isn't an authentic Mick Jagger, a familiar tune can work wonders on a world wanderer. Th Phra Athit and Th Sarasin are both filled with small live music bars. Other music venues, however, are scattered throughout town.

AD HERE THE 13TH Map pp254-5
13 Th Samsen; 🕙 **6pm-midnight; ferry Tha Phra Athit**

Next door to Khlong Banglamphu, this cramped neighbourhood joint features a soulful house band that plays at 10pm nightly. Their version of 'Me and Bobby McGee' will make you swear Janis Joplin has been reincarnated. Everyone knows each other, so don't be shy about mingling. At the time of research, the police had temporarily discontinued the live music until the correct 'papers' were filed.

AD MAKERS Map pp262-3
☎ **0 2652 0168; 51/51 Soi Lang Suan, Th Ploenchit;** 🕙 **5.30pm-midnight; Skytrain Ploenchit**

This brick box has a homely atmosphere of good times and good friends. A lot of patrons mix drinking and eating – two great pursuits. The house band here does all the classic rock favourites (brace yourself for a heartfelt 'Hotel California') as well as Thai folk.

BAMBOO BAR Map pp257-9
☎ 0 2236 0400; Oriental Hotel, Soi 38 (Oriental), Th Charoen Krung; ⏰ noon-midnight; Skytrain Saphan Taksin, ferry Tha Oriental

The Oriental's Bamboo Bar is famous for its live lounge jazz, which holds court in a colonial-era cabin of lazy fans, broad-leafed palms and rattan décor.

BROWN SUGAR Map pp260-1
☎ 0 2250 1825; 231/20 Th Sarasin; ⏰ 6pm-midnight; Skytrain Chitlom

Not to be overlooked is the strip of music bars along Th Sarasin, including this small jazz club. With a Crescent City informality, Brown Sugar gives inspired performances that are more bebop and brass than the city's usual smooth jazz bands. On Sunday nights, the high-powered musicians touring the luxury hotel network assemble here for impromptu jam sessions.

DALLAS PUB Map pp262-3
☎ 0 2255 3276; Soi 6, Siam Square; ⏰ 5pm-midnight; Skytrain Siam

Fiercely air-conditioned, Dallas Pub is a good warm-up spot for the nearby disco at Concept CM2 (p134). Songs-for-life bands play in the early evening, surrendering the stage to pop-fusion bands with bad hair and tight leather pants.

IMAGERIES BY THE GLASS Map pp264-5
☎ 0 2261 0426; 2 Soi 24, Th Sukhumvit; ⏰ 6pm-midnight; Skytrain Phrom Phong

Owned by Thai composer-musician Jirapan Ansvananada, Imageries boasts a huge sound board and closed-circuit TV for its stage shows, which welcome local and foreign bands of all genres. This is a classic Thai nightclub with politely seated spectators and very polished bands playing music that's verging on canned.

KITCHENETTE Map pp264-5
☎ 0 2381 0861; 1st fl, Dutchess Plaza, 289 Soi 55 (Thong Lor), Th Sukhumvit; ⏰ 5pm-midnight; Skytrain Thong Lor

With live folk music being played on the weekends, this older lesbian café attracts a mixed crowd.

METAL ZONE Map pp262-3
☎ 0 2255 1913; 82/3 Soi Lang Suan; ⏰ 7pm-midnight; Skytrain Chitlom

Never fear, child of the '80s, heavy metal lives onin Thailand. Amid dungeons-and-dungeons décor, there is plenty of head banging, lip jutting and tight-jean wearing. Aregular line-up of bands authentically reproduce everything from thrash to Goth to speed metal sounds, Ozzy squeal to Axel rasp, and a few convoluted Helmet tunes. The volume is perfect – loud enough for chest compression, but not quite able to extract blood from the ears.

The Soi Dogs gettin' down

RADIO CITY Map pp257-9

☎ 0 2266 4567; Soi Patpong 1; ☽ 8pm-1am;
Skytrain Sala Daeng

In the midst of Patpong's night market, Radio City has outdoor seating where you can whet a parched whistle and watch the parade of unrehearsed short stories. Beer is pricey, but the talented house band that performs old rock-and-roll tunes does a good job of earning its pay. The Thai Elvis and Tom Jones impersonators who perform here occasionally can really get the crowd going. Come late with a sufficient amount of social lubrication to enjoy the holiday-land cheesiness of the place.

SAXOPHONE PUB AND RESTAURANT
Map pp248-9

☎ 0 2246 5472; 3/8 Th Phayathai; ☽ 6pm-midnight;
Skytrain Victory Monument

Reminiscent of a German beer cellar, Saxophone's intimate space draws the Thai-*faràng* crowd into the laps of great jazz and blues musicians. Whether you're a beer-toast distance from the band or perched in the 2nd-floor alcove, the sounds are smooth and mellow on your traffic-weary ears. The music changes each night – jazz during the week; rock, blues and beyond on weekends. Well-loved reggae-fusion worships in the hall on Sunday night. Saxophone is on the southeast side of Victory Monument; from the Skytrain station's elevated walkway, descend the stairs near the night market.

TAWAN DAENG GERMAN BREWHOUSE Map pp246-7

☎ 0 2678 1114; 462/61 Th Narathiwat Ratchanakharin cnr Th Phra Ram III; ☽ 5pm-midnight;
access by taxi

A huge brewhouse that could accommodate a small village, Tawan Daeng hosts bands nightly, but most people come for the Wednesday performance of Fong Nam (see p32). Music starts at 8.30pm.

WITCH'S TAVERN Map pp264-5

☎ 0 2391 9791; 306/1 Soi 55 (Thonglor), Th Sukhumvit; ☽ 6pm-midnight; Skytrain Thong Lor

This spacious place is filled with leather couches and chairs arranged in clusters reminiscent of a hotel lobby. Jazz and folk bands start up around 8.30pm. At 10.30pm the house cover band takes to the stage, accepting requests from the audience. Ballads get the biggest round of applause from the mainly Thai crowd.

DISCOS & DANCE CLUBS

Bangkok is famous for its hi-tech discos, which have megawatt sound systems, giant-screen video and the latest in light-show technology. Absolute tackiness and heart-pounding music mean these über-discos will survive, although the tastes of local clubbers have evolved towards more intimate and stylish surroundings. But size doesn't matter when it comes to dancing your face off, and that Bangkok knows how to do.

Cover charges are around 400B on weeknights and 600B on weekends. Prices and the number of complimentary drinks will vary depending on how well you're dressed and the night of the week. Most places don't begin filling up until after 11pm.

BED SUPPERCLUB Map pp264-5

☎ 0 2651 3537; 26 Soi 11, Th Sukhumvit; cover 500B; ☽ 8pm-midnight; Skytrain Nana

You can't miss this place: it looks like a white alien egg and rivals the gaudiness of its neighbours' pseudo-Italian villas. Although liberally borrowing from the set of *2001: A Space Odyssey* with a sterile laboratory décor, the laws of gravity still apply. As the name suggests, there are beds (which are reserved hours in advance) for lounging with your friends, and a separate restaurant. At first embraced as the bee's knees, Bed is now everyone's favourite joke, perhaps due to the weak cocktails and crappy DJs. But if you stick to beer and need to let off steam, this is a stylish spot to see and be seen.

CAFÉ DEMOC Map pp254-5

☎ 0 2622 2571; 78 Th Ratchadamnoen; ☽ 8pm-midnight Tue-Sun; air-con bus 511 & 512, ordinary bus 2, 39, 10 & 12

Up-and-coming DJs present their turntable dexterity at this trendy club. Hip-hop, drum 'n' bass and tribal fill the nightly profiles. Keep watching for the monthly appearance of DJ Dragon.

CLUB 87 Map pp262-3

☎ 0 2690 9999; Conrad Hotel; 87 Th Withayu; ☽ 7pm-1am (disco); Skytrain Ploenchit

While most Bangkok dance clubs don't get started till 11pm, diehard Club 87 fans, who tend to be grown-up groovers rather than teen techno-heads, focus their entire evening here. Start in the 'studio' with Sambuca-smoked salmon, Sevruga caviar or Moroccan tofu salad, glide into the bar for drinks and when the mood strikes, the dance floor is only steps away.

CONCEPT CM2 Map pp262-3
☎ 0 2255 6888; basement, Novotel Bangkok on Siam Square, Soi 6, Siam Square; cover 200B; ☺ 8pm-midnight; Skytrain Siam
A stroke of marketing genius, Concept is the club equivalent of an all-in-one superstore. With karaoke, an Italian restaurant and a trance pit all under one roof, Concept satisfies those with short attention spans. The dance floor is frequented by visiting business people and the ubiquitous cadre of thin Thai girls. Live bands and DJs are featured throughout the week.

DANCE FEVER Map pp246-7
☎ 0 2247 4295; 71 Th Ratchadaphisek; ☺ 9pm-1am; ordinary bus 73, 136 & 137

Street Beats

Feeling like a night-time butterfly that would rather flit from one spot to another than be loyal to one spot? If you're having commitment issues, try these streets for a club buffet. A young crowd flocks to **Rama IX** (known as Royal City Ave, or RCA), a district of loud, flashy bars, for all-out drunken abandon – you remember the feeling, don't you? The best advice is to cruise the strip and congregate where the music suits you. Take bus 137, 168 or 179 to get there.

Like an ancient guild system, each *soi* off of **Th Silom** specialises in a different variety of night-time entertainment. Between the Japanese massage parlours and the ping-pong shows, these neighbouring *soi* turn the crowd itself into the entertainment. Soi 2 is Bangkok's most happening gay scene, packing every gay genre into a handful of clubs. **DJ Station** overflows with mixed groovers and money boys, while **Expresso Bar** offers a stylish wind-down.

More of a warm-up, Soi 4 is a rendezvous point for the paired and the pairable. In its Mediterranean-inspired spaces, **Tapas** offers small samplers for every taste. Take your pick of outdoor people-watching tables or the upstairs dance floor (cover 400B) filled with soulful sounds and sweaty bodies. Further down the cat-walk – er, *soi* – muscle boys and queens parade past **Telephone** and **Balcony Bar's** outdoor tables. Inside Telephone all the tables have a rotary phone so that patrons can call each other; please, no prank calls. You can expect to pay a cover charge of between 100B and 300B, and most clubs are open from 6pm to 1am. Take the Skytrain to Sala Daeng.

Very Thai, very loud and very young, this disco boasts a state-of-the-art sound and lighting system and giant video screens. It warrants a succession of stiff drinks.

DDM Map p256
Th Chao Fa, Banglamphu; ☺ 10pm-midnight (disco); Tha Phra Athit
This late-night dance club gets its fair share of Banglamphu regulars as well as the Japanese tourists staying in the dorm upstairs.

LUCIFER Map pp257-9
☎ 234 6902, 76/1-3 Soi Patpong 1; cover 130B; ☺ 9pm-1am; Skytrain Sala Daeng
This grottolike disco delivers the Miltonian side of Lucifer as a fun-loving hedonist. Nestled in the heart of Patpong, Lucifer kicks off the night with a few brave but terminally unhip travellers who wander in off the street. But the hardcore techno, pulsating black light and hired dancing girls bring together the tipsy band of misfits. By 11pm, the crowd shifts to a younger, prettier persuasion with serious dance-floor know-how. Another wave of recruits arrives at hook-up time when drunk *faràng* guys come to troll.

NARCISSUS Map pp264-5
☎ 0 2261 3991, 112 Soi 27, Th Sukhumvit; ☺ 9am-midnight; Skytrain Asoke
In keeping with its name, Narcissus is one of the city's most ostentatious clubs. It has stood the test of time, remaining a favourite of Bangkok's elite. Here, mediocrity is a dirty word; with its overly grand Art Deco fit-out, awesome sound system and international playbill (Oakenfold has brought the house down here almost annually), this place means business.

Q BAR Map pp264-5
☎ 0 2252 3274; 34 Soi 11, Th Sukhumvit; ☺ 9am-midnight; Skytrain Nana
Since its hyped opening in 1999, Q Bar has fast become Bangkok's venue of choice for anyone who is anyone, or at least has a cellphone. Weaned on New York City nightlife, Q Bar is a slick industrial space punctuated by suggestive neon lighting and spike heels. DJs drive a groovy beat from hip-hop to Latin, and everyone has their own dance moves, some of which are straight off a Nana stage. It boasts perhaps the largest range of drinks in Thailand – choose from 27 types of vodka and 41 brands of whisky/bourbon. Absinthe even resides somewhere behind the bar. Finish off the night with a potent *mojito* and a Cuban cigar.

Gay & Lesbian Bangkok

While stepping off the Western shelf is a gamble for many gays, Thailand's signature tolerance extends to homosexuality as well. Drawing from a diverse international and indigenous community, Bangkok's male-gay nightlife is out and open with go-go bars, late-night discos and *kàthoey* (transvestite and transsexual) cabarets. Night spots for Thai lesbians *(tom-dee)*, on the other hand, aren't as prominent (or segregated) and receive more police scrutiny.

Popular with gays and straights, Silom Soi 2 and Soi 4 (see boxed text opposite) have the city's highest concentration of gay clubs. Nearby, there's a cluster of seedier male-gay go-go bars around Soi Anuman Ratchathon, off Soi Tantawan, which joins Th Surawong opposite the Ramada Hotel.

Babylon Bangkok (Map pp260-1; ☎ 0 2213 2108; 50 Soi Nantha, near Soi 1/Atakanprasit, Sathon; ✆ 5am-11pm) is a four-storey gay sauna that has been described as one of the top 10 gay men's saunas in the world. Facilities include a bar, roof garden, gym, massage room, steam and dry saunas, and spa baths. The spacious, well-hidden complex also has accommodation.

Lesbian haunts include **Kitchenette** (p132), **Vega Café** (p125) and bars along **Th Phra Athit** (see boxed text, p131). For information on how to find out about gay and lesbian social events and entertainment, see p214.

GO-GO BARS

It is no secret that Bangkok makes male fantasies come true. From the hostess bars where pretty young things play flirty drinking games, to the clubs with live skin shows and massage parlours with 'happy endings', Bangkok as a sexual playground is both a novelty and a way of life. New male arrivals either dive in and never resurface or receive the proper aversion therapy to keep the scene at curiosity distance.

Looming large in the visitors' imagination is the notorious Patpong district of ping-pong and 'fuckey' shows. Along two narrow *soi* (Soi Patpong 1 and Soi Patpong 2, off Th Silom), blaring neon bars with poetic names such as King's Castle, Supergirls and Pussy Galore cater mainly to a gawking public (both male and female) with circuslike sexual exploits. In this accessible underworld, some tourists are duped into seeing 'free' sex shows in back-alley bars, where the inflated bills are enforced by muscled bouncers. The safer course is to stay on the main street, where prices are posted and patrons filter in and out freely.

The gay men's equivalent of Patpong can be found on nearby Soi Thaniya, Soi Pratuchai and Soi Anuman Ratchathon, where bars feature go-go dancers and live sex shows, which are usually better choreographed (think Cirque de Soleil with a bull's-eye) than the hetero equivalents in Patpong.

A more direct legacy of the Vietnam R&R days is Soi Cowboy (between Soi 21 and Soi 23, Th Sukhumvit), a strip of hostess and go-go bars targeted to the consumer, not the curious.

Nana Entertainment Plaza (Nana Plaza; Map pp264-5; Soi 4/Nana Tai, Th Sukhumvit) is a three-storey complex attracting a local (Thai and *faràng*) clientele for topless dancing and strip shows. Nana Plaza comes complete with its own guesthouses, used almost exclusively by Nana Plaza's female bar workers for illicit meetings. The 'female' staff at **Casanova** consists entirely of Thai transvestites and transsexuals; this is a favourite stop for foreigners visiting Bangkok for sex reassignment surgery.

Asian tourists – primarily Japanese, Taiwanese and Hong Kong males – flock to the Ratchada entertainment strip, part of the Huay Khwang district, along wide Th Ratchadaphisek between Th Phra Ram IX and Th Lat Phrao. Lit up like Las Vegas, this stretch of neon boasts huge, male-oriented, massage-snooker-and-karaoke and go-go complexes with names like Caesar's Sauna and Emmanuelle, which are far grander in scale and more expensive than any places in Patpong.

Patpong's Past

Although it is commonly believed that American GIs on R&R in Bangkok were the primary consumers of Patpong strip clubs, a *Metro* interview with the late Patpongphanit patriarch (the founder of the Patpong dynasty) gives the credit to international airline staff arriving in the 1950s. Curiously, this grove of neon was a banana plantation until it was sold to the Patpong-phanit family just before WWII.

THEATRE & DANCE

Bangkok's performing arts-venues host both traditional Thai and international theatre and op. The city's daily newspapers and monthly magazines maintain a calendar of cultural events. You can also call the **Cultural Information Service** (☎ 0 2247 0028) for a schedule in English.

BANGKOK PLAYHOUSE Map pp264-5

☎ 0 2679 8548; 284/2 Th Phetburi Tat Mai; air-con bus 512, ordinary bus 58, 60

Founded in 1993, this community theatre uses resident actors for the most part, but occasionally hosts touring troupes from abroad. It's a primary venue for *lákhon phûut* (contemporary theatre).

CHALERMKRUNG ROYAL THEATRE

Map pp252-3

☎ 0 2222 0434; 66 Th Charoen Krung at Th Triphet; air-con bus 508, ordinary bus 48

This royal theatre (alternatively known as Sala Chaloem Krung), housed in a Thai Art Deco building, provides a striking venue for *khŏn* (masked dance-drama based on stories from the *Ramakian*) performance. When it first opened in 1933, the Chalermkrung, funded by royalty, was the largest and most modern theatre in Asia, with state-of-the-art motion-picture projection

Dancers' costume, Erawan Shrine (above)

Shrine Dancing

Although scheduled performances are grand, lasting memories seem to be made from experiences that are unscripted. Traditional *lákhon kâe bon* (shrine dancing) is usually seen utterly by chance; if you hear the din of the drums and percussion, follow the sound to see an amazing spectacle. At **Lak Meuang** (Map p256; cnr Th Ratchadamnoen Nai & Th Lak Meuang) and **Erawan Shrine** (Map pp262-3; cnr Th Ratchadamri & Th Ploenchit), worshippers can commission costumed troupes to perform dance movements that are similar to classical *lákhon*, but more crude, as they are specially choreographed for ritual purposes.

technology and the first chilled-water air-con system in the region. Prince Samaichaloem, a former student of the École des Beaux-Arts in Paris, designed the hexagonal building.

The refurbished theatre's 80,000-watt audio system, combined with computer-generated laser graphics, enables the 170-member dance troupe to present a technologically enhanced version of traditional *khŏn*. The performances last approximately two hours, including intermission. Other Thai performing arts and film festivals also make appearances. The theatre requests that patrons dress respectfully, which means no shorts, tank tops or sandals. Bring a wrap or long-sleeved shirt in case the air-con is running full blast.

JOE LOUIS PUPPET THEATRE

Map pp260-1

☎ 0 2252 9683; Suan Lum Night Bazaar, 1875 Th Rama IV; tickets 600B; ⌚ shows 7.30pm & 9.30pm

The ancient art of Thai puppetry *(lákhon lék)* was rescued by the late Sakorn Yangkhiawsod, more popularly known as Joe Louis, in 1985. Joe's children now carry on the tradition. His creations are controlled by three puppeteers and can strike many humanlike poses. Modelled after the characters in the epics *Ramayana* and *Phra Aphaimani*, the puppets perform nightly at this air-conditioned theatre, conveniently located in the Suan Lum Night Bazaar.

NATIONAL THEATRE Map p256

☎ 0 2224 1342; Th Ratchini; tickets 40-80B; air-con bus 507 & 512, ordinary bus 39, 59, 123 & 201

Thailand's most traditional *lákhon* (dance-drama) and *khŏn* performances are held at the National Theatre (Rong Prakan Haeng Chat). The theatre's regular public roster schedules six or seven performances of traditional dance per month, usually on weekends. It also hosts international performances and choreographed events by national artists.

PATRAVADI THEATRE Map p256
☎ 0 2412 7287; www.Patravaditheatre.com; Soi Wat Rakhang, cnr Soi Tambon Wanglang 1, Thonburi; tickets 300-800B; ⊙ shows 7pm Fri-Sun; ferry from Tha Chang to Tha Wat Rakhang

Across the road from Supatra River House, Patravadi is Bangkok's only open-air theatre. Led by Patravadi Mejudhon, a famous Thai actress and playwright, the troupe's performances blend traditional Thai dance and themes with modern choreography, music and costume. Reservations are recommended. This is also the primary venue for the Bangkok International Fringe Festival, held in April/May.

THAILAND CULTURAL CENTRE
Map pp246-7
☎ 0 2247 0028; www.thaiculturalcenter.com; Th Ratchadaphisek btwn Th Tiam Ruammit & Th Din Daeng; ordinary bus 137, 136, 206

Occasionally, classical dance performances are held at this venue featuring a concert hall, art gallery and outdoor studios. Regional Thai concerts, featuring *lûuk thŭng* (Thai country music) and Khorat Song (Thai folk song), cycle through the yearly calendar. International dance and theatre groups are also profiled, especially during the International Festival of Dance & Music, which is held from late September to early October.

DINNER THEATRE
Another option for viewing Thai classical dance is through a dinner theatre especially designed for tourists. Most dinner theatres are heavily promoted through hotels to an ever-changing clientele, so standards are poor to fair. Recommended for short-term visitors only, dinner theatres can be worthwhile if you accept them as cultural tourist traps.

SALA RIM NAM Map pp257-9
☎ 0 2437 2918, 0 2437 3080; Oriental Hotel, Soi 38 (Soi Oriental); tickets 1700B; ⊙ dinner shows 7pm & 8.30pm; Skytrain Saphan Taksin, ferry Tha Oriental

The historic Oriental Hotel hosts a dinner theatre in a sumptuous Thai pavilion located across the river in Thonburi. Free shuttle boats transfer guests across the river from the hotel's dock. The price is well above average, reflecting the hotel's client base rather than the show's merits.

SUPATRA RIVER HOUSE Map p256
☎ 0 2411 0305, 266 Soi Wat Rakhang, cnr Tambon Wanglang 1, Thonburi; dishes 150-300B; ⊙ dinner shows 8.30-9pm Fri & Sat; cross-river ferry from Tha Chang to Tha Wat Rakhang

This stylishly restored teak house garners the famous dual-temple view of Wat Arun as well as the Grand Palace. An outdoor stage hosts dance performances by graduates of the affiliated Patravadi Theatre. The food and service, however, are hit and miss. If a dish doesn't arrive, don't ask about it during the meal; instead spare yourself the disappointment of finding that it has grown cold and lonely in the kitchen by requesting the item be removed from the bill at the end.

KÀTHOEY CABARET
At the city's popular cabaret shows, lady-boys *(kàthoey)* take their masterful gender-bending to the stage with elaborate costumes, MTV-style dance routines and rehearsed lip-synching to pop hits. **Calypso Cabaret** (Map pp262-3; ☎ 0 2261 6355, 0 2216 8937; 1st fl, Asia Hotel, 296 Th Phayathai; tickets 1000B; ⊙ shows 8.15pm & 9.45pm) and **Mambo Cabaret** (Map pp264-5; ☎ 0 2259 5715; Washington Square, Th Sukhumvit btw Soi 22 & Soi 24; tickets 600-800B; ⊙ shows 8.30pm & 10pm) do family- and tourist-friendly shows of pop and Broadway camp. A gay club, **Freeman** (Map pp260-1; ☎ 0 2632 8032; sub-soi between Soi 2 and Soi Thaniya, Th Silom; cover varies; ⊙ shows midnight) was named Bangkok's best cabaret show in 2003– it's more racy than family-friendly shows.

CINEMA
To offset the uncomfortable humidity, Bangkok's cinemas know how to pamper. These hi-tech, well-air-conditioned palaces offer VIP decadence (reclining seats and table service) in addition to the familiar fold-down seats and sticky floors.

All movies in Thai theatres are preceded by the Thai royal anthem, during which everyone is expected to stand respectfully.

Releases of Hollywood movies arrive in Bangkok's theatres in a timely fashion. Foreign films are usually censored for nudity and, occasionally, violence. Recently, Thai films, often subtitled in English, have been fuelling an emerging cinematic trend highlighted at the annual Bangkok International Film Festival, held in January (see p10).

Film buffs can go to **Alliance Française Bangkok** (Map pp260-1; ☎ 0 2670 4200; www.alliance -francaise.or.th; 29 Th Sathon Tai) and **Goethe Institut** (Map pp260-1; ☎ 0 2287 0942; 18/1 Soi Goethe, off Soi 1/Atthakarm Prasit, Th Sathon Tai); most films have English subtitles and are free or cost about 40B.

For movie listings and reviews, check the *Nation*, *Bangkok Post, Metro* and Movie Seer (www.movieseer.com).

At the cinemas listed here, English movies are subtitled in Thai rather than dubbed. Ticket prices range from 100B to 180B for regular seats up to 300B for VIP seats.

EGV Map pp262-3
☎ 0 2812 9999; www.egv.com; Siam Discovery Centre, 6th fl, Th Phra Ram I; Skytrain Siam
Also called Entertain Golden Village, this ultra-comfortable theatre shows mainstream films.

LIDO MULTIPLEX Map pp262-3
☎ 0 2252 6498; btwn Soi 2 & Soi 3, Th Phra Ram I, Siam Square; Skytrain Siam)
Art buffs should head for this older theatre, which shows independent movies.

MAJOR CINEPLEX Map pp262-3
☎ 0 2515 5555; Central World Plaza, 7th fl, Th Ratch-adamri; Skytrain Chitlom
For watching movies with all of the creature comforts, you'll want this new theatre with all the amenities.

SCALA Map pp262-3
☎ 0 2251 2861; Soi 1, Th Phra Ram I, Siam Square; Skytrain National Stadium
This is for patrons who enjoy an old-style theatre with grand décor in the heart of funky Siam Square.

SF CINEMA CITY Map pp262-3
☎ 0 2611 6444; 7th flr, MBK Centre, Th Phra Ram I; Skytrain National Stadium
Here is a multiplex with an abundance of blockbuster Hollywood showings.

SFV Map pp264-5
☎ 0 2260 9333; 6th fl, The Emporium, Th Sukhumvit cnr Soi 24
SFV is for travellers who want a cinema with all the comfort trimmings and varied screenings.

WATCHING SPORT

Thailand's indigenous sports are acrobatic tests of strength. In the case of *muay thai* (Thai boxing), the sport is followed with as much devotion as football is in Western countries. During an important match, every TV in the city is tuned in, and resulting cheers and jeers echo from inside homes and shops.

MUAY THAI (THAI BOXING)

The best of the best fight at Bangkok's two boxing stadiums: **Lumphini Stadium** (Sanam Muay Lumphini; Map pp260-1 Th Phra Ram IV) and **Ratchadamnoen Stadium** (Sanam Muay Ratch-adamnoen; Map pp254-5; Th Ratchadamnoen Nok). Lumphini Stadium is scheduled to move to a new location in the future.

Tickets at both stadiums cost 500B for 3rd class, 800B for 2nd class and 1500B for ringside seats. Be aware that these admission prices are more than double what Thais pay, and the inflated price offers no special service or seating. At Ratchadamnoen Stadium, foreigners are sometimes corralled into an area with an obstructed view. Feeling warm and fuzzy already? If you are mentally prepared for the jabs from the promoters, then you'll enjoy the real fight.

There is much debate about which seats are better. Ringside gives you the central action, but amid a subdued crowd where gambling is prohibited. The 2nd-class seats are filled with backpackers and numbers-runners who take bets from the crowd. Akin to being in a stock-exchange pit, hand signals communicating bets and odds fly between the 2nd- and 3rd-class areas. The 3rd-class area is the rowdiest section. Fenced off from the rest of the stadium, most of the die-hard fans follow the match (or their bets) too closely to sit down. If you're prepared for two men punching each other, then 3rd-class seats, can be a crowd diversion.

Fights are held throughout the week. Ratchadamnoen hosts matches on Monday, Wednesday and Thursday at 6pm and on Sunday at 5pm. Lumphini hosts matches on Tuesday, Friday and Saturday at 6pm. Aficionados say the best-matched bouts occur on Tuesday nights at Lumphini and Thursday nights at Ratchadamnoen. There are eight to 10 fights of five rounds each. The stadiums don't fill up until the main events, which start around 8pm or 9pm.

There are English-speaking 'staff' outside the stadium who will practically tackle you upon arrival. Although there have been a few reports of scamming, most of these assistants help steer visitors to the foreigners' ticket windows and hand out a fight roster; they can also be helpful in telling you which fights are the best match-ups. (Some say that welterweights, between 135lb and 147lb, are the best.) To keep everyone honest, however, remember to purchase tickets from the ticket window, not from a person outside the stadium.

The restaurants on the north side of Ratchadamnoen stadium are well known for their delicious *kài yâang* (grilled chicken) and other northeastern dishes.

TÀKRÂW

Once known as 'Siamese football', traditional *tàkrâw* players stand in a circle and keep the ball airborne by kicking it soccer-style. Points are scored for style, difficulty and variety of kicking manoeuvres. A common variation on *tàkrâw*, which is used in school and college or international competitions, is played with a volleyball net, using the same rules as in volleyball except that only the feet and head are permitted to touch the ball. At **Lumphini Park** (Map pp260-1; Th Rama IV; Skytrain Ratchadamri or Saladaeng) and **National Stadium** (Map pp248-9; ☎ 0 2214 0120; Th Phra Ram I; Skytrain National Stadium) it's great to see the players do aerial pirouettes, spiking the ball over the net with their feet. One option has players kicking the ball into a hoop 4.5m above the ground (basketball without hands or a backboard!)

HEALTH & FITNESS

You'll find many ways to burn off Thai sweets with Bangkok's array of sports facilities. Besides your own procrastination, the weather can be a barrier to outdoor fitness. Early mornings and late evenings provide enough of a relief from the direct sun for the exercise nuts.

SPORTS CLUBS & GYMS

Bangkok is a workout town, and it offers a diversity of sports facilities reflecting the international nature of its population. Most large hotels have gyms and swimming pools as do many large condos and residential complexes. The city's parks are also popular morning and evening workout zones, with joggers (or, to be more accurate, shufflers), people doing aerobics classes, football players and cyclists.

Some gyms have tennis courts, and the following options are also open to the public: **Central Tennis Court** (Map pp260-1; ☎ 0 2213 1909 ; 13 Soi 1, Atakanprasit, Th Sathon Tai) and **Santisuk Tennis Courts** (Map pp264-5; ☎ 0 2391 1830; Soi 38, Th Sukhumvit).

BRITISH CLUB Map pp257-9

☎ 0 2234 0247; 189 Th Surawong; Skytrain Sala Daeng
Open to citizens of Australia, Canada, New Zealand and the UK, or to others by invitation, the British Club's sports facilities include a pool, a golf driving range, and squash and tennis courts.

CALIFORNIA FITNESS Map pp257-9

☎ 0 2631 1122; cnr Th Convent & Th Silom; Skytrain Sala Daeng
Part of the 24-Hour Fitness network, this gaudy spot is more like a disco than a gym. Heart-pounding techno escapes out on to the street, suggesting more serious sweating than what you find inside. Exercise equipment looks out on to Th Convent, providing ogling opportunities from both sides of the fishbowl.

CAPITOL CLUB Map pp264-5

☎ 0 2661 1210; www.presidentpark.com; President Park, Soi 22-24, Th Sukhumvit; Skytrain Phrom Phong
Aerobics, rock climbing, swimming, tennis, squash, weights, fitness machines and yoga are all offered at this well-outfitted facility.

CLARK HATCH PHYSICAL FITNESS CENTRES Map pp262-3

☎ 0 2653 9000: 8th fl, Amari Watergate Hotel, 847 Th Phetburi; www.clarkhatchthailand.com
This top-class facility offers weight machines, aerobics classes, a pool, sauna and massage. Other locations include Amari Atrium Hotel (☎ 0 2718 2000; 4th fl) and Century Park (☎ 0 2246 7800; Th Ratchaprarop, 5th fl).

NATIONAL STADIUM Map pp248-9

☎ 0 2214 0120; Th Phra Ram I; Skytrain National Stadium
This stadium hosts international soccer matches as well as providing the public with access to swimming facilities, tennis courts and gyms.

RED BULL X PARK Map pp257-9

☎ 0 2670 8080; Th Sathon Tai, opposite Evergreen Laurel Hotel; ☽ 10am-9pm; Skytrain Chong Nonsi
A skate and BMX park for those daredevils into extreme sports.

SOI KLANG RACQUET CLUB Map pp264-5

☎ 0 2391 0963; 8 Soi 49, Th Sukhumvit; Skytrain Thong Lor
This club offers squash, tennis, racquetball, swimming, aerobics and gym facilities.

GOLF

Success in business goes hand-in-hand with success in golf, so finding well-tended courses in Bangkok is a snap. Most courses are outside the central city and require a car. Green fees range from 400B to 3000B, and it is customary to tip caddies 100B. A few noteworthy courses include **Bangkok Golf Club** (Map pp246-7; ☎ 0 2501 2828; 99 Th Tiwanon, Pathum Thani province), **KrungThep Kreetha Sports Club** (Map pp246-7; ☎ 0 2379 3716; Th Kurngthep Kreetha) and **Subhaphruek** (Map pp246-7; ☎ 0 2317 0801; Km 26, Th Bang Na-Trat).

JOGGING & CYCLING

Lumphini Park and Sanam Luang host early-morning and late-evening runners. Bangkok has several Hash groups, meeting for weekly runs through the outskirts of Bangkok. These include Bangkok HHH (men only), Bangkok Monday Hash (mixed) and the Harriettes (mixed). The Bangkok Hash House Mountain Bikers meet monthly on Sunday afternoon for a 20-30km mountain-bike ride on the outskirts of Bangkok or overnight trips outside Bangkok. For current contact numbers, check the Sports section of the *Bangkok Post* every Saturday or visit www.bangkokhhh.com.

SPAS

BANYAN TREE SPA Map pp260-1

☎ 0 2679 1200; www.banyantree.com; Banyan Tree Hotel and Spa, 21/100 Th Sathon Tai; from US$140
This hotel spa delivers modern elegance and world-class pampering. The womblike spa rooms look out over a silent and peaceful vision of Bangkok. Thai, Swedish and Balinese massages, body scrubs using aromatic oils and herbs with medicinal properties, an à la carte menu of relaxation and beauty treatments comprise the spa's offerings. Many visitors, especially newlyweds, purchase 'spa vacation' packages that include accommodation and spa treatments.

ORIENTAL SPA THAI HEALTH & BEAUTY CENTRE Map pp257-9

☎ 0 2439 7613; www.mandarinoriental.com; Oriental Hotel, 48 Soi 38 (Soi Oriental), Th Charoen Krung; from US$200; Skytrain Saphan Taksin, ferry Tha Oriental
Set in a traditional Thai teak home, the spa at the Oriental Hotel offers a full range of massage

Oriental Spa Thai Health & Beauty Centre

and health treatments, including a 40-minute 'jet lag massage' designed to reset your body clock. Privacy is the spa's main strength, with individuals' and couples' suites (shower, massage tables and steam room). Ranking high in the spa name game, the Oriental counts international celebrities such as George Bush among its clients. The spa complex is located across the river on the banks of Thonburi, but can be reached via ferry from the hotel pier.

PIROM SPA: THE GARDEN HOME SPA
Map pp262-3

☎ 0 2655 3525; www.piromspa.com; 78 Soi 1, Th Sukhumvit; à la carte from 800B, packages from 2800B; Skytrain Ploenchit or Nana

Using techniques from northern Thailand, where the women are renowned for their good looks, this spa offers an array of aromatherapy options, hydrotherapy baths, body wraps, facials and Thai massage. Set in a '60s-style house, Pirom's is near Bamrungrad Hospital.

TRADITIONAL THAI MASSAGE
Known to Thai locals as *nûat phaen boraan*, which seems more closely related to *muay thai* than to shiatsu, is based on ancient techniques for general health and healing. Involving stretching, pulling, bending and

manipulating pressure points, a Thai traditional massage will leave you sore but remarkably revitalised. Finding a Thai traditional massage parlour (as opposed to the sexy massage parlours) is easy; they are everywhere and have outgoing sales techniques. A simple errand in a massage neighbourhood means you must run the gauntlet of a chorus of 'Hello, massage?' The demand for massage is so high that quality can be inconsistent – the only thing 'ancient' about some places is the age of the masseuse or masseur. Even worse is the massage social hour, where soap operas or parlour gossip get more attention than you do.

BUATHIP THAI MASSAGE Map pp264-5
☎ 0 2251 2627; 4/13 Soi 5, Th Sukhumvit; 1hr Thai traditional massage 270B, oil 450B, foot 250B; ☽ 10am-midnight; Skytrain Nana

On a small sub-*soi* behind the Amari Boulevard Hotel, this tidy shopfront has a professional masseuse whose focused concentration could melt metal.

MARBLE HOUSE Map pp264-5
☎ 0 2651 0905; 3rd fl, Ruamchit Plaza, 199 Th Sukhumvit at Soi 15; 2hr traditional massage 400B, oil 1000B, foot 300B; ☽ 10am-midnight; Skytrain Sala Daeng

Marble House is on the level, even though the surrounding area is knee-deep in 'friendly' massages. Tucked away on the sleepy 3rd floor of Ruamchit Plaza, the Th Sukhumvit location sees fewer happenstance visitors and has a more affable staff than the **branch** on Soi Surawong Plaza (Map pp257-9; ☎ 0 2235 3519, 37/18-19 Soi Surawong Plaza, Th Surawong).

PHUNNEE FOOT MASSAGE Map pp264-5
☎ 0 2250 2699; 12/3 Soi 22, Th Sukhumvit; 1hr foot massage 250B; ☽ 10am-10pm; Skytrain Phrom Phong

A local chain, Phunnee is well known for its expert foot massages. Don't expect much from the décor, though: this is a standard-issue storefront with no personality.

PIAN MASSAGE Map p256
☎ 0 2629 0924; soi off Th Khao San, Banglamphu; 1hr foot massage 200B; ☽ 8-12.30am; ferry Tha Phra Athit, air-con bus 506 & 56

Well lit and constantly full, this Khao San darling does serious business with an easily impressed clientele. Thai traditional, Swedish and herbal massages are available.

RUEN-NUAD MASSAGE & YOGA

Map pp257-9

☎ 0 2632 2662; 42 Th Convent, Th Silom; ☺ 10am-10pm; 1hr traditional massage 350B, aromatherapy 750B, foot 350B; Skytrain Sala Daeng

The new generation in massage, Ruen-Nuad is set in a converted wooden house. It has partitioned massage stations, creating a mood of pampering and privacy typical of spa facilities, but at parlour prices.

SKILLS DEVELOPMENT CENTER FOR THE BLIND Map pp246-7

☎ 0 2583 7327; 78/2 Soi 1, Th Tiwanon, Pak Kred, North of central Bangkok; 1½hr massage without/with air-con 100/140B

This outreach centre trains the blind in the ancient techniques of Thai traditional massage, developing what many people consider to be expert masseuses. Although the massage might be memorable, getting out here is the primary adventure. Take the Chao Phraya Express north to Tha Nonthaburi, where you will connect to a Laem Thong boat (5.45am to 5.45pm) to Tha Pak Kret. From the pier, hire a motorcycle taxi to take you to the Skills Development Center (10B one way). You'll need a little Thai to pull this off, but Pak Kret villagers are pretty easy-going and willing to listen to foreigners massacre their language.

WAT PHO THAI TRADITIONAL MASSAGE SCHOOL Map p256

☎ 0 2221 2974; 2 Th Sanamchai; 1hr Thai massage 270B, oil 450B, foot 250B; ☺ 10am-6pm; ferry Tha Tien

The most traditional centre for Thai traditional massage is the school affiliated with Wat Pho. Once occupying a *săalaa* (open-sided meeting place) within the temple complex, the massage centre has moved to a fairly ordinary storefront closer to the river. If your love of massage has evolved into an addiction, consider enrolling in one of Wat Pho's massage courses.

YOGA

It is hard to believe that Thais need to be any more relaxed (wouldn't the next level be comatose?), but the urban frenzy has spawned a host of yoga studios. Of the many to choose from, two centrally located studios are: Yoga for Health (☎ 0 2224 4526; Thai-Bharat Cultural Lodge, Soi Damnoen Klang Tai, Th Ratchadamnoen, Banglamphu) and Yoga Elements Studio (☎ 0 2655 5671; www.yoga elements.com; 29 Vanissa Building, 23rd Floor, Soi Chitlom).

Shopping

Shopping

Regular visitors to Asia know that Bangkok beats Hong Kong and Singapore for deals on handicrafts, textiles, jewellery, art and antiques in terms of selection, quality and prices. But the city's intense urban tangle sometimes makes orientation a challenge. *Nancy Chandler's Map of Bangkok* (see p217) makes a good shopping companion, with annotations on all sorts of small, out-of-the-way shopping venues and markets. It is sold in book shops throughout the city.

Shopping is certainly a popular pastime, with hi-tech high-rises and low-tech pavement markets working in tandem to separate people and their baht. The offerings range from necessities and indulgences to oddities. Bargaining is part of the shopping culture at markets and small family-run shops where prices aren't posted. When engaging in this ancient sport, remember it is a game of finesse rather than force. The best approach is one of camaraderie. If you're interested in buying, ask the vendor the price and then ask if they could lower it. You can then counter with a lower sum that will tug the return offer closer to a comfortable range. Figures are sometimes volleyed back and forth at this point. Remember the basic rules of engagement – stay calm and cool. It is poor form to haggle over a difference of 10B.

Thais are generally so friendly and laid-back that some visitors are lulled into a false sense of security, forgetting that Bangkok is a big city with untrustworthy characters. While your personal safety is rarely at risk in Thailand, you may be unwittingly charmed out of your wallet. See p220 for more information about scams.

Tax Refunds

Thailand allows for value added tax (VAT) refunds, like many tourist-oriented countries, and some complicated rules apply, making refunding more challenging. First you need to qualify as a VAT recipient (non-Thais and nonairline crew). You must have spent at least 5000B on the goods, which must be bought at participating shops (a minimum 2000B spend per visit), and received the appropriate paperwork from the shop. You also must have been in Thailand for less than 180 days in a calendar year, be leaving the country by plane and apply at the airport departure hall. Call the **VAT Refund for Thailand Office** (☎ 0 2272 9387) for more information.

Shopping Areas

Siam Square has the greatest concentration of shopping malls for designer and department-store goods. Street markets for souvenirs and pirated goods can be found on Th Khao San, Th Sukhumvit and Th Silom. Shopping is considered entertainment to the extent that many of the street markets start doing business after offices close.

Opening Hours

Most family-run shops are open from 10am to 7pm daily. Street markets are either daytime (from 9am to 5pm) or night-time (from 8pm to 1am). Shopping centres are usually open from 10am to 10pm.

Best Shopping Options in Bangkok

- **Chatuchak Weekend Market** (p154) Best all-round stop for textiles, household gear and second-hand clothes.
- **Mahboonkrong** (MBK; p148) Best centre for hip teenage wear, cellphone accessories and wacky odds and ends.
- **River City Complex** (p152) Best one-stop shop for antiques.
- **Sampeng Lane** (p147) Best venue for being a shopping spectator.
- **Siam Discovery Center** (p150) & **Gaysorn Plaza** (p148) Best spots for chic home décor.
- **Th Khao San** (p145) Best spot to pick up a backpacker-hippie uniform

KO RATANAKOSIN

Generally the home of palaces and temples, this area doesn't have a great deal of shopping opportunities, but it is definitely the place to head for if you're after an excellent-quality *phrá khrêuang* (amulet).

AMULET MARKET

Map p256   *Outdoor Market*

Several small soi off Th Maharat, across from Wat Mahathat; ferry Tha Maharat, air-con bus 8 & 12

Whether browsing or buying, go through this amulet market, which sprawls along the broken pavement across from the temple and back into the sunless *soi* heading towards the river. The main part of the market runs like any commercial *soi*, with shop owners snacking and gossiping between serving customers. The street scene is seedier, drawing on a darker force, although these vendors – with their wares meticulously aligned on a quick getaway towel – attract monks and believers alike inspecting the small carvings for authenticity and power.

BANGLAMPHU

The place for outfitting yourself like a grungy backpacker, Banglamphu has wash-and-wear fisherman pants, bangles and faux dreadlocks as well as luggage for the trip home so you can carry all of those irreplaceable treasures. Prices on pavement market goods are best here because the thrifty backpackers keep expectations low.

APORIA BOOKS Map pp254-5   *Books*

☎ 0 2629 2919; 131 Th Tanao; ☾ 9am-8.30pm; ferry Tha Phra Athit, air-con bus 506, ordinary bus 56

On the east side of Th Tanao across from Th Khao San, Aporia offers an extensive selection of new and used books, including titles on religion and philosophy.

BANGLAMPHU MARKET

Map pp254-5   *Outdoor Market*

Th Chakkraphong; ☾ 9am-6pm; ferry Tha Phra Athit, air-con bus 506, ordinary bus 53 & 56

Spread out over several blocks, the Banglamphu market attracts a no-nonsense crew of street vendors selling snacks, handbags, brassieres, pyjamas, household items and night-blooming jasmine flower buds *(phuang malai)*. You many never come here on purpose, but passing through invariably leads to a purchase.

CHAROEN CHAIKARNCHANG SHOP

Map pp254-5   *Religious*

☎ 0 2222 4800; 87 Soi Nava, Th Bamrung Muang; air-con bus 508

Easily the largest and most impressive religious shop in the area. The workshop at the back produces gigantic bronze Buddha images for wáts all over Thailand.

JOHNNY'S GEMS

Map pp252-3   *Gemstones*

☎ 0 2224 4065; 199 Th Fuang Nakhon, cnr Th Charoen Krung; ☾ closed Sun; air-con bus 508, ordinary bus 56

A long-time favourite of Bangkok expats, Johnny's Gems is a reliable name in an unreliable business.

RIM KHOB FAH BOOKSTORE

Map pp254-5   *Books*

☎ 0 2622 3510; Democracy Monument, 78/1 Th Ratchadamnoen; ☾ 8.30am-7pm; air-con bus 511 & 512, ordinary bus 2, 39, 10 & 12

This English and Thai bookshop has lots of glossy books on Thai arts and culture. Without having to commit loads of baht, you can sample an array of slim scholarly publications from the Fine Arts Department on such heady topics as 'What is a Buddha Image?' or Thai traditional painting. There is also a small historic exhibit on Bangkok inside the shop with a great panorama of the city's skyscrapers viewed from the river.

Images of sitting Buddha for sale

Clothing Sizes

Measurements approximate only, try before you buy

Women's Clothing

Aus/UK	8	10	12	14	16	18
Europe	36	38	40	42	44	46
Japan	5	7	9	11	13	15
USA	6	8	10	12	14	16

Women's Shoes

Aus/USA	5	6	7	8	9	10
Europe	35	36	37	38	39	40
France only	35	36	38	39	40	42
Japan	22	23	24	25	26	27
UK	3½	4½	5½	6½	7½	8½

Men's Clothing

Aus	92	96	100	104	108	112
Europe	46	48	50	52	54	56
Japan	S		M	M		L
UK/USA	35	36	37	38	39	40

Men's Shirts (Collar Sizes)

Aus/Japan	38	39	40	41	42	43
Europe	38	39	40	41	42	43
UK/USA	15	15½	16	16½	17	17½

Men's Shoes

Aus/UK	7	8	9	10	11	12
Europe	41	42	43	44½	46	47
Japan	26	27	27½	28	29	30
USA	7½	8½	9½	10½	11½	12½

SHAMAN BOOKS Map pp254-5 *Books*

☎ 0 2629 0418; 71 Th Khao San; ☻ 8am-midnight; ferry Tha Phra Athit, air-con bus 506, ordinary bus 56

If you were to create a census, you'd discover used bookshops would run a close second behind beer stalls along Th Khao San. These well-thumbed paperbacks have encountered as much of Asia as many of the road-weary travellers. Shaman's has a wide mixture of new and used guidebooks, maps, novels and books on spirituality in several languages, although their prices are a bit higher than the norm.

SUKSIT SIAM Map pp254-5 *Books*

☎ 0 2225 9531; 113-5 Th Fuang Nakhon; air-con bus 508, ordinary bus 56

Opposite Wat Ratchabophit, this bookshop specialises in books on Thai politics, especially those representing the views of leading Thai social critic, Sulak Sivaraksa, and the progressive Santi Pracha Dhamma Institute (which has offices next door). The shop also has mainstream titles on Thailand and Asia, in both English and Thai.

TAEKEE TAAKON Map pp254-5 *Handicrafts*

118 Th Phra Athit; ☻ 10am-5pm Mon-Sat; ferry Tha Phra Athit

This shop has stunning Thai textiles from the country's main silk-producing areas (especially northern Thailand). Enjoy Northern Thai dishes at the few tables by the front windows.

TH KHAO SAN MARKET

Map pp254-5 *Outdoor Market*

Th Khao San; ☻ 10am-2am; ferry Tha Phra Athit, air-con bus 506, ordinary bus 56

The main guesthouse strip in Banglamphu is a day and night shopping bazaar. What have they got? What don't they have? Cheap T-shirts, wooden elephants, fuzzy puppets, bootleg CDs, hemp clothing, Thai axe pillows (a traditional Thai wedge-shaped pillow), fisherman pants and other goods that make backpackers go ga-ga – just to name a few. Ask around to find out which vendors sell the best-quality CDs, many skip so badly that they aren't worthy of a second career as a coaster. And don't leave without a new tattoo, body piercings and dreadlock extensions, and possibly a fake student ID card.

THEWET & DUSIT

This area isn't full of the bustling streets associated with other areas, which are so characteristic of Bangkok. Shopping here will be a more calmly paced experience.

THAI NAKORN Map pp250-1 *Handicrafts*

☎ 0 2281 7867; 79 Th Prachathipathai; ☻ closed Sun; air-con bus 511 & 512, ordinary bus 2, 39, 10 & 12

Near the Democracy Monument, this shop has been in business for 70 years. Nielloware and silverware are its specialities; the Royal family commissions silver ornaments from this business. Call ahead for directions as it is impossible to find without help.

Nielloware, from Europe via Nakhon Si Thammarat, has been created in Thailand for more than 700 years. Engraved silver is inlaid with niello – an alloy of lead, silver, copper and sulphur – to form black-and-silver jewellery designs, inspired by Thai classical dance motifs.

THEWET FLOWER MARKET

Map pp250-1 *Plants & Flowers*

Th Krung Kasem, off Th Samsen; ☻ 9am-6pm; ferry Tha Thewet

If you have any outdoor space to call your own, you should join in the city-wide fascination with container gardening. This quiet daytime market sells all the basics, from ferociously trimmed bougainvilleas to coconut-shell pots of orchids. Now all you have to do is add water.

CHINATOWN

The Phahurat and Chinatown districts have interconnected markets selling tonnes of fabrics, clothes and household wares, as well as a few places selling gems and jewellery. See p102 for a suggested walking route through one small sliver of this district.

NAKHON KASEM

Map pp252-3   *Outdoor Market*
Th Yaowarat & Th Chakrawat; 8am-8pm; ferry Tha Saphan Phut
Cooking equipment, spare electronic parts, and other bits you didn't know could be resold are available at this open-air market. During looser times, this was once known as the Thieves Market, selling the fruits of the five-finger discount.

PHAHURAT MARKET

Map pp252-3   *Outdoor Market*
Th Phahurat & Th Triphet, across from Old Siam Plaza; ferry Tha Saphan Phut
If it sparkles, then this market has it. Dealing mostly in textiles, Phahurat prefers boisterous colours, traditional Thai costumes, tiaras, sequins, wigs and other accessories to make you a Bollywood princess. Amid the shopping riot are great deals on traditional Thai textiles.

PAK KHLONG MARKET

Map pp252-3   *Flowers*
Th Chakkaphet & Th Atsadang; 24hr; ferry Tha Saphan Phut
The bright displays of baby roses, delicate orchids and button carnations are endless and so inexpensive that even a concrete-cell dweller on Th Khao San could buy a bouquet. Pak Khlong is also a big vegetable market. Go late at night when the postdrinking crowd arrives to squander their undrinkable baht.

SAMPENG LANE

Map pp252-3   *Outdoor Market*
Soi Wanit 1, Th Ratchawong; 8am-8pm; ferry Tha Ratchawong
Running roughly parallel to Th Yaowarat, Sampeng Lane is a narrow artery bisecting the commercial areas of Chinatown and Phahurat. The Chinatown portion of Sampeng is lined

with wholesale shops of hair accessories, pens, stickers, household wares and beeping flashing knick-knacks. As the *soi* enters Phahurat, the shops morph into a fabric centre – many operated by Indian (mostly Sikh) merchants. In the vicinity of Th Chakrawat gem and jewellery shops abound. Weekends are horridly crowded, and it takes a gymnast's flexibility to squeeze past the pushcarts, motorcycles and other roadblocks.

SAPHAN PHUT NIGHT BAZAAR

Map pp252-3   *Outdoor Market*
Th Saphan Phut; 8pm-midnight, closed Wed; ferry Tha Saphan Phut
Along the riverfront pavement on either side of the Memorial Bridge (Saphan Phut), this night market has loads of cheap clothes, late-night snacking and a lot of people-watching. Word is that the prices here are cheaper than at Chatuchak – how is that even feasible?

SIAM SQUARE & PRATUNAM

An unbelievable concentration of multistorey shopping malls cluster in Siam Square and Pratunam. From teeny-boppers to highrollers, everyone has a favourite centre for window shopping and splurges.

AMARIN PLAZA

Map pp262-3   *Shopping Centre*
Th Ploenchit; 10.30am-8.30pm; Skytrain Chitlom
Next door to the Erawan shrine, Amarin Plaza is anchored by Sogo, a Japanese department

---

From Nymph to Jumbo

In your hometown, you may be considered average-sized or petite, but based on the Thai measuring stick you're an extra large, making it hard to find clothes and shoes that fit. Many of the market and street vendors (except on Th Khao San) sell clothes in Thai sizes that qualify as preteen sizes if converted to Western charts. For foreign women, Thai clothes are out of proportion in the bust and hips, due to different body types. If you're larger than a US size 10 or an Australian size 12, you strike out altogether. Men will find that length and shoulder width will be their obstacles. This is why many people turn to custom orders through tailors or shop at department stores, such as Central, which carries larger sizes.

store. There is talk that the 1st floor will be developed into a showcase for modern Thai art and design, but so far it is only talk.

CENTRAL DEPARTMENT STORE

Map pp262-3 *Shopping Centre*
Th Phloenchit; 10am-9pm; Skytrain Chitlom

Central is a modern Western-style department store with locations throughout the city. Foreigner-sized clothing is one of the shop's strengths. The helpful sales staff will bluntly, but kindly, steer you to slimming colours and seemingly huge sizes to fit your sturdy frame. The camera department also gets recommended for quality equipment.

On the 6th floor, there is a large selection of Thai crafts, including damascene ware *(khraam)* and textiles, but prices are higher than the outdoor markets. Damascene ware is created when gold and silver wire is hammered into a cross-hatched steel surface to create exquisitely patterned bowls and boxes.

CENTRAL WORLD PLAZA

Map pp262-3 *Shopping Centre*
cnr Th Ploenchit & Th Ratchadamri; 10am-10pm; Skytrain Chitlom

Formerly named the World Trade Centre, this shopping centre is more family-oriented than its neighbours and is anchored by Isetan and Zen department stores, which have clothing shops reminiscent of Hong Kong's high-end boutiques. **Alta Moda** (1st floor) sells fabrics from top-end designers and vibrantly coloured silks.

DO RE ME

Map pp262-3 *Music*
0 2251 4351; 274 Siam Square, Th Phra Ram I; noon-9pm; Skytrain Siam

Blockbuster hits and one-hit wonders find their way into this organisationally liberated shop.

GAYSORN PLAZA

Map pp262-3 *Shopping Centre*
cnr Th Ploenchit & Th Ratchadamri; 10am-10pm; Skytrain Chitlom

Attached to the Chitlom skytrain station by a shaded walkway, Gaysorn spares shoppers from sullying themselves amid the street-level chaos. A *haute couture* catwalk, Gaysorn has spiralling staircases, all-white halls and mouthfuls of top-name designers. Thai fashion leaders, such as **Fly Now** (2nd floor), have also sewn themselves into this international collage. The top floor is an irresistible stroll of chic and antique home décor. **Triphum** (3rd floor) has mother-of-pearl inlaid cabinets, lacquerware scripture chests and other high-quality reproductions. **Ayodhya** (3rd floor) sells celadon pieces in spa-influenced colours.

MAHBOONKRONG (MBK)

Map pp262-3 *Shopping Centre*
cnr Th Phra Ram I & Th Phayathai; 10am-10pm; Skytrain National Stadium

Unadulterated consumerism and market-stall energy make MBK one of the most vibrant shopping centres in Bangkok. Popular with teenagers and university students, MBK is filled with cheap, shiny stuff, cellphone accessories,

Quirky reflections in the façade of Mahboonkrong shopping centre (MBK; above)

shoes, Paul Frank accessories and the middle-class Tokyu department store. Part of the fun is watching the shoppers' attempts at individualism by accessorising their mundane school uniforms with high slits or torturous heels.

MARCO TAILORS Map pp262-3 *Tailor*
☎ 0 2252 0689; Soi 7, Siam Square; ☷ 10am-5pm Mon-Fri; Skytrain Siam
Dealing solely in men's suits, Marco has a wide selection of banker-sensibility wools and cottons. They require at least two weeks and two fittings.

NARAYANA PHAND
Map pp262-3 *Souvenirs & Handicrafts*
☎ 0 2252 4670; 127 Th Ratchadamri; ☷ 10am-8pm; Skytrain Chitlom
Souvenir-quality handicrafts are given fixed prices and comfortable air-conditioning at this government-run facility. You won't find anything here that you haven't already seen at all of the tourist street markets, but it is a good stop if you're pressed for time or spooked by haggling.

PANTIP PLAZA
Map pp262-3 *Computer Equipment*
☎ 0 2656 5030; 604 Th Phetburi; ☷ 10am-10pm; Skytrain Phayathai
This is the best place to buy computer equipment and digital cameras. It has five storeys of computer shops and dozens of stalls selling computers and peripherals (both genuine and openly pirated software). Up on the 6th floor is **IT City** (☎ 0 2656 5030), a reliable computer megastore that gives VAT refund forms for tourists.

PENINSULA PLAZA
Map pp262-3 *Shopping Centre*
Th Ratchadamri; ☷ 10am-10pm; Skytrain Ratchadamri
Cathedral quiet, bar the clicking of heels and an occasional tinkling piano, the Peninsula Plaza is the most posh of Bangkok's shopping centres. It's the turf of the serious, luxury-brand heavyweights such as Louis Vuitton, Gianni Versace et al. But don't expect a designer bargain here – prices are comparable to those found in the Western counterparts of these shops.

PRATUNAM MARKET
Map pp262-3 *Outdoor Market*
Cnr Th Phetburi & Th Ratchaprarop; ☷ 9am-midnight; Skytrain Chitlom & Phayathai

Bookshop Chains
For new books and magazines, Asia Books and Bookazine have branches throughout the city.

Asia Books
Central World Plaza (Map pp262-3; ☎ 0 2255 6209; 3rd fl, Th Ratchadamri)

Emporium shopping centre (Map pp264-5; ☎ 0 2664 8545; 3rd floor, Th Sukhumvit)

Landmark Plaza (Map pp264-5; ☎ 0 2252 5839; 1st & 3rd floor)

Peninsula Plaza (Map pp262-3; ☎ 0 2253 9786; 2nd floor, Th Ratchadamri)

Siam Discovery Center (Map pp262-3; ☎ 0 2658 0418; 4th floor, Th Phra Ram I)

Th Sukhumvit (Map pp264-5; ☎ 0 2651 0428; 221 Th Sukhumvit btwn Soi 15 & Soi 17)

Thaniya Plaza (Map pp257-9; ☎ 0 2231 2106; 3rd floor, Th Silom)

Times Square (Map pp264-5; ☎ 0 250 0162; 2nd floor, Th Sukhumvit)

Bookazine
Siam Square (Map pp262-3; ☎ 0 2255 3778; 286 Th Phra Ram I, btwn Soi 3 & Soi 4, opposite Siam Center)

Silom Complex (Map pp260-1; ☎ 0 2231 3135; 2nd floor, cnr Th Silom & Th Phra Ram IV)

Sogo department store, Amarin Plaza (Map pp262-3; ☎ 0 2256 9304; 3rd floor, Th Ploenchit)

Th Sukhumvit (Map pp264-5; ☎ 0 2655 2383; north side btwn Soi 3 & Soi 5)

Starting from the corner of Th Phetburi and Th Ratchaprarop and filtering deep into the *soi* behind the shopfronts, Pratunam has everything you could ever dream of needing, such as cheap clothes, luggage, market-lady sarongs, bulk toiletries and souvenirs. To take a break, wander some of the *soi* off Th Phetburi for a sampling of this eclectic neighbourhood.

PRINYA DECORATION
Map pp262-3 *Furniture*
☎ 0 2318 1824; Th Phetburi at Soi 24; air-con bus 505 & 511
Rosewood and teak are fashioned into custom furniture designs reflecting Asian and European styles.

Buyer Beware

Guarantees are an important consideration if you're buying expensive items such as gems or electronic goods. Make sure the guarantee is international before you start haggling. A national guarantee is next to useless – are you going to return with a gem to Bangkok if you discover it's fake? Finally, make sure that the guarantee is filled out correctly with the shop's name and, if appropriate, the serial number of the item. For electronic goods, check the item's compatibility back home. You don't want a brand or model that has never found its way to your home country.

Antiques

Real Thai antiques are rare and costly. Most Bangkok antique shops keep a few antiques around for collectors, along with lots of pseudo-antiques or traditionally crafted items that look like antiques. The majority of shop operators are quite candid about what's really old and what isn't, but you should do your research. The **National Museum Volunteers Group** (☎ 0 2662 5523) can provide guidelines for detecting a fake. Reputable antique dealers will issue an authentication certificate with your purchase. Also be aware that regulations forbid the export of religious images and fragments (either antique or reproductions) without a licence. For more information, contact the **Department of Fine Arts** (☎ 0 2226 1661).

Gems & Jewellery

Thailand is one of the world's largest exporters of gems and ornaments, rivalled only by India and Sri Lanka. If you know what you are doing you can make some really good buys in both unset gems and finished jewellery. Buy from reputable dealers only, unless you're a gemologist. Be wary of special deals or 'one-day only' sales that set you up as a courier and promise you big money on the resale (see p220).

Reputable dealers are members of the Jewel Fest Club, established jointly by the Tourist Authority of Thailand (TAT) and the Thai Gem Jewellery Traders Association. When you purchase from a member shop, a certificate detailing your purchase will be issued and a refund is guaranteed (less 10–20%). A list of members offering government guarantees is available from TAT, or visit the association's website (www.thaigemjewelry.com) for buying information.

Tailor-Made Clothes

Tailors are as prolific as massage parlours in Bangkok and so are the scams. Workmanship ranges from shoddy to excellent, so it pays to ask around before committing yourself. And don't be fooled by the cut-rate specials, such as four shirts, two suits, a kimono and a safari suit all in one package – you'll be disappointed by the quality.

Before you engage a tailor on a custom job, assess their workmanship by commissioning them to copy an item of clothing (which will often cost a tenth of the price if based on a designer garment). Wear the piece for a while to make sure it can withstand wear and tear before returning with business. Once you find a tailor you trust, the next hurdle is selecting quality fabric. If the tailoring shop doesn't offer fabrics to your liking, you can supply your own material from another source. Be especially wary of 100% cotton claims, which are usually a blend of cotton and a synthetic. More than a few tailors will actually try to pass off full polyester or synthetics as cotton. Good quality silk, on the other hand, is plentiful.

Shirts and trousers can be turned around in 48 hours or less with only one fitting. But no matter what a tailor may tell you, it takes more than one or two fittings to create a good suit, and most reputable tailors will ask for two to five fittings. A sturdy custom-made suit will cost from US$200 (for synthetics or natural/synthetic blends) to US$400 (for 100% wool or cashmere). Tailor-made silk shirts should cost no more than US$25.

SIAM SQUARE

Map pp262-3 *Shopping Centre*
Th Phra Ram I, near Th Phayathai; Skytrain Siam
A network of some 12 *soi*, Siam Square requires an itty-bitty waist and near fluency in Thai before you can really appreciate what it has to offer. Small shops selling pop-hip styles, books, sporting goods and music attract more Chulalongkorn students than perhaps their university classes do. The plethora of fast-food restaurants will scratch unknown itches of homesickness.

SIAM CENTER & SIAM DISCOVERY

CENTER Map pp262-3 *Shopping Centre*
cnr Th Phra Ram I & Th Phayathai; ☺ 10am-10pm; Skytrain National Stadium & Siam
Across the road from frenetic MBK, Siam Center and the attached Siam Discovery Center feel almost monastic in hushed hallways. Thailand's first shopping centre, Siam Center was built in 1976 but hardly shows its age. In addition to the name-brand shops, the shopping centre has a large selection of eclectic and stylish home-furnishing shops, as well as

a branch of **Asia Books** (3rd floor). The 5th floor of Siam Discovery Center is dedicated to children's toys. **Mae Fah Luang** (4th floor) is a royally funded crafts shop selling handmade cotton and linen from villages formerly involved with poppy production. Men's fashions also find a comfortable home here.

THAI CRAFT VILLAGE

Map pp262-3   *Handicrafts*
Ground fl, President Tower, 973 Th Ploenchit;
🕑 **10am-10pm; Skytrain Chitlom**
Upscale Thai crafts are sold at this ground-floor arcade. Basketware, textiles, ceramics and hill-tribe crafts are some of the selections. There are also additional shops on the ascending floors of this shopping-hotel tower.

UTHAI'S GEMS

Map pp262-3   *Gems & Jewellery*
☎ **02 253 8582; 28/7 Soi Ruam Rudi, Th Ploenchit;**
Skytrain Ploenchit
You need to make an appointment to see Uthai's gems in this quiet neighbourhood. His fixed prices and good service make him a popular choice among expats.

SILOM & SURAWONG

Savvy shoppers with larger wallets prowl these streets looking for quality collector souvenirs. Fine silks, museum-quality antiques and not-so-perfect pirated goods are all easily accessible at the various shopping malls or street markets.

DESIGN THAI Map pp257-9   *Fabric*
☎ **0 2235 1553; 304 Th Silom; Skytrain Chong Nonsi**
This airy shop has an enchanting assortment of subdued-coloured Thai silks and cottons as well as Italian-cut ties and small silk gifts.

IMAGE QUALITY LAB

Map pp257-9   *Film Processing*
☎ **0 2266 4080; 160/5 ITF Building, Th Silom;**
🕑 **8.30am-6pm Mon-Fri, 8.30am-noon Sat; Skytrain
Chong Nonsi**
Follow the car park into the ITF building to reach a small island of shops, including IQ Lab. This photo-processing shop efficiently prepares professional-quality prints of most varieties of film. Another **branch** (☎ 0 2714 0644) is at 9/23-34 Thana Arcade, Soi 63, Th Sukhumvit.

JIM THOMPSON SILK CO

Map pp260-1   *Thai Silk*
☎ **0 2235 8930; 149/4-6 Th Surawong;** 🕑 **9am-6pm;
Skytrain Sala Daeng**
The surviving business of the main promoter of Thai silk, Jim Thompson shops sell colourful silk handkerchiefs, placemats, wraps and pillow cushions. The styles and motifs attract older, conservative tastes. There are also the gift shop at Jim Thompson's House, and a factory outlet on Soi 93, Th Sukhumvit. Their annual sales make the high-end product more attractive.

JULIE Map pp260-1   *Tailor*
1279 Th Charoen, near Th Silom; 🕑 **closed Sun; ferry
Tha Oriental**
This small shop can do reasonable reproductions of women's fashions. Remember to ask for two fittings and give the shop plenty of time to accommodate that request.

NIKS/NAVA IMPORT EXPORT

Map pp257-9   *Cameras*
☎ **0 2233 2288; 166/4-5 Th Silom;** 🕑 **11am-4pm
Mon-Fri; Skytrain Chong Nonsi**
On the northwest corner of Soi 12, Niks sells all types of professional equipment, including Nikon, Mamiya and Rollei.

MERMAN BOOKS Map pp260-1   *Books*
☎ **0 2231 3300; 4th fl, Silom Complex, 191 Th Silom;**
Skytrain Sala Daeng
A bookshop for the true lover of Asiana, this antiquarian shop, operated by a former *Bangkok Post* editor, collects all manner of out-of-print and rare books, along with plenty of new titles.

ORIENTAL PLACE (OP)

Map pp257-9   *Shopping Centre*
Soi Oriental, 30/1 Th Charoen Krung; 🕑 **10.30am-
7pm; ferry Tha Oriental, Skytrain Saphan Taksin**
In front of the Oriental Hotel, this upmarket complex has several good, if pricey, antique shops, specialising in antique silks, religious artefacts and curios. A branch of the royally funded **Chitlada Shop** sells indigenous handicrafts from rural areas of Thailand.

PATPONG NIGHT MARKET

Map pp257-9   *Outdoor Market*
Soi Patpong 1 & Soi Patpong 2, Th Silom; 🕑 **nightly;
Skytrain Sala Daeng**
You'll be faced with the distractions of strip clubs and shopping on this infamous street.

True to the street's illicit leanings, pirated goods make a prominent appearance even amid a wholesome crowd of families and straight-laced couples. Bargain with determination as first-quoted prices tend to be astronomically high compared to Th Khao San market.

RIVER CITY COMPLEX

Map pp252-3   *Shopping Centre*
Th Yotha, off Th Charoen Krung; ⏰ 10am-9pm, many shops close Sun; ferry Tha Si Phraya
Near the Royal Orchid Sheraton Hotel, this multistorey centre is an all-in-one stop for old-world Asiana. Several high-quality art and antique shops occupy the 3rd and 4th floors. **Acala** is a gallery of unusual Tibetan and Chinese artefacts. **Old Maps & Prints** proffers one of the best selections of one-of-a-kind, rare maps and illustrations, with a focus on Asia. Shipping is easy to arrange and bargaining is advisable.

SIAM BRONZE FACTORY

Map pp257-9   *Handicrafts*
☎ 0 2234 9436; 1250 Th Charoen Krung; ⏰ closed Sun; ferry Tha Oriental
Thailand has the oldest bronze-working tradition in the world. This factory produces bronze flatware, tableware and collector pieces. Prices are fixed. Make sure any items you buy are silicon-coated, otherwise they'll tarnish.

SILOM VILLAGE TRADE CENTRE

Map pp257-9   *Shopping Centre*
Soi 24, Th Silom; ⏰ 10.30am-7pm; ferry Tha Oriental
Behind the Silom Village Inn, this arcade of compact shops sells souvenir-quality reproduction antiques, including teak carvings, textiles and ceramics. The pace is relaxed and rarely crowded. **Artisan's** has Thai-style furniture, altar tables and wooden decorations. **Gems Garden** sells *khŏn* (masked dance-drama) masks.

SOI LALAI SAP

Map pp257-9   *Outdoor Market*
Soi 5, Th Silom; ⏰ 9am-8pm; Skytrain Sala Daeng
The 'money-dissolving *soi*' has a number of vendors selling all sorts of cheap clothing, watches and housewares during the day.

SUAN LUM NIGHT BAZAAR

Map pp260-1   *Outdoor Market*
Cnr Th Withayu & Th Phra Ram IV; ⏰ 3pm-midnight; ordinary bus 13, 17, 76 & 106
A new addition to Bangkok's neon nightscape, Suan Lum is a huge government-backed night market with around 3700 stalls selling modern Thai souvenirs, handicrafts and a few antiques. Stall openings are erratic and the centre seems to be excessive for the number of visitors it attracts. There are several outdoor beer gardens and the opening of the subway system should bring a boost in patronage.

A variety of ornaments on show at Siam Bronze Factory (above)

SUNNY CAMERA Map pp257-9   *Cameras*

☎ 0 2236 8365; 144/23 Th Silom; ⏰ 10am-6pm; Skytrain Chong Nonsi

For a wide range of camera models and brands, you could try Sunny Camera. There are other branches on the 3rd floor of the **Mahboonkrong** (☎ 0 2217 9293) and at 1267-1267/1 Th Charoen Krung (☎ 0 2235 2123).

TECK HENG BOOKSTORE
Map pp257-9   *Books*

☎ 02234 1836; 1326 Th Charoen Krung; ⏰ closed Sun; ferry Tha Oriental, Skytrain Saphan Taksin

Between the Shangri-La and Oriental hotels, this is the best independent bookshop in the neighbourhood, carrying an up-to-date variety of books on Southeast Asia.

TH SUKHUMVIT

Supplies for the recently arrived expat can be found at the shops that line never-ending Th Sukhumvit. Furniture, clothes and household knick-knacks hang out on upper Sukhumvit, while tourist souvenirs centre on Soi 11.

ELITE USED BOOKS Map pp264-5   *Books*

☎ 0 2258 0221; 593/5 Th Sukhumvit at Soi 33/1; Skytrain Phrom Phong

Near the Villa Supermarket, this bookshop stocks a decent selection of used foreign-language titles, including English, Chinese, French, German and Swedish.

EMPORIUM Map pp264-5   *Shopping Centre*

622 Th Sukhumvit, cnr Soi 24; ⏰ 10.30am-11pm; Skytrain Phrom Phong

This centre has six floors of what's hot (Prada, Miu Miu and Chanel), a well-stocked supermarket and a department store. **Kinokuniya** (3rd floor) is a well-rounded bookshop carrying English and Japanese titles, including the latest bestsellers and children's books. Thai crafts can be found on the 4th floor. Listening stations and varied CDs are available at **CD Warehouse** (3rd floor).

PATAYA FURNITURE COLLECTION
Map pp264-5   *Furniture*

☎ 0 2258 7280; 753-755 Th Sukhumvit at Soi 31; ⏰ 10am-6pm; Skytrain Phrom Phong

Modern interpretations of rattan and water hyacinth furniture are sold at this long-running shop. If you're looking for traditional rattan furniture, stroll Th Sukhumvit between Soi 35 and Soi 43 for a host of related shops.

NAGI SHOP Map pp264-5   *Antiques*

☎ 0 2661 6480; 131 Soi 21 (Soi Asoke), Th Sukhumvit; ⏰ 9am-5pm Tue-Sat; Skytrain Asoke

Next door to the Siam Society (p96), this small shop is an odd collection of antiques (textiles, buddhas, prints) from across Asia. Amid the treasures, older *faràng* (Westerners) can often be found discussing bygone days.

NANDAWANG Map pp264-5   *Handicrafts*

☎ 0 2258 1962; 108/3 Soi 23 (Soi Prasanmit), Th Sukhumvit; Skytrain Asoke

High-quality woven cotton clothing and household wares (tablecloths, napkins etc) are Nandakwang's speciality.

RASI SAYAM Map pp264-5   *Handicrafts*

☎ 0 2258 4195; 32 Soi 23 (Soi Prasanmit), Th Sukhumvit; Skytrain Asoke

Located in a shady wooden house, Rasi Sayam sells wall-hangings, *benjarong*, basketry and pottery that are made specifically for this shop by handicraft villages. Better than souvenirs, many items are *objet d'art*.

TH SUKHUMVIT MARKET
Map pp264-5   *Outdoor Market*

Th Sukhumvit btwn Soi 2 & Soi 12, Soi 3 & Soi 15; ⏰ 11am-10.30pm; Skytrain Nana

A market for the aficionado of fakeness, who knows the seriously big difference between a good faux Fendi handbag and one with dodgy stitching and a bum zip. Other top imitations: soccer kits (Becks, Giggsy and Zidane dominate), watches, sunglasses, Levis and jewellery. You'll also find stacks of nudie DVDs, Chinese throwing stars, penis lighters and other questionable gifts for your high-school-aged brother.

VILAI'S Map pp264-5   *Handicrafts*

☎ 0 2391 6106; 731/1 Soi 55 (Soi Thong Lor), Th Sukhumvit; Skytrain Thong Lor

This small shop has an attractive selection of lacquerware and fabrics that are frequently perused by clientele looking for quality.

GREATER BANGKOK

Markets really capture the hubbub of Bangkok. The big drawcard here is the renowned Chatuchak Weekend Market. Trendy fashions or traditional culture can be found at the following spots.

BO-BE MARKET

Map pp248-9   *Outdoor Market*

Th Krung Kasem; 🕙 **9am-6pm; Khlong Saen Saeb canal taxi, air-con bus 511, ordinary bus 53, 110 & 204**

This wholesale clothing market sells army surplus, camping gear, polyester catastrophes, old-lady brassieres, and high-fashion finds.

INTERNATIONAL SCHOOL BANGKOK

Map pp264-5   *Handicrafts*

☎ **0 2963 5800; 39/7 Soi Nichadathani Samakhi, Th Chaeng Wattana**

This college-preparatory school puts on a large charity sale of Thai handicrafts every sixth Saturday or so (except during its summer holiday from June to August). Quality varies from the rare to the mundane. Call for the fair schedule.

KHLONG TOEY MARKET

Map pp264-5   *Outdoor Market*

Cnr Th Phra Rama IV & Th At Narong; 🕙 **dawn to dusk; ordinary bus 115, 116 & 136**

Under the expressway, this all-purpose market is one of the city's cheapest and is best visited on Wednesday. In the days of yore, a whole section of the market sold items that had 'fallen off the boat', but these days everything has been carefully unloaded and tallied.

THAI CELADON Map pp246-7 *Handicrafts*

☎ **0 2229 4780; 8/3-8/5 Th Ratchadaphisek; ordinary bus 136, 137 & 206**

For quality Thai celadon, this showroom carries tableware, lamps and bowls. The annual sale in December is worth checking out.

CHATUCHAK WEEKEND MARKET

Map pp246-7   *Market*

Th Phahonyothin; 🕙 **8am-6pm Sat-Sun; air-con bus 502, 503, 509, 510, 512 & 513, ordinary bus 77, Skytrain Mo Chit**

Known in Thai as Talat Jatujak, this is the Disneyland of Thai markets; on weekends more than 15,000 stalls cater to an estimated 200,000 visitors a day. Everything is sold here, from live chickens and snakes to opium pipes and herbal remedies. Thai clothing such as the *phâakhamáa* (sarong for males) and the *phâasîn* (sarong for females), *kaang keng jiin* (Chinese pants) and *sêua mâw hâwm* (blue cotton farmer's shirt) are good buys. You'll also find musical instruments, hill-tribe crafts, religious amulets, antiques, flowers, clothes imported from India and Nepal, camping gear and military surplus. Second-hand clothes that look fresh off the rack from thrift

Chatuchak Weekend Market (below)

shops in New York's East Village are abundant at Chatuchak. You can affect a genuine 'bed-head musician' look on a real musician's salary here.

The best bargains of all are household goods such as pots and pans, dishes, drinking glasses etc. If you're moving to Thailand for an extended period, this is the place to purchase kitchen items. There is an information centre, a couple of banks with ATMs and foreign-exchange booths at the Chatuchak Park offices, near the northern end of the market's Soi 1, Soi 2 and Soi 3. The information centre also dispenses fold-out maps. Posted maps and toilets are conveniently located throughout the market. Plan to spend a full day, as there's plenty to see, do and buy.

On weekday mornings a vegetable, plant and flower market (Talat Phahonyothin) sets up opposite the south side of Chatuchak Weekend Market. One section of the latter, known as the **Aw Taw Kaw Market**, sells organically grown (no chemical sprays or fertilisers) fruits and vegetables.

Operated by the Asoke Foundation, the **vegetarian restaurant** near the Weekend Market is one of Bangkok's oldest. It's open only on weekends from 8am to noon and is an adventure to find. If you're successful, then this is a real treasure. Cross the footbridge above Th Kamphaeng Phet, heading away from the market, and towards the southern end of Th Phahonyothin. Take the first right onto a through street heading into the car park, and walk past nightclubs and bars. Turn right, and you'll see a new block of buildings selling bulk food stuff; you're getting closer because these are organic wholesalers (smell that 'health-food shop' scent?). The restaurant is at the end of this strip. Prices are ridiculously low (around 10B per dish) and you buy tickets at the front desk.

There is plenty of interesting and tasty food for sale within the market and you can listen to live music in the early evening.

1 Uniformed Royal Palace Guards marching towards the Grand Palace (p78) *2* Chakri Mahaprasat (Grand Palace Hall, p79) *3* Stunning gold façades on the buildings of Wat Phra Kaew (p78) *4* Temples need their guardians, Wat Phra Kaew (p78)

1 The prang (Khmer-style tower) is covered in a mosaic of Chinese porcelain at Wat Arun (Temple of Dawn, p77), named after Indian god of dawn, Aruna 2 Thai woman praying in Bangkok's Chinatown (p87) 3 Traditional Chinese dragon mural decorates a Chinatown temple on Sampeng Lane (p147) 4 An array of Hindu gods appear on the intricately carved detail of Sri Mariamman Temple (p95)

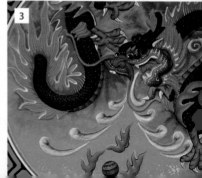

1 Traffic whizzes by the Democracy Monument (p81) in Banglamphu 2 The enormous MBK shopping centre (p148) fringed by a never-ending stream of city traffic 3 The Bangkok city skyline at dusk resembling a scene from Blade Runner 4 Bank of Asia building, known to locals as the 'Robot Building' (p93)

1 Thai boxers sweat it out in a hard-fought *muay thai* match at Lumphini Stadium (p138)
2 Playing a round of golf at one of Bangkok's many courses (p140)
3 Joggers making the most of the open spaces in Lumphini Park (p140) 4 Bending, twisting and pulling – some of the joys of traditional Thai massage (p141)

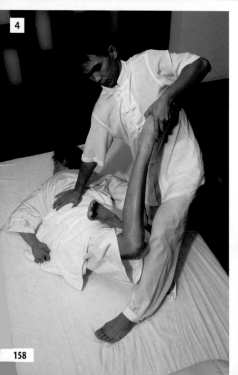

1 *Benchasiri Park in Khlong Toey (p72), takes two hours to reach by boat from Bangkok* 2 *Locals and visitors relax in Lumphini Park (p93)* 3 *Flying colourful kites in the gardens of Sanam Luang, Ko Ratanakosin (p76)* 4 *Elaborate detail on kites for sale in Sanam Luang*

1 The Q Bar, one of Bangkok's 'it' bars (p134) 2 Bar staff keep the drinks coming and the punters happy in Bangkok's drinking hot spots 3 Bangkok's notorious strip club district, Patpong (p135) 4 Megawatt sound systems, giant-screen video and the latest in light-show technology feature in Bangkok's superclubs (p133)

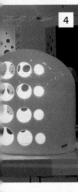

1 Thai-boxing shorts for sale at the Patpong Night Market (p151) *2* Be tempted by things that glisten – selling jewellery in Silom Village *3* Looking for an antique bargain? Bangkok's specialist antique stores abound *4* Groovy lamps for sale in a specialist shop in Emporium (p153), Th Sukhumvit

1 The restored Wat Chai Wattanaram at Ayuthaya Historical Park (p185) **2** Gnarled roots grow around a sculpture of Buddha's head at Wat Phra Mahathat, Ayuthaya (p185) **3** Sunset provides the backdrop to the Death Railway Bridge, the focus of The Bridge on the River Kwai film, in Kanchanaburi (p189) **4** Novice Buddhist monks partaking in study at Wat Phra Pathom, Nakhon Pathom (p198)

Sleeping

Sleeping

Bangkok has perhaps the best variety of places to stay of any Asian capital, which is one of the reasons why it's such a popular destination for roving world travellers. As accommodation is spread across the city it's easy to find a place close to where you want to be: the tourist shopping ghettos of Th Sukhumvit, Th Silom and Th Surawong, the backpackers' ghetto of Banglamphu (north of Th Ratchadamnoen Klang), the centrally located Siam Square area, boisterous Chinatown, the elegant hotels along the river or the old travellers centre around Soi Ngam Duphli, off Th Phra Ram IV.

Top-end hotels will maintain international luxury standards and have at least one pool either tropically landscaped or with city views, fitness and business centres, and sometimes a spa. Rooms typically have a dataport, IDD international phone, international cable channel, mini-bar and a safety box. Special perks are listed in the individual reviews. Rates usually include breakfast.

Mid-range hotels vary greatly in quality. They all have the look of a hotel back home – a door attendant, uniformed desk clerks and a well polished lobby – but without the predictability in room standards. Most rooms boast TV (with international channels), refrigerator, mini-bar, phone and a desk (Internet access is not always available). But at the mid-range level, there are always some unexpected quirks mainly in the décor or the quality of the bathroom. Some hotels have recently remodelled rooms that are bright and cheery, while others are worn and tired. For some reason curtains and bathrooms in Thailand's hotels age worse than a heroin junkie. Swimming pools and complimentary breakfasts are noted in the review.

Guesthouses or hotels in the Cheap Sleeps range will always provide a bed, a light and four walls starting out at the cheapest level with a fan and shared bath (typically cold-water shower). For a little more baht, you can have air-con and a private bathroom with hot shower. Not all guesthouses have a 24-hour staffed desk. This corner of the market can sometimes have some real bargains, but by and large rooms are 'simple', some might even say 'rustic'. Many guesthouses span the range from dorms to 500B-plus rooms. Above 500B, in every neighbourhood except Banglamphu, these rooms come with daily maid service and fresh towels.

Small chedi (stupas) decorate a pool at the Sukhothai Hotel (p175)

Banglamphu has the greatest concentration of budget options. Th Silom and Th Sukhumvit are the major business centres and have mid- to upper-budget range hotels. Interesting options in the low-end of the mid-range can be found in Siam Square and Chinatown. If not otherwise stated, hotels offer en-suite bathrooms.

Please note that luxury hotels typically quote their rates in US dollars, a holdover from the Asian currency crisis when the Thai baht was unstable.

LONG-TERM RENTALS

Staying in Bangkok for longer than a week? Consider basing your stay at a serviced apartment with weekly and monthly rates. These include furniture, daily cleaning services, bed and bath linens, a kitchenette (with refrigerator, microwave, hot plate and utensils) and direct dial telephones, all included in the basic rent. Usually an on-site business and fitness centre and in-room Internet access are also available.

Top Five Bangkok Sleeps

After looking into every hotel room that would let us in, here is a purely subjective list of the best the city has to offer.

- **Best Business Option** Swiss Lodge (p176) and Four Seasons Hotel (p171) Both are well located, have reliable staff and all the amenities to stay connected.
- **Best for Style** Sukhothai Hotel (p175) Where ancient Thai architecture merges with minimalist drama.
- **Best Foray into History** Oriental Hotel (p174) Every 19th-century writer who wandered through Asia stayed here, and the mystique of steamships and typewriters is still alive today.
- **Best Garden** Nai Lert Park (p172) Surrounded by a lush tropical garden that transports visitors far away from Bangkok's concrete jungle.
- **Best Luxury Option** Peninsula Hotel (p175) Regularly placed as one of the world's top hotels.

Where there is one executive residence, there are many, so the accommodation listed here are a cross-section. Right in the heart of Silom's business district, Siri Sathorn Executive Residence (p175) is a fashionable option. In the embassy district off Th Ploenchit, Chateau de Bangkok (p171) is a bit sterile, but the residential street is charming. Th Sukhmvit-bound business people might want to consider Rembrandt Towers (p178) or Grand President (p178). If you're looking for a little escapism from the city's business districts, check out Pathumwan House (p172), near Siam Square.

In addition to these options, check the 'Property Guide' in the *Bangkok Post* on Thursday for rental advertisements and listings.

BANGLAMPHU

Banglamphu, which includes the backpacker ghetto of Th Khao San, is a well-padded landing zone for jet-lagged travellers. It is generally easy to find a place to crash for very little baht. Also, you can't swing a *túk-túk* driver without hitting an inexpensive Internet shop, beer Chang stall or *phàt thai* vendor. If you're hanging out in the low end of the budget range, just show up and start hunting as most cheapies don't take reservations, although the high season, from December to February, is when you'd better take the first bed you come across as vacancy becomes scarce. The mid-range hotels take reservations and usually offer better rates through advance notice.

The neighbourhood is divided into three distinct districts centred around the following streets: Th Khao San, Soi Rambutri-Th Phra Athit and Th Samsen. In the early 1980s there were only two Chinese-Thai hotels on Th Khao San, the Nith Jaroen Suk (now called Nith Charoen Hotel) and the Sri Phranakhon (now the Khao San Palace Hotel). Now Khao San is synonymous with budget traveller culture, and there are hundreds of hotels and guesthouses.

A different-flavoured traveller enclave has developed on the *soi* heading towards the Chao Phraya River (Mae Nam Chao Phraya) where there is more mid-range accommodation. This area is within walking distance of Tha Phra Athit where you can catch express boats to major historical sites. Across Khlong Banglamphu from Th Khao San, Th Samsen cuts a path northward lined on either side by small branch-like *soi*. Home life spills out into these streets where mothers chase freshly bathed babies and neighbours shuffle to the nearest shopkeeper for sundries. The accommodation typically is converted homes with shared bathroom.

BUDDY LODGE Map pp254-5 *Hotel*
☎ 0 2629 4477, fax 0 2629 4744; www.buddylodge
.com; 265 Th Khao San; d 1800-2500B; ferry Tha Phra
Athit; air-con bus 506, ordinary bus 53; ✗ ☐

Leading the charge towards a gentrified tourist ghetto, this boutique hotel, smack dab on Khao San, has charming rooms accented with traditional Thai designs, like terra-cotta tiled floors and simple wood-panelled walls. The total effect is a romantic (and modernised) interpretation of breezy tropical manor houses. Despite the stylish décor, you won't feel out of place in your dusty sandals and fisherman pants.

NEW WORLD HOUSE APARTMENTS & GUEST HOUSE Map pp254-5 *Hotel*
☎ 0 2281 5596, fax 0 2282 5614; Th Samsen; d from
900/1200B without/with breakfast; ferry Tha Phra
Athit; air-con bus 506, ordinary 53

Facing the north side of Khlong Banglamphu off Th Samsen, this hotel offers both short and long-term room rentals. Rooms come with private hot-water shower, air-con and a small balcony. The hotel is popular with Muslim families.

ROYAL HOTEL Map pp254-5 *Hotel*
☎ 0 2222 9111–26, fax 0 2224 2083; cnr Th Ratchadamnoen Klang and Th Atsadang; d 1600B includes
breakfast; ferry Banglamphu; air-con bus 511; ✗ ☐

This is the third oldest hotel in Bangkok. Just a short walk from the Ko Ratanakosin sites, the Royal Hotel is inconveniently fenced in by fast-moving traffic, making an excursion on foot a death-defying feat. The Royal's 24-hour coffee shop is a favourite local rendezvous spot, and the daily buffet breakfast is quite good. This is one of the few upper mid-range places where there are as many Asian as non-Asian guests. Most taxi drivers know this hotel as the 'Ratana-kosin' (as the Thai sign on top of the building reads), not as the Royal.

WILD ORCHID VILLA
Map p256 *Guesthouse*
☎ 0 2629 4378; 8 Soi Chana Songkram; d with bathroom 600-650B; ferry Tha Phra Athit; air-con bus 506,
ordinary bus 53; ✗

Like an affordable resort, Wild Orchid sports an interior palette borrowed from a Mexican villa with arty baths and rooms situated to capture light. Some rooms have balconies, but nobody gets hot-water showers. A sunny outdoor patio restaurant gives tropical lizards plenty of sunning spots.

The Royal Hotel (below left)

VIENGTAI HOTEL Map pp254-5 *Hotel*
☎ 0 2280 5434, fax 0 2281 8153, 42 Th Rambutri; d
1600B; ferry Tha Phra Athit; air-con bus 506, ordinary
bus 53; ✗ ☐

Before Th Khao San was 'discovered', this was a basic Chinese-style hotel in a quiet neighbourhood minding its own business. Over the last decade or so the Viengtai has continually renovated its rooms and raised its prices until it now sits solidly in the mid-range of Bangkok hotels. With conservative hotel décor, Viengtai doesn't offer much in the way of personality (except for the caddy desk clerk), but comfort and quiet are givens.

CHEAP SLEEPS

Khao San has been afflicted with the Michael Jackson syndrome: a continuous series of facelifts rendering it shinier and plusher for plump wallets. Bare-bones digs reeking of dirty travellers are being replaced by high-rises with air-con and a lift. Savvy budgeters should shop around for the latest makeover or newcomer, which often offers incredibly cheap promotions. An interesting trend, however, is the 'bait-and-switch' lobby. New paint, fancy mirrors, tiled floors and other improvements are installed only in the lobby to serve as a lure, masking the still horrendously dirty rooms bearing smudge marks from two decades worth of sweaty palms.

For budget travellers happy to forfeit cleanliness, privacy and quiet for the sheer thrill of paying close to nothing, 150B specials are on or just off Th Khao San. They are simply small rooms with a toilet and a shower down the hall. If you don't plan on stumbling home in the wee hours, look for a room on one of the alleys of Th Khao San or Th Tanao. Th Rambutri, which runs roughly parallel to Th Khao San, also has a quieter mood.

BAAN SABAI Map p256 *Guesthouse*
☎ 0 2629 1599; 12 Soi Rongmai, s/d 170/270B, with bathroom d 500-550B; Tha Phra Athit, air-con bus 506, ordinary bus 53;

Resembling an old Bangkok-style building, Baan Sabai is aptly named for its relaxed atmosphere and a pleasant garden courtyard. The rooms are small but solid with modern baths and noise-proof concrete walls.

BARN THAI GUEST HOUSE
Map pp254-5 *Guesthouse*
☎ 0 2281 9041; 27 Trok Mayom; s 200/300B, d with bathroom 400B; ferry Tha Phra Athit; air-con bus 506, ordinary bus 53

Down a tiny alley is very quiet and secure Barn Thai, which is the converted home of an older, *rip-roy* (prim and proper) Thai woman named Churee. Although priced higher than normal for this area, it's kept very clean and the front gate is locked nightly at midnight. This is a great option for solo travellers who might be apprehensive about the unpredictable goings-on in this city and don't mind being well behaved.

BELLA BELLA HOUSE
Map p256 *Guesthouse*
☎ 0 2629 3090; 74 Soi Rambutri; s 170B, d 300-500B; ferry Tha Phra Athit; air-con bus 506, ordinary bus 53;

Just past the Soi Chana Songkhram, Bella Bella has great views on to the tiled roofs of the neighbouring temple. Rooms are spartan and clean with rickety beds, but the bathrooms are new and shiny. There is a downstairs restaurant.

CH II GUESTHOUSE
Map pp254-5 *Guesthouse*
☎ 0 2280 6284; 85-87 Soi Damnoen Klang Neua; s/d 120/170, with bathroom 200/250B; ferry Tha Phra Athit; air-con bus 506, ordinary bus 53

Built in a converted wooden house of cramped winding stairs and hallways, this guesthouse is a textbook example of a standard issue cheapie.

CHAI'S HOUSE Map p256 *Guesthouse*
☎ 0 2281 4901; 49/4-8 Soi Rongmai; s/d from 150/250B; ferry Tha Phra Athit; air-con bus 506, ordinary bus 53;

Take a right on the *soi* running beside Baan Sabai and you'll reach this family-run guesthouse with shared bathrooms. It's a security-conscious, quiet place with a sitting area out the front. All rooms have shared bathrooms. A 1am curfew is required of guests.

CLASSIC INN Map pp254-5 *Guesthouse*
☎ 0 2281 7129; 259 Th Khao San; d 250-350B; d with bathroom 390-450B; ferry Tha Phra Athit; air-con bus 506, ordinary bus 53;

The lobby at this guesthouse-hotel is more impressive than its rooms, but the solid concrete partitions provide a humane retreat from noise. There are all sorts of upgradeable amenities – private bath, air-con, hot water shower – if you're starved of creature comforts.

D&D INN Map pp254-5 *Guesthouse*
☎ 0 2629 5252; 68-70 Th Khao San; s/d 450/600B; ferry Tha Phra Athit; air-con bus 506, ordinary bus 53;

This place is always packed with huge new backpacks and equally fresh-faced arrivals. Each room has a TV, private bathroom and IDD phone.

KAWIN PLACE Map pp254-5 *Guesthouse*
☎ 0 2281 7511; 86 Th Khao San; s/d 250/350B, d with bathroom 550B; ferry Tha Phra Athit; air-con bus 506, ordinary bus 53;

Formerly Khao San Privacy Guest House, this impersonal guesthouse-hotel is down a *soi* off Th Khao San. The new building has well-polished wooden floors and gleaming bathrooms. The older wing has shared squat toilets.

KHAO SAN PALACE INN
Map pp254-5 *Guesthouse*
☎ 0 2282 0578; s with fan/air-con 280/400B, d from 350/530B; ferry Tha Phra Athit; air-con bus 506, ordinary bus 53;

Set back down an alley, Khao San Palace is a multistorey guesthouse with a spiffy lobby and a new wing of clean private baths. Skip the older wing with junky rooms. Even though this is moving towards mature digs, young bucks fill the open vacancies in their drunken, shirtless *joie de vivre*.

PRAKORP'S HOUSE

Map pp254-5 *Guesthouse*

☎ 0 2281 1345, fax 2629 0714; 52 Th Khao San; s/d 150/250B; ferry Tha Phra Athit; air-con bus 506, ordinary bus 53

This is one of the last old-style guesthouses on Th Khao San. Prakorp's is an old wooden house set back from the road, with wood-floored rooms and a small café at the front, overlooking Th Khao San. The entryway is obscured by the army-green umbrellas of the sarong and souvenir vendors set up on the street out front.

PRASURI GUEST HOUSE

Map pp254-5 *Guesthouse*

☎ & fax 0 2280 1428; s/d/tr with fan 220/280/360B, with air-con 380/450/530B; ferry Tha Phra Athit; air-con bus 506, ordinary bus 53

Venturing outside Th Khao San, follow Th Tanao across Th Din So into a neighbourhood of Chinese-style storefronts. At the first *soi* (Soi Phrasuli), hang a right to reach this guesthouse. Instead of the usual crowd of sunburned Europeans, Prasuri's downstairs restaurant is crowded with Thai schoolchildren on a lunch break. Despite the din of secondary-school gossiping, the rooms are quiet and clean and all have private bathroom.

RAJATA HOTEL Map pp254-5 *Hotel*

☎ 0 2281 8977; 46 Soi 6, Th Samsen; s/d 360/480B; ferry Tha Phra Athit; air-con bus 506, ordinary 53; ☒

Along this soi, there are several Thai 'no-tell' motels designed for hourly visitors who need lots of privacy (note the interior car park). Incongruously, backpackers make up a good portion of the clientele. Of the strip, Rajata is the best with crisp clean sheets and no stale smoke smell.

RIVER GUEST HOUSE

Map pp254-5 *Guesthouse*

☎ 0 2280 0876; 18/1 Soi 3 (Soi Wat Samphraya), Th Samsen; d 150-170B; ferry Tha Phra Athit; air-con bus 506, ordinary bus 53

Deep into serpentine *soi*, River Guest House has a friendly and relaxed mood with a popular common area for tale-swapping. The rooms are nothing special, however.

SIAM ORIENTAL Map pp254-5 *Guesthouse*

☎ 0 2629 0312; 190 Th Khao San; s with fan 280B, q 680B; ferry Tha Phra Athit; air-con bus 506, ordinary bus 53; ☒

Multistorey Siam Oriental has a variety of rooms, most with private bathroom, of varying sizes and amenities. There's a large restaurant and a lift.

TUPTIM BED & BREAKFAST

Map pp254-5 *Guesthouse*

☎ 0 2629 1535, fax 0 2629 1540, www.tuptimb-b .com; 82 Th Rambutri; s 250-400B; d 550B; ferry Tha Phra Athit; air-con bus 506, ordinary bus 53; ☒

All of Tuptim's rooms have shared gender-segregated toilets and hot-water showers.

VILLA GUEST HOUSE

Map pp254-5 *Guesthouse*

☎ 0 2281 7009; 230 Soi 1, Th Samsen; s/d 250/500B; ferry Tha Phra Athit; air-con bus 506, ordinary bus 53

This old teak house occupies a cosy garden amid the village life of Soi 1. Instead of the urban sounds of traffic, Villa wakes up to the sounds of roosters crowing or stiff-broomed sweeping and the smells of mesquite cooking fires. Villa adheres to the guesthouse maxims of shabby baths and thin sheets. With only 10 rooms all with shared bathroom and fan, Villa is often full and recommends making reservations.

THEWET & DUSIT

Thewet, the district north of Banglamphu near the National Library, is also popular with travellers, especially for families and the over-30 crowd. A series of guesthouses line the *soi* that lies directly across from Th Si Ayuthaya where it crosses Th Samsen. It's a lovely leafy area, but during the rainy season it is prone to flooding. These places are run by various members of the same extended family. Dusit has a few large package-tour hotels as well as Bangkok's only youth hostel.

THAI HOTEL Map pp254-5 *Hotel*

☎ 0 2629 2100, fax 0 2280 1299; 78 Th Prachatipatai; s/d 950/1250B; ordinary bus 9, 12, 56; ☒ ▢ ▣

A popular business option, Thai Hotel has modern standards and a reserved atmosphere.

A complimentary shuttle bus delivers guests to the area's attractions. Next door, a little open-air Chinese coffeeshop makes the best *kaafae yen* (iced Thai coffee) in the city.

TRANG HOTEL Map pp250-1 *Hotel*
☎ 0 2282 2141, fax 0 2280 3610; www.trang-hotel .co.th; 99/1 Th Wisut Kasat; d 1200-1400B; ferry Tha Thewet; ordinary bus 49; ⚡

This is a subdued mid-range option popular with families. Rooms with all the mod cons radiate from an interior pool courtyard and a shady outdoor sitting area. The hotel's landscaping blocks out the intrusion from the traffic-choked main road. The location is a drawback; you'll want to master the buses or be prepared for a lengthy walk to the nearest river ferry pier.

CHEAP SLEEPS
BANGKOK INTERNATIONAL YOUTH
HOSTEL Map pp250-1 *Hostel*
☎ 0 2282 0950, bangkok@ tyha.org; 25/2 Th Phitsanulok; dorm 120B; s/d 280/350B; ferry Tha Thewet; ordinary bus 16, 19; ⚡

East of Th Samsen is the Bangkok branch of this international network. The rooms are cramped and tired. One plus is the friendly common area of good-natured early risers from all over the globe. The tourist information desk in the lobby is staffed by local university students.

SRI AYUTTAYA GUEST HOUSE
Map pp250-1 *Guesthouse*
☎ 0 2282 5942; Soi Thewet, Th Si Ayuthaya; d 300B, with bathroom 380-450B; ferry Tha Thewet

Sri Ayuttaya has romantic rooms with pretty hardwood floors, exposed brick and other stylish touches.

CHINATOWN
Many visitors venture into this neighbourhood for a little more cultural immersion. Chinatown's hotels are unexciting high-rise buildings outfitted to suit the aesthetic tastes of visiting Chinese families: lots of mirrors and faux gold in the lobbies. But the rates and rooms communicate in the international language for 'good value'. The Indian district known as Phahurat is less expensive and caters to business travellers from the Indian subcontinent.

There are several budget choices around Bangkok's main train station, Hualamphong,

which is handy if you're making an early morning getaway. Watch your pockets and bags around the Hualamphong area. The cream of the razor artists operate here as the train passengers make good pickings.

BURAPHA HOTEL Map pp252-3 *Hotel*
☎ 0 2213 5459, fax 0 2226 1723; 160/14 Th Charoen Krung; d 550-600B; ferry Tha Saphan Phut; ⚡

On the western edge of Chinatown, Burapha has nice simple rooms and is popular with do-it-yourself exporters hitting the Sampeng Lane wholesale shops. You'll share the cramped elevator with huge plastic bags filled with goods en route to foreign soils. The hotel segregates its guests by nationality: the Westerners get one floor, Indians another and Chinese yet another.

GRAND VILLE HOTEL Map pp252-3 *Hotel*
☎ 0 2225 0050; 930 Th Maha Chai; s/d from 1700/1900B; pool; ferry Tha Saphan Phut

Popular with Indian and Chinese business travellers, Grand Ville is the 'swankiest' hotel in the neighbourhood. Rooms are huge and comparable in quality to mid-range chain hotels back home.

KRUNG KASEM SRIKUNG HOTEL
Map pp252-3 *Hotel*
☎ 0 2225 0132, fax 0 2225 4705; 1860 Th Krung Kasem; d 550B; ordinary bus 25, 35, 53; ⚡

Southwest of Hualamphong Railway Station, this high-rise has clean, sizeable rooms. Exterior rooms will pick up a lot of street noise but also garner a killer view of the circulating traffic around the train station.

MIRAMAR HOTEL Map pp252-3 *Hotel*
☎ 0 2226 3579, fax 0 2225 4994; 777 Th Maha Chai; d 750-850B; ferry Tha Saphan Phut; ⚡

A low-level business hotel, Miramar has sizeable rooms with functional (if outdated) bathrooms and the sweetest desk staff in the city. Opt for an interior room to escape the roar of traffic.

NEW EMPIRE HOTEL Map pp252-3 *Hotel*
☎ 0 2234 6990–6, fax 0 2234 6997; 572 Th Yaowarat; d 580-650B; ferry Tha Ratchawong; ⚡

Near the Th Charoen Krung intersection and a short walk from Wat Traimit, New Empire has a central Chinatown location and pleasant 'deluxe' rooms. The standard rooms are home to many long-term Chinese Thai who use the common hallway as a living room for visiting, smoking and hanging up laundry.

RIVER VIEW GUEST HOUSE

Map pp252-3   *Guesthouse*

☎ 0 2234 5429, fax 0 2237 5428; 768 Soi Phanurangsi, Th Songwat; d 700-800B; ferry Tha Si Phraya; ✿

River View has an awesome location in the Talat Noi area, between Silom and Chinatown, steps from the river. Stream-like *soi* turn in on themselves, connecting the guesthouse with the sturdy Jao Seu Kong Chinese shrine guarded by colourful dragon statues and grease-stained machine shops. Utterly disorienting, the *soi* tempt you into doing circles through the neighbours' living rooms, which extend into the narrow streets.

While most of the rooms have a river view (one of the cheapest in town), the bad news is that only the bed sheets are clean. River View is a tough one to find. From Charoen Krung heading north of Th Si Phraya, take a left on to Th Songwat (before the Chinatown Arch), then the second left onto Soi Phanurangsi. You'll start to see signs at this point and the road will become barely passable by car.

WHITE ORCHID Map pp252-3   *Hotel*

☎ 0 2226 0026, fax 0 2225 6403; 409-421 Th Yaowarat; d 1200-1700B; ferry Tha Ratchawong; ✿

Another solid choice, White Orchid is centrally located in Chinatown and has generous-sized rooms and tidy beds. The lobby is a house of mirrors, so be careful not to bump into yourself.

CHEAP SLEEPS
SRI HUALAMPHONG HOTEL

Map pp252-3   *Hotel*

☎ 0 2214 2610; 445 Th Rong Muang; d with bathroom 200B; ordinary bus 25, 35, 53; ✿

Along the eastern side of the railway line, Sri Hualamphong is a long-running and atmospheric spot with a grand ornamented staircase and terrace sitting area. Rooms are simple padlocked partitions.

SIAM SQUARE & PRATUNAM

Conveniently located on the Skytrain route, this area has a host of high-rise chains that offer predictable, yet sterile, Western standards. A devoted cast of *túk-túk* and taxi drivers throng the entrance zealously pouncing on every map-toting victim. If you're a pedestrian wanderer, you'll be happier at a smaller hotel that is less of a target.

With a glimpse into Bangkok's daily routine, Soi Kasem San 1, off Th Phra Ram I, has a cluster of nice guesthouses intermixed with lunch-time vendors and commuting office workers. Early-to-bed, early-to-rise travellers with do-it-yourself itineraries tend to congregate in this area.

Sleeping in Transit

Finding moderately priced accommodation in the airport area is difficult. Most of the hotels charge nearly twice as much as comparable hotels in the city just for the convenience.

Amari Airport Hotel (☎ 0 2566 1020, fax 0 2566 1941; www.amari.com; d from US$200; day-use from US$75; pool), connected to the airport by an air-conditioned walkway, is obviously the closest hotel to Bangkok International. The Amari offers nonsmoking rooms and an executive floor with huge suites.

Asia Airport Hotel (☎ 0 2992 6999, fax 0 2532 3193; 99/2 Moo 8, Th Phaholyothin; d from 2800B) is 3km north of the airport at Km 28. It provides a free shuttle bus to and from the airport.

Central Grand Plaza Bangkok (☎ 0 2541 1234, fax 0 2541 1087; 1695 Th Phahonyothin; d from 4000B) is a luxury-class hotel overlooking the Railway Golf Course and Chatuchak Park. There is a daily shuttle to Chatuchak Park and Mo Chit Skytrain station for trips into central Bangkok.

Comfort Suites Airport (☎ 0 2552 8921–9, fax 0 2552 8920; 88/117 Vibhavadi Rangsit Hwy; d 1400-1500B; pool), which is about five minutes south of the airport by car, has large rooms with all the amenities. Best of all, the hotel provides a free shuttle to/from the airport.

We-Train International House (☎ 0 2929 2222, fax 0 2929 2300, www.we-train.co.th; 501/1 Mu 3, Th Dechatungkha, Sikan, Don Muang; dorm 280B; d 610-1030B; pool) is the most inexpensive option. Operated by the nonprofit Association for the Promotion of the Status of Women, We-Train International House provides airport pick-up service with advance notice. Alternatively, you could visit the website for a printable map (with directions in Thai) to give to a taxi driver.

AMARI WATERGATE Map pp262-3 *Hotel*
☎ 0 2653 9000, fax 0 2653 9045; watergate@amari
.com; 847 Th Phetburi; s/d US$184/200; Skytrain
Chitlom; 🚗 🛒 🖳
Right in the centre of Bangkok's Pratunam district, this chain hotel has large rooms, great
views and is well situated for easy access to
shopping safaris in air-con bubbles or market
madness.

ASIA HOTEL Map pp262-3 *Hotel*
☎ 0 2215 0808, fax 0 2215 4360; www.asiahotel
.co.th; 296 Th Phayathai; s/d from 2900/3200B;
Skytrain Ratchathewi; 🚗 🛒
A first stop for those new to Asia, the Asia Hotel
is a full-sized hotel, with big rooms, all the amenities and good-sized bathrooms with a climb-
able bathtub. Quiet and predictable, this makes
for a nice landing pad after a long flight.

BAIYOKE SKY HOTEL Map pp248-9 *Hotel*
☎ 0 2656 3000, fax 0 2656 3555, www.baiyokehotel
.com; Baiyoke Tower II, 222 Th Ratchaprarop; s/d from
3000/3400B; Skytrain Phayathai; 🚗 🛒
Thailand's tallest tower, Baiyoke measures in
at a gangly 88 storeys tall. In its rush to grow
heavenward, Baiyoke's designers forgot to put
effort into the interior. Even the highly prized
skyzone rooms (floors 50–62) are gaudy and
flimsy. The views, bathtubs and Internet promotions transforms Baiyoke into a decent
package, considering the altitude. Guests also
have free access to the 77th-floor observatory.

BORAN HOUSE Map pp248-9 *Hotel*
☎ 0 2253 2252, fax 0 2253 3639; 487/48 Soi Wat-
tanasin, Th Ratchaprarop; s/d 850/950B; Skytrain
Ploenchit; 🚗
This small inn with apartment-style rooms
is tricky to find, tucked deep into a neighbourhood of maze-like *soi* where everyday
life extends from the open parlours to the
ever-narrowing streets. It can be reached by
walking east along the *soi* opposite the Indra
Regent (off Th Ratchaprarop).

CHATEAU DE BANGKOK
Map pp262-3 *Serviced Apartments*
☎ 0 2651 4400, fax 0 2651 4500; www.accorhotels
-asia.com; 29 Soi Ruam Rudi, Th Ploenchit; studios
from 44,000B, one bedroom from 64,000B per month;
Skytrain Ploenchit; 🚗 🛒 🖳
Owned by French hotel group Accor, Chateau
de Bangkok offers serviced studios (33–50 sq
metres) and one-bedroom apartments (56–84

The Baiyoke Sky Hotel (left)

sq metres) with standard hotel-style décor.
They claim the bed is a king, but even a joker
would know it is a queen. All but the smallest
studio has a galley kitchen with fridge and
microwave. The area is perfect for doing business with the nearby embassies.

CONRAD BANGKOK Map pp262-3 *Hotel*
☎ 0 2690 9999, fax 0 2690 9000; www.conradhotels
.com; 87 Th Withayu; from US$240; Skytrain Ploenchit;
🚗 🛒 🖳
This newcomer offers modern rooms decorated with Thai silks and painted in rust and
ochre earth tones. Bath aficionados should
search no further. Rooms have deep soak tubs
with an adjustable TV and in-room speakers
to combine watery pursuits with music and
television. Showers have ceiling-affixed rain
dispensers to turn bathing into a spa experience. The hotel even sends you home with a
complimentary stuffed elephant as a souvenir.
So far the hotel's dance club and lobby bar has
the whole town abuzz.

FOUR SEASONS HOTEL
Map pp262-3 *Hotel*
☎ 0 2250 1000, fax 0 2253 9195; www.fourseasons
.com; 155 Th Ratchadamri; d from US$190; Skytrain
Ratchadamri; 🚗 🛒 🖳
Bangkok's well-regarded Regent Hotel has been
adopted by the Four Seasons chain. This is classic

Thai architecture with a spectacular traditional mural descending a grand staircase and neck-craning artwork on the ceiling. Still boasting a formidable reputation in the business realm, the Four Seasons has an efficient 24-hour business centre. It should be noted, however, that standard rooms are situated around an outdoor (un-airconditoned) courtyard.

The Grand Hyatt Erawan Hotel (below)

GRAND HYATT ERAWAN

Map pp262-3 *Hotel*
☎ 0 2254 1234, fax 0 2254 6308; www.bangkok
.hyatt.com; cnr Th Ratchadamri & Th Ploenchit; d from
US$280; Skytrain Chitlom; 🔀 🔁 💻
The exterior of this grand hotel is an interesting mixture of Greek Revival and traditional Thai architecture. Inside an atrium jungle erases urban fatigue, and the mezzanine level displays some of the hotel's vast Thai art collection. Rooms have hi-tech gadgets such as reading lights that pull out of the wall and in-room temperature controls. European-style tubs with tall showerheads make the bathrooms fully functional. The rooms in the rear of the hotel overlook the prestigious Bangkok Royal Sports Club racetrack. For most top-end visitors it vies with the Four Seasons or the Novotel Bangkok on Siam Square for the best location in terms of transport and proximity to shopping.

HOLIDAY MANSION HOTEL

Map pp262-3 *Hotel*
☎ 0 2255 0099, fax 0 2253 0130; 53 Th Withayu; s/d
2500/2700B, includes breakfast; Skytrain Ploenchit;
🔀 🔁
This concrete building has a pleasant interior courtyard pool and huge rooms sporting electric blue décor. There is no difference between the deluxe and grand deluxe rooms, so don't upgrade. A solid mid-range option with business facilities, Holiday Mansion becomes more attractive when there are 50% promotions.

INDRA REGENT Map pp262-3 *Hotel*
☎ 0 2208 0033, fax 0 2208 0388; www.indrahotel.com;
120/126 Th Ratchaprarop; s/d from 2400/2600B, includes
breakfast; Skytrain Phayathai; 🔀 🔁
Similar to the Asia Hotel, the Indra lacks the front-door skytrain entrance, but many visitors seem unfazed by this. With multiroom accommodation and good business facilities, this hotel is made all the more attractive to families and corporate guests when it offers regular discount rates.

INTERCONTINENTAL BANGKOK

Map pp262-3 *Hotel*
☎ 0 2656 0444, fax 0 2656 0555, www.intercontinental
.com, 973 Th Ploenchit; d from US$240, suite from
US$500; Skytrain Chitlom; 🔀 🔁 💻
Formerly Le Meridien President Hotel & Tower, this modern scraper has standard rooms with huge beds, marble bathrooms, separate tub and shower (tall enough for over-sized foreigners) and a work desk.

PATHUMWAN HOUSE

Map pp262-3 *Serviced Apartments*
☎ 0 2612 3580, fax 0 2216 0180; 22 Soi Kasem San
1, Th Phra Ram I; d 1000-1400B daily, 24,000-40,000B
monthly; Skytrain National Stadium; 🔀
Tucked back in the crook of the *soi*, this high-rise of dubious architectural merit is mainly a long-term business hotel with weekly and monthly rates. Rooms are a decent size with kitchenette and a generous bed. In the front courtyard, a collection of caged birds greet the customers in Chinese, English, Japanese and Thai.

NAI LERT PARK Map pp262-3 *Hotel*
☎ 0 2253 0123, fax 0 2253 6509, www.swissotel
.com; 2 Th Withayu; d from US$200; Skytrain Ploenchit;
🔀 🔁 💻
Formerly an outpost of the Hilton chain, this highly ranked hotel has changed hands (and

names) to the Raffles International group. What does remain here is the exquisite garden with a private jogging track and a tropically landscaped pool which provides an instant remedy for jet lag.

NOVOTEL BANGKOK ON SIAM SQUARE Map pp262-3 *Hotel*
☎ 0 2255 6888, fax 0 2255 1824, www.novotel .co.th; Soi 6, Siam Square; d from 5100B; Skytrain Siam; 🛇 🖳 🖫

Another extremely well-located hotel for business or leisure is the Novotel. In fact, the Novotel is so reliable that you might forget you've travelled over an ocean or a continent. Rooms look exactly like high-end hotels back home. The deluxe rooms are more suited to business travellers as they have a desk and larger sitting area.

RENO HOTEL Map pp262-3 *Hotel*
☎ 0 2215 0026, fax 0 2215 3430; 40 Soi Kasem San 1; d from 900B, includes breakfast; Skytrain National Stadium; 🛇 🖳

This Vietnam War veteran is now an R&R option for the new millennium, where you can rest in simple rooms and recreate beside the pool. The licked-with-paint Reno has an attentive door attendant, leftover 1960s aesthetics and a shiny restaurant popular with well-scrubbed locals.

SIAM ORCHID INN Map pp262-3 *Hotel*
☎ 0 2555 3140, fax 0 255 3144; siam_orchidinn@ hotmail.com; 109 Soi Ratchadmri, Th Ratchadamri; d 1100-1200B, breakfast included; Skytrain Chitlom; 🛇

Opposite Central World Plaza, Siam Orchid is a petite anomaly in a super-sized neighbourhood. Well-appointed rooms boast all the standard amenities and are decorated with Thai antiques.

VIP GUEST HOUSE/GOLDEN HOUSE
Map pp262-3 *Hotel*
☎ 0 2252 9535, fax 0 2252 9538; www.goldenhouses .net; 1025/5-9 Th Ploenchit; d 1300B, includes breakfast; Skytrain Chitlom; 🛇

The shiny lobby of this small inn leads to rooms with mammoth-sized beds and parquet floors.

The Nose Knows

Top-end and some mid-range hotels have smoking and non-smoking floors. If you've got a nose for stale cigarette smoke, which has amazing endurance in the tropics, state your preference at the time of booking.

The baths, however, don't have bathtubs, only showers. VIP is down a little alley near the TOT office, at the corner of King's Antiques.

CHEAP SLEEPS

A-ONE INN Map pp262-3 *Guesthouse*
☎ 0 2215 3029; www.aoneinn.com; 25/13-15 Soi Kasem San 1; d 500-600B; Skytrain National Stadium; 🛇

A friendly place with laundry and Internet facilities. A-One gets a lot of return business. Rooms come with hot-water showers.

BED & BREAKFAST INN
Map pp262-3 *Guesthouse*
☎ 0 2215 3004; Soi Kasem San 1; s/d 400/500B, includes breakfast; Skytrain National Stadium; 🛇

The maze-like Bed & Breakfast Inn has rooms that are substantially smaller than those at the A-One Inn, but the rates include a European breakfast.

WENDY HOUSE Map pp262-3 *Guesthouse*
☎ 0 2216 2436, fax 0 2216 8053; d from 550B; Skytrain National Stadium; 🛇

This cheery place has small but well-scrubbed rooms and tiled baths that would make more expensive places look like novices. Rising up the price scale, you can add a fridge and TV. There are also daily newspapers for guests to read in the lobby and weekly rates available. If you're carrying unusually heavy bags, note there's no lift and the stairs are abnormally steep.

SILOM & SURAWONG

This business district has the city's greatest concentration of luxury hotels – all boasting coveted riverfront property. Moving east, hotels range from modest business to affluent business.

The main thoroughfares are incredibly urban, but narrow side streets lead to ethnic enclaves of Muslim and Korean neighbourhoods. This district is also home to the infamous red-light district of Patpong.

BANYAN TREE HOTEL Map pp260-1 *Hotel*
☎ 0 2679 1200, fax 02679 1199, www.banyantree .com; Thai Wah II Bldg, 21/100 Th Sathon Tai; d US$300; Skytrain Sala Daeng; air-con bus 15, 67; 🛇 🖳 🖫

Housed in the back of the Thai Wah II Building, a sleek wafer of a skyscraper, the Banyan Tree has translated the mood of a spa into a hotel, with the fragrance of gardenias, dimly lit corridors in woodland colours and a sunken lobby next to a languid fountain-and-rock garden. The suites are magnificent with separate work and sleep areas, two TVs and deep bathtubs. There is a free shuttle to Silom, overcoming the hotel's inconvenient location for pedestrians.

DUSIT THANI Map pp260-1 — Hotel

☎ 0 2200 9000, fax 02 2636 6400, www.dusit.com; 946 Th Phra Ram IV; d US$225-300; Skytrain Sala Daeng; 🅿 🅿 🖵
A long-running favourite of the business set, this massive tower hotel is a government enterprise. It offers good rooms and very stylish suites.

HOLIDAY INN SILOM BANGKOK
Map pp260-1 — Hotel

☎ 0 2238 4300, fax 0 2238 5289; www.bangkok-silom .holiday-inn.com; 981 Th Silom; d 4300B, suite 6800B; ferry Tha Oriental; Skytrain Surasak; 🅿 🅿 🖵
A freshly laundered, fashionably dressed set of Europeans confidently file out of this American chain unaware that the hotel's reputation stateside is a step above roadside. Reinvented here on Asian turf, the hotel does what it knows best – predictability.

LA RÉSIDENCE HOTEL Map pp260-1 — Hotel

☎ 0 2233 3301, fax 0 2237 9322; residence@loxinfo .co.th; 173/8-9 Th Surawong; d 1000-1500B, suite 2700B; Skytrain Chong Nonsi; 🅿 🅿
'Boutique' translates well into Thai. La Résidence is a hip boutique inn with playfully and individually decorated rooms. The standard is very small and fittingly decorated like a child's bedroom with lavender and green tiling. The next size up is more mature and voluptuous with blood red walls and modern Thai motifs.

MANOHRA HOTEL Map pp260-1 — Hotel

☎ 0 2234 5070, fax 0 2237 7662; 412 Th Surawong; d 1400B includes breakfast; ferry Tha Oriental; 🅿 🖵
This is a decent business-class hotel popular with Asian businesspeople. The rooms are adequate (although the showers are for a petite clientele), but they might be a tad musty for sensitive noses.

MONTIEN Map pp260-1 — Hotel

☎ 0 2233 7060, fax 0 2236 5218; www.montien.com; 54 Th Surawong; s/d 5800/6400B; Skytrain Sala Daeng; 🅿 🅿 🖵
The old guard of Thai high-end hotels, Montien receives patronage from the diplomatic

corps as well as government functions. From the rooms on the south wing, you can get a view of blazing Patpong. This is not the height of fashion or luxury, but the desk staff is kind and the costumed door attendants man their posts with precision. The hotel is heavily marketed in Sweden, which is the native home of the general manager.

NARAI HOTEL Map pp257-9 — Hotel

☎ 0 2237 0100, fax 0 2236 7161; www.narai.com; 222 Th Silom; s/d 3000/3500B, suites from 4800B; Skytrain Chong Nonsi; 🅿 🅿
Before booking into this hotel be sure to organise a handsome promotional discount. The rooms have hardwood floors and cosy beds, but the bathrooms are small and ageing quickly.

ORIENTAL HOTEL Map pp257-9 — Hotel

☎ 0 2659 9000, fax 0 2659 0000; www.mandarin oriental.com; 48 Soi Oriental, Th Charoen Krung; d from US$300, suites from US$900; ferry Tha Oriental; 🅿 🅿 🖵
The 124-year-old Oriental Hotel, right on Mae Nam Chao Phraya, is one of the most famous hotels in Asia, akin to Raffles in Singapore or the Peninsula in Hong Kong. Rated as one of the best hotels in the world, it is about the most expensive in Bangkok. The hotel management prides itself on providing highly personalised service – once you've stayed here the staff will remember your name, what you like to eat for breakfast, even what type of flowers you'd prefer in your room. The rooms evoke a romanticised version of those bygone steamship days when everyone dressed for dinner and English tea was the litmus test for a civilisation.

From the river, the Oriental Hotel looks more modern and less classic – the original Author's Wing is dwarfed by the Tower (built in 1958) and River (1976) wings. A landscaped annexe directly across the river from the hotel harbours the spa, a sports centre with jogging track, air-conditioned tennis and squash courts, and classrooms for the Thai Cooking School and Thai Culture Programme.

It's worth wandering in, if only to see the lobby (no shorts, sleeveless shirts, backpacks or sandals allowed). Be sure to stroll through the Author's Wing, which has historic photos of the royal family and an effervescent sense of literary history. The riverside patio is also a fabulous place to catch an evening drink. See boxed text opposite.

From Literati to Glitterati

A simple boarding house for waylaid European traders, the Oriental's first incarnation in the late 19th century had more in common with the guesthouses on Th Khao San than with the regal structure it is today. It was traded unceremoniously by the original owners, two Danish sea captains, to Hans Niels Anderson, the founder of the formidable East Asiatic Company, which operated between Bangkok and Copenhagen. Anderson hoped to transform the hotel into a civilised palace of grand architecture and luxury standards. Shrewdly he hired an Italian architect, S. Cardu, to design what is now the Author's Wing, which was the city's most fantastic building not constructed by the king.

The rest of the hotel's history lies with its famous guests. A Polish-born sailor named Joseph Conrad stayed here in between jobs on sailing vessels and steamships in 1888. The hotel brought him good luck: he got his first command on the ship *Otago*, from Bangkok to Port Adelaide, which in turn gave him ideas for several early stories. W. Somerset Maugham stumbled into the hotel with an advanced case of malaria contracted during his overland journey from Burma. In his feverish state, he heard the German manager arguing with the doctor about how a death in the hotel would hurt business. Maugham's recovery and completion of *Gentleman in the Parlour: A Record of a Journey from Rangoon to Haiphong* gave lasting literary appeal to the hotel. Other notable guests have included Noël Coward, Graham Greene, John le Carré, James Michener, Gore Vidal and Barbara Cartland. Some modern-day writers claim that an Oriental stay will overcome writers block.

PENINSULA HOTEL Map pp257-9 *Hotel*
☎ 0 2861 2888, fax 0 2861 1112; pbk@peninsula.com; 333 Th Charoen Nakhon; d from US$280, suite from US$420; private ferry dock near the Oriental Hotel; ⛅ 🏊 🖥

Rimming Mae Nam Chao Phraya, the Peninsula Hotel is one of the highest-ranking luxury hotels in the world. The lobby feels like an Asian interpretation of a mausoleum – polished marble hallways with squat squared hallways, a hushed sense of privilege and well-poised guests of distinguished pedigree. Being on the Thonburi side of the river, the Peninsula faces Bangkok's high-rises, and guests don't have to dodge incoming vehicles upon leaving or entering the premises. A complimentary ferry service shuttles guests to and from Bangkok.

Tastefully decorated, the rooms and suites boast oversized executive work desks and private fax numbers. The Peninsula is also known for its affiliated golf course.

ROYAL ORCHID SHERATON
Map pp257-9 *Hotel*
☎ 0 2266 0123, fax 0 2236 8320; 2 Soi Captain Bush, Th Si Phraya; d from US$230; ferry Tha Si Phraya; ⛅ 🏊 🖥

Next door to the River City shopping complex, the Sheraton provides a hassle-free shopping experience. It's known for crisp, efficient service, and the business centre is open 24 hours.

SHANGRI-LA HOTEL Map pp257-9 *Hotel*
☎ 0 2236 7777, fax 0 2236 8579; www.shangri-la.com; 89 Soi Wat Suan Phlu, Th Charoen Krung; d from US$210, suites from US$330; ferry Tha Oriental; Skytrain Saphan Taksin; ⛅ 🏊 🖥

Another riverside hotel, the Shangri-La strives for a New Asia aesthetic with minimalist, almost forgettable, décor. It's within the luxury sphere, yet families won't feel like bulls in a china shop.

SILOM VILLAGE INN Map pp257-9 *Hotel*
☎ 0 2635 6810, fax 0 2635 6817; csilom-village-inn@ thai.com; 286 Th Silom; rooms from 1800B; ferry Tha Oriental; ⛅ 🖥

Like a mini-resort in the midst of busy Silom, this hotel is part of a greater beast known as Silom Village Trade Centre, an outdoor arcade of shops and restaurants. Guests frequently grab a drink in the open-air pavilion to watch TV or passers-by. All rooms come with the usual upper mid-range amenities, and generous discounts explain why they are frequently full.

SIRI SATHORN EXECUTIVE RESIDENCE
Map pp260-1 *Serviced Apartment*
☎ 0 2266 2345, fax 0 2267 5555; 27 Soi Sala Daeng 1, Th Silom; studio 65,000B, one bedroom 75,000-85,000B per month; Skytrain Sala Daeng; ⛅ 🏊 🖥

Affiliated with the Sukhothai Hotel, this boutique executive residence offers stylish city roosts in the heart of the Silom business district. With great views, the accommodation feels more like an apartment; they even lack that particular hotel smell. Studios are 57 square metres and bedrooms are 60-95 square metres.

SUKHOTHAI HOTEL Map pp260-1 *Hotel*
☎ 0 2287 0222, fax 0 2287 4980; www.sukhothai.com; 13/3 Th Sathon Tai; d US$280, suites US$395; ⛅ 🏊 🖥

Many luxury hotels try so hard to emulate the West that they end up looking like bad parodies. Not the Sukhothai. Of all the luxury hotels,

Entrance to the Swiss Lodge (below)

this one dips deep into Thailand's architectural heritage to produce a unique expression. Modelled after Thailand's ancient capital, Sukhothai resembles the temple monuments of colonnaded antechambers with deliberate views of exterior ponds and serene Buddha figures. The rooms are exquisitely decorated and have hardwood floors and reasonably sized bathrooms. The only drawback is that the hotel's location discourages pedestrian excursions.

SWISS LODGE Map pp257-9   *Hotel*
☎ 0 2233 5345, fax 0 2236 9425; www.swisslodge.com; 3 Th Convent; d 4300-5190B includes breakfast; Skytrain Sala Daeng; 🅇 🅇 🅇

With only 57 rooms, Swiss Lodge is an intimate inn with large-scale amenities. Rooms are new, showers are tall, beds are comfortable, and staff is on the mark. Soundproof windows further enhance the attraction for people doing business along this busy corridor.

TOWER INN Map pp257-9   *Hotel*
☎ 0 2237 8300-4, fax 0 2237 8286; www.towerinn bangkok.com; 533 Th Silom; s 2700B, d from 2900B; Skytrain Chong Nongsi; 🅇 🅇

This multistorey hotel has several floors of large, updated rooms that are popular with repeat business travellers. Pass on staying here, however, if they usher you to one of the older rooms that haven't been remodelled.

TRINITY SILOM HOTEL Map pp257-9 *Hotel*
☎ 0 2231 5050, fax 0 2231 5417; 425/15 Soi 5, Th Silom; s 1700-2100B, d 1900-2300B; suites from 2500B; Skytrain Chong Nonsi; 🅇 🅇

Another business option, Trinity Silom has simple comfortable rooms and suites. It's behind the headquarters of Bangkok Bank.

CHEAP SLEEPS
ANNA'S CAFÉ & BED
Map pp257-9   *Guesthouse*
☎ 0 2632 1323; 44/16 Th Convent; dm 350B, d 850B, family room 950B; Skytrain Sala Daeng; 🅇

Don't let people tell you differently: this is a guesthouse, just like you'd find in Banglamphu. Due to the geography, Anna's is sometimes labelled a 'boutique B&B' and enjoys inflated prices as a result. The rooms are plain and simple, private rooms have en suite bathrooms and the family room sleeps four. The attached café serves European and Thai cuisine.

BANGKOK CHRISTIAN GUEST HOUSE
Map pp260-1   *Guesthouse*
☎ 0 2233 2206, fax 0 2237 1742; reservations@bcgh .org; 123 Sala Daeng Soi 2, Th Convent; s/d/tr 1000/1400/ 1800B, includes breakfast; Skytrain Sala Daeng; 🅇

After a complete renovation, Bangkok Christian is once again open and full of guests. Although it is a Christian guesthouse, it is still steps away from Patpong's strip clubs, proving that vice and morality are dependent companions. Lunch and dinner are also available at low prices.

INTOWN RESIDENCE Map pp257-9 *Hotel*
☎ 0 2639 0960, fax 0 2236 6886; 1086/6 Th Charoen Krung btw Th Si Phraya & Soi 30; d 600-700B; ferry Tha Si Phraya; 🅇

Sleeping – Silom & Surawong

Once you get off Th Charoen Krung into the neighbourhood's soi, this hotel's merits become clear. This is a Muslim, mainly Indian, area which subtly twists the misconception of Thailand's homogeneity. Intown's rooms are unremarkable, but the desk staff is very friendly.

NIAGARA HOTEL Map pp257-9 *Hotel*
☎ 0 2233 5783; 26 Soi 9 (Suksavitthaya), Th Silom; Skytrain Chong Nonsi; d 680B; ⊠
From the outside Niagara looks like another shady no-tell motel, but its interior reveals one of the best bargains in Silom. The rooms are immaculate with gleaming white bathrooms (the shower curtains are brand-spanking new), the rock-hard bed is graced with a plush comforter and a fresh coat of paint brings cheer to the institutional setting. A dubious perk is the three channels of 24-hour pornography on the compact TV – it beats pay-per-view. The neighbourhood, a mix of Thais and Koreans, adds a necessary touch of ordinary life to this otherwise sterile district. If you need a cab, hailing a ride on Th Sathon will bypass congested Silom.

PINNACLE HOTEL Map pp260-1 *Hotel*
☎ 0 2287 0111, fax 0 2287 3420; www.pinnaclehotels.com; 17 Soi Ngam Duphli, Th Phra Ram IV; d 2000-2400B with breakfast; bus air-con 507, ordinary 13, 14, 74, 109, 115 and 116; ⊠ ⊡
Out of sync with the rest of the neighbourhood, the Pinnacle Hotel is a mid-range business option with comfortable and modern rooms. Amenities include a fitness centre with sauna, steam room and outdoor rooftop Jacuzzi.

SALA THAI DAILY MANSION
Map pp260-1 *Guesthouse*
☎ 0 2287 1436; 15 Soi Si Bamphen; d 200B with shared bath; bus air-con 507, ordinary 13, 14, 74, 109, 115 and 116
This is a friendly guesthouse at the end of a quiet alley lined with family guesthouses and container gardens. There are basic rooms (bed, light, walls), which have shared bathrooms. There is a pleasant sitting area with TV on the 3rd floor and a breezy rooftop terrace.

WOODLANDS INN Map pp257-9 *Hotel*
☎ 0 2235 3894, fax 0 2237 5493; www.woodlandsinn.org; 1158/5-7 Soi 32, Th Charoen Krung; s/d 570/750B; ferry Tha Si Phraya; ⊠
North of the main post office, Woodlands has basic box rooms with lumpy beds and clean bath. Like Intown (see earlier), the neighbourhood outshines the accommodation.

TH SUKHUMVIT
Staying in this area puts you in the newest part of Bangkok and the furthest from old Bangkok near the river. Taxis take longer to get here because of the one-way street system. On the other hand the Skytrain runs all the way from the start of Th Sukhumvit at Th Ploenchit to well beyond the Eastern Bus Terminal.

South of Soi Asoke is the tourist sector where, among other more salubrious activities, you will encounter the hedonistic pursuits of the 1960s – R&R days live on with girlie bars and hired Thai girlfriends. Otherwise Th Sukhumvit has the general mix of tourists, Thais, expats and businesspeople.

CITY LODGES Map pp264-5 *Hotel*
Two locations: ☎ 0 2253 7705, fax 0 2255 4667; Soi 9, Th Sukhumvit, Skytrain Nana; and ☎ 0 2254 4783, fax 0 2255 7340; Soi 19, Th Sukhumvit, Skytrain Asoke; s/d 1300/1500B daily, s/d 26,400/28,200B; ⊠
Favourites among middle-class business travellers, both locations are small inns operated by the larger Amari chain. Rooms are adequate and are mere steps away from the Skytrain. You might want to request a room at the back to avoid street noise.

FEDERAL HOTEL Map pp264-5 *Hotel*
☎ 0 2253 0175, fax 0 2253 5332; federalhotel@hotmail.com; 27 Soi 11, Th Sukhumvit; d from 900B; Skytrain Nana; ⊡ ⊠
Club Fed, as the holidaying sex tourists call it, was once an R&R stop for American GIs that has upgraded to enjoy a slightly improved reputation. The upstairs rooms are comfortably decorated with rattan furniture and generously sized beds. The ground levels, however, should be avoided as these occasionally flood in the rainy season and aren't worth the price. The main attractions are the frangipani-lined pool and time-warped American-style coffee shop.

FORTUNA HOTEL Map pp264-5 *Hotel*
☎ 0 2251 5121, fax 0 2253 6282; 19 Soi 5, Th Sukhumvit; s 1200B, d 1500B includes breakfast; Skytrain Ploenchit & Nana; ⊡ ⊠
Near Little Arabia, this is a friendly mid-sized hotel popular with Japanese business people. Rooms have a surprising amount of personality compared with the typical hotel, and the Fortuna manages to shield guests from the nearby girlie-bar scene.

LANDMARK HOTEL Map pp264-5 *Hotel*
☎ 0 2254 0404, fax 0 2253 4259; 138 Th Sukhumvit, btw Soi 4 & Soi 6; d from US$169, suites from $235; Skytrain Nana; 🛇 💻 🕭

The revolving door at this corporate hotel hasn't stopped turning with working travellers, thanks to a business centre that never sleeps. But it's not all business suits and briefcases these days. Khakis and waist packs belonging to package holidaymakers are starting to appreciate the practical Landmark.

NOVOTEL LOTUS BANGKOK
Map pp264-5 *Hotel*
☎ 0 2261 0111, fax 0 2262 1700; www.novotellotus .com; 1 Soi 33, Th Sukhumvit; d from 4800B; Skytrain Phrom Phong; 🛇 💻 🕭

Accor's second Bangkok branch is a well-designed modern creation with a soothing lotus pond in the centre of the lobby. Rooms are plush and private. There are also exquisite suites on a semi-private floor with a terrace.

REMBRANDT HOTEL Map pp264-5 *Hotel*
☎ 0 2261 7100, fax 0 2261 7017; www.rembrandt bkk.com; 19 Soi 18, Th Sukhumvit; d from US$125, suites from US$250; Skytrain Asoke & Phrom Phong; 🛇 💻 🕭

This tastefully decorated hotel has large rooms and the city's best Mexican and Indian restaurants (see Señor Pico's of Los Angeles p125 and Rang Mahal p124). Another advantage is the proximity to Queen Sirikit National Convention Centre, off Soi 16.

REMBRANDT TOWERS
Map pp264-5 *Serviced Apartments*
☎ 0 2261 5900, fax 0 261 5958; 22 Soi 20, Th Sukhumvit; studio from 40,000B, one bedroom from 68,000B per month; Skytrain Asoke & Phrom Phong; 🛇 💻 🕭

Affiliated with the Rembrandt Hotel, these serviced apartments offer well-designed studios (25–40 sq metres) and one bedroom apartments (50–95 sq metres) with spiffy bathrooms. A fully stocked kitchenette appears in the one bedrooms, while a microwave, electric kettle and other necessities are provided in the studio. Don't be shocked to find that the lobby is more ostentatious than the rooms.

ROYAL ASIA LODGE & PARADISE
Map pp264-5 *Hotel*
☎ 0 2251 5514, fax 0 2253 2554; www.royalasialodge .com; 91 Soi 8, Th Sukhumvit; d 900B; suite 1300B; Skytrain Nana; 🛇 🕭

At the end of a peaceful residential *soi*, Royal Asia has quiet, comfortable rooms well removed from the area's constant hustle and bustle. Suites have a kitchenette. A free shuttle service provides transport to Th Sukhumvit.

WESTIN GRANDE SUKHUMVIT
Map pp264-5 *Hotel*
☎ 0 2651 1000, fax 0 2255 2441, www.westin.com /bangkok; 259 Th Sukhumvit at Soi 19; US$95-110; Skytrain Asoke; 🛇 💻 🕭

This modern monstrosity has been fully renovated to discard its old image as the Delta Grand Pacific. Unlike the rock-hard beds found in most Thai hotels, the Westin presents the trademarked 'Heavenly' beds, which are, as the name suggests, soft and cosy like the eternal reward of living a good life. Bathrooms have separate bathtub and shower with a shower head that is *faràng*-sized (western-sized).

WINDSOR SUITES & WINDSOR HOTEL Map pp264-5 *Hotel*
Suites: ☎ 0 2262 1234, fax 0 2262 1212; suites from 6000B; hotel: ☎ 0 2258 0160, fax 0 2258 1491; s/d from 2000/2400B; www.windsorsuiteshotel.com; 8-10 Soi 20 (Soi Nam Phung), Th Sukhumvit; Skytrain Phrom Phong; 🛇 💻 🕭

With hotel rooms and suites segregated into different buildings, the Windsor is popular with group tours and corporate travellers. Suites have kitchenettes with hardwood floors and marble bath (although the showerhead is a little short), and long-term visitors get their own floor. Hotel rooms are fairly standard.

MAJESTIC SUITES Map pp264-5 *Hotel*
☎ 0 2656 8220, fax 0 2656 8201; www.majesticsuites .com; 110-110/1 Th Sukhumvit btw Soi 4 & Soi 6; s/d 1165/1500B; Skytrain Nana; 🛇

Love-for-money gets thick over in this part of Th Sukhumvit, but Majestic's hermetically sealed rooms deliver privacy and quiet. The hotel is small and friendly and rooms that face Sukhumvit have a bird's-eye view of the street's traffic-snarled grandeur.

GRAND PRESIDENT
Map pp264-5 *Serviced Apartments*
☎ 0 2651 1200, fax 0 2651 3835; 14-16 Soi 11, Th Sukhumvit; www.presidentpark.com; studio from 10,500/32,600B weekly/monthly, one bedroom from 21,000/64,600B weekly/monthly; Skytrain Nana; 🛇 💻 🕭

These executive apartments are top of the professional line with studios (26–32 sq metres) and one bedrooms (50–60 sq metres). Of the two, the best option is the Royal Suite, which has a generous work area.

CHEAP SLEEPS

ATLANTA Map pp264-5   *Guesthouse*
☎ 0 2252 6069, 0 2252 1650, fax 0 2656 8123; 78 Soi 2/Soi Phasak, Th Sukhumvit; d fan/air-con 485/665B; Skytrain Ploenchit;

The oldest hotel in the Th Sukhumvit area, the Atlanta enjoys cult-like status with return budget travellers who shun the Banglamphu 'tourist' scene. The mid-century lobby and jungle-landscaped pool are obviously more beguiling than the worn-out rooms of dubious cleanliness. To its credit, however, this is one of the only budget options in Sukhumvit and it offers lots of quirky amenities, like traditional Thai dance performances, old-fashioned letter-writing desks in the lobby, each with its own light and fan, and an enforced policy barring sex tourists.

For the uninitiated, a visit to The Atlanta café is recommendable over a night's stay. The subdued coffee shop features a heavily annotated menu (itself a crash course in Thai cuisine), a selection of British, German and French newspapers, a sound system playing Thai, classical and jazz (including an hour of King Bhumibol's compositions beginning at noon), and evening video selections that include film classics with Thailand themes (such as *Changi* and *Bridge on the River Kwai*). The Nana Skytrain station is about 15 minutes away on foot.

This hotel was started as the Atlanta Club in the 1950s by Dr Max Henn, a former secretary to the Maharajah of Bikaner and owner of Bangkok's first international pharmacy.

GOLDEN PALACE HOTEL
Map pp264-5   *Hotel*
☎ 0 2252 5115, fax 0 2254 1538; 15 Soi 1, Th Sukhumvit; d from 550B; Skytrain Ploenchit;

This L-shaped, aquamarine-coloured building is also a strong budget contender, despite its institutional façade. The rooms are a decent size, and the daily rate is fair.

MIAMI HOTEL Map pp264-5   *Hotel*
☎ 0 2253 0369, fax 0 2253 1266, miamihtl@asiaaccess .net.th; 2 Soi 13, Th Sukhumvit; s/d 650/700B; Skytrain Nana;

This laissez-faire joint has changed very little since the days when the GIs were in Bangkok,

The freeze-framed Miami Hotel (below)

and it shows in the lumpy beds and rustic bathrooms. But the strange down-and-out charm appeals to folks who spent too many hungover weekends watching war movies on TV or who claim to be collecting material for a 'novel'. Discounts are given for long-term stays should you join these lounge lizards.

SUK 11 Map pp264-5   *Hostel*
☎ 0 2253 5927, fax 0 2253 5929; www.suk11.com; dorm 250B, s without/with bath 450/500B, d 550/600; Skytrain Nana

Sukhumvit's primary outpost of backpacker culture, Suk 11 is tucked down a little sub-*soi* off Soi 11 that instantly creates a calm oasis amid the concrete jungle. The rickety wooden sitting area is serenaded by tranquil tunes and decorated with a small flower garden.

GREATER BANGKOK
Staying outside the centre of Bangkok is not recommended if you need to do a daily commute. The Victory Monument area, however, is one exception thanks to the conveniently located Skytrain station. North of Th Sukhumvit, Ratchadaphisek hosts an Asian-targeted business and entertainment area.

ARTISTS PLACE Map pp246-7 *Guesthouse*

☎ 0 2862 0056, fax 0 2862 0074; 63 Soi Thiam Bunyang, off Soi Krung Thonburi 1, Th Krung Thonburi; s/d 150/200B

You could hardly be further from the tourist track than at this quirky spot in Thonburi. This family-style place has a communal kitchen, rooftop sitting area and artist's studio space. The guesthouse offers free laundry and luggage storage services. It is tricky to find, so call ahead for directions.

BANGKOK MARRIOTT RESORT & SPA

Map pp246-7 *Hotel*

☎ 0 2476 0022, fax 0 2476 1120; 257/1-3 Th Charoen Nakhon; d from US$100, suites from $200; hotel shuttle boat from Tha Sathon, Tha Oriental; 🔀 🔝 🖳

Set amid the lushest landscaped gardens by the river, the Marriott really is a place where you can get away from it all. Because it's downriver from the main action, it gives you the perfect excuse not to leave the divine poolside area.

CENTURY PARK HOTEL

Map pp246-7 *Hotel*

☎ 0 2246 7800, fax 0 2246 7197; www.century parkhotel.com; 9 Th Ratchaprarop; s/d 4000/4500B; Skytrain Victory Monument; 🔝 🔀

Just north of Siam Square, in the Victory Monument area, Century Park is a semi-plush high-rise. Despite its location in front of the expressway, there is a lot of wandering to do in the neighbourhood, and the hotel provides daily shuttle service to the area's attractions.

MERCHANT COURT HOTEL

Map pp246-7 *Hotel*

☎ 0 2694 2223, fax 0 2694 2223; info@merchantcourt .th.com; 202 Th Ratchadaphisek; s/d from 5000/5500B; 🔀 🔝 🖳

This well-appointed hotel managed by Singapore's Raffles International occupies one of the two tower blocks of Le Concorde Building. Rooms on floors set aside for executives offer two phone lines, ergonomically designed writing desk and chair, and optional personal computer and fax/printer. When the subway is finished, there will be a station right in front of this hotel.

ROYAL PRINCESS Map pp248-9 *Hotel*

☎ 0 2281 3088; 269 Th Lan Luang; d 2000-2400B, suites from 4000B; 🔝 🔀 🖳

In a charming neighbourhood of shophouses and unhurried activity, Royal Princess is a large corporate hotel with tennis courts and a shady swimming pool. Being on the eastern rim of Banglamphu makes for a marathon walk to the area's attractions, but it is close enough to be an inexpensive cab ride.

SIAM BEVERLY HOTEL Map pp246-7 *Hotel*

☎ 0 2275 4397, fax 0 2290 0170; 188 Th Ratchadaphisek; d from 1800B, including breakfast; 🔀 🔝 🖳

In the Ratchada district, Siam Beverly is next to the Le Concorde building and close to several upmarket entertainment centres. It's fairly affordable, the service is friendly, and the rooms have all the amenities if not all the luxury.

SIAM CITY HOTEL Map pp246-7 *Hotel*

☎ 0 2247 0123, fax 0 2247 0165, siamcity@siam hotels.com; 477 Th Si Ayuthaya; s/d from US$155/165; Skytrain Phayathai; 🔝 🔀 🖳

This independently owned and operated hotel has large, well-maintained rooms with all the amenities. This is a great place for dedicated shoppers as it is a mere Skytrain stop away from Siam Square's shopping malls. The lobby features a bas-relief sculpture by the Queen's personal artist depicting the famous Thai kings and their great accomplishments.

THAI HOUSE Map pp246-7 *Guesthouse*

☎ 0 2903 9611, fax 0 2903 9354, www.thaihouse .co.th; 32/4 Mu, 8 Tambon Bang Meuang, Amphoe Bang Yai; d from 1200B

North of central Bangkok in Nonthaburi (about 40 minutes away by Chao Phraya Express) is this traditional Thai home surrounded by fruit trees that has been converted into a guesthouse. There are no worries about searching for food: cooking courses are taught on the premises. From Tha Chang, take a public boat to Bang Yai, Nonthaburi, via Khlong Bangkok Noi. Once you reach the public pier in Bang Yai, charter a boat for 100B to Thai House's own pier – all the boat pilots know it.

Excursions

Excursions

When you've had enough of Bangkok's intensity, there are several spots outside the city where you can escape for day trips or overnight visits. These are all reachable by bus or train and give an interesting look at provincial Thailand, where fashion is dictated by the market racks, business signs aren't in English, and children might be surprised to see a foreigner. In addition to their tourist attractions, these towns revolve around the local food markets – from the daytime produce markets for kitchen basics and takeaway food, to the night markets for socialising and dining. Bangkok's outlying areas also have many theme parks and animal attractions that will entertain children sick of humouring their parents.

NATURE

West of Bangkok, limestone hills rise out of the sun-parched land like a ruined city of mountain worshippers. Kanchanaburi (p189) is the best base for exploring this area of water-falls, caves and tropical jungle. Long lazy bike rides will take you past shaggy fields of sugar cane being harvested by hand and lovingly tended spirit houses guarding uninhabited woods. Well-regarded organised tours take visitors on whirlwind outings by land, water and rail. Incongruous with the peaceful natural setting is Kanchanaburi's unfortunate role in WWII as the site of a Japanese-run prisoner of war (POW) camp for Allied soldiers. Through this dramatic landscape the POWs were forced to build a supply railway. The remaining memorials to the men who died are touching examples of humanity's shared struggle against violence.

CULTURE

Thailand's long-reigning ancient capital, Ayuthaya (p184) is a Unesco World Heritage Site and a major pilgrimage site for anyone interested in Thai history. The remaining red-brick temples, which resisted the Burmese siege in the 18th century and are now resisting the pull of gravity, provide a glimpse into an exotic city that bewitched European traders venturing aboard sailing vessels in the heyday of the Asian trade route. Ayuthaya is also a popular spot for the celebration of Loi Krathong. Nearby Bang Pa-In, a royal summer palace, is a surviving homage to the world's architectural styles that convened near this port city.

Meuang Boran, an architectural museum in Samut Prakan (p203), has reproduced Thailand's great monuments into a tastefully arranged park. Explorable by bicycle, the peaceful grounds and impressive structures will inspire further flung excursions throughout the country.

Nakhon Pathom (p198) is believed to be the country's oldest city, as evidenced by the world's tallest Buddhist monument, Phra Pathom Chedi, whose original structure dates to the 6th century.

Wat Yai Chai Mongkhon, Ayuthaya (p187)

Theme Parks

Just outside Bangkok a host of theme parks, most of them kid-oriented, can be visited most easily through tour operators who pick you up from your hotel.

DreamWorld (☎ 0 2533 1946; www.dreamworld-th.com, Thai only; Km 7 Rangsit Nakornnayok, Thanya Buri; combination tickets 1000-1200B; ☼ 10am-5pm Mon-Fri, 10am-7pm public holidays) Has roller coasters, paddle boats, stunt shows, go-carts and an artificial snow world.

Rose Garden Country Resort (☎ 0 3432 2588; www.rose-garden.com; Km 32 Th Phetkasem, Sam Phran; adult/child 840/420B; ☼ 8am-6pm, cultural show at 2.45pm) A canned Thai cultural village with demos of handicrafts, dancing, traditional ceremonies and martial arts. There's also a resort hotel, swimming pools, tennis courts, a three-hectare lake, elephant rides and a golf course, as well as a namesake rose garden (with 20,000 bushes).

Samphran Elephant Ground & Zoo (☎ 0 2284 1873; Km 30 Th Phetkasem, Sam Phran; adult/child 250/150B adult/child; ☼ 8am-5.30pm) A kilometre from the Rose Garden is a nine-hectare animal zoo with elephant round-ups and crocodile shows.

Siam Park (☎ 0 2919 7200; 99 Th Serithai, off Th Ramintra, Khannayao; adult/child 200/150B; 10am-6pm Mon-Fri, 10am-7pm weekends & public holidays) A water park with artificial waves, giant water slides and a flow pool. There is also an amusement park, small zoo and playground.

BEACHES

With its emerald seas, languid breezes and blonde strips of sand, **Ko Samet** (p194) is an easy weekend getaway for urban warriors. Small bungalows dot the various bays, which are connected by footpaths traversing rocky outcrops. You can claim a piece of sand and watch the day expire, dine at beachside barbecues and listen to the music of the hidden insects.

JOURNEYS

Although slow going, the train to **Kanchanaburi** (p189) passes a steady parade of green fields, modest wooden huts, melancholy water buffalo and tiny villages seemingly swallowed up by the surrounding countryside. If you take the train beyond Kanchanaburi to Nam Tok, you travel over portions of the railway constructed by Allied POWs during their imprisonment in the Japanese forced-labour camp.

The famous floating market at **Damnoen Saduak** (p199), although very touristy, makes for an easy journey to the riverine hinterlands. After a brief spin through the obligatory floating market, long-tail boats can also cruise the surrounding canals, which serve as primary arteries for their inhabitants. Other floating markets commence around the town of **Samut Songkhram** (p201), which is linked to Damnoen Saduak by beautiful tropical scenery.

AYUTHAYA
พระนครศรีอยุธยา

You wouldn't know it by the surviving city, but Ayuthaya was once a dazzling and powerful capital with influence outside the small Siamese kingdom. Built in 1350 at the confluence of three rivers (Chao Phraya, Pa Sak and Lopburi), this island city was courted by foreign interests, extended its control deep into present-day Laos, Cambodia and Myanmar, and held sway over the region for 400 years. Perhaps its strength derived from its auspicious namesake, Ayodhya (Sanskrit for 'unassailable' or 'undefeatable'), the home of Rama in the Indian epic *Ramayana*.

Such an immortal name invited disaster. European companies conspired with and against each other to control trade with Ayuthaya. In the late 17th century a Greek advisor to King Narai even plotted an unsuccessful coup. But it was the Burmese who, after several attempts, eventually conquered and destroyed the city in 1767 astride their battle-trained elephants. The surviving Thai army fled south to re-establish control in Thonburi.

The famed capital suffered greatly at the hands of the invading Burmese army. Many of the city's temples were levelled, and the sacred Buddha figures were decapitated as if they were enemy combatants. Although Thailand's Fine Arts Department has done extensive restoration work on the ancient capital, it is still rare to find an unscarred Buddha amid Ayuthaya's ruins.

What Ayuthaya might lack in preservation it makes up for with its rich history. This was no place for obscure kings cloaked in untranslatable myths; Ayuthaya was a cosmopolitan centre with well-documented political intrigue. Its proximity to Bangkok allows for a day's shot of culture and history with a painless return home. And who could pass up a visit to a Unesco World Heritage Site?

Getting a handle on the religious and historical importance of the temples is difficult without some preliminary research. **Ayuthaya Historical Study Centre** has informative, professional displays that paint an indispensable picture of the ancient city. Also purchase the Ayuthaya pamphlet (15B) for sale at Wat Phra Si Sanphet's admission kiosk for post-ruins reading. Other museums in town include **Chao Sam Phraya National Museum**, which features a basic roundup of Thai Buddhist sculpture with an emphasis on Ayuthaya pieces, and **Chantharakasem National Museum**, which is a museum piece in itself. Chantharakasem was built by the 17th king of Ayuthaya, Maha Thammaracha, for his son Prince Naresuan, who later became one of Ayuthaya's greatest kings and ruled from 1590 to 1605. Among the exhibits is a collection of gold treasures from Wat Phra Mahathat and Wat Ratburana.

The **Ayuthaya Historical Park** is separated into two geographical districts. Ruins 'on the island', in the central part of town between Th Chee Kun and Th U Thong, are best visited on bicycle; those 'off the island', opposite the river from the centre, are best visited on an evening boat tour. You can also take a bicycle across the river by boat from the pier near Phom Phet fortress, inside the southeast corner of the city centre.

On the Island

Wat Phra Si Sanphet was once the largest temple in Ayuthaya and was used as the royal temple-palace by several kings. Built in the 14th century, the compound contained a 16m standing Buddha coated with 250kg of gold, which was melted down by the Burmese conquerors. It is mainly known for the *chedi* (stupas) erected in the Ayuthaya style, which has come to be identified with Thai art more than any other style. The adjacent **Wat Phra Mongkhon Bophit**, which dates to the 1950s, houses a huge bronze seated Buddha, the largest in Thailand.

Wat Phra Mahathat, on the corner of Th Chee Kun and Th Naresuan, has one of the first *prang* (Khmer-style tower) built in the capital. One of the most photographed sites in Ayuthaya is a Buddha head engulfed by fingerlike tree roots. Across the road, **Wat Ratburana** contains *chedi* and murals that are not quite as dilapidated.

Neighbouring **Wat Thammikarat** features overgrown *chedi* ruins and lion sculptures.

Loi Krathong Minus the Stinky Canal

Ayuthaya holds one of the country's largest Loi Krathong festivals, in which small boats are launched into waterways on the full moon of the 12th lunar month, usually November. This is a perfect opportunity to give your *krathong* (small lotus-shaped floats made from banana leaves and topped with incense, flowers, coins and candles) a more provincial sendoff far from Bangkok's stinky canals.

Ayuthaya's celebrations vary from quiet, family-friendly events to rollicking live music shows. A full army of food vendors covers every available corner. The highlight of the festival is the launching of *krathong* out into the junction of the Lopburi and Pa Sak rivers. *Krathong* can be purchased at the pier (or you can make your own from materials for sale). Thai tradition says that any couple who launch a *krathong* together are destined to be lovers – if not in this lifetime then the next.

Other events include outdoor stages offering *li-keh* (folk plays with dancing and music), Thai pop, cinema and *lákhon chaatrii* (dance-drama) all at the same time – the din can be deafening! Fireworks are also a big part of the show.

At the **Royal Folk Arts & Crafts Centre** (☎ 0 3536 6252; 24km west of Ayuthaya; admission 100B) in Bang Sai, festivities centre on traditional costumes and handmade *krathong*. If you can put together a small group, any of the hotels or guesthouses in Ayuthaya can arrange a trip to the Loi Krathong in Bang Sai.

CENTRAL AYUTHAYA

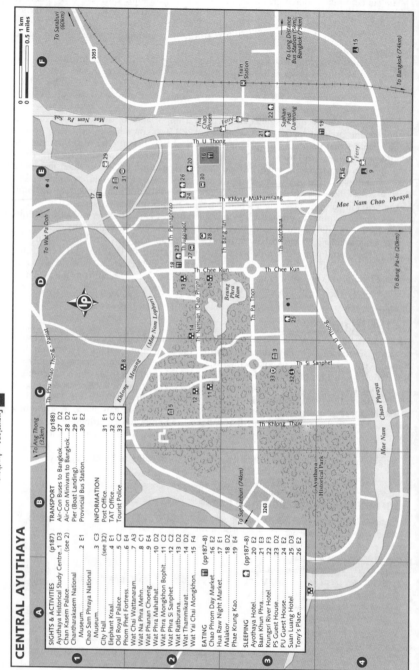

SIGHTS & ACTIVITIES	(p187)
Ayothaya Historical Study Centre...1	D3
Chan Kasem Palace...(see 2)	
Chantharakasem National	
Museum...2	E1
Chao Sam Phraya National	
Museum...3	C3
City Hall...(see 32)	
Elephant Kraal...4	E1
Old Royal Palace...5	C2
Phom Phet Fortress...6	E4
Wat Chai Wattanaram...7	A3
Wat Na Phra Mehn...8	C1
Wat Phanan Choeng...9	E4
Wat Phra Mahathat...10	D2
Wat Phra Monghkon Bophit...11	C2
Wat Phra Si Sanphet...12	C2
Wat Ratburana...13	D2
Wat Thammikarat...14	D2
Wat Yai Chai Mongkhon...15	F4

EATING	(pp187–8)
Chao Phrom Day Market...16	E2
Hua Raw Night Market...17	E1
Malakor...18	D2
Phae Krung Kao...19	E4

SLEEPING	(pp187–8)
Ayothaya Hotel...20	E2
Baan Khun Phra...21	E3
Krungsri River Hotel...22	F3
PS Guest House...23	D2
PU Guest House...24	E2
Suan Luang Hotel...25	D3
Tony's Place...26	E2

TRANSPORT	(p188)
Air-Con Buses to Bangkok...27	D2
Air-Con Minivans to Bangkok...28	D2
Pier (Boat Landing)...29	E1
Provincial Bus Station...30	E2

INFORMATION	
Post Office...31	E1
TAT Office...32	C3
Tourist Police...33	C3

Off the Island

Southeast of town on Mae Nam Chao Phraya, **Wat Phanan Choeng** was built before Ayuthaya became a Siamese capital. The temple's builders are unknown, but it appears to have been constructed in the early 14th century, so it's possibly Khmer. The main *wihǎan* (central sanctuary) contains a highly revered 19m sitting Buddha image from which the wát derives its name. The temple is dedicated to Chinese seafarers involved in the Thai-Chinese trade route during Ayuthaya's heyday, and on weekends it is crowded with Buddhist pilgrims from Bangkok who pay for lengths of saffron-coloured cloth to be ritually draped over the image.

The ruined Ayuthaya-style tower and *chedi* of **Wat Chai Wattanaram**, on the western bank of Mae Nam Chao Phraya, have been restored. Photographers favour this spot at sunset.

Wat Yai Chai Mongkhon is southeast of the town proper, and can be reached by white-and-green minibus No 6 (5B). It's a quiet place built in 1357 by King U Thong and was once famous as a meditation centre. The compound contains a very large *chedi*, and there is a community of *mâe chii* (Buddhist nuns) residing here.

North of the city, the **Elephant Kraal** is a restoration of the wooden stockade once used for the annual roundup of wild elephants. A huge fence of teak logs planted at a 45-degree angle enclosed the elephants. The king had a raised observation pavilion for the thrilling event.

North of the old royal palace *(wang lǔang)* grounds is a bridge to **Wat Na Phra Mehn**. This temple is notable because it escaped destruction in the 1767 Burmese capture, though it has required restoration over the years. The main *bòt* (central chapel) was built in 1546 and features fortresslike walls and pillars. During the 18th-century Burmese invasion, Burma's King Along Phaya chose this site to fire a cannon at the palace; the cannon exploded and the king was fatally injured, thus ending the sacking of Ayuthaya. The *bòt* interior contains an impressive carved wooden ceiling and a splendid 6m-high sitting Buddha in royal attire. (The figure's ornate clothing is an artistic characteristic unique to the Ayuthaya period; other representations of Buddha typically depict monastic robes.) Inside a smaller *wíhǎan* behind the *bòt* is a green-stone, European-pose (sitting in a chair) Buddha from Ceylon, said to be 1300 years old. The walls of the *wíhǎan* show traces of 18th- or 19th-century murals.

Sights & Information

Ayuthaya Historical Park At many of the ruins a 30B admission fee is collected from 8am to 6.30pm.

Ayuthaya Historical Study Centre (☎ 0 3524 5124; Th Rotchana; adult/student 100/50B; ⏲ 9am-4.30pm Mon-Fri, 9am-5pm Sat & Sun)

Chantharakasem National Museum (☎ 0 3525 1586, Th U-Thong, north-east corner of town; admission 30B; ⏲ 9am-4pm Wed-Sun)

Chao Sam Phraya National Museum (☎ 0 3524 1587; Th Rotchana & Th Si Sanphet; admission 30B; ⏲ 9am-4pm Wed-Sun)

Long-tail boat trip (400B for 2-hr evening trip) You can complete a semicircular tour of the island and see some of the less accessible ruins, which include Wat Phanan Choeng and Wat Chai Wattanaram, as well as river life. PU Guest House arranges tours or you can hire a boat at the pier.

Tourist Authority of Thailand (TAT; ☎ 0 3524 6076; Th Si Sanphet; ⏲ 9am-5pm) Provides maps, bus schedules and information about Loi Krathong festivities.

Tourist Police (☎ 0 3524 1446; Th Si Sanphet)

Eating & Sleeping

Food prices and quality tend to be disappointing in Ayuthaya because of the tourist tide.

Ayothaya Hotel (☎ 0 3523 2855, fax 0 3525 1018; 12 Soi 2, Th Naresuan; d 1100-3500B; 🔲 🔲) Across from the provincial bus station, this is a more upmarket place where rooms have air-con, bathroom, fridge and cable TV.

Baan Khun Phra (☎ 0 3524 1978; 48/2 Th U Thong; dm/s/d 150/250/350B) Formerly known as Reuan Doem, this 80-year-old teak house is the most atmospheric place to stay in Ayuthaya. Besides rooms, there are beds in a four-bed dorm. Rooms come with ceiling fans and shared bathroom. The place was recently given a tasteful renovation and is decorated with the friendly owner's antique collection. A very good restaurant extends from the river side of the house.

Hua Raw Night Market and **Chao Phrom Day Market** (both on Th U Thong) These markets have Muslim-style roti as well as popular Thai wok-wonders.

Krungsri River Hotel (☎ 0 3524 4333, fax 0 3524 3777; 27/2 Th Rotchana; d from 1600B; 🔲) This is a nine-storey hotel, Ayuthaya's flashiest, with decked-out rooms and suites. It has a bar/coffee house, Chinese restaurant, beer garden, fitness centre, pool, bowling alley and snooker club.

Malakor (Th Chee Kun; dishes 35-50B) Opposite Wat Ratburana, this restaurant is located in a two-storey wooden house with a charming view of the temple. It has good, cheap Thai dishes, plus an excellent selection of coffees.

Phae Krung Kao (Th U Thong; dishes 60-100B; ☽ 10am-2am) On the southern side of the bridge, this floating restaurant is so popular that Thai locals even rouse their geriatric grandmas for a night out celebrating here.

PS Guest House (☎ 0 3524 2394; 23/1 Th Juggrapat; d without bathroom 120-180B) On a back road parallel to Th Naresuan and off Th Chee Kun, this quirky place has odd-sized rooms in a homey two-storey building surrounded by a quiet neighbourhood. The manager and staff speak English well.

PU Guest House (☎ 0 3525 1213; 20/1 Soi Thaw Kaw Saw, off Th Naresuan; d from 250B) At the end of the *soi*, this well-run spot has massive amounts of tourist informa-tion, clean rooms with varying amenities, and a friendly café.

Suan Luang Hotel (☎ /fax 0 3524 5537; Th Rotchana; d 500B; ⌘) Also functioning as a training facility for students completing majors in tourism courses at the neighbouring Rajabhat University, this five-storey hotel has passable air-con rooms with fridge, TV and private bathrooms.

Tony's Place (☎ 0 3525 2578; Soi Thaw Kaw Saw, off Th Naresuan; dm without bathroom 80B, d 160-300B)

Transport

Distance from Bangkok 85km

Direction North

Travel Time Two hours by bus; 1½ hours by train

Bus 1st class air-con (52B) and 2nd-class air-con (41B) buses depart Bangkok's Northern (Mo Chit) bus terminal to Th Naresuan in Ayuthaya every 20 minutes between 5am and 7pm. On Th Naresuan in Ayuthaya, a minivan service shuttles to Bangkok every 20 minutes from 5am to 5pm for 45B.

Train From Bangkok's Hualamphong station, north-bound trains leave roughly every 30 minutes between 6.20am and 9.30am, and 6pm and 10pm. The 3rd-class fare is 20B. From Ayuthaya's train station, the quickest way to reach the city is to walk straight west to the river, where you can take a short ferry ride (3B) across to Tha Chao Phrom. Alternatively, a *túk-túk* (motorised pedicab) to any point in old Ayuthaya should be around 30B to 40B.

Boat See p73 for details on boat tours to Ayuthaya.

Getting Around Guesthouses rent bicycles for 50B per day or motorcycles for 250B; *túk-túk* tours cost 200B per hour.

Tony's is a sprawling establishment, which has an ener-getic party atmosphere with a busy patio restaurant and bar. Rooms are dependable, and some have balconies.

Excursions – Ayuthaya

Detour: Bang Pa-In

บางปะอิน

This postcard-perfect palace lies just 24km south of Ayuthaya. A hodgepodge of international architectural styles reflects the eclectic tastes of King Mongkut (1851-1868) and his son and heir King Chulalongkorn (Rama V; 1868-1910), who both used the residence as a retreat from the summer rains. The winged-eaved Thai-style pavilion, the ornate Chinese-style Wehat Chamrun Palace and a Swiss chalet mansion (which was the preferred residence of King Chulalongkorn) can be viewed. A flamboyant lookout tower (Withun Thatsana) gave the king fine views over the gardens and lakes. There are various other buildings, towers and memorials in the grounds, plus an interest-ing topiary garden where the bushes have been trimmed into the shape of a small herd of elephants. Wat Niwet Thamaprawat, across the river south of the palace grounds, looks much more like a Gothic Christian church than anything from Thailand.

Bang Pa-In can be reached by blue *sǎwngthǎew* (pick-up truck, 12B, 45 minutes) from Ayuthaya's Chao Phrom Market on Th Naresuan. From Bangkok there are buses (40B) every half-hour from the Northern Bus Terminal. You can also reach Bang Pa-In by two morning trains from Bangkok (3rd class 20B). Tour groups love Bang Pa-In so try to visit later in the day.

Chao Phraya Express Boat (☎ 0 2623 6001, 0 2623 6143 – hotline; tour 350B; ☽ 8am-5.30pm) does a tour every Sunday from Tha Maharat in Bangkok to Bang Pa-In and Bang Sai's Royal Folk Arts & Crafts Centre. For more expensive, all-inclusive river cruises to Bang Pa-In, which include tours of old Ayuthaya, see p73.

KANCHANABURI

อ.เมืองกาญจนบุรี

Leafy Kanchanaburi (pronounced 'kan-cha-NA-buri') is nestled beside craggy limestone mountains, sugar-cane plantations and Mae Nam Khwae Yai (Big Kwai River). The peaceful setting belies the town's tragic past as the site of a WWII POW camp and the infamous Death Railway Bridge. Today visitors come to pay their respects to the fallen Allied soldiers, relax at the riverside guesthouses or explore the scenic countryside. In fact, Kanchanaburi provides a better retreat into provincial Thailand than over-stimulated Ayuthaya.

Despite its leisurely charm, Kanchanaburi is a major stop for package tourists from China and Japan, who blaze through in air-con buses, stop off at the Death Railway Bridge and the war cemetery, and then hurry off to the nearby sapphire mines or one of the big waterfalls before heading north to Chiang Mai or back to Bangkok. Another contemptible component of Kanchanaburi's tourist landscape is the all-night disco and karaoke barges popular with van tours from Bangkok. Out-of-tune crooners and shoddy stereo systems disrupt the tranquillity many backpackers are hoping to find at riverside guesthouses. Guesthouse operators are full of empty promises about how the barges only go out on weekends or stop after midnight. If only Asia had a mute button, everyone could enjoy the river.

Kanchanaburi was originally established by Rama I as a first line of defence against the Burmese who, it was commonly believed, might use the old invasion route through the Three Pagodas Pass on the Thai-Burmese border. The pass is still a popular smuggling route into Burma today.

During WWII, the Japanese used Allied POWs to build the **Death Railway** along this same invasion route, though in reverse, along Mae Nam Khwae Noi (Small Kwai River) to the pass. Sixteen thousand Allied prisoners died as a result of brutal treatment by their captors, a story chronicled in Pierre Boulle's book *The Bridge on the River Kwai* and popularised by a movie based on the book. If the Thais in Kanchanaburi don't seem to have heard of such a river, it's because the wrong pronunciation was imported abroad. Thais pronounce River Kwai (more accurately spelled 'Khwae' (tributary), like 'quack' without the '-ck'. The bridge is a popular sightseeing destination, despite its rather unspectacular appearance (yup, that's a bridge). Actually the structure that has posed for a million snapshots is a post-war reconstruction; the original was bombed in 1945 by Allied planes. Only the curved portions of the bridge are original. Little remains of the original Death Railway. West of Nam Tok, Karen and Mon tribespeople carried off most of the track to use in the construction of local buildings and bridges.

Death Railway to Nam Tok

You can travel a portion of the POW-built railway, including the part that crosses the bridge over Mae Nam Kwae, aboard a Nam Tok–bound train from Kanchanaburi. The route passes through a treacherous landscape that fiercely resisted manual submission during the railway's construction. Because a return trip takes four hours (plus a two-hour layover at Nam Tok), many people opt for an organised tour, which includes one-way travel on the train and van pick-up at the terminus followed by sightseeing at additional sites. If you'd prefer to do it yourself, there is one morning train that leaves the Kanchanaburi station at 10.50am for the two-hour trip. At Nam Tok, you'll have only 20 minutes to catch the last returning train at 1pm.

Near to the bridge is a privately owned museum recently renamed **WWII & JEATH War Museum** to capitalise on guidebooks' endorsements of another museum by a similar name in town. The collection might be the oddest assortment of memorabilia under one roof, but the building affords picture-postcard views of the bridge.

Before you trek out to the Death Railway Bridge, get a little history under your belt at the **Thailand-Burma Railway Centre** and the **Kanchanaburi Allied War Cemetery**. Professional exhibits outline Japanese aggression in Southeast Asia during WWII and Japan's plan to connect Rangoon (in Burma, now known as Myanmar) with Bangkok via rail for transport of military supplies. From 1942, captured Allied soldiers as well as Burmese and Malay prisoners were transported to the jungles of Kanchanaburi to build 415km of railway. Japanese engineers estimated that it would take five years to link Thailand and Burma by rail, but the Japanese army forced the POWs to complete the railway in only 16 months. Much of it was built in difficult terrain

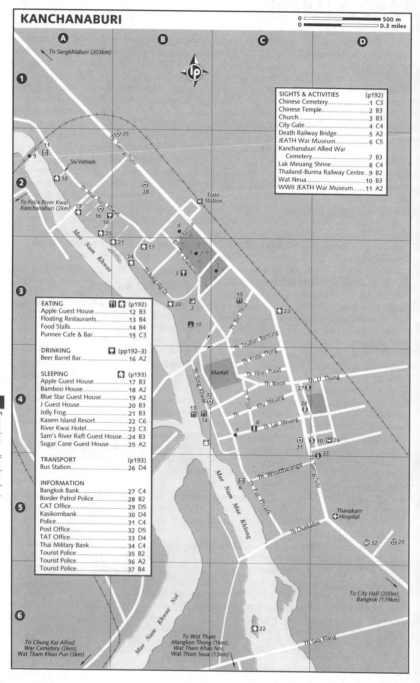

KANCHANABURI

0 — 500 m
0 — 0.3 miles

To Sangkhlaburi (203km)

Th Saengchuto

Soi Vietnam

Th Mae Nam Khwae

To Felix River Kwai
Kanchanaburi (2km)

Mae Nam Khwae

Train
Station

Th Rong Hip O

Th Chaokunnen

Th Pak Praek

Th Ban Neua

Th Tesaban Bamrung

Th Kratai Thong

Th Hiran Prasit

Market

Th Bovon

Th Prasit

Khu Meuang

Th U Thong

Th Lak Meuang

Th Saeng Chuto

Mae Nam Mae Khlong

Th Wisutththarangsi

Th Pak Phraek

Th Saengchuto

Th Chukkadon

Thanakarn
Hospital

To City Hall (200m);
Bangkok (139km)

Mae Nam Khwae Noi

To Chung Kai Allied
War Cemetery (2km);
Wat Tham Khao Pun (3km)

To Wat Tham
Mangkon Thong (1km);
Wat Tham Khao Noi;
Wat Tham Seua (13km)

Th Sala Klang

that required high bridges and deep mountain cuttings. The rails were finally joined 37km south of Three Pagodas Pass; a Japanese brothel train inaugurated the line. The Death Railway Bridge was in use for 20 months before the Allies bombed it in 1945.

Across the street from the museum, the **Kanchanaburi Allied War Cemetery** is the final resting place of only a small portion of the total number of prisoners who died during the construction of the railway. It is estimated that more than 100,000 men died, 16,000 of whom were Western POWs, mainly from Britain and Holland. Lovingly tended, the cemetery is a touching gift from the Thai people to the countries whose citizens died on their soil.

Another less visited cemetery, **Chung Kai Allied War Cemetery**, is a short and scenic bike ride from central Kanchanaburi. As in the more visited cemetery in town, the Chung Kai burial plaques carry names, military insignia and short epitaphs for Dutch, British, French and Australian soldiers.

If you still have emotional energy, the **JEATH War Museum** is a heartfelt testament to the atrocities of war. The museum operates in the grounds of a local temple and has reconstructions of the bamboo huts that were used by the POWs as shelter. The long huts contain various photographs taken during the war, drawings and paintings by POWs, maps, weapons and other war memorabilia. The acronym JEATH represents the fated meeting of Japan, England, Australia/America, Thailand and Holland at Kanchanaburi during WWII.

The limestone hills surrounding Kanchanaburi are famous for their temple caves, an underground communion of animistic spirit worship and traditional Buddhism. Winding arteries burrow into the guts of the caves past bulbous calcium deposits and altars for reclining or meditating Buddhas, surrounded by offerings from devout pilgrims. An easy bike ride from town, **Wat Tham Khao Pun** is one of the closest cave temples, and is safe to visit despite its tragic past. This temple was the site of the 1995 murder of a British tourist by a drug-addicted monk living at the wat. Kanchanaburi residents,like the rest of Thailand – were mortified by the crime, and many now refer to the cave as 'Johanne's Cave' in memory of the victim. The monk was defrocked and sentenced to death (commuted to life imprisonment without parole by the king in 1996).

Wat Tham Mangkon Thong (Cave Temple of the Golden Dragon) has long been an attraction because of the 'floating nun' – a *mâe chii* who meditated while floating on her back in a pool of water. The old nun finally passed away, but a disciple continues the tradition – sort of. Despite what her predecessor was known for, the current floating nun doesn't meditate but instead strikes Buddha-like poses based on traditional mudras. It's very popular with Chinese and Korean tour groups. Just in case you thought the nun was doing this for

The famous floating Nun of Wat Tham Mangkhon Thong, Kanchanaburi (above)

spiritual reasons, a sign informs visitors that she doesn't float for less than 200B. If a tour group of 20 or more people is here for the show, you're in luck – you only have to pay 10B. Is it worth it? Yes, but only if you happen to be here when a tour group is around; watching the Asian tourists' reactions to the floating nun's poses is more engaging than watching the nun go through her routine – with each new pose there's a frenzy of camera flashes. Most tour groups visit this temple around 5pm.

A long flight of stairs with dragon-sculpted handrails leads up the craggy mountainside behind the main *bòt* to a complex of limestone caves. Follow the string of light bulbs through the front cave.

There are also myriad outdoor activities such as river kayaking, elephant trekking, waterfall spotting and bamboo rafting – you name it, Kanchanaburi has it. To take part, many visitors sign up for tours through guides in town. As soon as you check in to a guesthouse, a friendly guide will introduce you to all of the available options.

You might notice the fish-shaped street signs in Meuang Kan (an alternate name for Kanchanaburi) – they represent *plaa yîisòk*, the most common food fish in Mae Nam Mae Klong and its tributaries.

Sights & Information

Chung Kai Allied War Cemetery (3km from TAT office; admission free; ☷ 7am-6pm) From Th Lak Meuang, take the bridge across the river through picturesque corn and sugar-cane fields until you reach the cemetery on your left.

Death Railway Bridge (2km from town) Best visited by bicycle, following the river north. You can also travel over the bridge by train en route to Nam Tok (see boxed text p189).

JEATH War Museum (Th Pak Phraek; admission 30B; ☷ 8.30am-4.30pm) The war museum is at the end of Th Wisuttharangsi (Visutrangsi), near the TAT office. The common Thai name for this museum is *Phiphitháphan Sŏngkhram Wát Tâi* (Wat Tai War Museum).

Kanchanaburi Allied War Cemetery (Th Saengchuto; admission free; ☷ 7am-6pm) It's only a 15-minute walk

from the River Kwai Hotel, or you could catch a *sǎwngthǎew* or orange minibus (No 2) anywhere along Th Saengchuto going north – the fare is 5B.

TAT office (☎ 0 3451 1200; Th Saengchuto, near the bus terminal; ☷ 8.30am-4.30pm) Provides a great provincial map with information about trips outside Kanchanaburi, as well as bus and train schedules.

Thailand-Burma Railway Centre (☎ 0 3451 0067; 73 Th Jaokannun; adult/child 60/30B; ☷ 9am-5pm)

Wat Tham Khao Pun (3km from TAT office; admission by donation; ☷ 7am-4pm) This temple is about 1km southwest of the Chung Kai cemetery across the railroad tracks and midway up the hill. It's best reached by bicycle.

Wat Tham Mangkon Thong (3km from TAT office; admission 10-200B; ☷ 7am-4pm) Take a *sǎwngthǎew* (5B) down Th Saengchuto heading south-east of town to the City Hall, then take a motorcycle taxi (10B to 20B) down Th Mae Nam Klong over the river to the temple. Alternatively, you could bike here following the roads that border the river to the Mae Nam Khlong bridge; the route is flat and passes sugar-cane fields, karst formations, wooden houses, cattle and rock quarries.

WWII & JEATH War Museum (Th Mae Nam Khwae; admission 30B; ☷ 9am-5pm) Near the Death Railway Bridge; best reached by bicycle.

Eating & Drinking

Apple Guest House (☎ 0 3451 2017; Th Rong Hip Oi; dishes 50-120B; ☷ 8am-10pm) This guesthouse restaurant introduces newcomers to Thai food without being condescending. Both the *kaeng mátsàmàn* (Muslim-style curry) and *phàt thai* (rice noodles stir-fried with egg, tofu and peanuts) are highly recommended. Apple also does what is perhaps the best banana pancake in Thailand.

Beer Barrel (Th Mae Nam Khwae; ☷ 6pm-midnight) Deep in a thicket of trees, this mazelike bar of gigantic wooden tables is a soothing elixir after a day of doing nothing. Before

The Chung Kai Allied War Cemetery

Transport

Distance from Bangkok 130km

Direction West

Travel Time 1½ to 3 hours

Minivans Tourist vans leave from Th Khao San and drop off passengers at commissioning guesthouses in Kanchanaburi (190B).

Bus Regular buses leave from Southern Bus Terminal, Thonburi (air-con 79B, every 20 minutes until 7pm) to Kanchanaburi's bus station on Th Saengchuto.

Train More scenic but slower than the bus, the train leaves from Bangkok Noi station in Thonburi twice a day (7.30am and 1.30pm, 25B) to Kanchanaburi's train station, just off Th Saengchuto. Kanchanaburi is a stop on the Bangkok Noi–Nam Tok line, which includes Nakhon Pathom (see p198) and the Death Railway Bridge (p189). To return to Bangkok, there is one morning and one afternoon departure.

Getting Around Kanchanaburi is very accessible by bicycle, which can be hired at most guesthouses (50B per day). For areas outside of town, rent a motorcycle (150B to 200B per day) from the Suzuki dealer near the bus terminal. *Săamláw* within the city cost 30B a trip. Regular *săwngthăew* (5B) cruise Th Saengchuto, but be careful you don't accidentally 'charter' one.

you suspect the beer of playing tricks on you, there really is a white horse and an overpreened ostrich living in the far corner of the bar, but they are publicity shy.

Floating restaurants (Th Song Khwae; dishes 100-200B; 6-11pm) Down on the river there are several large floating restaurants where the quality of the food varies but it's hard not to enjoy the atmosphere. Most cater to Thais out for a night of drinking and snacking.

Food stalls (Th Song Kwae; dishes 30-60B; 6-11pm) Opposite the floating restaurants are some restaurants that are just as good but less expensive. This is where the bus drivers grab a meal while waiting for their tour groups to return.

Punnee Café & Bar (☎ 0 3451 3503; Th Ban Neua; dishes 50-180B) A local legend, Punnee serves Thai and European food to expat tastes and advertises the coldest beer in town. Lots of information on Kanchanaburi is available here.

Sleeping

The most scenic places to stay are the floating guesthouses along the river, but these are also the loudest, thanks to the nightly disco and karaoke barges. A pair of good earplugs and a night of imbibing will help to block out the bass sounds. A *săamláw*

(three-wheeled pedicab) or motorcycle taxi from the bus or train stations to the river area and most guesthouses should cost from 20B to 30B.

Apple Guest House (☎ 0 3451 2017; Th Rong Hip Oi; s/t bungalows 200/250B) Despite no water view, Apple Guest House manages to keep a full house. Sitting under a huge mango tree near the Th Mae Nam Khwae intersection, Apple offers single- or double-bed bamboo bungalows. All have clean toilet and shower, fan and screened doors for better ventilation. One-day Thai cooking courses are offered.

Bamboo House (☎ 0 3462 4470; 3-5 Soi Vietnam, Th Mae Nam Khwae; d 200-350B; 🔀) If you want to stay out near the Death Railway Bridge (and away from the floating discos), Bamboo House is a good option; the only drawback is the cranky *soi* dogs that hang around the top of the street.

Blue Star Guest House (☎ 0 3451 2161; Th Mae Nam Khwae; d 150-380B; 🔀) The interior rooms (150B) here have a funky décor with faux stones that line the walls. A wooden boardwalk lined by stilted bamboo tree houses reminiscent of an Ewok village leads to the river.

J Guest House (☎ 0 3462 0307; Th Rong Hip Oi; d with bath 100B) In a hyacinth-choked lagoon, J's is the scrap-heap village you've always dreamed of building with loot pilfered from construction sites. These rickety particle-board sheds are so undignified that you won't feel guilty cracking a beer at dawn.

Jolly Frog Backpacker's (☎ 0 3451 4579; 28 Soi China, off Th Mae Nam Kwae; d 200-290B; 🔀) Jolly Frog is a well-oiled 'bamboo motel' popular with those who are counting every baht.

Kasem Island Resort (☎ 0 3451 3359, 0 2255 3604 in Bangkok; d 750-1250B; 🔀 🖵) Sitting on an island in the middle of Mae Nam Mae Klong about 200m from Tha Chukkadon, Kasem Island Resort has tastefully designed thatched cottages and house rafts. There are facilities for swimming, fishing and rafting, as well as an outdoor bar and restaurant. The resort has an office near Tha Chukkadon where you can arrange a free shuttle boat out to the island.

River Kwai Hotel (☎ 0 3451 3348, fax 0 3451 1269; 284/3-16 Th Saengchuto; d 1300B; 🔀 🖵) Kanchanaburi's original 1st-class hotel is comparable in quality to a mid-range number in Bangkok.

Sam's River Raft Guest House (☎ 0 3462 4231; 48 Th Rong Hip Oi; d 250-350B; 🔀) New and spiffy bamboo rooms with polished wooden floors sit on the river, while cheaper interior rooms escape the noise. The staff is young and sassy.

Sugar Cane Guest House (☎ 0 3462 4520; 22 Soi Pakistan, off Th Mae Nam Khwae; d 250-550B; 🔀) This friendly spot has comfortable rooms on a raft with a wide veranda, as well as bungalows and a riverside restaurant. Raft rooms are all doubles with private bathroom; the expensive rooms have beds with box springs (a rarity in guesthouses).

KO SAMET

เกาะเสม็ด

A glorious release from concrete, the island of Ko Samet has wide sandy beaches and an endless expanse of ocean less than half a day's journey from the capital city. Ko Samet is also a relatively dry island, making it an excellent place to visit during the rainy season. Of course, all of this makes it very popular with everyone – Thais, foreigners, even stray dogs – especially on weekends or holidays. During these times, people outnumber beds and new arrivals claim space on floors of beach restaurants, on the beach – just about everywhere. If you're plotting a beach getaway, opt for September rather than March.

Ko Samet earned a permanent place in Thai literature when classical Thai poet Sunthorn Phu set part of his epic *Phra Aphaimani* on its shores. The story follows the travails of a prince exiled to an undersea kingdom governed by a lovesick female giant. A mermaid assists the prince in his escape to Ko Samet, where he defeats a giant by playing a magic flute. Today the poem is immortalised on the island by a **mermaid statue** built on a rocky point separating Ao Hin Khok and Hat Sai Kaew.

In the early 1980s, Ko Samet began receiving its first mortal visitors: young Thais in search of a retreat from city life. At that time there were only about 40 houses on the island. Rayong and Bangkok speculators saw the sudden interest in Ko Samet as a chance to cash in on an up-and-coming Phuket and began buying up land along the beaches. No-one bothered about the fact that Ko Samet had been a national marine park since 1981. When *faràng* (Westerners) soon followed, spurred on by rumours that Ko Samet was similar to Ko Samui '10 years ago' (one always seems to miss it by a decade, eh?), the National Parks Division stepped in and built a visitors office on the island, ordered that all bungalows be moved back behind the tree line and started charging admission to the park.

Except at the admission gate, the regulating hand of the National Parks Division is almost invisible, as many attempts to halt encroachment have been successfully defeated by resort operators or developers. One lasting measure is the ban on new accommodation (except where it replaces old sites), ensuring that bungalows are spread thinly over most of the island.

Ko Samet by Any Other Name

Formerly Ko Kaew Phitsadan (Vast Jewel Isle) – a reference to the abundant white sand – this island became known as Ko Samet (Cajeput Isle) after the *samèt* (cajeput) tree that grows in abundance here and is very highly valued as firewood throughout Southeast Asia. Locally, the *samèt* tree has also been used in boat-building.

The northern end of the island is where most of the development is located, but compared to Bangkok even the densest part of Ko Samet seems as sparsely populated as the Australian outback. Most boats from the mainland arrive at **Na Dan Pier**, where there is one 7-Eleven and a few Internet shops (without which this could be called 'wilderness'). Closest to the pier is **Hat Sai Kaew** (Diamond Beach), the most developed stretch of beach on the island and the best place for nightlife. Wealthy Bangkokians file straight into Hat Sai's air-con bungalows with their designer sunglasses and designer dogs.

Around the next headland is a scruffier set of beaches (**Ao Hin Khok**, **Ao Phai** and **Ao Phutsa**), fittingly claimed by the backpackers.

South of Ao Phutsa, which is palm-shaded, the beaches are separated from one another by fairly steep headlands linked by narrow footpaths that make a great postnap ramble. Quiet **Ao Nuan** and **Ao Cho** (Chaw) have beaches that aren't voluptuous enough to attract crowds.

Immediately to the south is the prom queen of the bunch: **Ao Wong Deuan**, whose graceful stretch of sand supports an entourage of screaming jet skis, sardine-packed sun-worshippers and honky-tonk bars akin to those in Pattaya.

Thai college kids claim **Ao Thian** (Candlelight Beach) for all-night guitar jam-sessions. Further south is a castaway's dream of empty beaches and gentle surf, and the starting point for languid walks to the western side of the island to see fiery sunsets.

The only beach on the western side of the island is **Ao Phrao** (Coconut Beach), which hosts the island's only luxury resort and moonlights as 'Paradise Beach' to those escaping winter climates, eager for a postcard holiday.

KO SAMET

| 0 | 1 km |
| 0 | 0.5 miles |

To Ban Phe (7km)
Laem Noi Na
To Ban Phe (5km)
Ao Wiang Wan
To Ban Phe (11km)

Laem Phra

Ao Kham

Na Dan Pier
Na Dan

Ao Phrao
Hat Ao Phrao
7
10

Laem Ya/Ko Samet National Park

22

Hat Laem Yai

24
12
Laem Yai

25
3 15 16
19 9
2
Hat Sai Kaew

6 11
Ao Hin Khok

17
8
Ao Phai

20
Ao Phutsa (Ao Thap Thim)

Laem Rua Taek

5
Ao Nuan

1
23
Ao Cho

14
Ao Wong Deuan

21

Hat Saeng Thian

13
Ao Thian

Ao Thai (Gulf of Thailand)

18
Ao Wai

Ao Kiu Na Nai

4
Ao Kiu Na Nok

Laem Khut

Ao Karang

EATING	(pp196)
Bamboo Restaurant	1 B3
Naga Bungalows	2 C2
Toy Restaurant	(see 16)
White Sand Bungalows	3 C2

SLEEPING	(pp196–7)
Ao Kiu Coral Beach	4 A6
Ao Nuan Bungalows	5 B3
Ao Phai Hut	6 C2
Ao Prao Resort	7 B2
Ao Putsa	8 B3
Coconut Bungalows	9 C2
Dome Bungalows	10 B2
Jep's Inn	11 C2
Laem Yai Seaview	12 C2
Lung Dam Resort	13 B4
Malibu Garden Resort	14 B4
Ploy Talay	15 C2
Saikaew Villa	16 C2
Samed Villa	17 B3
Sametville Resort	18 B5
Tok's Little Hut	19 C2
Tub Tim	20 B3
Vongdeuan Resort	21 B4

INFORMATION	
Johnny's Internet Café	(see 9)
Ko Samet Health Centre	22 C2
National Park Branch Office	23 B3
National Park Main Office	24 C2
Post Office	25 C2

Sights & Information

ATMS & Currency Exchange – There are no ATMs on the island. Some guesthouses on Ao Phutsa offer currency exchange.

Boat Trips (per person 500-600B) Several bungalows on the island can arrange boat trips to nearby reefs and uninhabited islands, such as Ko Thalu and Ko Kuti.

Ko Samet Health Centre (btwn Hat Sai Kaew and Na Dan) Small public clinic with English-speaking doctors for minor health problems.

National Park Entrance Gates (two offices: Hat Sai Kaew & Ao Wong Deuan; adult/child 200/100B; ☽ dawn to dusk)

Post Office (Ao Hin Khok, next to Naga Bungalows; ☽ 8.30am-4.30pm Mon-Fri, 8.30am-noon Sat) Post restante and Internet access.

Eating

Most guesthouses have restaurants, and many offer beachside dining in the evenings.

Ao Prao Resort (☎ 0 3864 4101; Ao Prao; dishes 200-300B; ☽ 8am-10pm) The fancy open-air terrace restaurant at this resort is probably the best eatery on the island.

Bamboo Restaurant (Ao Cho; dishes 80-150B; ☽ 8am-10pm) This restaurant offers inexpensive but tasty food and good service.

Naga Bungalows (☎ 0 3865 2448; Ao Hin Khok; dishes 150-200B; ☽ 8am-10pm) This guesthouse-restaurant has a fantastic bakery, with warm rolls, croissants and doughnuts in the morning, and great sandwiches and pizza throughout the day. There are plenty of tofu dishes on the menu and weekly buffet meals.

White Sand Bungalows (☎ 0 3864 4000; Hat Sai Kaew; dishes 150-200B; ☽ 6-10pm) The restaurant here is a very good bet, especially when the seafood barbecue is offered – check the chalkboard out front for the nightly offerings.

Sleeping

Because of demand, Ko Samet's prices aren't always reflective of amenities. A ramshackle hut starts at 250B, and with air-con this can climb to 700B. Reservations aren't always honoured, so at peak times it is advisable to arrive early and poised for foraging.

Since this is a national park, camping is allowed on any of the beaches, but guest-house operators on the beach discourage campers from setting up nearby. There is one hassle-free area by the park entrance area. Bring your own gear as rentals are not available.

Transport

Distance from Bangkok 200km

Direction Southeast

Travel Time 4 hours

Bus Air-con buses to Rayong (117B, 2½ hours, every 30 minutes) leave Bangkok's Eastern Bus Terminal from 4am to 10pm and return from 3am to 9pm. Ordinary buses to Rayong (87B, four hours, every half-hour) leave from the same terminal from 4.30am to 10pm.

Săwngthăew (15B, 30 minutes, every 15 minutes) from Rayong bus station go to Ban Phe (where you catch the boat to Ko Samet).

Boat Most travellers catch a boat to Ko Samet from Ban Phe's Nuanthip pier. From here, boats go to Na Dan Pier (100B return), but there are also boats to Ao Wong Deuan (120B return), Ao Phrao (120B return) and Ao Wai (200B return). There is a boat from Ban Phe to Ao Kiu (200B return), but it is not as frequent; it waits until it has about seven passengers. Since Ao Kin is less popular than other areas, you might have to wait a while.

Boat schedules vary depending on the season, so prepare to wait an hour or more unless it's very busy.

If you already have a place of accommodation in mind and a large enough group (eight to 12 people), it can actually be cheaper to hire a speedboat (800B to 1200B, depending on which beach you go to and what time of day or night you hire it).

HAT SAI KAEW

Coconut Bungalows (☎ 0 3865 1661; d 500-1500B; ☒) Has 30 bungalows with fan or air-con, TV and fridge. Each bungalow has a small veranda and chairs.

Laem Yai Seaview (☎ 0 3865 1956; d 800-1200B; ☒) Has wooden bungalows with attached bathroom but not much else in the way of amenities. Electricity is on from 6pm to 6am.

Ploy Talay (☎ 0 3864 4212; d 500-800B; ☒) This place has a range of beachside bungalows; the cheaper ones are older and less comfortable.

Saikaew Villa (☎ 0 3865 1852; d 700-1650B; ☒) A huge, top-end place near the prettiest part of the beach. Breakfast is included. Try to get a room away from the noisy generators.

AO HIN KHOK & AO PHAI

Ao Phai Hut (☎ 01 213 6392; Ao Phai; s/d 500/600B) Comfortable bungalows in a pretty garden setting of humming insects and pecking chickens. If you don't like what

Bamboo Restaurant lit up at night on Ao Cho beach, Ko Samet (opposite)

you see here, follow the road until it becomes a foot path that hugs the shore connecting all the bays to one another.

Jep's Inn (☎ 0 3864 4112; Ao Hin Khok; d 500-1500B;) Jep's has 14 nicely designed bungalows. Its restaurant (which doesn't play videos in the evenings) is also quite good, and there's a shaded dining area right at the edge of the beach.

Samed Villa (☎ 0 3864 4094; Ao Phai; d 600-900B;) Come here for well-maintained, tree-shaded bungalows with large verandas. Smaller units have private bathrooms, and larger bungalows suit family accommodation. There is 24-hour electricity, and some of the bungalows have great sea views.

Silver Sand (☎ 0 1996 5720; Ao Phai; d 300-500B;) This establishment has about 40 comfortable bun-galows, with their own verandas, and 24-hour electricity. There is also a beach bar.

Tok's Little Hut (☎ 0 3864 4073; Ao Hin Khok; d 300-500B) This was one of the island's first bungalow operations. There are very simple but comfortable bungalows (no air-con options), and the price depends on proximity to the generator.

AO PHUTSA (AO THAP THIM) & AO NUAN

Ao Nuan Bungalows (Ao Nuan; d 200-400B) If you blink, you'll miss this beach and the secluded rustic huts scattered about the hillside. They all have shared bathrooms and intermittent electricity. The food here is quite good (vegetarians will appreciate it), and the eating area is set in an imaginatively arranged garden. It's a five-minute walk over the headland from Ao Phutsa.

Ao Putsa (☎ 0 1450 3075; Ao Phutsa; d 500B) This place has well-worn huts, but some of them are quite close to the water, making them pretty good value.

Tub Tim (☎ 0 1218 7759; Ao Phutsa; d 500-1200B;) At the southern end of the beach, Tub Tim has older, smaller bungalows on a shady hillside and newer, more spacious wooden bungalows with sea views and air-con.

Know Your Neighbours

Between Ao Hin Khok and Ao Phai you might see what looks like a Thai 'gathering of the tribes' – a colourful outpost presided over by Chawalee, a free-spirited Thai woman who has lived on this beach since long before the bungalows were built.

AO WONG DEUAN & AO THIAN

Lung Dam Resort (☎ 0 3865 1810; Ao Thian; d 500-600B)
This is good for low-budget romance – the huts are built of scrap and junk, both organic and otherwise. It all looks as if it belonged to some settlement of castaways marooned on a deserted island. During the high season, the restaurant sets up on the beach for drinks under the stars.

Malibu Garden Resort (☎ 0 3864 4020; Ao Wong Deuan; bungalows 950-1850B; 🍽) This resort has well-built brick or wooden bungalows; the more expensive rooms have a fridge and TV. Breakfast is included. The resort has its own boat to Ban Phe that leaves two to three times a day.

Vongdeuan Resort (☎ 0 1942 7220; Ao Wong Deuan; bungalows 800-1100B; 🍽) This is the best of Ao Wong Deuan, and is quite extravagant by Ko Samet standards. All bungalows have flush toilets and 24-hour electricity.

OTHER EASTERN BEACHES

Ao Kiu Coral Beach (☎ 0 3865 2561; Ao Kiu; tents 300B, d 300-800B; 🍽) There are only two bamboo huts

remaining here, but there are better-equipped cement huts and tents that can be rented.

Sametville Resort (☎ 0 3865 1681; Ao Wai; d 800-1500B; 🍽) Sametville is very private and offers a fine combination of upscale accommodation and isolation. Most bookings are made by phone, but you could try your luck by talking to someone at one of the Ban Phe piers.

AO PHRAO

Ao Prao Resort (☎ 0 3864 4101; d 2800-5200B; 🍽 🖥) This enchanting resort is the only luxury lodging on the island. Amenities include cable TV, room service, childcare, massage and possibly the best restaurant on the island (see p196). Prao Divers, at the resort, provides diving, windsurfing, kayaking and boat trips. If needed, private transfer to/from Bangkok can be arranged as well.

Dome Bungalows (☎ 0 3865 1377; d 700-1000B; 🍽) Dome has 22 bungalows built on the hillside. Breakfast is included. A pleasant restaurant on the premises features a menu of Thai and Western dishes.

NAKHON PATHOM
อ.เมืองนครปฐม

Nakhon Pathom is a typical provincial Thai city whose only visible link to its claim that it's the country's oldest city is the Phra Pathom Chedi. The town is worth a quick look if you are in this neck of the woods during a trip to Damnoen Saduak, but there's not enough to see to interest most visitors for very long.

Occupying the centre of town, **Phra Pathom Chedi** is the tallest Buddhist monument in the world, rising to 127m. The original monument, buried within the massive orange-glazed dome, was erected in the early 6th century by the Theravada Buddhists of Dvaravati, but in the early 11th century the Khmer king, Suryavarman I of Angkor, conquered the city and built a Brahman *prang* over the sanctuary. The Burmese of Bagan, under King Anuruddha, sacked the city in 1057 and the *prang* lay in ruins until King Mongkut had it restored in 1860. There's a Chinese temple attached to the outer walls of the *chedi*, next to which outdoor *lí-keh* (partly improvised, often bawdy folk play featuring dancing, comedy, melodrama and music) is sometimes performed. On the eastern side of the monument, in the *bòt*, is a Dvaravati-style Buddha seated in a European pose similar to the one in Wat Na Phra Mehn in Ayuthaya. It might, in fact, have come from Phra Mehn.

The *wát* surrounding the *chedi* enjoys the kingdom's highest temple rank, Ratchavoramahavihan, one of only six temples so honoured in Thailand. Rama VI's ashes are interred in the base of the Sukhothai-era Phra Ruang Rochanarit, a large standing Buddha image in the *wát's* northern *wíhǎan*.

Phra Pathom Chedi, Nakhon Pathom

Sights & Information

Day Market (btwn train station & Phra Pathom Chedi; 🕐 6am-4pm daily) Keep an eye out for *khâo lăam* (sticky rice and coconut steamed in a bamboo joint), which is reputed to be the best in Thailand. There are many good, inexpensive food vendors and restaurants in this area too.

Phra Pathom Chedi Museum (admission 20B; 🕐 9am-4pm Wed-Sun) This museum contains interesting Dvaravati sculpture.

Tang Ha-Seng (no Roman-script sign; 71/2-3 & 59/1-2 Th Thesa; dishes 50B) This is an old, reliable, stand-by, located east of the *chedi*, that does inexpensive Chinese meals.

Rathchaphruek (no Roman-script sign; Th Ratchad-amnoen, near Soi 5; dishes 100B) Located directly west of Phra Pathom Chedi, this open-air restaurant has a pleasant setting with good, medium-priced Thai food. If you catch this place on a slow day, your only dining companions will be posters of Kiss, the Beatles and other rock stars.

Transport

Distance from Bangkok 56km

Direction West

Travel Time 1 hour

Bus From Thonburi's Southern Bus Terminal, air-con buses Nos 997 and 83 (35B) depart for Nakhon Pathom throughout the day. To return to Bangkok, catch one of the idling buses from Th Phayaphan on the canal side of the road, a block from the train station. In Nakhon Pathom, buses to Damnoen Saduak floating market (No 78) depart from southeast of Phra Pathom Chedi.

Train Express and rapid trains (30B to 40B) leave Bangkok's Hualamphong station in the morning (7.45am and 9.25am) and hourly between 1pm and 7pm. Ordinary trains (3rd class 22B) leave from Thonburi's Bangkok Noi station at 7.45am and 1.50pm. For an afternoon return, there are two Hualamphong-bound trains (5.15pm and 7.00pm) and one Bangkok Noi–bound train (4.20pm).

DAMNOEN SADUAK

ตลาดน้ำดำเนินสะดวก

Wooden canoes laden with multicoloured fruit and vegetables, paddled by Thai women wearing indigo-hued clothes and wide-brimmed straw hats – this quintessential picture of Thailand might have wooed you to this country, but this photo is more than 20 years old and is a piece of history rather than a current snapshot. An updated version would show row upon row of souvenir stands lining the canals and boatloads of tourists glued to their cameras. The floating fruit vendors are still there, but the piles of exotic colours have diminished to a few lacklustre, overpriced bunches of bananas.

Should you scratch the famous Damnoen Saduak Floating Market *(tàlàat náam)* off of your list? Despite its decay, the floating market can still be fun, if you catch it early. The best advice is to arrive in Damnoen Saduak the night before, staying at the conveniently located **Noknoi** hotel and getting up around 7am to see the market. By 9am the package tours from Bangkok arrive, draining what little authenticity is left. It is almost impossible to beat the tours if you travel from Bangkok, especially on a weekday.

Damnoen Saduak Floating Market, which is more than 100 years old, is the town's only remaining market – despite what the operators say. Minor markets, such as Talat Hia Kui and Talat Khun Phitak, once offered a more traditional experience, but these have gone.

Beyond the market, the **residential canals** are quite peaceful and can be explored by hiring a boat for a longer duration. South of the floating market are several small family businesses that welcome tourists; these include a Thai candy maker, a pomelo farm and a knife crafter.

Excursions – Damnoen Saduak

Transport

Distance from Bangkok 65km

Direction Southwest

Travel Time 2 hours

Bus Air-con bus Nos 78 and 996 (52B) go direct from Thonburi's Southern Bus Terminal to Damnoen Saduak every 20 minutes, beginning at 6.30am. Most buses will drop you off at a pier along Khlong Hia Kui or Khlong Damnoen Saduak, where you can hire a boat directly to the floating market. The regular bus stop is in town just across the bridge. A yellow *săwngthăew* (5B) does a frequent loop between the floating market and the bus stop in town.

The scenery between Damnoen Saduak and Samut Songkhram makes a trip between the two a worthwhile excursion (see p201).

Sights & Information

Damnoen Saduak Floating Market (also known as Ta lat Tom Khen; Khlong Damnoen Saduak; ☾ 7am-midday) You can hire a boat from any pier that lines Th Sukhaphiban 1, which is the land route to the floating market area. The going rate is 150B to 200B per person per hour. If the boat operator wants to charge you more, keep shopping.

Damnoen Saduak Tourist Information Office (across from the floating market, Th Sukhaphiban 1; ☾ 9am-5pm)

This office can organise transport to access outlying canal sites if you want a two- to three-hour tour. It also arranges for home-stays and other canal trips.

Sleeping

Noknoi (Little Bird; ☎ 0 3225 4382; across the highway from the bus stop; d 180-350B; ✳) A clean and quiet option, Noknoi is about a 15-minute walk from the floating market.

SAMUT SAKHON
อ.เมืองสมุทรสาคร

Samut Sakhon, popularly known as Mahachai because it straddles the confluence of Mae Nam Tha Chin and Khlong Mahachai, is a bustling port town, just several kilometres from the Gulf of Thailand. A few rusty cannons pointing towards the river testify to the town's crumbling fort, built to protect the mouth of Mae Nam Chao Phraya from foreign invaders. Before the arrival of European traders in the 17th century, the town was known as Tha Jiin (Chinese Pier) because of the large number of Chinese junks that called here.

A few kilometres west of Samut Sakhon, further along Hwy 35, is the Ayuthaya-period **Wat Yai Chom Prasat**, which is renowned for the intricately carved wooden doors on its bòt. You can easily identify the wát from the road by the tall Buddha figure standing at the front.

Jao Mae Kuan Im Shrine at Wat Chawng Lom is a 9m-high fountain in the shape of the Mahayana Buddhist Goddess of Mercy, and it is popular with regional tour groups. The colourful image, which pours a constant stream of water from a vase in the goddess's right hand, rests on an artificial hill into which a passageway is carved, leading to another Kuan Im shrine.

Sights & Information

Jao Mae Kuan Im Shrine (☾ sunrise to sunset; Wat Chawng Lom; admission 20B) To get here from the ferry terminal at the harbour end of Th Sethakit (Tha Mahachai), take a ferry (2B) to Tha Chalong, and from there take a motorcycle taxi (10B) for the 2km ride to Wat Chawng Lom.

Wat Yai Chom Prasat (☾ 9am-6pm; Hwy 35; admission 20B) To reach here from Samut Sakhon, board a westbound bus (3B) heading towards Samut Songkhram. The wát is about a 10-minute ride from the perimeter of town.

Eating

Khrua Chom Ao (☎ 0 3442 2997; dishes 60-200B) About a five-minute walk from Wat Chong Lom, down the road running along the side of the temple opposite the statue of the Chinese goddess Kuan Im, is this open-air seafood restaurant with a view of the gulf. Locals prefer Khrua Chom Ao to Tarua.

Tarua Restaurant (Ferry Terminal Building, Th Sethakit; dishes 60-200B) Occupying three floors of the ferry building, this seafood restaurant offers an English-language menu.

Transport

Distance from Bangkok 28km
Direction Southwest
Travel Time 1½ hours
Bus Air-con bus No 976 from the Southern Bus Terminal in Thonburi leaves for Samut Sakhon (25B) throughout the day. Buses also run between Samut Sakhon and Samut Songkhram (ordinary/air-con 15/22B, one hour).

Train Samut Sakhon is nearly midway along the 3rd-class, short-line 'Mahachai' train route that runs between Thonburi's Wong Wian Yai station and Samut Songkhram. Wong Wian Yai can be reached via cross-river ferry from Bangkok's Tha Si Phraya. Take a cab from here to the station, which is a straight ride along Th Charoen Rat; be sure the driver understands that you are going to 'Wong Wian Yai' not 'Bangkok Noi'.

The fare to Samut Sakhon (Mahachai) is 10B; there are several morning departures a day starting at 5.30am. To return to Bangkok, there are hourly afternoon departures until 7pm. You can continue to Samut Songkhram by crossing the river by ferry to another train line.

SAMUT SONGKHRAM

อ.เมืองสมุทรสงคราม

Commonly known as 'Mae Klong', Samut Songkhram lies along a sharp bend in Mae Nam Mae Klong, just a few kilometres from the Gulf of Thailand. Owing to flat topography and abundant water sources, the area surrounding the capital is well suited to the steady irrigation needed to grow guava, lychee and grapes. Along the highway from Thonburi, visitors will pass a string of artificial sea-lakes used in the production of salt. A profusion of coconut palms makes the area look unusually lush, considering its proximity to Bangkok.

Samut Songkhram would make a good jumping-off point for early morning forays to the Damnoen Saduak floating market, 20 minutes away by bus.

The capital itself is a fairly modern city with a large market area between the train line and bus terminal. The sizable **Wat Phet Samut Worawihan**, in the centre of town near the train station and river, contains a renowned Buddha image called Luang Phaw Wat Ban Laem – named after the *phrá sàksìt* (holy monk) who dedicated it, thus transferring mystical powers to the image.

At the mouth of Mae Nam Mae Klong, not far from town, is the province's most famous tourist attraction: a bank of fossilised shells known as **Don Hoi Lot**. These shells come from *hǎwy làwt*, clams with a tubelike shell. The shell bank is best seen late in the dry season when the river surface has receded to its lowest height (typically April and May). Many seafood restaurants have been built at the edge of Don Hoi Lot, encroaching on a crab-eating macaque habitat.

Wat Satthatham, 500m down the road from Don Hoi Lot, is notable for its *bòt* constructed of golden teak and decorated with 60 million baht worth of mother-of-pearl inlay. The inlay completely covers the temple's interior and depicts scenes from the *Jataka* above the windows and the *Ramakian* below.

King Buddhalertla (Phuttha Loet La) Naphalai Memorial Park, a 10-minute walk from Amphawa Floating Market, is a museum housed in a collection of traditional central Thai houses set on four landscaped acres. Dedicated to King Rama II, a native of the Amphawa district, the museum contains a library of rare Thai books, antiques from early 19th-century Siam and an exhibition of dolls depicting four of Rama II's theatrical works *(Inao, Manii Phichai,*

Intricate flower garlands for offerings, Samut Songkhram (above)

Wild Goose Chase: DIY Floating Markets

The communities south of Bangkok, where the land meets the Gulf of Thailand, are crisscrossed by canals, creating the perfect environment for traditional Thai floating markets. Visiting these markets on your own, rather than joining a tour, will involve a love of pre-dawn excursions and a lot of investigative skills. The **Amphawa Floating Market** (*Talàat Náam Ampháwaa*), about 7km northwest of Samut Songkhram, convenes daily in front of Wat Amphawa from 6am to 8am, but is best on weekends. There are other floating markets that meet in the mornings on particular lunar days, including **Tha Kha Floating Market** (second, seventh and 12th days of the waxing and waning moons). Tha Kha convenes along an open, breezy *khlong* lined with greenery and old wooden houses.

These floating markets can be visited by chartered long-tail boat from the Mae Klong Market pier in Samut Songkhram; rates are highly negotiable, ranging from 250B for an hour to 500B all morning. Pretend that you're not really interested in going and the rate might drop. **Baan Tai Had Resort** (☎ 0 3476 7220; 1 Moo 2, Th Wat Phuang Malai-Wat Tai Had) rents kayaks for exploring these canals.

Ramakian, Sang Thong). Behind the houses is a lush botanical garden and beyond that is a dramatic-arts training hall.

Pinsuwan Benjarong Complex is a small factory in a modern house that produces top-quality *benjarong*, the traditional five-coloured Thai ceramics. Here you can watch craftspeople painting the intricate arabesques and ornate floral patterns for which *benjarong* is known. This isn't the glossy stuff you see at Chatuchak Weekend Market in Bangkok but the real thing.

Sights & Information

Don Hoi Lot To get to Don Hoi Lot you can hop into a *săwngthăew* in front of Somdet Phra Phuttalertla Hospital at the intersection of Th Prasitwatthana and Th Thamnimit; the trip takes about 15 minutes. Or you can charter a boat from the Mae Klong Market pier *(thâa tàlàat mâe klawng)*, a scenic journey of around 45 minutes.

King Buddhalertla (Phuttha Loet La) Naphalai Memorial Park (Km 63, Route 35; admission 20B; ☽ park 9am-6pm, museum 9am-6pm Wed-Sun) To get here from Amphawa Floating Market, walk over the bridge and follow the road through the gardens of Wat Amphawan Chetiyaram.

Pinsuwan Benjarong Complex (☎ 0 3475 1322; ☽ 9am-4pm) You can reach the complex, which is 1km from King Buddhalertla park, by motorcycle taxi (10B).

Sleeping & Eating

Alongkorn 1 Hotel (☎ 0 3471 1017; 541/15 Th Kasem Sukhum; d 200B) & **Alongkorn 2 Hotel** (☎ 0 3471 1709; 540 Th Pomkaew; d 200B) These sister hotels have basic accommodation.

Mae Klong Hotel (☎ 0 3471 1150; 546/10-13 Th Phet Samut; d 150-200B) Opposite Wat Phet Samut Worawihan on Th Si Champa, Mae Klong is a simple spot in the centre of town. The owners speak some English and can provide information about the area.

Meng Khao Mu Daeng (☎ 0 3471 3422; 467 Th Phet Samut; dishes 30B) This friendly spot does excellent *khâo mùu daeng* (red pork over rice) as well as *khâo nâa pèt*

(duck over rice). Clippings from a *Matichon* restaurant review on the wall attest to the duck's greatness.

Suan Ahan Tuk (Don Hoi Lot; dishes 100-200B) An extensive Thai and Chinese menu.

Transport

Distance from Bangkok 74km

Direction Southwest

Travel Time 2 hours

Bus Regular buses from the Southern Bus Terminal in Thonburi to Damnoen Saduak also stop at Samut Songkhram (45B). There are also many daily buses to Samut Sakhon (ordinary/air-con 15/22B, one hour). Buses and taxis park at the intersection of Th Ratchayat Raksa and Th Prasitphatthana.

Train Samut Songkhram is the southernmost terminus of a 70km railway, starting from Thonburi (Wong Wian Yai) station (see p200 for directions to the station), passing Samut Sakhon, where you cross the river to another rail line for the trip's last leg. To reach Samut Songkhram, you need to leave Wong Wian Yai no later than 8.30am; there are only two morning departures (7.30am and 10am) from Samut Sakhon to Samut Songkhram. The 3rd-class train costs 10B. To return there are two departures (11.30am and 3.30pm). The station is a five-minute walk from the bus terminal, where Th Kasem Sukhum terminates at Th Prasitphatthana near the river.

SAMUT PRAKAN
อ.เมืองสมุทรปราการ

At the mouth of Mae Nam Chao Phraya, where it empties into the Gulf of Thailand, Samut Prakan (sometimes referred to as Meuang Pak Nam) is home to the Ancient City and a crocodile farm – two interesting attractions worth a day's hiatus from Bangkok.

Just outside Samut Prakan, the **Ancient City** (Meuang Boran) will challenge your preconceptions that Thailand is infested with soot-stained concrete buildings, dusty roads and screaming motorcycles. Billed as the largest open-air museum in the world, the Ancient City covers more than 80 hectares of peaceful countryside scattered with 109 scaled-down facsimiles of many of the kingdom's most famous monuments. The grounds have been shaped to replicate Thailand's general geographical outline, with the monuments located accordingly.

Ancient City, Samut Prakhan

Visions of Las Vegas and its corny replicas of world treasures might spring to mind, but the Ancient City has architectural integrity and is a preservation site for classical buildings and art forms. For students of Thai architecture or those who want an introduction to the subject, it's worth a day's visit. It's also a good place for long, undistracted walks or bicycle rides (rental 50B), as it's usually quiet and never crowded. There is lots of open space for picnics, if you want to pick up some food from the market in central Samut Prakan, or you can enjoy a leisurely meal of *sômtam* (spicy salad) in an open-air pavilion catching cool breezes and listening to the rhythm of the mortar and pestle mixing your dish's ingredients.

Transport

Distance from Bangkok 30km

Direction South

Travel Time 2 hours

Bus Ordinary bus No 25 (3.50B) and air-con bus Nos 507, 508 and 511 (16B) ply regular routes between central Bangkok's Th Sukhumvit and Pak Nam (central Samut Prakan). If traffic is horrendous, consider catching the Skytrain's Sukhumvit line to On Nut station and then catching the aforementioned buses on the road heading out of Bangkok; you can also catch the Skytrain at On Nut heading back into Bangkok as well.

Getting Around The bus station in Samut Prakan is located on Th Srisamut in front of the harbour and the market. Note where the Bangkok bus drops you off because Samut Prakan has very few streets signs in Roman script. *Sǎwngthǎew* and minibuses to the town's attractions are usually parked nearby. The Ancient City is 3km from central Samut Prakan on the Old Sukhumvit Hwy. From Samut Prakan take a green minibus (No 36, 6B), which passes the entrance to the Ancient City; nervous types should sit on the left side of the bus to watch for the 'Muang Boran' sign. To return to town, cross the main highway and catch a white *sǎwngthǎew* (No 36, 5B), which can also drop you off at the road leading to the Crocodile Farm.

To reach the crocodile farm from central Samut Prakan, take the blue *sǎwngthǎew* No S61, admission 10B; this will go directly to the gate. If you are coming from the Ancient City, catch a white *sǎwngthǎew* (No 36, 5B) to the farm's access road and then a motorcycle taxi (10B) to the entrance. Bicycles are only useful for touring the Ancient City, and you can rent bicycles at the Ancient City's entrance booth.

Samut Prakan Crocodile Farm & Zoo has more than 30,000 crocs who spend their time wallowing in mud. It also harbours elephants, monkeys and snakes. The farm has trained-animal shows – which include croc wrestling and elephant performances – and the reptiles get their dinner between 4pm and 5pm.

Sights & Information

Ancient City (☎ 0 2323 9253; Old Sukhumvit Hwy, just outside Samut Prakan; adult/child 50/20B; ☀ 8am-5pm)

Samut Prakan Crocodile Farm & Zoo (☎ 0 2387 0020; adult/child 300/200B; ☀ 7am-6pm)

Directory

Directory

TRANSPORT

AIR

You can fly to Bangkok direct from an extensive list of cities in Europe, Asia, the USA and Australia. Thailand's national carrier is **Thai Airways International** (www.thaiair.com), which also operates many domestic air routes. Bangkok is one of the cheapest cities in the world to fly out of, due to the Thai government's relaxed restrictions on air fares and aggressive competition between airlines and travel agencies.

Airlines – International

Air Asia (AK; ☎ 0 2515 9999; www.airasia.com; Bangkok International Airport)

Air Canada (AC; ☎ 0 2670 0400; www.aircanada.ca; Suite 1708, Empire Tower, River Wing West, South Sathon Road, Yannawa, Sathon)

Air France (AF; ☎ 0 2635 1191; www.airfrance.com; 20th fl, Vorawat Bldg, 849 Th Silom)

Air India (AI; ☎ 0 2254 3280; www.airindia.com; 12th fl, One Pacific Place, 140 Th Sukhumvit)

Air New Zealand (NZ; ☎ 0 2254 8440; www.airnz.co.nz; 14th fl, Sindhorn Bldg, 130-132 Th Withayu)

American Airlines (AA; ☎ 0 2263 0225; www.aa.com; 11th fl, Ploenchit Tower, Th Ploenchit)

Cathay Pacific Airways (CX; ☎ 0 2263 0606; www.cathay pacific.com; 11th fl, Ploenchit Tower, 898 Th Ploenchit)

China Airlines (CI; ☎ 0 2253 4242; www.china-airlines.com; 4th fl, Peninsula Plaza, 153 Th Ratchadamri)

Garuda Indonesia (GA; ☎ 0 2679 7371–2; www.garuda -indonesia.com; 27th fl, Lumphini Tower, 1168/77 Th Phra Ram IV)

Japan Airlines (JL; ☎ 0 2692 5151/60; www.jal.co.jp; JAL Bldg, 254/1 Th Ratchadaphisek)

KLM Royal Dutch Airlines (KL; ☎ 0 2679 1100 ext 2; www.klm.com; 19th fl, Thai Wah Tower II, 21/133-134 Th Sathon Tai)

Lufthansa Airlines (LH; ☎ 0 2264 2490/2402; www .lufthansa.com; 18th fl, Q House, Asoke Bldg, 66 Soi 21, Th Sukhumvit)

Malaysia Airlines (MH; ☎ 0 2263 0565/71; www.malay siaairlines.com; 20th fl, Ploenchit Tower, 898 Th Ploenchit)

Qantas Airways (QF; ☎ 0 2636 1747; www.qantas.com .au; 14th fl, Abdulrahim Place, 990 Th Phra Ram IV)

Singapore Airlines (SQ; ☎ 0 2236 0440; www.singapore air.com; 12th fl, Silom Center Bldg, 2 Th Silom)

Swiss (LX; ☎ 0 2636 2150; www.swiss.com; 21st fl, Abdulrahim Place, 990 Th Phra Ram IV)

Thai Airways International (TG; ☎ 0 2628 2000; www .thaiair.com; 89 Th Vibhavadi Rangsit)

United Airlines (UA; ☎ 0 2253 0558; www.united.com; 14th fl, Sindhorn Bldg, 130-132 Th Withayu)

Airlines – Domestic

Until recently domestic airline choices were limited, but Thailand is now going through a period of air route deregulation, which has resulted in several low-fare, no-frills airline start-ups. Listed below are the ones most likely to last.

Air Asia (AK; ☎ 0 2515 9999; www.airasia.com; Bangkok International Airport)

Air Andaman (2Y; ☎ 0 2229 9555; www.airandaman.com; 16th fl, Sirirat Bldg, Th Rama IV)

Bangkok Airways (PG; ☎ 0 2265 5555; www.bangkokair .com; Queen Sirikit National Convention Center, 99 Th Vibhavadi Rangsit)

Orient Thai Airlines (OX; ☎ 0 2267 3210–5; www.orient -thai.com; 17th fl, Jewelry Trade Center Bldg, 919/298 Th Silom)

PB Air (9Q; ☎ 0 2261 0220; www.pbair.com; 17th fl, UBC II Bldg, 591 Soi 33, Th Sukhumvit)

Phuket Air (9R; ☎ 0 2679 8999; www.phuketairlines.com; 34th fl, Lumpini Tower, 1168 Th Rama IV)

Thai Airways International (TG; ☎ 0 2628 2000; www .thaiair.com; 89 Th Vibhavadi Rangsit)

Airport

Bangkok International Airport (BIA; Map pp246-7), 25km north of the city at Don Muang, has two international terminals (Terminal 1 and Terminal 2) and one domestic terminal.

Foreign-exchange booths on the ground floor of the arrival hall and in the departure lounge of both international terminals give a good rate of exchange, so there's no need to wait until you're in the city centre to change money if you need Thai currency. ATMs can also be found in the arrival and departure halls.

Left-luggage facilities (⊗ 5am-midnight; 70B per item for up to 24hr, then 35B for each additional 12hr) are available in the departure hall in both terminals.

Air services are set to shift to New Bangkok International Airport (NBIA; also known as Suvarnabhumi Airport), 30km east of Bangkok at Nong Ngu Hao, in September 2005. See www.suvarnabhumiairport.com for the latest information.

To reach the city from BIA, choose one of the following options.

AIRPORT BUS

A special Airport Bus operates from Bangkok International Airport to central Bangkok for 100B, with services every 15 minutes from 5.30am to 12.30am. There's an Airport Bus desk on the forecourt between Terminal 1 and Terminal 2, and another in front of the domestic terminal. To catch an Airport Bus back to the airport, just wait at one of the designated stops, which are signposted with relevant lines indicated, and buy a ticket on board the bus. The four routes are:

A-1 To Th Charoen Krung via Pratunam, Th Ratchadamri, Th Silom and Th Surawong.

A-2 To Sanam Luang via Th Phayathai, Th Lan Luang, Th Ratchadamnoen Klang and Th Tanao (close to Th Khao San in Banglamphu). In the reverse direction, it stops on Th Phra Athit.

A-3 To the Phrakhanong district via Th Sukhumvit, including the Eastern Bus Terminal.

A-4 To Hualamphong train station via Th Ploenchit, Th Rama I, Th Phayathai and Th Rama IV, passing Siam Square.

MINIVAN FROM BANGLAMPHU

If you're heading to the airport from Banglamphu, all the hotels and guesthouses can book you on to air-con minivans to the airport. These pick up from hotels and guesthouses and leave every hour on the hour from 4am to 1am (60–80B, 1½ hours).

PUBLIC BUS

Cheapest of all are the public buses to Bangkok that stop on the highway in front of the airport, but these are slow and crowded, and conductors usually won't allow you on board with bulky luggage. The fares range from 3.50B to 13B, depending on the distance and whether the bus is air-conditioned. Ordinary bus No 59 passes Th Khao San and the Democracy Monument in Banglamphu. Air-con buses are faster, and you might actually get a seat. Useful routes include:

No 4 Th Silom.

No 10 Victory Monument, Southern Bus Terminal.

No 13 Th Sukhumvit, Eastern Bus Terminal.

No 29 Northern Bus Terminal, Victory Monument, Siam Square and Hualamphong Railway Station.

TAXI & LIMOUSINE

For public metered taxis, walk directly to the public taxi desk on the forecourt in front of Terminal 1 or the domestic terminal. You'll have to join the queue and obtain a receipt from the efficient desk staff, which will include details of where you want to go (in Thai) and the licence-plate number of the cab that will take you (in English).

Cabs booked through this desk always use their meters, but you must also pay a 50B official airport surcharge and reimburse drivers for any charges if you use the city tollway; drivers will always ask your permission to use the tollway.

The taxi touts in the arrivals lounge work for limousine taxi companies, usually with Mercedes or large Toyota sedans, charging flat fares of 400B to 800B to central Bangkok.

TRAIN

The walkway that connects Terminal 1 to the Amari Airport Hotel also provides access to Don Muang train station, which has regular trains to Hualamphong Railway Station every 15 minutes or so from 5am to 8pm (3rd-class ordinary/express 5/30B, one hour). To get to Banglamphu from Hualamphong Railway Station, pick up ordinary bus No 53 from the Th Rong Muang side of the station.

Flight Bookings
FROM ASIA

STA Travel proliferates in Asia, with branches in Bangkok (☎ 0 2236 0262; www.statravel .co.th), Singapore (☎ 6737 7188; www.statrav el.com.sg), Hong Kong (☎ 2736 1618) and Japan (☎ 03 5391 2922; www.statravel.co.jp). Another resource in Japan is **No 1 Travel** (☎ 03 3205 6073; www.no1-travel.com); in Hong Kong try **Four Seas Tours** (☎ 2200 7777; www .fourseastravel.com/english).

FROM AUSTRALIA & NEW ZEALAND

To locate **STA Travel** branches in Australia, call ☎ 1300 733 035 or visit www.statravel.com.au. **Flight Centre** (☎ 133 133; www.flightcentre.com .au) has offices throughout Australia. For online bookings, try www.travel.com.au.

Both **Flight Centre** (☎ 0800 243 544; www
.flightcentre.co.nz) and **STA Travel** (☎ 0508
782 872; www.statravel.co.nz) also have
branches throughout New Zealand. The site
www.travel.co.nz is recommended for online
bookings.

FROM CANADA

Travel Cuts (☎ 1-888-359 2887; www.travelcuts
.com) is Canada's national student travel agency.
For online bookings try www.expedia.ca and
www.travelocity.ca.

FROM CONTINENTAL EUROPE

Recommended agencies in France include:

Anyway (☎ 0892 893 892; www.anyway.fr in French)

Lastminute (☎ 0892 705 000; www.lastminute.fr in
French)

Nouvelles Frontières (☎ 0825 000 747; www.nouvelles
-frontieres.fr in French)

OTU Voyages (www.otu.fr in French) This agency specialises in student and youth travellers.

In Germany, recommended agencies include:

Expedia (www.expedia.de in German)

Just Travel (☎ 089 747 3330; www.justtravel.de)

Lastminute (☎ 01805 284 366; www.lastminute.de in
German)

STA Travel (☎ 01805 456 422; www.statravel.de in German) For travellers under the age of 26.

One recommended Italian agent is **CTS Viaggi**
(☎ 06 441111; www.cts.it in Italian), specialising in student and youth travel.
In the Netherlands try **Airfair** (☎ 020 620
5121; www.airfair.nl in Dutch).
Recommended agencies in Spain include
Barcelo Viajes (☎ 902 11 62 26; www.barcelo
viajes.com in Spanish) and **Nouvelles Frontières**
(☎ 902 17 09 79).

FROM INDIA

Here are recommended agencies.

STIC Travels (Delhi ☎ 11-233 57 468, Mumbai 22-221 81
431; www.stictravel.com) Has offices in various Indian cities.

Transway International (www.transwayinternational.com).

FROM THE MIDDLE EAST

Here is a list of recommended agencies.

Al-Rais Travels (Dubai; www.alrais.com)

Egypt Panorama Tours (Cairo; ☎ 2-359 0200; www.ep
tours.com)

Israel Student Travel Association (ISTA; Jerusalem;
☎ 02-625 7257)

Orion-Tour (Istanbul; www.oriontour.com; ☎ 212 232
6300)

FROM SOUTH AMERICA

Here is a list of recommended agencies.

ASATEJ (Argentina; ☎ 011- 4114 7595; www.asatej.com
in Spanish)

Student Travel Bureau (Brazil; ☎ 3038 1555; www.stb
.com.br in Spanish)

IVI Tours (Venezuela; ☎ 0212-993 6082; www.ividiomas
.com in Spanish)

FROM THE UK

Discount air travel is big business in London.
Advertisements for many travel agencies
appear in the travel pages of the weekend
broadsheet newspapers, in *Time Out,* in the
Evening Standard and in the free magazine
TNT.

Here are recommended travel agencies:

Bridge the World (☎ 0870 443 2399; www.b-t-w.co.uk)

Flightbookers (☎ 0870 010 7000; www.ebookers.com)

Flight Centre (☎ 0870 499 0040; www.flightcentre.co.uk)

North-South Travel (☎ 01245 608 291; www.north
southtravel.co.uk) Donates part of its profit to projects in
the developing world.

Quest Travel (☎ 0870 442 3542; www.questtravel.com)

STA Travel (☎ 0870 160 0599; www.statravel.co.uk) For
travellers under the age of 26.

Trailfinders (www.trailfinders.co.uk)

Travel Bag (☎ 0870 890 1456; www.travelbag.co.uk)

FROM THE USA

Discount travel agents in the USA are known
as consolidators (although you won't see a
sign on the door saying 'Consolidator'). San
Francisco is the ticket consolidator capital of
America, but some good deals can be found in
Los Angeles, New York and other big cities.
The following agencies are recommended
for on-line bookings:

www.cheaptickets.com

www.expedia.com

www.itn.net

www.lowestfare.com

www.orbitz.com

www.sta.com (for travellers under the age of 26)

www.travelocity.com

BOAT

Although many of Bangkok's canals (khlong) have been paved over, there is still plenty of transport along and across Mae Nam Chao Phraya and up and down adjoining canals.

The **Chao Phraya Express Boat** (☎ 0 2623 6001, 0 2623 6143 – hotline; www.chaophrayaboat .com) runs between Tha (Pier) Wat Ratchasingkhon in the south and Tha Nonthaburi in northern Bangkok. There are services every 15 minutes from 6am to 6.40pm daily; fares range from 6B to 10B. At peak times there are also express services, which fly yellow or orange flags and stop at fewer stops, charging from 9B to 25B. A special tourist boat runs between Tha Banglamphu and Tha Sathon every 30 minutes between 9am and 4pm for 10B to 25B; you can get a one-day pass for unlimited travel for 75B.

There are also dozens of cross-river ferries, which charge 2B for the crossing and run every few minutes until late at night.

Canal taxi boats run along Khlong Saen Saeb (Banglamphu to Bang Kapi), Khlong Phrakhanong (Sukhumvit to Sinakharin University campus), Khlong Bang Luang/Khlong Lat Phrao (Th Phetburi Tat Mai to Saphan Phahonyothin) and Khlong Phasi Charoen in Thonburi (Kaset Bang Khae port to Saphan Rama I). These boats are mostly used by daily commuters and pull into the piers for just a few seconds – jump straight on or you'll be left behind. Fares range from 5B to 15B.

BUS

You can save a lot of money in Bangkok by using the public buses, which are run by the **Bangkok Mass Transit Authority** (BMTA; ☎ 184, 0 2246 0973; www.bmta.co.th) – the website has information on all bus routes. Ordinary (nonaircon) buses have a blue or red stripe and cost 3.50B (5B on blue-stripe buses) for any journey under 10km. Blue air-con buses cost 6B to 16B, depending on the distance travelled; orange air-con buses cost 8B to 18B. Small air-con microbuses cost 20B regardless of the distance travelled.

Pick up a copy of Bangkok Thailand (also known as Tour 'n Guide Map), which features all the Bangkok bus routes, at any bookshop.

Be careful with your belongings while riding Bangkok buses. Bag-slashers and pickpockets are common on ordinary buses, particularly around the Hualamphong Railway Station area. Some public buses operate as 'lady-buses' and will carry only women – you can usually tell straight away whether a bus is a lady-bus.

CAR & MOTORCYCLE

You'll need to have nerves of steel to drive yourself around Bangkok, and we really don't recommend it. The traffic is chaotic, the roads are poorly signposted, and random contraflows mean that you can suddenly find yourself facing a wall of cars coming the other way.

Rental

If you still want to give it a go, all the big car-hire companies have offices in Bangkok. Rates start at around 1500B per day for a small car, including basic insurance; personal accident cover is an extra 100B per day. An International Driving Permit and passport are required for all rentals.

A few reliable Bangkok car-rental companies include the following:

Avis Rent-A-Car (☎ 0 2255 5300–4; www.avisthailand .com; 2/12 Th Withayu) Branches at Bangkok International Airport and Grand Hyatt Erawan Hotel.

Budget Car Rental (☎ 0 2203 9200; www.budget.co.th; 19/23 Bldg A, Royal City Avenue, Th Phetburi Tat Mai) Also at Bangkok International Airport.

Hertz (☎ 0 2267 5161; 4th fl, Charn Issara Tower, 942/127 Th Rama IV)

National Car Rental (☎ 0 2928 1525; http://smtrentacar .com; SMT Rent-a-Car, Amari Airport Hotel, 727 Th Si Nakharin)

Parking

Finding a parking space in Bangkok can be a hassle. You can often park on the street for a small fee, but unless you can read Thai road signs this will always be bit of a gamble. It's usually safer to use the car parks at the big shopping centres or the private car parks in the central business district. Most mid-range and top-end hotels offer parking for guests.

SKYTRAIN

The **BTS Skytrain** (rót fai fáa; ☎ 0 2617 7300; www .bts.co.th) allows you to soar above Bangkok's legendary traffic jams in air-conditioned comfort. Services are fast, efficient and cheap, although the Skytrain can become busy during the morning and afternoon rush hours.

There are two lines. The Silom line runs from Saphan Taksin, at the intersection of Th Charoen Krung and Th Sathon, to National Stadium on Th Rama I. The Sukhumvit line runs from On Nut, at the southeastern end of Th Sukhumvit, to Mo Chit, near Chatuchak Weekend Market on Th Phahonyothin. The two lines intersect at Siam station (also called Central). Plans to extend the existing lines probably won't bear fruit for a few more years.

Fares range from 10B to 40B, and trains run from 6am to midnight. Ticket machines take only coins, but change is usually available from window attendants. There are useful one-day (100B) and three-day (280B) passes that allow unlimited transport by Skytrain. If you buy the three-day pass, you'll get a free Bangkok map and guide.

SUBWAY (METRO)

A new subway system *(rót fai fáa mahǎanákhawn)*, operated by the **Metropolitan Rapid Transit Authority** (MRTA; ☎ 0 2246 5733, 0 2246 5744; www.mrta.co.th) and nicknamed 'the Metro', is set to open in August 2004. First to operate will be the 20km Blue Line from Hualamphong Railway Station to Bang Seu. The route features 21 stations, including four interchange stations linking up with the Skytrain. Fares will cost 15B to 38B depending on distance travelled.

TAXI

Bangkok taxis almost all use their meters, and most have wonderful air-con and working seat belts. You can flag them down anywhere. The meter charge is 35B for the first 2km, then 4.50B per kilometre for the next 10km, 5B per kilometre for 13km to 20km and 5.50B per kilometre for any distance greater than 20km. If traffic is moving slowly, a small per-minute surcharge kicks in. Freeway tolls – 30B to 70B depending on where you start – must be paid by the passenger. A 24-hour 'phone-a-cab' service, **Siam Taxi** (☎ 0 2377 1771), is available for an additional 20B over the regular metered fare.

During the morning and afternoon rush hours, taxis might refuse to go to certain destinations because of the traffic; if this happens, just try another cab. Around Th Khao San and other tourist areas, some cabbies might try to charge a flat fee – just walk away and find another cab.

From the Southern Bus Terminal, almost every taxi charges a flat fee of 200B to 300B into town.

It is possible to hire a taxi all day for 1500B to 2000B, depending on how much driving is involved.

Motorcycle Taxi

With traffic almost permanently gridlocked in central Bangkok, motorcycle taxis have become the only reasonable way to get around during the rush hour. However, taking a motorcycle taxi through the Bangkok traffic is not for the faint-hearted. The kamikaze drivers routinely drive against the flow of traffic, and the average journey will involve half a dozen incidents in which you are just millimetres away from a gruesome death. That said, passengers do get helmets in Bangkok and there are good hospitals nearby! Fares range from 10B for a short hop to 60B for a longer cross-town trip – we leave the decision in your hands.

TÚK-TÚK

Called *sǎamláw khrêuang* by the Thais – *túk-túk* is 'foreigner talk' – these putt-putting little three-wheelers are best for short trips, preferably at night, when the pollution won't sour your alfresco trip as much. They're really worth catching only for the novelty appeal because they're not much cheaper than metered taxis. You have to bargain – about 40B for a short hop is a fair price.

Beware of any *túk-túk* driver who offers to take you sightseeing for only 10B or 20B an hour. His sole purpose will be to guide you to shady gem or tailor shops hoping for commissions.

PRACTICALITIES

ACCOMMODATION

The Sleeping chapter (pp164-80) contains our recommendations for places to stay in the city, arranged by neighbourhood. The neighbourhoods are further broken down into mid-range and top-end hotels, listed alphabetically, followed by budget recommendations under 'Cheap Sleeps'.

Bangkok hotels enjoy a relatively high occupancy rate year-round, but space can be particularly tight during the two peak seasons, November–March and July–August. Seasonal discounts are occasionally available at top-end hotels in May, June and September only.

Fancier hotels oriented towards business travellers sometimes offer weekend rates that are slightly lower than weekday rates.

Booking Services

For mid-range and top-end hotels, discounts of 30% to 50% per night can easily be obtained through many Thai travel agencies. At Bangkok International Airport, in the arrival halls of both the international and domestic terminals, the **Thai Hotels Association** (THA; ☎ 0 2996 7725; www.thaihotels.org) can also arrange discounts. If you're travelling with Thai International Airways (THAI), ask about special discounts at affiliated hotels.

Web-based booking services also regularly run Internet specials for mid-range and top-end hotels. User-friendly booking sites with plenty of options include www.bangkok.com and www.asiatravel.com.

BUSINESS

Business Hours

Most government offices are open from 8.30am to 4.30pm on weekdays, but closed from noon to 1pm for lunch. In recent years the government has pushed for a 'no lunch closing' policy – you might even see signs posted to this effect – but in reality government employees pay no attention and you will almost surely be disappointed if you expect to get anything done during the noon to 1pm lunch hour.

Regular bank hours in Bangkok are 9.30am to 3.30pm Monday to Friday, but several banks have special foreign-exchange offices that are open longer hours (generally from 8.30am until 8pm) every day of the week. Note that all government offices and banks are closed on public holidays (see p216).

Commercial businesses usually operate between 8.30am and 5pm on weekdays and sometimes Saturday morning as well. Larger shops usually open from 10am to 6.30pm or 7pm, but smaller shops may open earlier and close later. Hours for restaurants and cafés vary greatly. Some open as early as 8am, others around 11am and still others are open in the evenings only. Some close as early as 9pm and others stay open all night. Bars, by law, can't open before 4pm and must close by 1am.

CHILDREN

Thais love children and in many instances will shower attention on your offspring, who will find ready playmates among their Thai counterparts and a temporary nanny service at practically every stop.

For the most part, parents needn't concern themselves too much about health concerns, although it is worth laying down a few ground rules – such as frequent hand-washing – to head off potential medical problems. All the typical health precautions apply (see p214). Children should especially be warned not to play with animals, as rabies is relatively common in Thailand.

Nappies, formula and other infant requirements are readily available at Bangkok supermarkets, pharmacies and convenience stores.

Check out Lonely Planet's *Travel With Children* for further advice.

Fun for Kids

Bangkok has plenty of attractions for children. Among the most recommended are the centrally located Dusit Zoo (p85), World Ice Skating (p91), the Bangkok Doll Factory & Museum (p90), the Children's Discovery Museum (p97) and, on the outskirts of the city, Safari World (p98). Queen Saovabha Memorial Institute (Snake Farm; p93), Lumphini Park (p93) and Samphran Elephant Ground & Zoo (p184) are other good options.Most shopping centres offer free children's play centres on their uppermost floors. These areas often have banks of video-game machines off to one side.

CLIMATE

At the centre of the flat, humid Mae Nam Chao Phraya River delta, Bangkok sits at the same latitude as Khartoum and Guatemala City, and can be as hot as the former and as wet as the latter.

The southwest monsoon arrives between May and July and lasts into October. This is followed by a dry period from November to May, which begins with lower relative temperatures until mid-February (because of the influence of the northeast monsoon, which bypasses this part of Thailand but results in cool breezes),

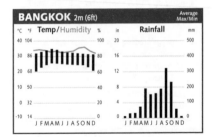

Directory – Practicalities

followed by much higher relative temperatures from March to May.

It usually rains most during August and September, though it can flood in October since the ground has reached full saturation by then. If you are in Bangkok in early October, you may find yourself in hip-deep water in certain parts of the city. An umbrella can be invaluable – a raincoat will just make you hot.

See City Calendar (pp10–12) for recommendations on best times of year to visit.

COURSES
Cooking

Amaze your friends back home with your deft preparations of *yam* (hot and tangy salad) and *làap* (spicy minced-meat salad) after attending a Thai culinary course at one of the following.

Blue Elephant Cooking School (Map pp257-9; ☎ 0 2673 9353; www.blueelephant.com/school; 233 Th Sathon Tai) The latest entry into the fierce cooking-school competition, with a state-of-the-art teaching kitchen.

Oriental Hotel Cooking School (Map pp257-9; ☎ 0 2437 6211, 0 2437 3080; 48 Soi 38 (Soi Oriental), Th Charoen Krung) Plush and famous, this is where visiting celebs typically learn how to turn out a *kaeng khĭaw-wăan* (sweet green curry).

Thai House (☎ 0 2903 9611; fax 0 2903 9354; pip_thaihouse@hotmail.com, Tambon Bang Meuang, Amphoe Bang Yai, Nonthaburi) Popular residential cooking course about 40 minutes north of Bangkok by boat. The programme includes all meals, four nights' accommodation, and transfer to and from central Bangkok.

Language

Tuition at most Thai language schools averages around 250B per hour for group classes, more for private tutoring. We recommend the following.

American University Alumni (AUA) Language Center (Map pp262-3; ☎ 0 2252 8170; 179 Th Ratchadamri) One of the largest private language-teaching institutes in the world.

Thai Language Academy (☎ 0 2631 2712; 10th fl, Kamol Sukosol Bldg, 317 Th Silom) Opened in 2003 by a group of experienced Thai language teachers from other schools, TLA has quickly gained a loyal following.

Union Language School (☎ 0 2233 4482; 109 Th Surawong) Generally recognised as having the most rigorous course, with a balance of structure-oriented and communication-oriented methodologies.

Meditation

Although at times Bangkok might seem like the most unlikely Buddhist city on earth, there are several places where interested foreigners can learn about Theravada Buddhist meditation. Instruction and accommodation are free of charge.

Wat Mahathat (Map p256; ☎ 0 2222 6011; Tha Phra Chan) The International Buddhist Meditation Centre at Wat Mahathat provides meditation instruction several times daily at Section 5, a building near the monks' residences. There is also a special Saturday session for foreigners at the Dhamma Vicaya Hall. Air-con bus Nos 8 and 12 pass near the wát; the nearest Chao Phraya Express pier is Tha Maharat.

World Fellowship of Buddhists (Map pp264-5; ☎ 0 2661 1284; Benjasiri Park, Soi 24, Th Sukhumvit) A clearing house for information on Theravada Buddhism as well as dialogue between various schools of Buddhism. The centre hosts meditation classes from 2pm to 5.30pm on the first Sunday of every month.

Yoga

Bikram Yoga Bangkok (☎ 0 2652 1333; 29/1 14th fl, Soi Lang Suan, Th Ploenchit)

Iyengar Yoga Studio (☎ 0 2714 9924; Fiftyfifth Plaza, 3rd fl, Soi 55, Th Sukhumvit 55)

CUSTOMS

Thailand prohibits the importation of illegal drugs, firearms and ammunition (unless registered in advance with the Police Department), and pornographic media. A reasonable amount of clothing for personal use, toiletries and professional instruments are allowed in duty-free, as is one still or one movie or video camera with five rolls of still film or three rolls of movie film or video tape. Up to 200 or 250g of tobacco cigarettes can be brought into the country without paying duty. One litre of wine or spirits is allowed in duty-free.

Electronic goods such as personal stereos, calculators and computers can be a problem if the customs officials have reason to believe you're bringing them in for resale. As long as you don't carry more than one of each, you should be OK.

For information on currency import or export, see Exchange Control (p219).

Be sure to check the import regulations in your home country before taking or sending back a large quantity of high-valued Thailand purchases.

Antiques & Art

When leaving Thailand, you must obtain an export licence for any antiques or objects of art you want to take with you. Export licence applications can be made by submitting two front-view photos of the object(s), with no more than five objects to a photo, and a photocopy of your passport, along with the object(s) in question, to the Department of Fine Arts (DFA; Map pp250-1), Bangkok National Museum. Allow three to five days for the application and inspection process to be completed.

Buddhas or other deity images (or any part thereof) to be exported require a permit from the Ministry of Commerce as well as a licence from the DFA. The one exception to this is the small Buddha images (*phrá phim* or *phrá khrêuang*) that are meant to be worn on a chain around the neck. These may be exported without a licence as long as the reported purpose is religious.

DISABLED TRAVELLERS

Bangkok presents one large, ongoing obstacle course for the mobility-impaired. With its high curbs, uneven pavements and nonstop traffic, movement around the city can be particularly difficult. Many streets must be crossed via pedestrian bridges flanked with steep stairways, while buses and boats don't stop long enough for even the mildly disabled. Rarely are there any ramps or other access points for wheelchairs.

A few of the most expensive top-end hotels make consistent design efforts to provide disabled access to their properties. Other deluxe hotels with high employee-to-guest ratios are usually good about providing staff help where building design fails. For the rest, you're pretty much left to your own resources.

Organisations

Access Foundation (☎ 516-887 5798; PO Box 356, Malverne, NY 11565, USA)

Accessible Journeys (☎ 610-521 0339; www.disability travel.com; 35 West Sellers Ave, Ridley Park, Pennsylvania, USA)

Mobility International USA (☎ 541-343 1284; info@miusa.org; PO Box 10767, Eugene, OR 97440, USA)

Society for Accessible Travel & Hospitality (☎ 212-447 7284; www.sath.org; Suite 610, 347 Fifth Ave, New York, NY 10016, USA)

ELECTRICITY

Electric current is 220V, 50 cycles. Electrical wall outlets are usually of the round, two-pin type. Some outlets accept plugs with two flat pins, and some will accept either flat or round pins. Any electrical supply shop will carry adaptors for international plugs, as well as voltage converters.

EMBASSIES & CONSULATES

Countries with diplomatic representation in Bangkok include the following:

Australia (Map pp260-1; ☎ 0 2287 2680; 37 Th Sathon Tai)

Cambodia (Map pp262-3; ☎ 0 2254 6630; 185 Th Ratchadamri, Lumphini)

Canada (Map pp260-1; ☎ 0 2636 0540; 15th fl, Abdulrahim Bldg, 990 Th Rama IV)

EU (Map pp262-3; ☎ 0 2255 9100; Kian Gwan House II, 19th fl, 1410/1 Th Withayu)

France (Embassy; Map pp257-9; ☎ 0 2266 8250–6; 35 Soi 36, Th Charoen Krung)

France (Consulate; Map pp260-1; ☎ 0 2287 1592, 29 Th Sathon Tai)

Germany (Map pp260-1; ☎ 0 2287 9000; 9 Th Sathon Tai)

Indonesia (Map pp262-3; ☎ 0 2252 3135; 600-602 Th Phetburi)

Laos (Map pp246-7; ☎ 0 2539 6679; 520/1-3 Soi 39, or Soi Pracha Uthit, Th Ramkhamhaeng)

Malaysia (Map pp262-3; ☎ 0 2679 2190–9; 33-35 Th Sathon Tai)

Myanmar (Map pp257-9; ☎ 0 2234 4789; 132 Th Sathon Neua)

Netherlands (Map pp262-3; ☎ 0 2254 7701, 0 2252 6103–5; 106 Th Withayu)

New Zealand (Map pp262-3; ☎ 0 2254 2530–3; 19th fl, M Thai Tower, All Seasons Place, 87 Th Withayu)

Singapore (Map pp257-9; ☎ 0 2286 2111; 9th & 18th fls, Rajanakam Bldg, 183 Th Sathon Tai)

South Africa (Map pp257-9; ☎ 0 2253 8473; 6th fl, Park Place, 231 Th Sarasin)

Switzerland (Map pp262-3; ☎ 0 2253 0156–60; 5 Th Withayu Neua)

UK & Northern Ireland (Map pp262-3; ☎ 0 2305 8333; 1031 Th Withayu)

USA (Map pp262-3; ☎ 0 2205 4000; 120-122 Th Withayu)

Vietnam (Map pp262-3; ☎ 0 2251 5836–8; 83/1 Th Withayu)

EMERGENCY

Ambulance (via Police) ☎ 191

Fire ☎ 195

Police ☎ 191

Tourist Assistance Center ☎ 0 2282 8129

Tourist Police ☎ 1155

GAY & LESBIAN TRAVELLERS

Thai culture is very tolerant of homosexuality, both male and female. The nation does not have laws that discriminate against homosexuals, and the gay and lesbian scene in Bangkok is pretty much out in the open. On the whole, lesbians and gays are accepted without comment.

Organisations & Publications

Utopia (www.utopia-asia.com/thaibang.htm), once a gay and lesbian centre consisting of a guesthouse, bar, café and gallery, is now mostly a Web presence with lots of Bangkok information.

Anjaree Group (☎ 0 2668 2185; www.anjaree .org) is Thailand's only lesbian society. It sponsors various group activities and produces a Thai-only newsletter. Bilingual Thai-English websites of possible interest to visiting lesbians include www.lesla.com.

Gay men may be interested in the **Long Yang Club** (☎ 0 2266 5479; www.longyangclub.com /thailand), a 'multicultural social group for male-oriented men who want to meet outside the gay scene', with branches all over the world. The Thailand chapter hosts various events in Bangkok.

The monthly **Metro** (www.bkkmetro.com) magazine stays abreast of gay and lesbian happenings in the capital.

HEALTH

Travel health depends on your predeparture preparations, your daily health care while travelling and how you handle any medical problem that does develop. While the potential dangers can seem quite frightening, in reality few travellers experience anything more than an upset stomach.

Bangkok and the surrounding regions of central Thailand are entirely malaria-free, so you won't need to worry about taking any antimalarial medication if you don't plan to venture beyond that area.

Before You Go

Pack medications in their original, clearly labelled containers. A signed and dated letter from your physician describing your medical conditions and medications, including generic names, is also a good idea. If carrying syringes or needles, be sure to have a physician's letter documenting their medical necessity. If you have a heart condition bring a copy of your ECG taken just prior to travelling.

If you take any regular medication bring double your needs in case of loss or theft. In Bangkok you can buy many medications over the counter without a doctor's prescription, but it can be difficult to find some of the newer drugs, particularly the latest antidepressant drugs, blood pressure medications and contraceptive pills.

Basic Rules

FOOD

Beware of ice cream that is sold in the street or anywhere it might have been melted and refrozen; if there's any doubt, steer well clear. Raw or undercooked shellfish such as mussels, oysters and clams should be avoided, as should undercooked meat.

If a place looks clean and well run and the vendor also looks clean and healthy, then the food is probably safe. In general, places that are packed with travellers or locals will be fine, while empty restaurants are questionable. The food in busy restaurants is cooked and eaten quite quickly with little standing around, and is probably not reheated.

WATER

All water served in restaurants or to guests in offices or homes in Bangkok comes from purified sources. It's not necessary to ask for bottled water unless you prefer it. Reputable brands of Thai bottled water or soft drinks are generally fine. Try to purchase glass water bottles, however, as these are recyclable (unlike the plastic ones).

Fruit juices are made with purified water and are safe to drink. Milk in Thailand is always pasteurised.

Ice is generally produced from purified water under hygienic conditions and is therefore theoretically safe. The rule of thumb is that if it's chipped ice, it probably came from an ice block (which may not have been handled well), but if it's ice cubes or 'tubes', it was delivered from the ice factory in sealed plastic.

Internet Resources

There is a wealth of travel-health advice on the Internet. For further information, **Lonely Planet** (www.lonelyplanet.com) is a good place to start. The **World Health Organization** (WHO; www.who.int/ith) publishes a superb book called *International Travel & Health*, which is revised annually and is available on line at no cost. Another website of general interest is **MD Travel Health** (www.mdtravelhealth.com), which provides complete travel-health recommendations for every country and is updated daily. The **Centers for Disease Control and Prevention** (CDC; www.cdc.gov) website also has good general information.

Medical Problems & Treatment

In Thailand medicine is generally available over the counter, and the price will be much cheaper than in the West. However, be careful when buying drugs, particularly where the expiry date might have passed or correct storage conditions might not have been followed.

AIR POLLUTION

Pollution is something you'll become very aware of in Bangkok, where heat, dust and motor fumes combine to form a powerful brew of potentially toxic air. Air pollution can be a health hazard, especially if you suffer from lung diseases such as asthma. It can also aggravate coughs, colds and sinus problems, and cause eye irritation or infections. Consider avoiding very polluted areas if you think they might jeopardise your health, or invest in an air filter.

HEAT

Bangkok can be hot and humid throughout the year. For most people it takes at least two weeks to adapt to the hot climate. Swelling of the feet and ankles is common, as are muscle cramps caused by excessive sweating. You can prevent these by avoiding dehydration and excessive activity in the heat. Take it easy when you first arrive. Taking salt tablets isn't a good idea (they aggravate the gut), but drinking rehydration solution or eating salty food helps. Treat cramps by stopping activity, resting, rehydrating with double-strength rehydration solution and gently stretching.

Dehydration is the main contributor to heat exhaustion. Symptoms include feeling weak, headache, irritability, nausea or vomiting, sweaty skin, a fast, weak pulse and a normal or slightly elevated body temperature. Treatment involves getting out of the heat and/or sun, fanning the victim and applying cool, wet cloths to the skin, laying the victim flat with their legs raised and rehydrating with water containing a quarter teaspoon of salt per litre. Recovery is usually rapid, and it is common to feel weak for some days afterwards.

Heat stroke is a serious medical emergency. Symptoms come on suddenly and include weakness, nausea, a hot, dry body with a body temperature of more than 41°C, dizziness, confusion, loss of coordination, seizures, and eventually collapse and loss of consciousness. Seek medical help and commence cooling by getting the victim out of the heat, removing their clothes, fanning them and applying cool, wet cloths or ice to their body, especially to the groin and armpits.

Prickly heat is a common skin rash in the tropics, caused by sweat being trapped under the skin. The result is an itchy rash of tiny lumps. Treat it by moving out of the heat and into an air-conditioned area for a few hours, and by having cool showers. Creams and ointments clog the skin so they should be avoided. Locally bought prickly-heat powder can be helpful.

HIV & AIDS

Infection with the human immunodeficiency virus (HIV) might lead to acquired immune deficiency syndrome (AIDS), which is a fatal disease. Any exposure to blood, blood products or body fluids could put the individual at risk. The disease is often transmitted through sexual contact or dirty needles – tattooing, vaccinations, acupuncture and body piercing can potentially be as dangerous as intravenous drug use if the equipment is not clean.

In Thailand around 95% of HIV transmission occurs through sexual activity, and the remainder through natal transmission or through illicit intravenous drug use. HIV/AIDS can also be spread through infected blood transfusions, although this risk is virtually nil in Thailand due to rigorous blood-screening procedures.

SARS & AVIAN INFLUENZA

During the 2003 world SARS epidemic, no cases of infection occurred in Thailand.

In 2004 parts of the capital were quarantined to stop the possible spread of avian influenza (bird flu), but no human infections occurred in the city. In about a dozen other provinces in Thailand, however, several cases of human infection turned up and there were eight recorded deaths. The primary risk of contracting bird flu comes from handling live poultry. Contrary to myth, eating chicken or other poultry does not put one at risk of avian flu infection.

HOLIDAYS

The two holiday times that most affect Bangkok travel are Chinese New Year (usually late February or early March) and Songkran (mid-April). For up to a week before and after these holidays, all public transport in or out of the city might be booked up. Because it's peak season for foreign tourists visiting Thailand, December and January can also be very tight.

See p10 for detailed information on individual festivals and holidays. Government offices and banks close down on the following public holidays.

New Year's Day 1 January

Chakri Day (commemorates the founder of the Chakri dynasty, Rama I) 6 April

Coronation Day (commemorates the 1946 coronation of the King and Queen) 5 May

Khao Phansa (beginning of Buddhist rains retreat, when monks refrain from travelling away from their monasteries) July (date varies)

Queen's Birthday 12 August

Chulalongkorn Day 23 October

Ok Phansa (end of Buddhist rains retreat) October/November (date varies)

King's Birthday 5 December

Constitution Day 10 December

INTERNET ACCESS

The Internet is easily accessed in Bangkok. Most travellers make use of Internet cafés and free Web-based email such as **Yahoo** (www .yahoo.com) or **Hotmail** (www.hotmail.com). For the visitor who needs to log on only once in a while, these are a less expensive alternative to getting your own account – and it certainly beats lugging around a laptop. The going rate is 1B or 2B per on- and off-line minute, although we've seen a few places where slower connections are available at 0.50B per minute.

Th Khao San (Map pp254-5) has the highest concentration of access points in the city (more than 40 at last count), so if it's choice you want, head there. Other good areas for Internet centres include Th Silom, Th Ploenchit and Siam Square. Additionally, many Bangkok guesthouses and hotels offer Internet access.

Plugging In Your Portable Computer

RJ11 phone jacks are the standard in most hotels, though in older hotels and guesthouses the phones might still be hard-wired. In the latter case you might be able to use a fax line in the office, since all fax machines in Thailand are connected via RJ11 jacks. Some places will allow guests to use the house fax line for laptop modems, provided on-line time is kept short.

Temporary Internet accounts are available from several Thai ISPs. One of the better ones is WebNet, offered by **Loxinfo** (www.loxinfo.co.th). You can buy a block of 30 hours (380B) or 63 hours (750B), good for up to one year.

LEGAL MATTERS

In general, Thai police don't hassle foreigners, especially tourists. If anything, they generally go out of their way not to arrest a foreigner breaking minor traffic laws, taking the approach that a friendly warning will suffice.

One major exception is drug laws. Most Thai police view drug-takers as a social scourge and consequently see it as their duty to enforce the letter of the law; for others it's an opportunity to make untaxed income via bribes. Which direction they'll go often depends on drug quantities – small-time offenders are sometimes offered the chance to pay their way out of an arrest, while traffickers usually go to jail.

Be extra vigilant about where you dispose of cigarette butts and other refuse when in Bangkok. A strong antilittering law was passed in Bangkok in 1997, and police won't hesitate to cite foreigners and collect fines of 2000B.

If you are arrested for any offence, the police will allow you to make a phone call to your embassy or consulate in Thailand if you have one, or to a friend or relative. There's a whole set of legal codes governing the length of time and manner in which you can be detained by the police before being charged or put on trial, but the police have a lot of discretion. As a foreigner, the police are more likely to bend these codes in your favour than the reverse. However, as with police worldwide, if you don't show respect to the men in brown you will only make matters worse.

Tourist Police

The best way to deal with most serious hassles regarding rip-offs or thefts is to contact the Tourist Police, who are used to dealing with foreigners, rather than the regular Thai police. The Tourist Police maintain a hotline 24 hours a day – dial ☎ 1155 from any phone in Thailand to lodge complaints or to request assistance with regard to personal safety. You can also call this number between 8.30am and 4.30pm daily to request travel information.

The Tourist Police can be very helpful in cases of arrest. Although they typically have no jurisdiction over the kinds of cases handled by regular cops, they might be able to help with translation or with contacting your embassy.

Visiting Prisoners

If you would like to visit someone who is serving a prison sentence in Bangkok, you should contact the prisoner's Bangkok embassy, tell the consular staff the prisoner's name and ask them to write a letter requesting you be permitted to see that prisoner. The embassy can provide directions to the prison and tell you the visiting hours. Usually visiting is allowed only a couple of days a week. Don't try going directly to the prison without a letter from the prisoner's embassy, as you might be refused entry.

Over the last several years visiting imprisoned foreigners in Bangkok has become something of a fad. With the resulting increase in inquiries, both embassy and prison staff are tightening up on the release of prisoner information. The Thai corrections system does not accept the Western notion that anonymous prisoners should receive visitors, although exceptions are sometimes made for missionaries.

For the latest information on visitation policies, contact your embassy in Bangkok.

MAPS

A map is essential for finding your way around Bangkok, and there are many competing for your attention. Lonely Planet's comprehensive *Bangkok City Map,* in a handy, laminated, fold-out sheet-map form, includes a walking tour and is fully indexed.

A bus map is the best way to navigate Bangkok's economical bus system. The most popular is the durable *Tour 'n Guide Map (Bangkok Thailand),* aka the 'blue map', which shows all bus routes and some walking tours. It's regularly updated, but inevitably some bus routes will be wrong, so take care. Other similar maps include the *Bangkok Bus Map,* with lots of sightseeing tips, and *Latest Tour's Map to Bangkok & Thailand* (a 'blue map' clone).

The Tourism Authority of Thailand (TAT) publishes and distributes the free *City Map of Bangkok,* a folded sheet map on coated stock with bus routes, major hotels, the latest expressways, sightseeing, hospitals, embassies and more. Separate inset maps of popular areas are useful. You can pick it up at the airport TAT desk or at any Bangkok TAT office (see p224).

The long-running, often-imitated and never-equalled *Nancy Chandler's Map of Bangkok* contains information on out-of-the-way places and where to buy unusual things around the city. A new edition is released every year. Another contender on the market, Groovy Map's *Bangkok by Day,* combines an up-to-date bus map, Skytrain and MRTA subway routes, the usual sightseeing features, and a short selection of restaurant and bar reviews. Groovy Map publishes two other maps, *Bangkok by Night* (covering nightlife) and *Bangkok Expressway/Skytrain.*

MEDICAL SERVICES

Bangkok is Thailand's prominent health-care centre, with three university research hospitals, more than a dozen public and private hospitals, and hundreds of medical clinics. The Australian, US and UK embassies maintain up-to-date lists of doctors who can speak English. For doctors who speak other languages, contact the relevant embassy.

Here is a list of Bangkok's better hospitals:

Bangkok Adventist (Mission) Hospital (Map pp248–9; ☎ 0 2281 1422, 0 2282 1100; 430 Th Phitsanulok)

Bangkok Christian Hospital (Map pp257–9; ☎ 0 2233 6981–9, 0 2235 1000; 124 Th Silom)

Bangkok General Hospital (Map pp264–5; ☎ 0 2318 0066, 0 2310 3000; www.bgh.co.th; 2 Soi 47, Th Phetburi Tat Mai)

Bangkok Nursing Home (Map pp260–1; ☎ 0 2233 2610–9; 9 Th Convent)

Bumrungrad Hospital (Map pp264–5; ☎ 0 2667 1000; www.bumrungrad.com; 33 Soi 3, Th Sukhumvit)

Phayathai Hospital 1 (Map pp248–9; ☎ 0 2245 2620; 364/1 Th Si Ayuthaya)

Samitivej Hospital (Map pp264–5; ☎ 0 2381 6728; 133 Soi 49, Th Sukhumvit)

St Louis Hospital (Map pp257–9; ☎ 0 2212 0033; 215 Th Sathon Tai)

Should you need urgent dental care, suggested contacts in Bangkok include the following:

Dental Polyclinic (☎ 0 2314 4397; 2111/2113 Th Phetburi Tat Mai)

Dental Polyclinic (☎ 0 2662 2402; 593/6 Th Sukhumvit)

Siam Dental Clinic (☎ 0 2252 6660; 412/11-12 Soi 6, Siam Square)

For urgent eye care, the best choices are: **Pirompesuy Eye Hospital** (☎ 0 2252 4141; 117/1 Th Phayathai) and **Rutnin Eye Hospital** (☎ 0 2258 0442; 80/1 Soi Asoke).

There are many Chinese doctors and herbal dispensaries in the Sampeng district, close to Th Ratchawong, Th Charoen Krung, Th Yaowarat and Th Songwat. The **Pow Tai Dispensary** (572–574 Th Charoen Krung) has been preparing traditional Chinese medicines since 1941.

MONEY

The basic unit of Thai currency is the baht. There are 100 satang in one baht. Coins come in denominations of 25 satang, 50 satang,1B, 5B and 10B. Older coins have Thai numerals only, while newer coins have Thai and Arabic numerals.

Paper currency comes in denominations of 10B (brown), 20B (green), 50B (blue), 100B (red), 500B (purple) and 1000B (beige). A 10,000B bill was on the way when the 1997 cash crunch came, but has been tabled for the moment. The 10B bill is being phased out in favour of the 10B coin and has become rather uncommon.

See p19 for more information about the Thai economy.

ATMs & Credit/Debit Cards

Debit cards issued by a bank in your own country can be used at ATMs around the city to withdraw cash (in Thai baht only) directly from your account back home. There are plenty of ATMs, and they're easy to find. You can use MasterCard debit cards to buy baht at foreign-exchange desks at either Bangkok Bank or Siam Commercial Bank. Visa debit cards can buy cash through the Thai Farmers Bank exchange services.

Credit cards as well as debit cards can be used for purchases at many shops, hotels and restaurants. The most commonly accepted cards are Visa and MasterCard, followed by AmEx and Japan Card Bureau (JCB). To report a lost or stolen card, call the following telephone hotlines in Bangkok.

AmEx (☎ 0 2273 5050)

MasterCard (☎ 001 800 11 887 0663)

Visa (☎ 001 800 441 3485)

Bargaining

Items sold by street vendors, in markets and in most shops are flexibly priced – that is, the price is negotiable. The only places where you'll see fixed prices in Bangkok are department stores. If the same kind of merchandise is offered in a department store and a small shop or market, it's a good idea to check the department store price for a point of reference.

Whether at guesthouses or five-star hotels, room rates can sometimes be bargained down, particularly outside Bangkok's peak season, November to March.

Thais respect a good haggler. Always let the vendor make the first offer, then ask 'Is that your best price?' or 'Can you lower the price?' This usually results is an immediate discount from the first price. Now it's your turn to make a counter-offer; always start low, but don't bargain at all unless you're serious about buying. Negotiations continue back and forth until a price is agreed upon – there's no set discount from the asking price, as some vendors start ridiculously high, others closer to the 'real' price.

It helps if you've done your homework by shopping around, and the whole process becomes easier with practice. Keep the negotiations relaxed and friendly, and speak slowly and clearly (but not in a condescending manner). Vendors will almost always give a better price to someone they like.

Changing Money

Banks or legal moneychangers offer the optimum foreign-exchange rates. When buying baht, US dollars are the most readily accepted currency and travellers cheques receive better rates than cash. Generally, British pounds and euros are second to the US dollar in acceptability. As banks charge up to 23B commission and duty for each travellers cheque cashed, you'll save on commissions if you use larger cheque denominations. See Business Hours (p211) for information on bank opening hours.

American Express card-holders can get advances in travellers cheques. The Amex agent is **SEA Tours** (Map pp248-9; ☎ 0 2216 5783; 8th fl, Suite 88–92, Payathai Plaza, 128 Th Phayathai).

See the inside front cover for exchange rates. Current exchange rates are printed in the *Bangkok Post* and the *Nation* every day, or you can walk into any Thai bank and ask to see a daily rate sheet.

Exchange Control

By Thai law, any traveller arriving in Thailand is supposed to carry at least the following amounts of money in cash, travellers cheques, bank draft or letter of credit, according to visa category: Non-Immigrant Visa, US$500 per person or US$1000 per family; Tourist Visa, US$250 per person or US$500 per family; Transit Visa or no visa, US$125 per person or US$250 per family. Your funds might be checked by authorities if you arrive on a one-way ticket or if you look as if you're at 'the end of the road'.

There is no limit to the amount of Thai or foreign currency you may bring into the country. Upon leaving Thailand, you're permitted to take no more than 50,000B per person without special authorisation; exportation of foreign currencies is unrestricted. An exception is made if you're going to Cambodia, Laos, Malaysia, Myanmar or Vietnam, where the limit is 500,000B.

It's legal to open a foreign-currency account at any commercial bank in Thailand. As long as the funds originate from abroad, there are no restrictions on their maintenance or withdrawal.

NEWSPAPERS & MAGAZINES

Two well-respected English-language newspapers are published daily in Thailand and distributed in most provincial capitals throughout the country: the *Bangkok Post* in the morning and the *Nation* in the afternoon. The *Bangkok Post* is Thailand's oldest English-language newspaper, established in 1946. Both papers publish online (see p17). The Singapore edition of the *International Herald Tribune* is widely available in Bangkok.

English-language magazine publishing in general faltered, and several magazines failed, after the 1997 economic crash in Thailand.

Published by Bangkok expats, *Farang* aims itself squarely at the backpacker market, with coverage of the city's travel and party scenes. *Metro* takes a more casual tack, with listings on art, culture, cuisine, film and music in Bangkok. The monthly *Le Gavroche* offers news and features on Thailand for the Francophone community.

Popular international magazines are available in specialist bookshops (see p149).

POST

Thailand has a very efficient postal service, and both domestic and international postal rates are very reasonable. Bangkok's **main post office (Communications Authority of Thailand, CAT)** (Map pp257-9) on Th Charoen Krung is open from 8am to 8pm on weekdays and from 8am to 1pm on weekends and holidays.

A 24-hour international telecommunications service (including telephone, fax, telex and telegram) is located in a separate building to the right and slightly in front of the main post office building.

The easiest way to reach the main post office is via the Chao Phraya Express, which stops at Tha Meuang Khae at the river end of Soi Charoen Krung 34, next to Wat Meuang Khae, just south of the post office.

Packaging

There's an efficient and inexpensive packaging service at the main post office, or you could simply buy the materials at the counter and do it yourself. The parcel counter is open from 8am to 4.30pm on weekdays and from 9am to noon on Saturday. When the parcel counter is closed (weekday evenings and Sunday mornings), an informal packing service (using recycled materials) is open behind the service windows at the centre rear of the building.

Branch post offices throughout the city also offer parcel services.

Couriers

DHL Worldwide (☎ 0 2658 8000; 22nd fl, Grand Amarin Tower, Th Phetburi Tat Mai)

Federal Express (☎ 0 2367 3222; 8th fl, Green Tower, Th Phra Ram IV)

UPS (☎ 0 2712 3300; 16/1 Soi 44/1, Th Sukhumvit)

Receiving Mail
POSTE RESTANTE

Bangkok's poste-restante service is reliable, though with the popularity of email these days few tourists use it. When you receive mail, you must show ID, sign your name and write your passport number, the number of the letter and date of delivery in the book provided. The poste-restante counter at the main post office on Th Charoen Krung is open from 8am to 8pm on weekdays and from 8am to 1pm on weekends. Branch post offices throughout Bangkok also offer poste-restante service.

AMERICAN EXPRESS

The Amex agent **SEA Tours** (Map pp248-9; ☎ 0 2216 5783; 8th fl, Suite 88-92, Payathai Plaza, 128 Th Phayathai; ☼ 8.30am-noon & 1-4.30pm

Mon-Fri, 8.30-11.30am Sat) will take mail on behalf of Amex card-holders. It won't accept courier packages that require your signature.

RADIO

Bangkok has around a hundred FM and AM stations. Some of the Bangkok FM stations feature some surprisingly good music programmes with British, Thai and American DJs. Looking for *lûuk thûng* (Thai country) music? Station Luk Thung 90 FM broadcasts classic and new *lûuk thûng* styles. For Thai alternative, tune into Fat Radio 104.5 FM.

The BBC World Service, Radio Canada, Radio Japan, Radio New Zealand, Singapore Broadcasting Company and Voice of America all have English- and Thai-language broadcasts over short-wave radio. The frequencies and schedules, which change hourly, appear in the *Bangkok Post* and the *Nation*.

SAFETY

By and large, Bangkok is a very safe place with little street crime to speak of. Beware of crafty pickpockets on public buses, particularly in the area around Hualamphong Railway Station.

Scams

Thais are generally so friendly and laid-back that some visitors are lulled into a false sense of security that makes them vulnerable to scams and con schemes of all kinds. Con artists tend to haunt first-time tourist spots, such as the Grand Palace area, Wat Pho and Siam Square (especially near Jim Thompson's House).

Most scams begin the same way: a friendly Thai male (or, on rare occasion, a female) approaches a lone visitor and strikes up a seemingly innocuous conversation. Sometimes the con man says he's a university student or teacher; at other times he might claim to work for the World Bank or a similarly distinguished organisation. If you're on the way to Wat Pho or Jim Thompson's House, for example, he may tell you it's closed for a holiday or repairs. Eventually the conversation works its way around to the subject of the scam – the better con men can actually make it seem as though you initiated the topic.

The scam itself almost always incorporates gems, tailor shops or card playing. With gems, the victim is invited to a gem and jewellery shop – your new-found friend is picking up some merchandise for himself and you're just along for the ride. Somewhere along the way he usually claims to have a connection in your home country (what a coincidence!) with whom he has a regular gem export-import business. One way or another, the victim is convinced that they can turn a profit by arranging a gem purchase and reselling the merchandise at home. After all, the jewellery shop just happens to be offering a generous discount today.

There are seemingly infinite variations on the gem scam, almost all of which end up with the victim purchasing small, low-quality sapphires and posting them to their home country. Once you return home, of course, the cheap sapphires turn out to be worth much less than what you paid for them. Many have invested and lost virtually all their savings.

Even if you were able to return your purchase to the gem shop in question, chances are slim to none they'd give a full refund. The con artist who brings the mark into the shop gets a commission of 10% to 50% per sale – the shop takes the rest. The Thai police are usually of no help, believing that merchants are entitled to whatever price they can get. The main victimisers are a handful of shops who get protection from certain high-ranking government officials.

At tailor shops the objective is to get you to order poorly made clothes at exorbitant prices. The tailor shops that do this sort of thing are adept at delaying delivery until just before you leave Thailand, so that you don't have time to object to poor workmanship. The way to avoid this scam is to choose tailor shops yourself and not offer any more money than a small deposit – no more than enough to cover your chosen fabrics – until you're satisfied with the workmanship.

The card-playing scam starts out very similarly: a friendly stranger approaches the lone traveller on the street, strikes up a conversation and then invites him or her to the house of his relative for a drink or meal. After a bit of socialising, a friend or relative of the con arrives on the scene; it just so happens a little high-stakes card game is planned for later that day. Like the gem scam, the card-game scam has many variations, but eventually the victim is shown some cheating tactics to use with help from the 'dealer', some practice sessions take place and finally the game gets under way. The mark is allowed to win a few hands first, then somehow loses a few, gets bankrolled by one of the friendly Thais, and then loses the Thai's money. Suddenly your new-found buddies aren't so friendly any more – they want the money you lost. Sooner or later you end up cashing in most or all of your travellers cheques or making a costly visit to an ATM. Again the police won't take any action – in this case because gambling is illegal in Thailand and you've broken the law by playing cards for money.

Other minor scams involve *túk-túk* drivers, hotel employees and bar girls who take new arrivals on city tours; these almost always end in high-pressure sales pushes at silk, jewellery or handicraft shops. In this case greed isn't the ruling motivation – it's simply a matter of weak sales resistance.

Follow the TAT's number 1 suggestion to tourists: disregard all offers of free shopping or sightseeing help from strangers – they will invariably take a commission from your purchases. You might also try lying whenever a stranger asks how long you've been in Thailand – if it's only been three days, say three weeks! The con artists rarely prey on anyone except new arrivals.

You should contact the Tourist Police if you have any problems with consumer fraud. Call ☎ 1155 from any phone.

TAXES & REFUNDS

Thailand has a 7% value-added tax (VAT) that's added to many goods and services. Visitors to Bangkok who hold valid tourist visas and who depart by air may apply for a VAT refund on purchases made at certain designated shops and department stores. Refunds are available only at the departure halls of Thailand's international airports, where you must fill out a VAT refund application and present it to customs officers along with purchased goods and receipts.

Larger hotels will usually add a 10% hotel tax, and sometimes an 8% to 10% service charge as well, to your room bill.

TELEPHONE & FAX

The telephone system in Thailand, operated by the government-subsidised but privately owned Telephone Organisation of Thailand (TOT) under the Communications Authority of Thailand (CAT), is efficient if costly, and from Bangkok you can direct-dial most major centres with little difficulty.

The telephone country code for Thailand is 66. Thailand no longer uses separate area codes for Bangkok and the provinces, and all phone numbers in the country use eight digits (preceded by 0 if you're dialling domestically).

When dialling Thailand from outside the country, you must first dial whatever international access code is necessary, followed by 66 and then the phone number in Thailand.

For directory assistance, dial ☎ 13.

Mobile Phones

TOT authorises the use of private cellphones tuned to GSM networks. If you bring your own mobile phone, roaming is not usually a problem, though it can be quite expensive.

Two cellular operators in Thailand, Orange and DTAC, will allow you to use their SIM cards in an imported phone, as long as your phone isn't SIM-locked. Rates depend on the calling plan you choose, but are typically around 3B per minute anywhere in Thailand. Mobile-phone shops dealing in such cards can easily be found in most shopping centres in Bangkok.

Major hotels in Bangkok can arrange the rental of handsets and SIM cards for 150B to 250B a day, depending on how many days you need them. Call rates are 6B to 12B per minute.

Fax

CAT and TOT offices in Bangkok offer fax services in addition to regular phone services. There's no need to bring your own paper, as these offices supply their own. International faxes typically cost 100B to 130B for the first page, and 70B to 100B per page for the remaining pages, depending on the size of the paper and the destination.

Larger hotels with business centres offer the same telecommunication services, but always at higher rates.

International Calls

To direct-dial an international number from a private phone, simply dial ☎ 001 before the number (except for calls to Malaysia and Laos; see p222). For operator-assisted international calls, dial ☎ 100.

A service called Home Country Direct is available at Bangkok's main post office (Map pp257-9), Bangkok International Airport (Map pp246-7), Queen Sirikit National Convention Center (Map pp264-5), Sogo department store (Map pp262-3), and the Banglamphu (Map pp254-5) and Hualamphong (Map pp252-3) post offices. Home Country Direct phones offer easy one-button connection to international operators in about 40 countries around the world.

Alternatively you can direct-dial Home Country Direct access numbers from any private phone (most hotel phones won't work) in Thailand. Dial ☎ 001 999 followed by:

Australia (Telstra)	61 1000
Australia (Optus)	61 2000
Canada	15 1000
Canada (AT&T)	15 2000
Denmark	45 1000
Finland	358 1000
France	33 1000
Germany	49 1000
Israel	972 1000
Italy	39 1000
Japan	81 0051
Korea	82 1000
Netherlands	31 1035
New Zealand	64 1066
Norway	47 1000
Singapore	65 0000
Sweden	46 1000
Switzerland	41 1000
UK (BT)	44 1066
UK (MCL)	44 2000
USA (AT&T)	11 1111
USA – Hawaii	14424
USA (MCI)	12001
USA (Sprint)	13877

Hotels generally add surcharges (sometimes as much as 50% above the CAT rate) for international long-distance calls, so it's always cheaper to call abroad from a CAT telephone office. A useful CAT office stands next to the main post office (Map pp257-9). You can also make long-distance calls and send faxes at the TOT office (Map pp262-3) on Th Ploenchit – but this office accepts cash only, and no reverse-charge or credit-card calls can be made.

Depending on where you are calling, reimbursing someone later for a reverse-charge call to your home country might be less expensive than paying CAT/TOT charges – it is worth comparing rates at source and destination.

Private long-distance phone offices with international service always charge more than the government offices, although their surcharges are usually lower than hotel rates.

Whichever type of phone service you use, the least expensive time of day to make calls is from midnight to 5am (30% discount on standard rates), followed by 9pm to midnight or 5am to 7am (20% discount). You pay full price from 7am to 9pm (this rate is reduced by 20% on Sunday).

If you're calling from someone's private phone, you must dial the international access code (☎ 001) before dialling the country code, area code and phone number you wish to reach.

MALAYSIA & LAOS
CAT does not offer long-distance services to Malaysia or Laos. To call these countries you must go through the TOT. For Laos, you can direct-dial ☎ 007 and country code 856, followed by the area code and number you want to reach. Malaysia can be dialled direct by prefixing the Malaysian number (including area code) with the code 09.

International Phonecards
A CAT-issued, prepaid international phonecard, called ThaiCard, comes in 300B and 500B denominations and allows calls to many countries at standard CAT rates. You can use the ThaiCard codes from either end, eg calling the UK from Thailand or calling Thailand from the UK.

Lenso phonecards covers international phone calls from yellow Lenso International Cardphones, wall phones found in airports, shopping centres and in front of some post offices. Cards come in two denominations, 250B and 500B, and are sold in convenience stores and some supermarkets. You can also use most major credit cards with Lenso phones and dial AT&T direct-access numbers (though rates are high).

Internet Phone
The cheapest way to call internationally is via the Internet, and many Internet cafés in Bangkok are set up to allow Internet phone calls. Most charge only the regular per-minute or per-hour fees they charge for any other kind of Internet access, if the call itself is a free call. A few charge extra for Internet phone calls, and of course if the call isn't free you will pay for both Internet time and the call – but this is still often less expensive than using CAT.

CAT itself offers the PhoneNet card, which comes in a 1000B denomination only and allows you to call overseas via Voice over Internet Protocol for a 20% to 40% saving over regular rates. The difference with PhoneNet is that you can call from any phone, ie you don't call from a computer. Cards are available from any CAT office.

Payphones & Phonecards

There are three kinds of public payphones in Thailand: red, blue and green. The red phones are for local calls, the blue are for both local and long-distance calls (within Thailand), and the green ones are for use with phonecards.

Local calls from payphones cost 1B for 164 seconds (add more coins for more time). Local calls from private phones cost 3B, with no time limit. Some hotels and guesthouses have private payphones that cost 5B per call. Long-distance rates within the country vary from 3B to 12B per minute, depending on the distance.

For use with the green card phones, domestic TOT phonecards are available at the information counter or gift shops of Bangkok International Airport, major shopping centres and 7-Elevens. TOT phonecards come in 50B, 100B, 200B and 500B denominations, all roughly the same size as a credit card.

TELEVISION

Thailand has five VHF TV networks based in Bangkok, all but one government-operated. The single private network, ITV, is owned by the current prime minister's family, so even this one cleaves to the government line politically. All telecast a mixture of news, music, documentaries and dramatic series. Some English programming is available – check the TV schedules in the *Bangkok Post* and the *Nation* for details.

Satellite & Cable TV

UBC (www.ubctv.com) is the only cable company in Thailand, carrying six English-language movie channels (censored for language, nudity and violence), four sports channels, imported TV series, three music channels (MTV Asia, Channel V and VH1), CNN International, CNBC, NHK, BBC World Service Television, the Discovery Channel and all the standard Thai networks. You can access further information on UBC's website or in the Bangkok dailies.

Thailand has its own ThaiCom 1 and 2 satellites as uplinks for AsiaSat and as carriers for the standard Thai networks and Thai Sky (TST). The latter includes five channels offering news and documentaries, Thai music videos

and Thai variety programmes. Other satellites tracked by dishes in Thailand include China's Apstar 1 and Apstar 2. Additional transmissions from these and from Vietnam, Myanmar and Malaysia are available with a satellite dish.

TIME
Time Zone

Thailand's time zone is seven hours ahead of GMT/UTC. Thus, noon in Bangkok is 9pm the previous day in Los Angeles (except during Daylight Savings Time, when it's 10pm), midnight in New York (except during Daylight Savings Time, when it's 1am), 5am in London, 6am in Paris, 1pm in Perth, and 3pm in Sydney and Melbourne.

At government offices and local cinemas, times are often expressed according to the 24-hour clock, eg 11pm is written as 2300.

Thai Calendar

The official year in Thailand is reckoned from 543 BC, the beginning of the Buddhist Era, so that 2004 AD is 2547 BE, 2005 AD is 2548 BE etc. All dates in this book refer to the Western calendar.

TIPPING

Tipping is not normal practice in Bangkok, although they're used to it in expensive hotels and restaurants; don't bother elsewhere. The exception is loose change left from a largish Thai restaurant bill; for example, if a meal costs 288B and you pay with a 500B note, leave the 12B coin change on the change tray. It's not so much a tip as a way of saying 'I'm not so money-grubbing as to grab every last baht'.

TOURIST INFORMATION

Operated by the Bangkok Metropolitan Administration (BMA), the **Bangkok Tourist Bureau** (BTB; Map pp254-5; ☎ 0 2225 7612; http://bangkoktourist.bma.go.th; 17/1 Th Phra Athit; ⏰ 9am-7pm) has a friendly and informative staff. As well as stocking a wealth of brochures, maps and event schedules, staff can assist with the chartering of boats at the adjacent pier.

A **BTB tourist information booth** (Map pp254-5; ☎ 0 2281 5538) next to the Chana Songkhram police station on Th Chakraphong, near the corner of Th Khao San, distributes local bus maps (2B). BTB also has counters in Bangkok International Airport, opposite Wat Suthat and

Wat Phra Kaew, and at most major shopping centres.

The **Tourist Authority of Thailand** (TAT; ☎ 0 2250 5500; www.tourismthailand.org; 1600 Th Phetburi Tat Mai, Makkasan, Ratchathewi) has useful, informative and well-produced brochures on sightseeing as well as cultural topics. The TAT's **information compound** (Map pp254–5; ☎ 0 2282 9773; Th Ratchadamnoen Nok; ⏰ 8am–4.30pm), near the Ratchadamnoen Stadium, is more convenient. The TAT also maintains a 24-hour **Tourist Assistance Center** (☎ 1155) in the compound for matters relating to theft and other mishaps, run by its paramilitary arm, the Tourist Police (see p216).

The TAT also has information desks at Bangkok International Airport in the arrivals area of Terminal 1 (☎ 0 2504 2701) and Terminal 2 (☎ 0 2504 2669); both are open from 8am to midnight.

TAT Offices Abroad

Australia (☎ 02-9247 7549; fax 02-9251 2465; info@thailand.net.au; Level 2, 75 Pitt St, Sydney, NSW 2000)

France (☎ 01-53 53 47 00; fax 01-45 63 78 88; tatpar@wanadoo.fr; 90 Ave des Champs Elysées, 75008 Paris)

Germany (☎ 069-138 1390; tatfra@tat.or.th; Bethmannstrasse 58, D-60311 Frankfurt am Main)

Hong Kong (☎ 2868 0732; fax 2868 4585; tathkg@tat .or.th; 1601 Fairmont House, 8 Cotton Tree Dr, Central)

Japan Tokyo (☎ 03-3218 0337; fax 03-3218 0655; tattky@tat.or.th; South Tower 2F, Room 259, Yurakucho Denki Bldg, 1-7-1 Yurakucho, Chiyoda-ku, Tokyo 100) Osaka (☎ 06-6543 6654; fax 06-6543 6660; info@tatosacom; Technoble Yotsubashi Bldg 3F, 1-6-8 Kitahorie, Nishi-ku, Osaka 550-0014)

Malaysia (☎ 603-216 23480; fax 603-216 23486; sawatdi@po.jaring.my; Suite 22.01, Level 22, Menara Lion, 165 Jalan Ampang, 50450 Kuala Lumpur)

Singapore (☎ 65-235 7901; fax 65-733 5653; tatsin@singnet.com.sg; c/o Royal Thai embassy, 370 Orchard Rd, 238870 Singpore)

Taiwan (☎ 2502 1600; fax 2502 1603; tattpe@ms3.hinet .net; 13th fl, Boss Tower, 111 Sung Chiang Rd)

UK (☎ 020-7925 2511; tatuk@tat.or.th; 3rd fl, Brook House, 98-99 Jermyn St, London SW1Y 6EE)

USA (☎ 212-432 0433, 1-800 THAI LAND; fax 212-269 2588; tatny@tat.or.th; 61 Broadway, Suite 2810, New York, NY 10006)

USA (☎ 323-461 9814; fax 323-461 9834; tatla@ix.netcom .com; 1st fl, 611 North Larchmont Blvd, Los Angeles, CA 90004)

VISAS

The Royal Thai Ministry of Foreign Affairs lists its visa policies at www.mfa.go.th/web/12.php.

Tourist Visa Exemption

The Thai government allows 39 nationalities, including most European countries, Australia, New Zealand and the USA (see www.mfa .go.th/web/12.php for a detailed list), to enter the country without a visa for 30 days at no charge.

Citizens of Brazil, Korea and Peru may enter Thailand without a visa, in accordance with intergovernmental agreements, for a maximum stay of 90 days for purposes of tourism or temporary business only.

Without proof of an onward ticket and sufficient funds for their projected stay, any visitor can be denied entry, but in practice your ticket and funds are rarely checked if you're dressed neatly.

A few nationalities, eg Hungarians, must obtain a visa in advance of arrival or they'll be turned back. Check with a Thai embassy or consulate if you plan on arriving without a visa.

Tourist Visas

If you plan to stay in Thailand for more than a month, you should apply for the 60-day Tourist Visa (US$30). One passport photo must accompany all applications.

Transit Visas

Citizens from a list of 14 nations, including the People's Republic of China, Taiwan and several countries in Central and South Asia, can obtain a 15-day Transit Visa (1000B). You might be required to show you have 10,000B per person or 20,000B per family to obtain this visa.

Non-Immigrant Visas

The Non-Immigrant Visa is good for 90 days, must be applied for in your home country, costs around US$60 and is not difficult to obtain if you can offer a good reason for your visit. Business, study, retirement and extended family visits are among the purposes considered valid. If you want to stay longer than six months, this is the one to get: you can buy two back-to-back 90-day visas, and when the first expires, leave the country and come back in on the second visa. If you plan to apply for a Thai work permit, you'll need to possess a Non-Immigrant Visa first.

The Non-Immigrant Business Visa (usually abbreviated by Thai immigration officials to 'non-B') allows unlimited entries to Thailand for one year. The only hitch is that you must leave the country at least once every 90 days to keep the visa valid. However, a 90-day non-B can be extended to a full year if you're able to obtain a work permit during the first 90 days.

Visa Extensions & Renewals

It is possible to extend sixty-day Tourist Visas by up to 30 days at the discretion of Thai immigration authorities. The Bangkok **Immigration Office** (Map pp260-1; ☎ 0 2287 3101) is on Soi Suan Phlu, Th Sathon Tai, although you can apply at any immigration office in the country. The fee for extension of a Tourist Visa is 1900B. Bring along one photo and one copy each of the photo and visa pages of your passport. Usually only one 30-day extension is granted.

The 30-day no-visa stay can be extended for seven to 10 days (depending on the immigration office) for 1900B. You can also leave the country and return immediately to obtain another 30-day stay. There is no limit on how often you can do this, nor is there a minimum interval that you must spend outside the country.

Extension of the 15-day Transit Visa is allowed only if you hold a passport from a country that has no Thai embassy.

If you overstay your visa, the usual penalty is a fine of 200B for each extra day, with a 20,000B limit. Fines can be paid at the airport or in advance at the **Bangkok Immigration Office** (Map pp260-1; ☎ 0 2287 3101; Immigration Bureau, Room 416, 4th fl, Old Bldg, Soi Suan Phlu, Th Sathon Tai). If you've overstayed only one day, you don't have to pay. Children under 14 travelling with a parent do not have to pay the penalty.

WOMEN TRAVELLERS

Contrary to popular myth, Thailand doesn't receive a higher percentage of male visitors than most other countries. In fact around 40% of all visitors are women, a higher ratio than the worldwide average as measured by the World Tourism Organization. This is on a par with Singapore and Hong Kong, and ahead of all other Asian countries. The overall increase for women visitors has climbed faster than that for men every year since 1993.

Everyday incidents of sexual harassment are much less common in Thailand than in India, Indonesia or Malaysia, and this might lull women familiar with those countries into thinking that Thailand is safer than it is. However, virtually all incidents of attacks on foreign women in Thailand have occurred outside Bangkok, typically in remote beach or mountain areas. If you're a woman travelling alone, try to pair up with other travellers when travelling at night. Make sure hotel and guesthouse rooms are secure at night – if they're not, demand another room or move to another hotel or guesthouse.

WORK

Bangkok's status as the heart of the Thai economy provides a variety of work opportunities for foreigners, although in general it's not as easy to find a job as in more developed countries. As in the rest of East and Southeast Asia, there is a high demand for English speakers to provide instruction to Thai citizens. This is not due to a shortage of qualified Thai teachers with a good grasp of English grammar, but rather a desire to have native speaker models in the classroom.

Teaching English

Those with academic credentials such as teaching certificates or degrees in English as a second language get first crack at the better-paying jobs, such as those at universities and international schools. But there are perhaps hundreds of private language-teaching establishments throughout the city that hire non-credentialed teachers by the hour. Private tutoring is also a possibility. International oil companies pay the highest salaries for English instructors, but are also quite choosy.

If you're interested in finding teaching work, start with the English-language *Greater Bangkok Metropolitan Telephone Directory* yellow pages. Check all the usual headings – Schools, Universities, Language Schools (nearly a hundred listings in Bangkok alone) and so on.

A website maintained by an English as a Foreign Language teacher in Bangkok, www .ajarn.com, has tips on where to find teaching jobs and how to deal with Thai classrooms, as well as current job listings.

Other Jobs & Volunteering

Voluntary and paying positions with organisations that provide charitable services in

Directory – Practicalities

education, development or public health are available for those with the right education and/or experience. Some contacts are:

Australian Volunteers International (☎ 03-9279 1788, 1800 331 292; www.australianvolunteers.com; Melbourne, Australia)

US Peace Corps (☎ 800-424 8580; www.peacecorps.gov; Washington DC, USA)

Voluntary Service Overseas (VSO; ☎ 020-8780 7200; www.vso.org.uk; London, UK)

Voluntary Service Overseas (VSO; ☎ 613-234 1364, 1 888 876 2911; www.vsocanada.org; Ottawa, Canada)

Volunteer Service Abroad (☎ 04-472 5759; www.vsa .org.nz; Wellington, New Zealand)

The United Nations backs some ongoing projects in the nation. In Bangkok, try calling.

Food & Agriculture Organization (☎ 0 2281 7844)

Unesco (☎ 0 2391 0577)

Unicef (☎ 0 2280 5931)

United Nations Development Programme (☎ 0 2282 9619)

UN World Food Program (☎ 0 2280 0427)

World Health Organization (☎ 0 2282 9700)

Busking is illegal in Thailand, where it is legally lumped together with begging.

Work Permits

All work in Thailand requires a Thai work permit. Thai law defines work as 'exerting one's physical energy or employing one's knowledge, whether or not for wages or other benefits', so theoretically even volunteer and missionary work requires a permit.

Work permits should be obtained through an employer, who may file for the permit before the employee enters Thailand. The permit itself is not issued until the employee enters Thailand on a valid Non-Immigrant Visa (see p224).

For information about work permits, contact any Thai embassy abroad or check the Ministry of Foreign Affairs website (www.mfa .go.th/web/12.php).

Language

Language

It's true – anyone can speak another language. Don't worry if you haven't studied languages before or that you studied a language at school for years and can't remember any of it. It doesn't even matter if you failed English grammar. After all, that's never affected your ability to speak English! And this is the key to picking up a language in another country. You just need to start speaking.

Learn a few key phrases before you go. Write them on pieces of paper and stick them on the fridge, by the bed or even on the computer – anywhere that you'll see them often.

You'll find that locals appreciate travellers trying their language, no matter how muddled you may think you sound. So don't just stand there, say something! If you want to learn more Thai than we've included here, pick up a copy of Lonely Planet's comprehensive and user-friendly *Thai Phrasebook*.

PRONUNCIATION
Tones

In Thai the meaning of a single syllable may be altered by means of different tones. For example, depending on the tone, the syllable *mai* can mean 'new', 'burn', 'wood', 'not?' or 'not'.

The following chart represents tones to show their relative pitch values:

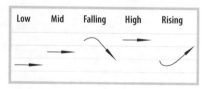

Low	Mid	Falling	High	Rising

The tones are explained as follows:

low tone – 'flat' like the mid tone, but pronounced at the relative bottom of one's vocal range. It is low, level and with no inflection, eg *bàat* (baht – the Thai currency).

mid tone – pronounced 'flat', at the relative middle of the speaker's vocal range, eg *dii* (good); no tone mark is used.

falling tone – sounds as if you are emphasising a word, or calling someone's name from afar, eg *mâi* (no/not).

high tone – pronounced near the relative top of the vocal range, as level as possible, eg *máa* (horse).

rising tone – sounds like the inflection used by English speakers to imply a question – 'Yes?', eg *săam* (three).

Consonants

The majority of consonants correspond closely to their English counterparts. The combinations **kh**, **ph** and **th** are all aspirated versions of **k**, **p** and **t** respectively. Aspirated consonants are pronounced with an audible puff of breath. A similar differentiation in English is heard in the 't' in 'pit' and 'tip'.

SOCIAL
Meeting People

Hello.
sà·wàt·dii (khráp/   สวัสดี(ครับ/ค่ะ)
  khâ)
Goodbye.
laa kàwn   ลาก่อน
Please.
kà·rú·naa   กรุณา
Thank you (very much).
khàwp khun (mâak)   ขอบคุณ(มาก)
Yes.
châi   ใช่
No.
mâi châi   ไม่ใช่
I
phŏm/dì·chăn (m/f)   ผม/ดิฉัน
you
khun   คุณ
Do you speak English?
khun phûut phaa·săa   คุณพูดภาษา
  ang·krìt dâi mǎi?   อังกฤษได้ไหม
Do you understand?
khâo jai mǎi?   เข้าใจไหม
I understand.
khâo jai   เข้าใจ
I don't understand.
mâi khâo jai   ไม่เข้าใจ

Could you please ...?
khăw ... dâi măi? ขอ...ได้ไหม
  repeat that
  phûut ìik thii พูดอีกที
  speak more slowly
  phûut cháa long พูดช้าลง
  write it down
  khĭan hâi เขียนให้

Going Out
What's on ...?
mii à·rai tham ...? มีอะไรทำ...
  locally
  thăew thăew níi แถวๆนี้
  this weekend
  săo aa·thít níi เสาร์อาทิตย์นี้
  today
  wan níi วันนี้
  tonight
  kheun níi คืนนี้

Where are the ...?
... yùu thîi năi? ...อยู่ที่ไหน
  clubs
  nai kláp ไนท์คลับ
  gay venues
  sà·thăan ban· สถานบันเทิงเกย์
    thoeng keh
  places to eat
  ráan aa·hăan ร้านอาหาร
  pubs
  phàp ผับ

Is there a local entertainment guide?
mii khûu meu sà·thăan ban·thoeng
  baw·rí·wehn níi măi?
มีคู่มือสถานบันเทิงบริเวณนี้ไหม

PRACTICAL
Question Words
Who?
khrai? ใคร
What?
a·rai? อะไร
When?
mêua rai? เมื่อไร
Where?
thîi năi? ที่ไหน
How?
yàang rai? อย่างไร

Numbers & Amounts

0	sŭun	ศูนย์
1	nèung	หนึ่ง
2	săwng	สอง
3	săam	สาม
4	sìi	สี่
5	hâa	ห้า
6	hòk	หก
7	jèt	เจ็ด
8	pàet	แปด
9	kâo	เก้า
10	sìp	สิบ
11	sìp·èt	สิบเอ็ด
12	sìp·săwng	สิบสอง
13	sìp·săam	สิบสาม
14	sìp·sìi	สิบสี่
15	sìp·hâa	สิบห้า
16	sìp·hòk	สิบหก
17	sìp·jèt	สิบเจ็ด
18	sìp·pàet	สิบแปด
19	sìp·kâo	สิบเก้า
20	yîi·sìp	ยี่สิบ
21	yîi·sìp·èt	ยี่สิบเอ็ด
22	yîi·sìp·săwng	ยี่สิบสอง
30	săam·sìp	สามสิบ
40	sìi·sìp	สี่สิบ
50	hâa·sìp	ห้าสิบ
60	hòk·sìp	หกสิบ
70	jèt·sìp	เจ็ดสิบ
80	pàet·sìp	แปดสิบ
90	kâo·sìp	เก้าสิบ
100	nèung ráwy	หนึ่งร้อย
1000	nèung phan	หนึ่งพัน
2000	săwng phan	สองพัน
10,000	nèung mèun	หนึ่งหมื่น
100.000	nèung săen	หนึ่งแสน
1,000,000	nèung láan	หนึ่งล้าน

Days

Monday	wan jan	วันจันทร์
Tuesday	wan ang·khaan	วันอังคาร
Wednesday	wan phút	วันพุธ
Thursday	wan phà·réu·hàt	วันพฤหัสฯ
Friday	wan sùk	วันศุกร์
Saturday	wan săo	วันเสาร์
Sunday	wan aa·thít	วันอาทิตย์

229

Banking

I'd like to ...
yàak jà ...
อยากจะ...

change money
lâek ngoen
แลกเงิน

change some travellers cheques
lâek chék doen thaang
แลกเช็คเดินทาง

Where's the nearest ...?
... thîi klâi khiang yùu thîi nǎi?
...ที่ใกล้เคียงอยู่ที่ไหน

automatic teller machine
tûu eh·thii·em
ตู้เอทีเอ็ม

foreign exchange office
thîi lâek ngoen tàang prà·thêt
ที่แลกเงินต่างประเทศ

Post

Where is the post office?
thîi tam kaan prai·sà·nii yùu thîi nǎi?
ที่ทำการไปรษณีย์อยู่ที่ไหน

I want to send a ...
yàak jà sòng ...
อยากจะส่ง...

fax
fàak   แฟกซ์
parcel
phát·sà·dù   พัสดุ
postcard
prai·sa·nii·yá·bàt   ไปรษณียบัตร

I want to buy ...
yàak jà séu ...
อยากจะซื้อ...

an envelope
sawng jòt·mǎi   ซองจดหมาย
a stamp
sa·taem   แสตมป์

Phones & Mobiles

I want to buy a phone card.
yàak jà séu bàt thoh·rá·sàp
อยากจะซื้อบัตรโทรศัพท์
I want to make a call to ...
yàak jà thoh pai ...
อยากจะโทรไป...
reverse-charge/collect call
kèp plai thaang
เก็บปลายทาง

I'd like a/an ...
tâwng kaan ...
ต้องการ...

adaptor plug
plák tàw
ปลั๊กต่อ
charger for my phone
khrêuang cháat sǎm·ràp thoh·rá·sàp
เครื่องชาร์จสำหรับโทรศัพท์
mobile/cell phone for hire
châo thoh·rá·sàp meu thěu
เช่าโทรศัพท์มือถือ
prepaid mobile/cell phone
thoh·rá·sàp meu thěu bàep jài lûang nâa
โทรศัพท์มือถือแบบจ่ายล่วงหน้า
SIM card for the ... network
bàt sim sǎm·ràp khreua khài kǒrng ...
บัตรซิมสำหรับเครือข่ายของ...

Internet

Where's the local Internet café?
ráan in·toe·nét yùu thîi nǎi?
ร้านอินเตอร์เนตอยู่ที่ไหน

I'd like to ...
yàak jà ...
อยากจะ...

check my email
trùat ii·mehn   ตรวจอีเมล
get online
tàw in·toe·nét   ต่ออินเตอร์เนต

Transport

What time does the ... leave?
... jà àwk kìi mohng?
...จะออกกี่โมง

bus
rót meh   รถเมล์
ferry
reua khâam fâak   เรือข้ามฟาก
train
rót fai   รถไฟ

What time's the ... bus?
rót meh ... maa kìi mohng?
รถเมล์...มากี่โมง

first
khan râek   คันแรก
last
khan sùt thái   คันสุดท้าย
next
khan tàw pai   คันต่อไป

Are you free? (taxi)
wâang mǎi?   ว่างไหม

Please put the meter on.
pòet mí·toe dûay   เปิดมิเตอร์ด้วยหน่อย
nòy
How much is it to ...?
pai ... thâo·rai?   ไป...เท่าไร
Please take me to (this address).
khǎw phaa pai ...   ขอพาไป...

FOOD

breakfast
  aa·hǎan cháo   อาหารเช้า
lunch
  aa·hǎan thîang   อาหารเที่ยง
dinner
  aa·hǎan yen   อาหารเย็น
snack
  aa·hǎan wâang   อาหารว่าง

Can you recommend a...
náe·nam ... dâi mǎi?
แนะนำ...ได้ไหม
  bar/pub
  baa/phàp   บาร์/ผับ
  café
  ráan kaa·fae   ร้านกาแฟ
  restaurant
  ráan aa·hǎan   ร้านอาหาร

*For more detailed information on food and
dining out, see the 'Food' chapter (p39) and
the 'Eating' chapter (p105).*

EMERGENCIES

It's an emergency!
pen hèt chùk chǒen!
เป็นเหตุฉุกเฉิน
Could you please help me/us?
chûay dâi mǎi?
ช่วยได้ไหม

Call the police/a doctor/an ambulance!
taam tam·rùat/mǎw/rót phá·yaa·baan dûay!
ตามตำรวจ/หมอ/รถพยาบาลด้วย
Where's the police station?
sà·thǎa·nii tam·rùat thîi klâi khiang yùu
thîi nǎi?
สถานีตำรวจที่ใกล้เคียงอยู่ที่ไหน

HEALTH

Where's the nearest ...?
... thîi klâi khiang yùu thîi nǎi?
...ที่ใกล้เคียงอยู่ที่ไหน
  chemist (night)
  ráan khǎi yaa   ร้านขายยา
  doctor/dentist
  mǎw/mǎw fan   หมอ/หมอฟัน
  hospital
  rohng phá·yaa·   โรงพยาบาล
  baan

I need a doctor (who speaks English).
tâwng kaan mǎw (thîi phûut phaa·sǎa
ang·krìt dâi)
ต้องการหมอ(ที่พูดภาษาอังกฤษได้)

Symptoms

I have (a) ...
pǒm (m)/dì·chǎn (f) ...
ผม/ดิฉัน...
  diarrhoea
  pen rôhk tháwng   เป็นโรคท้องร่วง
  rûang
  fever
  pen khâi   เป็นไข้
  headache
  pùat hǔa   ปวดหัว
  pain
  jèp pùat   เจ็บปวด

Glossary

baht – Thai currency
BMA – Bangkok Metropolitan Administration
BTS – Bangkok Mass Transit System
CAT – Communications Authority of Thailand
faràng – foreigner of European descent
Isan – *isǎan*; general term for North-Eastern Thailand, from the Sanskrit name for the medieval kingdom Isana, which encompassed parts of Cambodia and North-Eastern Thailand.
khlong – *khlawng*; canal
MRTA – Metropolitan Rapid Transit Authority
Ratanakosin – style of architecture present in the late 19th to early 20th century, which combines traditional Thai and European forms; also known as 'old Bangkok'
reua hǎang yao – longtail boat
rót fai fáa – BTS Skytrain
rót fai fáa máhǎanákhawn -- MRTA subway
Soi – *sawy;* lane or small road
TAT – Tourist Authority of Thailand
Tha – *thâa*; pier
THAI – Thai Airways International
Thanon – *thanǒn* (abbreviated 'Th' in this guide); road or street
TOT – Telephone Organisation of Thailand
Trok – *tràwk*; alleyway
wát – Buddhist temple, monastery

Behind the Scenes

THE LONELY PLANET STORY

The story begins with a classic travel adventure: Tony and Maureen Wheeler's 1972 journey across Europe and Asia to Australia. There was no useful information about the overland trail then, so Tony and Maureen published the first Lonely Planet guidebook to meet a growing need.

From a kitchen table, Lonely Planet has grown to become the largest independent travel publisher in the world, with offices in Melbourne (Australia), Oakland (USA), London (UK) and Paris (France).

Today Lonely Planet guidebooks cover the globe. There is an ever-growing list of books and information in a variety of media. Some things haven't changed. The main aim is still to make it possible for adventurous travellers to get out there – to explore and better understand the world.

At Lonely Planet we believe travellers can make a positive contribution to the countries they visit – if they respect their host communities and spend their money wisely.

THIS BOOK

This 6th edition of Bangkok was researched and written by Joe Cummings and China Williams. Joe also wrote all the previous editions. This guide was commissioned in Lonely Planet's Melbourne office and produced in Melbourne. The project team included:

Commissioning Editors Mary Neighbour & Kalya Ryan
Coordinating Editors Melissa Faulkner & Stephanie Pearson
Coordinating Cartographer Chris Thomas
Coordinating Layout Designer Cris Gibcus
Assisting Editors & Proofreaders Kate Evans, Cathryn Game, Charlotte Harrison, Lucy Monie & Nina Rousseau
Assisting Cartographers Wayne Murphy, Amanda Sierp
Cover Designer Gerilyn Attebery
Series Designer Nic Lehman
Series Design Concept Nic Lehman and Andrew Weatherill
Managing Cartographer Corie Waddell
Managing Editors Dan Caleo & Stephanie Pearson
Layout Manager Kate McDonald
Mapping Development Paul Piaia
Project Manager Chris Love
Language Content Coordinator Quentin Frayne
Regional Publishing Manager Kate Cody
Series Publishing Manager Gabrielle Green
Special thanks goes to Bruce Evans for his advice regarding Thai language matters.

Cover photographs The underside of a hand-painted red umbrella, Chris Mellor (top); Monk collecting alms in Bangkok, Kraig Lieb/Lonely Planet Images (bottom); Dusit Hall in Grand Palace, Bangkok, Bill Wassman/Lonely Planet Images (back)

Internal photographs by Richard l'Anson/Lonely Planet Images except for the following: p2 (#1), p201, p203 Richard Nebesky; p51 (#1), p155 (#1) Chris Mellor; p51 (#3) Dominic Bonuccelli; p52 (#1) John Elk III; p52 (#2), p157 (#2) Andrew Lubran; p52 (#4) Paul Piaia; p53 (#2) Bill Wassman; p53 (#3) p197 Frank Carter; p53 (#4), p57 (#3) Joe Cummings; p54 (#1, 4), p55 (#1, 2, 3, 4) Jerry Alexander; p54 (#2), p156 (#1) Kraig Lieb; p56 (#4) Sara-Jane Cleland; p57 (#2) Anders Blomqvist; p57 (#4), p158 (#4), p183 Lee Foster; p58 (#2) John Borthwick; p86, p156 (#2) Tom Cockrem; p155 (#3) Glenn Beanland; p157 (#1), p157 (#3), Ryan Fox; p162 (#1) Nicholas Reuss; p162 (#2) Juliet Coombe; p162 (#3), p191 Bill Wassman; p192, Dennis Johnson. All images are the copyright of the photographers unless otherwise indicated. Many of the images in this guide are available for licensing from Lonely Planet Images: www .lonelyplanetimages.com.

ACKNOWLEDGMENTS

Many thanks to the following for the use of their content:
Salvatore Besso's impressions are reproduced from the English translation of the original Italian, titled *Siam and China* by C. Mathews, Simpkin, Marshall, Hamilton, Kent & Co. Ltd (1914), London.

THANKS
CHINA WILLIAMS

Many thanks to my husband for so generously helping me investigate Bangkok's top-end restaurants. Thanks also to Mason, Luka, Big Mike, Jon Wu, and Nim for their Bangkok know-how. Also thanks to the coordinating author, Joe Cummings, who can answer such frivolous questions as why stray dogs wear T-shirts during the cold season, and to the talented LP production team.

JOE CUMMINGS

A varied bunch of Bangkokians helped out with investigations into what makes our capital so sweet and so sour. Special thanks are due to Cameron Cooper, Jim Algie and other staff at *Farang* magazine; Nima Chandler; Korakot 'Nym' Punlopruksa; Benjawan Sudhikarn & Leon Dolle; Frederic Meyer; Kaprice Kea; Pong & the Ad Here gang. Thanks also to Mick for a night on the town I'll never forget.

OUR READERS

Many thanks to the travellers who used the last edition and wrote to us with helpful hints, useful advice and interesting anecdotes. Your names follow:

Stephen Amrol, Niels Bjerg, Alfredo Borlongan, Andrew Bruce, Norm Cappell, Martin Conway, Hugh Cropp, Neil Cullen, John Dowd, Robert

Eklund, Karen Ferguson, Lisa Fleming, Henk Hilkmann, Margaret Hyder, Massoud Javadi, Alec Johnson, Brenda Kemp, Robert Kemp, James & Kasia Kilvington, Louise Martin, Lachlan McKenzie, Margaret McLaughlin, Kazuya Miyashita, Gail Mowat, Mariska Oosterkamp, Lee O'Shea, Florian Poltz, Timothy Reilly, Felix Reychman, Lliane & Manfred Satlot, Christine Sydneysmith, Martijn van Elzakker, Janet Vulevich, Jim Wilkins, Rebecca J Wood, Grace Yee

SEND US YOUR FEEDBACK

We love to hear from travellers — your comments keep us on our toes and help make our books better. Our well-travelled team reads every word on what you loved or loathed about this book. Although we cannot reply individually to postal submissions, we always guarantee that your feedback goes straight to the appropriate authors, in time for the next edition. Each person who sends us information is thanked in the next edition — and the most useful submissions are rewarded with a free book.

To send us your updates — and find out about LP events, newsletters and travel news — visit our award-winning website: www.lonelyplanet.com.

Note: We may edit, reproduce and incorporate your comments in Lonely Planet products such as guide-books, websites and digital products, so let us know if you don't want your comments reproduced or your name acknowledged. For a copy of our privacy policy visit www.lonelyplanet.com/privacy.

Notes

Notes

Notes

Index

See also separate indexes for Eating (p243), Shopping (p243) and Sleeping (p243).

Index

000 map pages
000 photographs

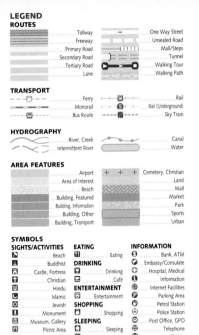

LEGEND

ROUTES

Tollway	One Way Street
Freeway	Unsealed Road
Primary Road	Mall/Steps
Secondary Road	Tunnel
Tertiary Road	Walking Tour
Lane	Walking Path

TRANSPORT

Ferry	Rail
Monorail	Rail (Underground)
Bus Route	Sky Train

HYDROGRAPHY

River, Creek	Canal
Intermittent River	Water

AREA FEATURES

Airport	Cemetery, Christian
Area of Interest	Land
Beach	Mall
Building, Featured	Market
Building, Information	Park
Building, Other	Sports
Building, Transport	Urban

SYMBOLS

SIGHTS/ACTIVITIES	EATING	INFORMATION
Beach	Eating	Bank, ATM
Buddhist	**DRINKING**	Embassy/Consulate
Castle, Fortress	Drinking	Hospital, Medical
Christian	Café	Information
Hindu	**ENTERTAINMENT**	Internet Facilities
Islamic	Entertainment	Parking Area
Jewish	**SHOPPING**	Petrol Station
Monument	Shopping	Police Station
Museum, Gallery	**SLEEPING**	Post Office, GPO
Picnic Area	Sleeping	Telephone
Point of Interest	Camping	Toilets
Ruin	**TRANSPORT**	**GEOGRAPHIC**
Shinto	Airport, Airfield	Lighthouse
Sikh	Bus Station	Lookout
Skiing	Cycling, Bicycle Path	Mountain
Winery, Vineyard	General Transport	National Park
Zoo, Bird Sanctuary	Taxi Rank	Waterfall

NOTE: Not all symbols displayed above appear in this guide.

Map Section

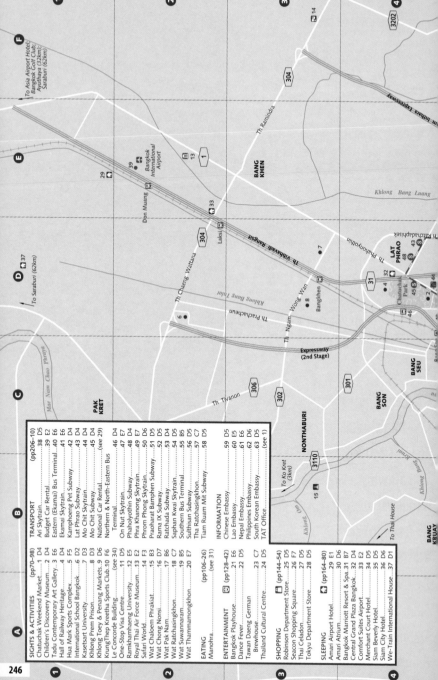

SIGHTS & ACTIVITIES	(pp70–98)
Chatuchak Weekend Market	1 D4
Children's Discovery Museum	2 D4
Tadu Contemporary Art Gallery	3 E6
Hall of Railway Heritage	4 D4
Hua Mark Sports Complex	5 F5
International School Bangkok	6 D2
Kasetsart University	7 D3
Khlong Prem Prison	8 D3
Khlong Toey & Penang Markets	9 D6
KrungThep Kreetha Sports Club	10 F6
Le Concorde Building	11 D5
One-Stop Visa Centre	(see 34)
Ramkhamhaeng University	12 E5
Royal Thai Air Force Museum	13 E2
Safari World	14 F3
Wat Chaloem Phrakiat	15 B3
Wat Chong Nonsi	16 D7
Wat Pak Nam	17 B6
Wat Ratchasingkhon	18 C7
Wat Suwannaram	19 B5
Wat Thammamongkhon	20 E7

EATING	(pp106–26)
Manohra	(see 31)

ENTERTAINMENT	(pp128–42)
Bangkok Playhouse	21 E6
Dance Fever	22 D5
Tawan Daeng German Brewhouse	23 C7
Thailand Cultural Centre	24 D5

SHOPPING	(pp144–54)
Robinson Department Store	25 D5
Seacon Shopping Square	26 F7
Thai Celadon	27 D5
Tokyu Department Store	28 D5

SLEEPING	(pp164–80)
Amari Airport Hotel	29 E1
Amari Atrium	30 D6
Bangkok Marriott Resort & Spa	31 B7
Central Grand Plaza Bangkok	32 D4
Comfort Suites Airport	33 E2
Merchant Court Hotel	34 D5
Siam Beverly Hotel	35 D5
Siam City Hotel	36 D6
We-Train International House	37 D1

TRANSPORT	(pp206–10)
Ari Skytrain	38 D5
Budget Car Rental	39 E2
Eastern (Ekamai) Bus Terminal	40 E6
Ekamai Skytrain	41 E6
Kamphoeng Pet Subway	42 D4
Lat Phrao Subway	43 D4
Mo Chit Skytrain	44 D4
Mo Chit Subway	45 D4
National Car Rental	(see 29)
Northern & North-Eastern Bus Terminal	46 D4
On Nut Skytrain	47 E7
Phaholyothin Subway	48 D4
Phra Khanong Skytrain	49 E7
Phrom Phong Skytrain	50 D6
Praoharat Bamphen Subway	51 D5
Rama IX Subway	52 D5
Ratchada Subway	53 D4
Saphan Kwai Skytrain	54 D5
Southern Bus Terminal	55 B5
Sulthisan Subway	56 D5
Tha Ratchasingkhon	57 C7
Tiam Ruam Mit Subway	58 D5

INFORMATION	
Chinese Embassy	59 D5
Lao Embassy	60 E5
Nepal Embassy	61 E6
Philippines Embassy	62 D6
South Korean Embassy	63 D5
TAT Office	(see 1)

0 [====] 5 km
0 [====] 3 miles

BANG KAPI ⑤

• 10

□ 26 Rama IX Royal Park ⑦

To Subhapruek Golf Course; Chonburi (48km)

Th Lat Phrao

(336)

Th Ramkhamhaeng • 5

12 •

Th Si Nakharin

Khlong

Prakhanong

Th Phetburi Tat Mai

Soi 77

Soi 101

Th Lat Phrao

(34)

To Samut Prakan (8km)

Soi 103 (Soi Udom Suk)

⑥

Th Phra Ram IX

ⓞ 60 Soi 39 (Soi Pracha Uthit)

63 Th Thian Ruammit

KHLONG TAN

□ 3

Th Phetburi Tat Mai

61

Soi 63 (Ekamai)

Soi 71

PHRA KHANONG

🚇 47

20

Soi 101

49

BANGNA

To Samut Prakan (8km)

Th Phra Ram IX

□ 34 35

28

51 ⓢ

56 ⓢ

HUAY KHWANG

58 59

25 ⓢ

27 🚇

22 24

Th Sukhumvit

52

Soi 55 (Thong Lor)

Soi 21 (Asoke)

□ 36

30

Samitivej Hospital ✚

41 40

62

50

Th Phra Ram IV

9

Th Phra Ram IV

Khlong Saen Saeb

KHLONG TOEY

PORT

38

Th Vibhavadi Rangsit

Th Phetchaburi

Th Ratchaprarop

Lumphini Park

THUNG MAHAMEK

Expressway (1st Stage)

3

See Central Bangkok Map (p248–9)

Th Ratchadaphisek

16

Mae Nam Chao Phraya

Th Ratchawithi

Chitralada Palace

SI YAN

Samsen

DUSIT

BANGLAMPHU

Th Phetburi

Th Phra Ram I

Hualamphong

Th Phra Ram I

TROK CHAN

Th Chan

23

Expressway (1st Stage)

303

PHRA PRADAENG

KO RATANAKOSIN

CHINATOWN

Th Charoen Nakhon

Wong Wian Yai

THONBURI

Wat Arun

RATBURANA

Th Ratchada III

Th Rama III

THANON TOK

57

18

31

Th Taksin

Th Sukhawat

To Rose Garden; Nakhon Chaisi; Nakhon Pathom (35km)

TALING CHAN

55

19 Thonburi (Bangkok Noi)

Santiwong

Khlong Bangkok Noi

BANGKOK NOI

(338)

17

4

DAO KHANONG

Th Phetkasem

Khlong Bangkok Yai

BANG KHUN THIAN

Khlong Dao Khanong

Floating Market •

Khlong Sanam Chai

35

To Samut Sakhon (19km)

To Nakhon Pathom (32km) ⑤

Skytrain & Station

Subway & Stations Under Construction (Due to open 2004)

⑤ ⑥ ⑦ ⑧

247

CENTRAL BANGKOK

1

To Southern
Bus Terminal
(4km)

Th Ratwithi

Th Samsen

Th Si Ayuthaya

Amphon
Park

Th Ratchasima

Th Ratwi

Th Rama V

DUSIT

Dusit
Zoo

Chitral
Park

Saphan Phra
Ram VIII

25

Th Luk Luang

Th Phitsanulok

Th Uthong Nai

Th Krung Kasem

Th Samsen

Th Wisut Kasat

Th Prachathipok

Th Rama

See Thewet & Dusit Map (pp2

Santichaiprakan
Park

2

Th Phra Pin Klao

Th Phra Athit

Khlong Banglamphu

Banglamphu
Market

Th Phra Sumen

Th Chakraphong

Th Bowonniwet

Th Ratchadamnoen Nok

Th Nakorn Sawan

Royal
Turf Club

Th Phitsanulok

Th Luk Luang

Khlong Bangkok Noi

Saphan
Phra Pin
Klao

BANGLAMPHU

Th Ratchini

Th Chao Fa

Th Din So

Th Maha Chai

Th Lan Luang

Th Krung Kasem

To Wat
Suwannaram
(1km)

Thonburi
(Bangkok Noi)

Thammasat
University

Th Na Phra That

Th Ratchadamnoen Klang

PHRA
NAKHON

Th Atsadang

Th Tanao

Th Chakkaphatdi

22

26

Th Phrannok

Sanam
Luang

Th Ratchini

Th Feuang Nakhon

Th Botphram

Th Tri Thong

See Banglamphu Map (p254-5)

Th Bamrung Meuang

Bo-Be
Market

3

Th Na Phra Lan

Th Kanlaya Namit

Th Luang

Th Wora Chak

Th Yukhon

POM PRAP
SATTRU PHAI

Th Luang

KO
RATANAKOSIN

Th Maha Rat

Th Thai Wang

Th Charoen Krung

PHAHURAT

Th Ban Mo

Nakhon Kasem
Thieves Market

Th Charoen Krung

Th Suapa

Th Mittaphap

Th Krung Kasem

Th Rong Meuang

Th Rama VI

Th Charoen M

BANGKOK
NOI

Th Arun Amarin

Khlong Mon

See Ko Ratanakosin Map (p256)

Th Sanam Chai

CHINATOWN

Th Triphet

Talat
Saphan Han
Market

Th Chakrawat

Th Chakraphet

Th Maitri

Khlong Padung Krung Kasem

Th Phayathai

Th Isaraphap

Khlong Chaeng

10

4

Th Wang Doem

24

Th Chakkaphet

29

Th Saphan

Phut

Th Ratchawong

Th Yaowarat

Th Songsawat

SAMPHAN
THAWONG

Th Phra Ram IV

Hualamphong

Hualamphong

12

7

Phra Pokklao
Bridge

Mae Nam Chao Phraya

Th Charoen Krung

Th Charoen Trimit

BANGKOK YAI

5

Th Prachathipok

Th Somdet Chao Phraya

Th Tha Din Daeng

See Chinatown (p252-3)

Th Itsaraphap

Th Charoen Nakhon

Th Maha Phruthanam

BANGK

Th Charoen Krung

Th Intharaphitak

Th Intharaphitak

Wong
Wian
Yai

Mittraphab
Hospital

Th Lat Ya

Th Rama VI

Thoet Thai Rd

Wong Wiam
Yai Market

Th Charoen Rat

KHLONG SAN

Th Phayathai

Th Mahesak

Th Surak

Bangkhlo

Expressway

11

6

Wong Wian Yai

Th Taksin

Th Krung Thonburi

THONBURI

Saphan Taksin

Saphan Taksin

Sura

248

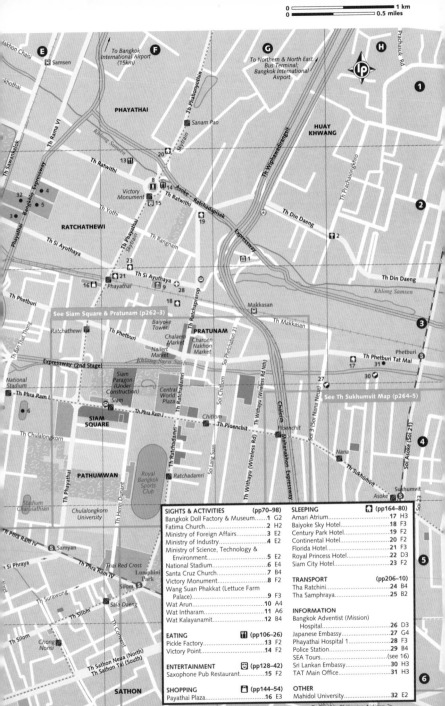

SIGHTS & ACTIVITIES (pp70–98)
Bangkok Doll Factory & Museum......**1** G2
Fatima Church............................**2** H2
Ministry of Foreign Affairs............**3** E2
Ministry of Industry....................**4** E2
Ministry of Science, Technology &
Environment...........................**5** E2
National Stadium.......................**6** E4
Santa Cruz Church.....................**7** B4
Victory Monument.....................**8** F2
Wang Suan Phakkat (Lettuce Farm
Palace)................................**9** F3
Wat Arun...............................**10** A4
Wat Intharam..........................**11** A6
Wat Kalayanamit......................**12** B4

EATING (pp106–26)
Pickle Factory..........................**13** F2
Victory Point...........................**14** F2

ENTERTAINMENT (pp128–42)
Saxophone Pub Restaurant...........**15** F2

SHOPPING (pp144–54)
Payathai Plaza.........................**16** E3

SLEEPING (pp164–80)
Amari Atrium...........................**17** H3
Baiyoke Sky Hotel.....................**18** F3
Century Park Hotel....................**19** F2
Continental Hotel......................**20** F2
Florida Hotel............................**21** F3
Royal Princess Hotel...................**22** D3
Siam City Hotel........................**23** F2

TRANSPORT (pp206–10)
Tha Ratchini...........................**24** B4
Tha Samphraya.......................**25** B2

INFORMATION
Bangkok Adventist (Mission)
Hospital...............................**26** D3
Japanese Embassy.....................**27** G4
Phayathai Hospital 1...................**28** F3
Police Station..........................**29** B4
SEA Tours.........................(see **16**)
Sri Lankan Embassy...................**30** H3
TAT Main Office.......................**31** H3

OTHER
Mahidol University....................**32** E2

THEWET & DUSIT

See Banglamphu Map (p254–5)

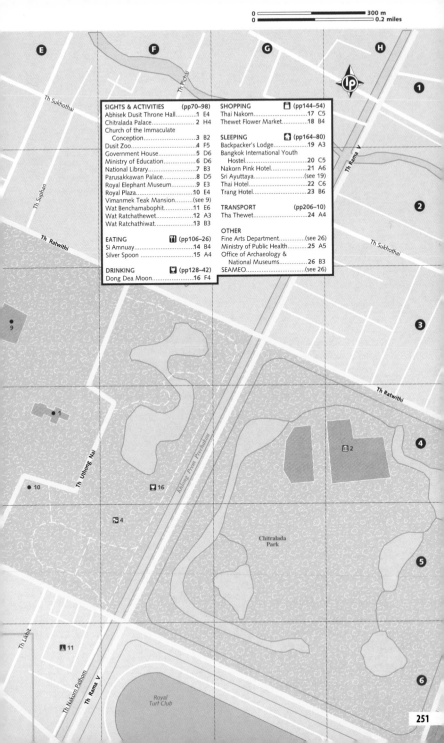

SIGHTS & ACTIVITIES (pp70–98)
Abhisek Dusit Throne Hall..........**1** E4
Chitralada Palace.......................**2** H4
Church of the Immaculate
  Conception...........................**3** B2
Dusit Zoo..................................**4** F5
Government House.....................**5** D6
Ministry of Education.................**6** D6
National Library.........................**7** B3
Parusakkawan Palace.................**8** D5
Royal Elephant Museum.............**9** E3
Royal Plaza...............................**10** E4
Vimanmek Teak Mansion..........(see 9)
Wat Benchamabophit.................**11** E6
Wat Ratchathewet.....................**12** A3
Wat Ratchathiwat......................**13** B3

EATING (pp106–26)
Si Amnuay.................................**14** B4
Silver Spoon **15** A4

DRINKING (pp128–42)
Dong Dea Moon........................**16** F4

SHOPPING (pp144–54)
Thai Nakorn..............................**17** C5
Thewet Flower Market...............**18** B4

SLEEPING (pp164–80)
Backpacker's Lodge....................**19** A3
Bangkok International Youth
  Hostel..................................**20** C5
Nakorn Pink Hotel.....................**21** A6
Sri Ayuttaya...........................(see 19)
Thai Hotel.................................**22** C6
Trang Hotel...............................**23** B6

TRANSPORT (pp206–10)
Tha Thewet..............................**24** A4

OTHER
Fine Arts Department...............(see 26)
Ministry of Public Health..........**25** A5
Office of Archaeology &
  National Museums................**26** B3
SEAMEO..................................(see 26)

CHINATOWN

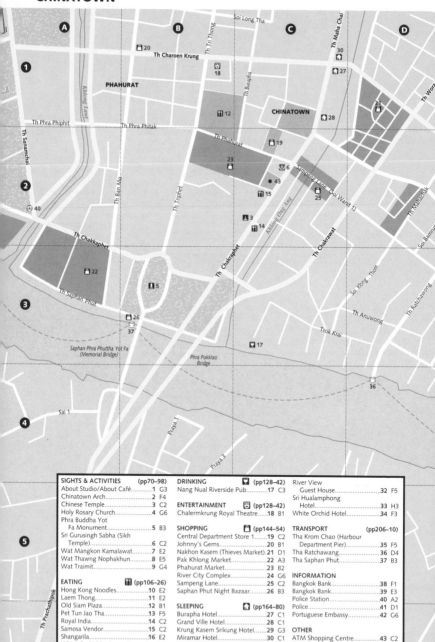

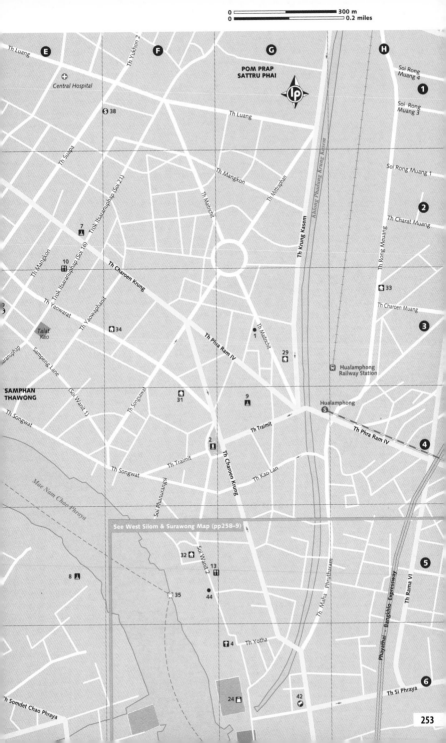

0 ——————— 300 m
0 ——————— 0.2 miles

E **F** **G** **H**

Th Luang

POM PRAP
SATTRU PHAI

Soi Rong
Muang 4

Central Hospital

Soi Rong
Muang 3

1

$5 38

Th Sukao

Th Luang

Th Mangkon

Soi Rong Muang 1

Th Mitraphan

Th Krung Kasem

Th Charat Muang

2

Th Rong Meuang

Trok Itsaranuphap (Soi 21)

7

Th Mangkon

Th Charoen Krung

Trok Itsaranuphap (Soi 16)

33

10

Th Matichti

Khlong Thailang Krung Kasem

Th Yaowarat

Th Charoen Muang

3

3

Th Yaowaphanit

Th Phra Ram IV

34

1 ● Th Matichit

Talat
Kao

Th Matichit

Hualamphong
Railway Station

Sampeng Lane

29

Th Phra Ram IV

SAMPHAN
THAWONG

(Soi Wanit 1)

31

9

Hualamphong

$

Th Songwat

Th Traimit

Th Songwat

2

Th Traimit

Th Phra Ram IV

4

Th Songwat

Th Kao Lan

Th Charoen Krung

Mae Nam Chao Phraya

Soi Phanurangsi

See West Silom & Surawong Map (pp258–9)

32

Soi Wanit 2

13

5

Th Rama VI

8

35

44

Th Maha Phruthaiam

Phayathai – Bangchlo – Expressway

4

Th Yotha

6

24

42

Th Si Phraya

Th Somdet Chao Phraya

253

BANGLAMPHU

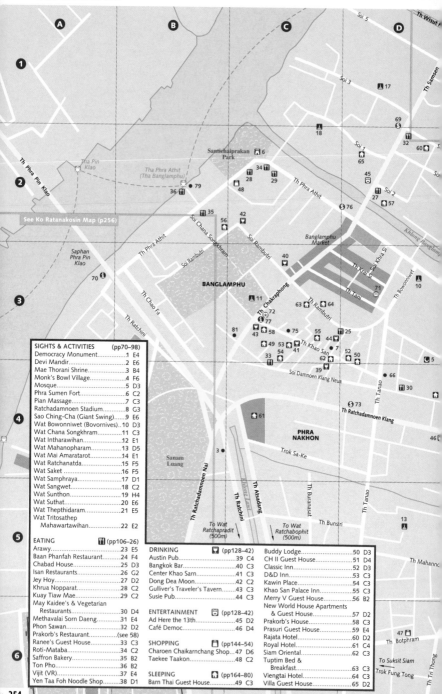

INFORMATION

OTHER

KO RATANAKOSIN

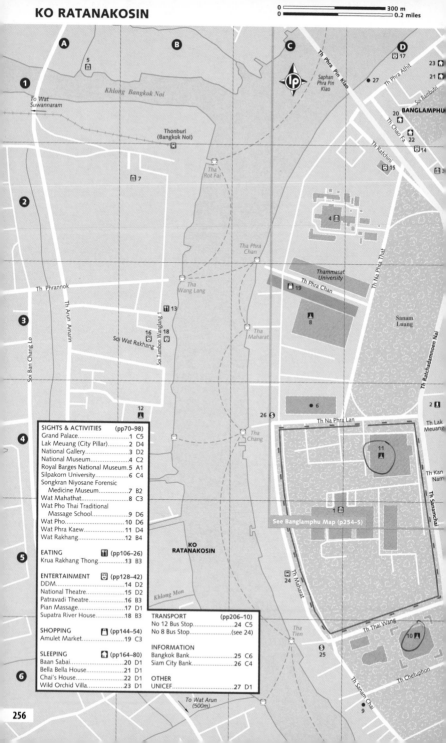

0		300 m
0		0.2 miles

Khlong Bangkok Noi

To Wat Suwannaram

Thonburi (Bangkok Noi)

BANGLAMPHU

Th Phra Pin Klao

Saphan Phra Pin Klao

Tha Rot Fai

Th Phrannok

Th Arun Amarin

Soi Ban Chang Lo

Soi Wat Rakhang

Soi Tambon Wanglang 1

Tha Phra Chan

Tha Wang Lang

Tha Maharat

Tha Chang

Tha Tien

Tha Phra Chan

Thammasat University

Sanam Luang

Th Na Phra That

Th Ratchadamnoen Nai

Th Na Phra Lan

Th Lak Meuang

Th Kan Nam

Th Sanamchai

KO RATANAKOSIN

Khlong Mon

Th Maharat

Th Thai Wang

Th Chetuphon

Th Sanam Chai

To Wat Arun (500m)

SIGHTS & ACTIVITIES (pp70–98)
Grand Palace......................................1 C5
Lak Meuang (City Pillar)......................2 D4
National Gallery.................................3 D2
National Museum................................4 C2
Royal Barges National Museum.5 A1
Silpakorn University.............................6 C4
Songkran Niyosane Forensic
 Medicine Museum.............................7 B2
Wat Mahathat....................................8 C3
Wat Pho Thai Traditional
 Massage School................................9 D6
Wat Pho..10 D6
Wat Phra Kaew..................................11 D4
Wat Rakhang......................................12 B4

EATING (pp106–26)
Krua Rakhang Thong.........................13 B3

ENTERTAINMENT (pp128–42)
DDM...14 D2
National Theatre................................15 D2
Patravadi Theatre...............................16 B3
Pian Massage.....................................17 D1
Supatra River House..........................18 B3

SHOPPING (pp144–54)
Amulet Market...................................19 C3

SLEEPING (pp164–80)
Baan Sabai..20 D1
Bella Bella House...............................21 D1
Chai's House......................................22 D1
Wild Orchid Villa...............................23 D1

TRANSPORT (pp206–10)
No 12 Bus Stop..................................24 C5
No 8 Bus Stop.............................(see 24)

INFORMATION
Bangkok Bank....................................25 C6
Siam City Bank..................................26 C4

OTHER
UNICEF..27 D1

256

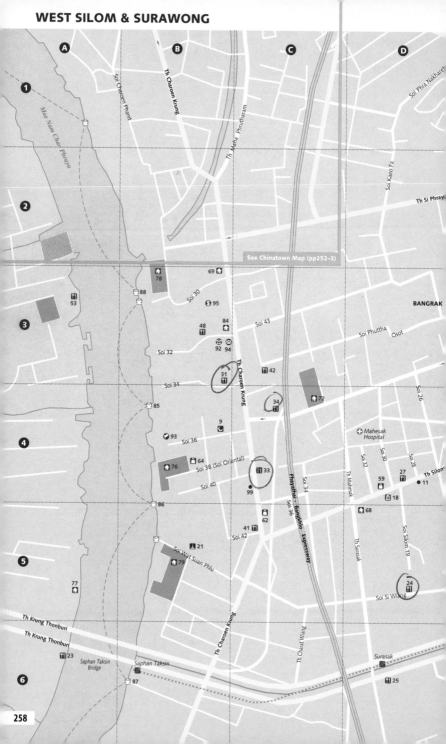

Mae Nam Chao Phraya

Soi Charoen Phanit

Th Charoen Krung

Th Maha Phrudharam

Soi Phra Nakharet

Soi Kaeo Fa

Th Si Phray

See Chinatown Map (pp252–3)

BANGRAK

78

69

88

53

95

84

48

43

92 94

Soi 32

Soi 30

Th Charoen Krung

Soi 43

Soi Phuttha Osot

42

31

Soi 34

85

34

72

Soi 26

9

93

Soi 36

Mahesak Hospital

76

64

Soi 38 (Soi Oriental)

Soi 32

Soi 30

Soi 28

33

Soi 40

99

59

27

11

18

Th Silom

62

86

68

Phayathai – Bangkhlo Expressway

Soi 34

Spa 36

Th Mahesak

41

Soi 42

21

77

79

Soi Wat Suan Phlu

Th Surasak

Soi Silom 19

24

Soi Si Wiang

Th Krung Thonburi

Th Krung Thonburi

23

Saphan Taksin Bridge

Saphan Taksin

87

Th Charoen Krung

Th Charat Wiang

Surasak

25

0 — 300 m
0 — 0.2 miles

E **F** **G** **H**

See Siam Square &
Pratunam Map (pp262–3)

Sol Chulalongkorn 42

Th Phayathai

Chulalongkorn
University

Th Henri Dunant

Soi 11
Soi 15

Th Phra Ram IV

Samyan **S**
🏠 71

Soi Chulalongkorn 60

🍴 52

1

● 15

Thai Red Cross

Th Naret

● 7
● 20
● 61

73
🏠

Patpong
Night
Market

Th Surawong

Soi 6 (Soi ThanTawan)

🍴 46

● 13
40
57
58

Soi Patpong 1
Soi Patpong 2

🍴 39
47 🍴
🏨 55
54
Silom Soi 2
56 🍴
67
45

Th Thaya

Sala Daeng

2

Soi Sarp

Sol Santi Phap

Sol Surawong

🍴 50

Th Decho

🏠 70
Soi 7

Soi Anuman Rachathon

🍴 51
38 🍴
60
89 ✚
66
5
4
32 🍴
35 37 🍴
Th Convent

3

● 91

Soi 12
Soi 14
Soi 16
Soi 18

Soi 9
(Soi Sukavitthaya)

65 🏠
82 🏠
10 ●

Soi 7
Soi 5 (Soi Lalaisap)

Th Silom

🏠 81

Th Convent

Soi 77 (Soi Pradit)

74

14 🌙
44 🍴

🍴 19

Th Pan

Soi 13 (Trok Vaithi)
Soi 11

Th Chong Nonsi

Chong Nonsi 🏛

🍴 29

83 🏠

Soi Silom 3
Soi Phiphat 2
Soi Phiphat 2

90 🍴

30 🍴
17
22 🍴

4

See East Silom Map (pp260–1)

75 🏠
Soi 10

Soi Phiphat 1

🍴 43

Th Pan

Soi Saukca Witthaya

Soi 12
8
1
63
36 🏛

🍴 26

96 🍴

● 3

Soi Pikun

Th Sathon Neua (North)
Th Sathon Tai (South)

97 🍴

● 2
● 6

● 16

5

98 ✚

Soi St Louis 2
Soi St Louis 3

Th Witthaya

Th Naradhiwat Rajanagarindra (Chong Nonsi)

🍴 49

● 12

(Soi 7) Soi Phra Phinij

SATHON

Soi Suanphlu 1

6

Soi Pichai 2

259

See Siam Square &
Pratunam Map (pp262–3)

A **B** **C** **D**

12

1

30

13
36
Th Sarasin

Soi Lang Suan

10

Skytrain
Th Ratchadamri

Chulalongkorn
Hospital

Lumphini
Park

Th Withayu (Wireless Rd)

2

3
14
Silom
S
37

16
18
22

35

Th Silom
19
Th Sala Daeng

Th Phra Ram IV

31

3

Soi Sala Daeng 2
21

Soi Yommarat

Soi Sala Daeng

Soi Sala Daeng 2

Lumphini
S

Soi Sala Daeng 1

25

2

33
26

4

Th Convent

29
4

Th Sathon Neua (North)
1

Th Sathon Tai (South)
27

32

Soi 1 (Atakarnprasit)

5
Soi Co...

28

38

15

8
9

5

Soi Phra Phinit

Soi Nantha

SATHON

Soi Suanphlu 1

Soi Suan Phlu
34

6

Soi Ngam Duphli

E **F** **G** **H**

SIGHTS & ACTIVITIES (pp70–98)
Alliance Française Bangkok...........**1** B4
Central Tennis Court....................**2** D4
Charn Issara Tower.......................**3** A2
Christ Church..............................**4** A4
Goethe Institut...........................**5** D4
Lumphini Tower..........................**6** F4
Sanam Muay Lumphini **7** E4

EATING 🍴 (pp106–26)
Colonade................................(see 26)
Folies Café Patisserie.................(see 1)
Just One...................................**8** D5
Lobby Salon.............................(see 26)
Mali Restaurant..........................**9** D5
Ngwan Lee Lang Suan................**10** C1
Ratsstube.................................**11** D4
Sara-Jane's...............................**12** D1

DRINKING 🍷 (pp128–42)
Brown Sugar.............................**13** C1
DJ Station.................................**14** A2
Espresso Bar............................(see 14)

ENTERTAINMENT 🎭 (pp128–42)
Babylon Bangkok.......................**15** D5
Freeman...................................**16** A2
Joe Louis Puppet Theatre............**17** E3

SHOPPING 🛍 (pp144–54)
Robinson Department Store.......**18** A2
Silom Center...........................(see 18)
Silom Complex.........................**19** A3
Suan Lom Night Bazaar.............**20** E3

SLEEPING 🛏 (pp164–80)
Bangkok Christian Guest House.**21** A3
Dusit Thani Hotel......................**22** A2
Pinnacle Hotel..........................**23** E4
Sala Thai Daily Mansion............**24** F6
Siri Sathorn Executive Residence.**25** B4
Sukhothai Hotel........................**26** C4

TRANSPORT (pp206–10)
Hertz.......................................(see 3)

INFORMATION
Australian Embassy....................**27** B4
Austrian Embassy......................**28** D5
Bangkok Nursing Home..............**29** A4
Cambodian Embassy..................**30** B1
Canadian Embassy.....................**31** B3
Danish Embassy.........................**32** D4
French Consulate......................(see 1)
German Embassy.......................**33** C4
Immigration Office....................**34** B6
Merman Books........................(see 19)
Police......................................**35** D2
South African Embassy..............**36** C1
Tourist Police...........................**37** A2
USIS..**38** A5

🎭 17

23
🏠

Bon Kai
Market

Bon Kai
S

● 6

Th Phra Ram IV

🏠 24

See Th Sukhumvit Map (p264–5)

1
2
3
4
5
6

SIAM SQUARE & PRATUNAM

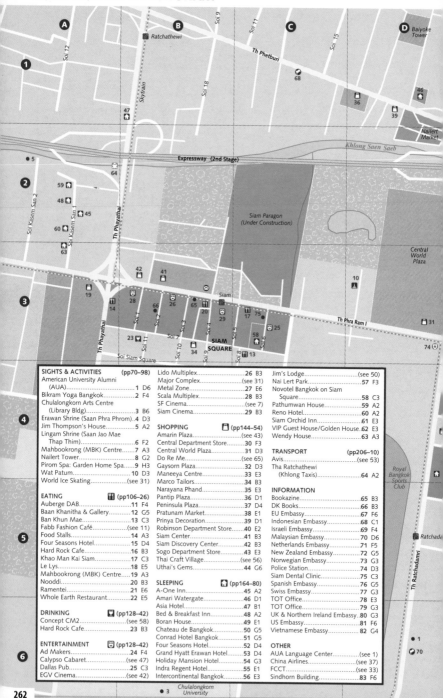

Soi 12 · Ratchathewi · Th Phetburi · Baiyoke Tower

Khlong Saen Saeb

Expressway (2nd Stage)

Siam Paragon (Under Construction)

Central World Plaza

Th Phra Ram I

SIAM SQUARE

Soi Siam Square

Nailert Market

Central Bangkok Sports Club

Royal Bangkok Sports Club

Chulalongkorn University

See West Silom & Surawong Map (p258–9)   See East Silom Map (p260–1)

0 _____ 300 m
0 _____ 0.2 miles

Th Makkasan **H**

E   Soi Wattanawong   **G**

55 ⌂

38

Th Ratchaprarop

PRATUNAM

F

1

Charoen
Nakhon
Market

49

Soi Phetchaburi 31

Soi Phetburi 35

Th Phetburi

Soi 32

Khlong Saen Saep   **2**

40

8 ●

6

Th Withayu Neua (Wireless Rd Nth)

57

73

See Th Sukhumvit Map (p264–5)

Gaysorn   61

79

Soi Chitlom

Soi Somkhit

Soi 1

9   **3**

77

President
Tower

56   78   62

30

54

80

43   33

Th Ploenchit

Chitlom

11

2

Ploenchit

Skytrain

4

Mahatlek Luang 1

24   69

Soi Lang Suan

82

Soi Ruam Rudi

Chalerm Mahanakhon Expressway

Soi 2

Mahatlek Luang 2

18

71

Soi Tonson

Th Withayu (Wireless Rd)

51

Soi 1

50

5

22

Soi 2

12

76

72

Mahatlek Luang 3

44   Soi 3

21

81

6

27

83

67

Soi Ruam Rudi

263

A B C D

1 2 3 4 5 6

93
91
75
60
54
25
32
73
26
84
76
Ploenchit
14
1
77
66 28
49
70
7
31 16
58 79 78 94
37
72
36
67
27
Nana
80
33
5 18
15
90
30
34 13
86 59
68 65
71
83
11 52
64 63
Asoke
Sukhumvit
Soi Cowboy
20
22
88 17
87 8
82 23
50 19
41 40
29
55

KHLONG
TOEY

See Siam Square & Pratunam Map (pp262–3)

See East Silom Map (pp260–1)

Chalem Mahanakhon Expressway

Th Sukhumvit

Th Ratchadaphisek

Sirikit Centre
9

Bon Kai
Market
Bon Kai

Th Phra Ram IV

To Eva Air;
Philippine Airlines;
Air Andaman
(100m)

63

Soi 1
Soi 3 (Soi Nana Neua)
Soi 5
Soi 7
Soi 9
Soi 11
Soi 13
Soi 15
Soi 19
Soi Asoke (Soi 21)
Soi 23 (Lak Khet)
Soi 25
Soi 27
Soi 29 (Lak Khet)
Soi 4 (Nana Tai)
Soi 6
Soi 8
Soi 10
Soi 12
Soi 16
Soi 18
Soi 20
Soi 22
Soi Ruam Rudi
Soi 1
Soi 2
Soi 3
Soi Polo
Soi Polo
Soi Phlukchit
Soi 2
Soi Saphan Khu
Soi Suan Sawat
Skytrain